GROUP 9 (associates left to right)
^   Bitwise exclusive OR: **x ^ y**

GROUP 10 (associates left to right)
¦   Bitwise OR: **x¦y**

GROUP 11 (associates left to right)
&&   Logical AND: **x && y**

GROUP 12 (associates left to right)
¦¦   Logical OR: **x¦¦y**

GROUP 13 (associates right to left)
?...:   Conditional: **x ? y : z**

GROUP 14 (associates right to left)
=   assignment: **i = j**
*=   * assignment: **k *= 2 (k = k*2)**
/=   / assignment: **m /= n (m = m/n)**
%=   % assignment: **i %= d (i = i%d)**
+=   + assignment: **x += y (x = x + y)**
−=   − assignment: **w −= x (w = w − x)**
<<=   << assignment: **z <<= 2 (z = z<<2)**
>>=   >> assignment: **z >>= 3 (z = z>>3)**
&=   & assignment: **a &= b (a = a&b)**
^=   ^ assignment: **c ^= d (c = c^d)**
¦=   ¦ assignment: **e¦= f (e = e¦f)**

GROUP 15 (associates left to right)
,   Comma expressions: **exp1, exp2, exp3**

MASTERING
QUICKC

MASTERING QUICKC®

STAN KELLY-BOOTLE

 SYBEX® SAN FRANCISCO • PARIS • DÜSSELDORF • LONDON

Acquisitions Editor: Dianne King
Developmental Editor: Vince Leone
Copy Editor: Rhoda Simmons
Technical Editor: Jon Forrest
Word Processors: Chris Mockel, Scott Campbell
Book Designer: Julie Bilski
Chapter Art and Layout: Suzanne Albertson
Technical Art: Jeff Giese
Screen Graphics: Sonja Schenk
Typesetter: Winnie Kelly
Proofreader: Sylvia Townsend
Indexer: Ted Laux
Cover Designer: Thomas Ingalls + Associates
Cover Photographer: David Bishop
Screen reproductions produced by XenoFont

For Crispin, Luke, Samuel, Tim, and Toni

► ACKNOWLEDGMENTS ►

It is meet and proper to record here my gratitude to the people who helped me produce this book.

At the top of my thank-you stack is the wonderful team at SYBEX. Once again, it was a real joy working with Dr. Rudolph Langer, one of those rare computer book executives well-versed in both computer and book lore. Since we have both been computing since the 1950s, it was fun to be able to discuss the incunabula of both trades!

Together with Dianne King, Dr. Langer coaxed me into the *Mastering QuickC* project and encouraged me through a sequence of deadlines with the minimum of life-threatening coercion.

Vincent Leone was again my developmental editor. The tales you hear of stormy editor/author interaction are not entirely true! In our case, a fruitful rapport has smoothed out the occasional stylistic logomachies and my less obtrusive Briticisms have been retained. My sincere thanks to Vincent for his unfailing guidance and attention to detail—in particular, the spotting of all my missing semicolons (I hope), spurious hyphens, and redundant commas. However, I reluctantly accept the blame for any errors that may have escaped him and Rhoda Simmons, the doyenne of copy editors.

Praise also to word processors Chris Mockel and Scott Campbell, typesetter Winnie Kelly, proff-reder Sylvia Townsend, artist Suzanne Albertson, and indexer Ted Laux.

I would like to thank my colleagues and fellow columnists at *UNIX Review* and *Computer Language* for helpful, informal discussions and input over the years, especially Steve Bourne, Ken Arnold, Tim Parker, Dave Burnette, Mark Compton, Ken Broadhurst, Dave Chandler, Bob Toxen, and Eric Allman. SYBEX author Michael Young has also been a ready source of advice.

There is, of course, an ongoing debt of gratitude from all Cfarers to the pioneers at Bell Labs who started it all and have kept it growing: Dennis Ritchie, Brian Kernighan, Ken Thompson, and Bjarne Stroustrup.

Penultimately, my thanks to Bill Gates, Greg Lobdell, and all the software genii at Microsoft, without whom, as they say, this book would have been far less bulky.

Finally, to my *bien aimée* wife, Iwonka: your loving patience will be long remembered.

► CONTENTS AT A GLANCE ►

► *TABLE OF CONTENTS* ►

► *INTRODUCTION* ►

There are three reasons for learning the C language: fun, profit, and everybody's doing it. The recent surge in popularity can be traced to several interconnected factors.

C is a "portable" language with an emerging ANSI standard, and C development packages have become available at reasonable prices on a wide range of hardware platforms. Indeed, it is difficult to think of a computer, large or small, that does not have the support of at least one C compiler.

In the case of the IBM PC (and compatible) range, recent years have seen something of a price war between Microsoft and Borland to capture the lion's share of the PC "language" market. The user has certainly benefited as these two vendors have played "leapfrog" by offering better price/performance and functionality with successive releases.

Although the millions of PCs and clones sold since 1981 naturally led to an enormous market for applications software, it was by no means obvious when IBM launched the personal computer with PC-DOS (a version of Microsoft's MS-DOS) that advanced language development tools would generate a market beyond the relatively small group of software houses. The PC came bundled with a BASIC interpreter (also developed by Microsoft) that was considered, at the time, quite adequate to meet the demands of hobbyist, nonprofessional, and departmental programmers. It is not easy to determine if the unexpected growth of this market led to the price reductions or whether falling prices fueled the surge in demand. The two trends clearly went hand in hand to upset most market predictions.

Programmers now accept without question that professional, high-level-language development packages are available for less than $150 or so. Not so many years ago, a prophecy along these lines would have been dismissed as ludicrous.

► *HISTORY LESSON* ►

While hardware costs had been declining dramatically since the first UNIVAC sale, the unquestioned assumption was that software, being human-labor intensive, was bound to move as rapidly in the opposite direction, if only to ensure that your total data-processing budget remained comfortably stable!

The flaw in this hypothesis emerged with the simple notion that you can amortize the considerable costs of developing sound, easy-to-use software by expanding the customer base with aggressive pricing and marketing. The latter is required, initially at least, to overcome the fixation that decent systems software is expensive and difficult to use if you don't have a degree in computer science. The size of the potential user base, of course, had expanded rapidly during the early 1980s with the advent of the IBM PC and its many bandwagoneers. The simple arithmetic of recovering a software investment of $3 million reveals that 1000 mainframe users must each spend $3000, whereas 30,000 PC users need spend only $100. Profit and support costs complicate the figures, but the principle is clear.

► *Success* ►

The success of Borland's Turbo Pascal proved that there was indeed an untapped market for professional PC compilers outside the traditional software development houses. That market, perhaps, was resigned to the fact that at one end of the spectrum compilers were slow, free, suspect, and unsupported, while at the other end they were competent and desirable but priced for the full-time, $50-an-hour programmer. The scene has now changed irreversibly with Microsoft's QuickC and Borland's Turbo C breaking the $100 barrier.

► *The IDEs March On* ►

For the learner, the "casual" user, and the full-time professional, these products offer more just than a compiler and linker. The new keyword is *IDE,* the Integrated Development Environment. Source code entry and editing, syntax checking, compiling, linking, running, and source-level debugging were all brought into the one package and were available through pop-up, easily navigated, windowed menus. Traditionally, these activities called for separate specialized software packages, often from different suppliers, inflating the total development costs and leading to the familiar "who did what?" debates when things went wrong.

► *The C Mystique* ►

Among all the computer languages, dead and alive, C holds a unique place—people either love it to distraction or detest it to distraction. There are no neutrals here! UNIX, the operating system closely associated with C (indeed, UNIX is largely written in C), has engendered the same dichotomy since it emerged with C from Bell Labs in the mid-1970s and migrated to the world's best campuses. UNIX and C have become de facto standards in many government and engineering fields—initially on minicomputers and mainframes but gradually moving into the microcomputer arena as CPUs became more powerful and capable of supporting larger memories.

► *Why C?* ►

Although C is particularly powerful as a systems programming language (its original pupose), it has proved to be efficient and economic in wider contexts. Perhaps portability is C's most widely touted property. The portability of C programs stems from the language's use of function libraries for such machine-dependent operations as I/O—an area that bedeviled the growth of a single-standard BASIC or Pascal. Since C is a small-core language (unlike, say, PL/1 or Ada), there are surprisingly few keywords to learn. On the other hand, C is richer in operators than most languages (for example, there are several operators that work at the bit level).

The critics cannot gainsay this success. C is undoubtedly the language of choice for most systems programmers, yet the snipers usually overlook the fact that you cannot have a powerful systems programming language without some attendant dangers. C offers you access at the machine level with a rare blend of efficiency and elegance, but sometimes the conciseness of the language encourages a cryptic cleverness that hinders maintainability.

The migration of C to the PC-DOS (MS-DOS) environment has not been easy. The architecture of the Intel 8088/86 family is not ideally suited to a language such as C in which pointers play a leading, some say frightening, role. To keep the pointer arithmetic clean and tidy, pointers should point to large, linear memories. The segmented memory space of the PC forces compiler writers to provide different memory models for different pointer dispositions—and the user, too, needs to be concerned over the sizes of code and data segments.

Another cloud on the horizon became visible as C moved away from UNIX to other environments. Compilers were emerging with slight but disconcerting differences in their interpretations of the syntax and semantics of C, which had been spelled out by Brian W. Kernighan and Dennis M. Ritchie in 1978. Because these specifications were the work of a few talented individuals, rather than the tedious output of a committee of t-crossers and i-dotters, ambiguities came to light leading to diverse dialectic offshoots, threatening the prized portability of C.

A committee of the American National Standards Institute (ANSI) was formed to resolve these differences. The task of Technical Committee X3J11 was and is to draw up a set of standards for C. As I write, ANSI C is not yet formally cast in stone, but enough data have emerged to point C compiler writers and C programmers in the right direction.

► *Why QuickC?* ►

The Microsoft QuickC package evolved from the Microsoft Optimizing C Compiler, currently at Version 5.1. The latter is aimed at the professional developer who, according to ancient traditions, uses an independent text editor and needs complex command-line compilers, linkers, librarians, and Make facilities to maintain close control over all stages of large-scale projects. With Microsoft's preeminent position as creator of MS-DOS, MS-Windows, Xenix, MASM (the macro assembler), and OS/2 (the "software platform of the future"), it is not surprising that C 5.1 and its predecessors are established as industry leaders, in spite of strong competition from many quarters, notably C products from Borland, Aztec, and Lattice.

QuickC offers a less powerful but more "user friendly" IDE interface, allowing beginners to concentrate on the programming aspects of C while delegating most of the housekeeping chores. In fact, this approach has turned out to be beneficial to professionals as well. For several years now, QuickC has been supplied as part of the larger, optimizing C 5.1 package, giving developers the option of testing ideas and strategies and setting up prototypes with QuickC before refining and optimizing programs with the larger compiler. Code produced with QuickC is fully compatible with the C 5.1 compiler and can be debugged using Microsoft's CodeView debugger. Moving in the other direction requires some care since C 5.1 has several non-QuickC features.

QuickC is complete and ready to go: just type QC to invoke QC.EXE, the IDE compiler. You get an ANSI C-conforming compiler/linker (with extensions that can be "switched off" for maximum portability) supporting five memory models (from small to huge). You can generate math coprocessor instructions for 8087/80287 chips or do floating-point emulation by software. You get a full-screen, interactive, customizable editor (with built-in aids for C source indentations) offering elaborate on-line help screens (both context sensitive and via topic indexes), pull-down menus, and various types of windows (up to five of which can be displayed simultaneously). The IDE gives you an independent Notepad facility with full cut and paste between windows.

QuickC has an integrated source-level debugger offering single-stepping and step over, pause on breakpoints, continuous display of selected watch values, and pause on selected watch conditions. You can record each debugging session in history files and replay them at any time. There is also an animation feature that lets you step through a program at any of three preset speeds.

QuickC also includes extensive Make utilities to check on file interdependencies and automate the compilation/linking process following changes to one or more component files.

In addition to the QC.EXE IDE compiler/linker, the package includes QCL.EXE, a completely independent command-line compiler free from mollycoddling menus and windows. This is not quite as comprehensive as the CL.EXE command-line compiler/linker provided with C 5.1, but it does offer more options than QC.EXE.

Among the other utilities that come with QuickC are LIB, a free-standing library manager; LINK, a stand-alone DOS-compatible linker; and NMAKE, a stand-alone Make utility.

In addition, QuickC lets you write in-line assembly-language code and allows you to link mixed modules written in assembly language, Pascal, FORTRAN, and other high-level languages.

QuickC Version 2 has several important enhancements over the previous version: The Help system has been considerably extended; more memory models are supported; and the graphics libraries now offer Hercules video-adapter support, MS-Windows fonts support, and high-level presentation graphics tools.

Following the C wars that I mentioned earlier, QuickC Version 2, the subject of this book, is clearly Microsoft's response to Borland's Turbo C

Version 2. Both products have their pros and cons. Turbo C has an edge in compilation/execution speed and documentation, but QuickC's windows, help, mouse-support, and PG (presentation graphics) features are superior. (I refer you to the February 1989 issue of *Computer Language* for a comprehensive comparision of 11 DOS-based C compilers.)

► *JOIN THE ELITE* ►

QuickC has already attracted a wide range of programmers, amateur hobbyists, part-timers, and professional software writers. If you have bought QuickC, either alone or as part of C 5.1, then this book will help you exploit its many features. If not, perhaps you will be encouraged to join the club.

Many users will, of course, be hardy types to whom C is the native tongue. My book may be helpful to them as far as picking up some of the special QuickC features, especially the unique presentation graphics tools; however, as will be clear from the gentle pace of the exposition, I have in mind the thousands of newcomers to the big wide world of C. I therefore assume you have only a few basic DOS skills but no prior experience of C or any other structured language. I also assume you can perform such feats as loading diskettes the right way up; creating directories; copying files; and locating the Alt, Ctrl, and Enter keys.

Previous exposure via BASIC, say, to such programming fundamentals as constants, variables, conditional **goto**s and loops, and subroutine calls will not prove a hindrance. Unlike Professor Edsger W. Dijkstra, I believe that BASIC users *can* seek repentance, win salvation, and start anew!

Obviously, the ever-nagging problem facing all computer-book authors is how to enlighten the uninitiated without boring the socks off the cognoscenti. As a possible solution, each chapter ends with a summary, so that readers can quickly map their lacunae to the appropriate sections.

I have included some appendices, which cover material that would have broken the thread of the discourse. The chapter contents reveal a fairly logical journey from simple to complex objects. Chapter 9 is devoted to QuickC graphics; Chapter 10 covers libraries and multifile programs; and finally, Chapter 11 deals with QuickC's debugging facilities.

This book is really part 1 of "mastering" QuickC. You and your creativity form parts 2, 3, and ever onward. QuickC provides the paint and brushes for your PC canvas; this book opens the paintbox and tells you which end of the brush goes into the paint. To become a master of C in the tradition of a Ritchie, Kernighan, Bourne, Holub, Harbison, Steele, Pike, Plum, or Plauger, you need to start daubing away as soon as possible.

Here's to your ever-growing fluenC!

Stan Kelly-Bootle
Mill Valley, California, and Bargemon, Provence

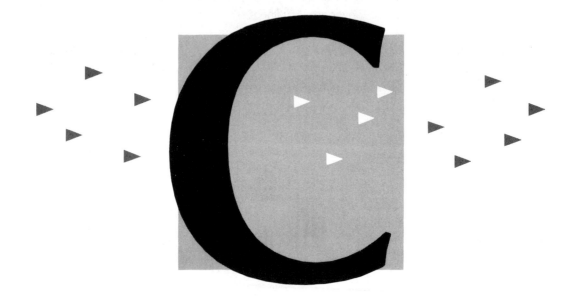

FIRST FALTERING STEPS

► *CHAPTER 1* ►

If you have not yet installed QuickC on your PC, please consult Appendix B and the *Up and Running* booklet supplied by Microsoft.

Your QuickC package contains two C compilers: QC.EXE, the integrated development system with built-in editor, linker, and debugger; and QCL.EXE, a stand-alone, command-line compiler/linker. I will concentrate on the QC part of QuickC in this chapter. Later on, you'll see the extra tricks possible with QCL.

Learning how to create a sequence of statements that your QuickC compiler will accept as valid is clearly a good starting point. There are two aspects to this.

First you'll learn the mechanics of the QuickC integrated environment, how to navigate the menus, select options, enter and edit your source code, and invoke the compiler and linker.

Then there are the syntactical rules of the C language, which spell out with precision exactly which strings of symbols are permissible.

I will first cover briefly the major steps needed to create and run a QuickC program. Some basic vocabulary will be established, so feel free to skim and skip according to your level of experience. The key points will be amplified later, so beginners should not be discouraged if new words and concepts fly by in rapid succession.

► *SOURCE CODE—EXTENSION .C* ►

The text of a program, called its *source code*, is a sequence of statements spelling out in fine detail the actions you want the machine to take. Before a program can be run, it must be translated by the QuickC compiler and then linked using the QuickC linker.

C source code is usually stored in files with the extension .C. So, to find out what source code files you have in your current directory, you can type DIR *.C and press Enter to get

```
C>DIR *.C
GETDAT   C      561    1-09-89    1:04p
```

CHKIP	C	1191	1-29-89	11:21a
HELLO	C	95	10-13-87	1:32p

3 file(s) 16889856 bytes free

which shows the names, sizes (in bytes), and date/time stamps of each file. Each of these files contains sequences of ASCII characters that can be displayed, printed, or edited, hence the general term *text* files. The full ASCII code is given in Appendix A.

The ANSI C standard does not specify how the character set should be encoded, but most implementations, including QuickC, have opted for the ASCII set, so characters are stored and manipulated by their numeric ASCII codes. For now, simply note that the 7-bit ASCII code gives 128 combinations, including both printable symbols and nonprintable control codes.

► DIRECTIVES AND INCLUDE FILES ►

In addition to the normal program statements that you enter in the .C files, there are several *directives* you can provide. They are readily recognized since they usually appear at the start of the .C file with the prefix # followed by the particular directive's name and its *arguments*. As you might guess, directives direct the compiler in various ways. In fact, there is a *preprocessing* phase that handles all the directives before the compilation itself gets under way.

An important example, familiar to most BASIC users, is the **#include** directive with a file name as its argument:

#include <*filename*>

tells the preprocessor to load the contents of the text file ***filename*** as though it formed part of your .C file at that point. Your .C file itself is not physically changed. You can set up your own include files to avoid repetitive typing. Initially, though, you will be using **#include** with some of the 25 special files provided by Microsoft for your convenience. These have the extension .H (for *header*) and they supply frequently needed definitions and declarations in accordance with ANSI C standards. Before too long you will come to know and love these .H files—they not only save you much drudgery, they also serve in the great cause of endowing C programs with their widely acclaimed portability.

Include files can be *nested*—that is, an include file may contain further include files, and so on, to a depth of 16.

You can picture the process as follows:

HELLO.C → preprocessor → HELLO.C + *<included-files>*

► *OBJECT CODE—EXTENSION .OBJ* ►

The compilation process, applied to your .C and .H files, produces *object code* files with the extension .OBJ. These files contain binary code that cannot be meaningfully displayed or printed, although you might find some recognizable ASCII characters embedded therein.

Object files contain machine language instructions that make sense only to the Intel 8088/6, 80286, or 80386 microprocessor that powers your PC:

HELLO.C + *<included-files>* → QuickC compiler → HELLO.OBJ

However, one more step is needed before you can run (or execute) the HELLO program. This is the *linking* process.

► *EXECUTABLE CODE—EXTENSION .EXE* ►

The linking process takes one or more .OBJ files and, true to its name, *links* them to produce one *executable* file with the extension .EXE. The linker can also automatically pull in code from standard precompiled *libraries* provided by Microsoft (or specialist libraries offered by a growing number of software vendors) to make programming easier for you. You are also allowed to create your own libraries. Your program can use any of these precanned library *functions* and leave it to the linker to incorporate their .OBJ code into the final product, namely, the .EXE file.

In simple cases with one .C file and one .OBJ file, the .EXE file is usually given the same name:

HELLO.C → preprocessor → HELLO.C + *<included-files>* → compiler
→ HELLO.OBJ + *<library-code>* → linker → HELLO.EXE

When you are linking several .OBJ files, you will normally find that one of them has the key name that naturally goes with the final .EXE file name:

FILECOMP.OBJ/GETOPT.OBJ + *<library-code>* → linker →
FILECOMP.EXE

Later on, you'll see how .MAK files and program lists are used to tell the linker which .OBJ files to link and how to name the final .EXE file. QuickC offers flexibility for professional developers in areas where the beginner might prefer to have no choice! We will often dogmatically insist on certain default actions until the reasons for the alternatives emerge.

Readers with wider DOS experience may want to know that if your program meets certain size restrictions, you can use the DOS EXE2BIN utility to translate your .EXE files into the faster, more compact .COM format.

Don't be unduly alarmed if your first small .C files seem to generate unexpectedly large .EXE files. They are carrying much baggage from the libraries. As your programs get more complex, this overhead will represent a much smaller percentage of the executable code.

► THE MANDATORY FIRST PROGRAM ►

Brian W. Kernighan and Dennis M. Ritchie, in their canonical book *The C Programming Language* (Englewood Cliffs, New Jersey: Prentice-Hall, 1978), started a tradition that most of the 10,000 subsequent C books have followed. K&R (as the book is widely known) offers as its "Getting Started" program HELLO.C, the sole purpose of which is to display **hello, world** on the screen.

Simple though it is, HELLO.C actually illustrates nine major elements of the C language. Before you get to this exciting demonstration, I'll take you on a quick tour of the QuickC integrated environment and show you the basics of program loading, editing, and running.

► INSTALLATION REMINDER ►

To simplify the exposition, I will assume you have a hard disk known as C:. If you are using two floppies or a hard disk other than C:, please make the necessary adjustments in what follows. If you have followed the hard-disk installation procedures given in the QuickC *Up and Running* manual, you should now have the following files available in the C:\BIN directory:

1. QC.EXE (the integrated development compiler), SETUP.EXE (the installation program), and the help files. (QCL.EXE, the command-line version of QC.EXE, will also be here, but we will not be using it until later.)

2. All the *.H (include) files in directory C:\INCLUDE.

3. The combined SLIBCE.LIB file in C:\LIB produced by SETUP when you select the default small memory model with math emulator. (To avoid tedious digressions, I am assuming the recommended default hard-disk installation setup. If you have different drive or directory names, simply adjust the following instructions accordingly. For details on the SETUP installation program, see Appendix B.)

My own system happens to use QuickC with a hard-disk partition called E:-, so show no surprise if you see E:\BIN etc. on some of the screen illustrations.

► *EXPLORING THE INTEGRATED QC ENVIRONMENT* ►

QuickC is only three keystrokes away. Type QC or qc at the C> prompt and press Enter, and you will soon see the screen shown in Figure 1.1, the QuickC main menu screen.

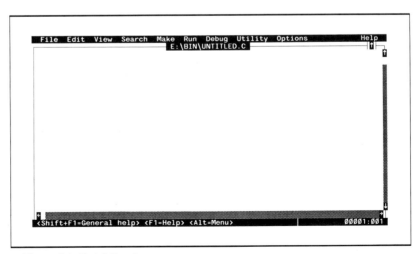

► *Figure 1.1:* QuickC main menu screen

▶ *The Small Print Enlarged* ▶

This is a timely moment to remind you to sign and send in the QuickC registration card. Also, reread the Microsoft copyright and licensing material. Microsoft Corporation has removed any of the so-called excuses and rationalizations for piracy. If you are violating any of its conditions, you should rectify the situation before proceeding. More specifically, erase any illegal copy diskettes and purchase your own copy of QuickC—you will sleep soundly tonight, and in the morning your acne will have disappeared.

Note that there are five basic areas in the main QuickC screen:

1. Main menu bar (the top highlighted strip)

2. Title bar (showing the name of the source code being edited)

3. Source window (awaiting your keystrokes)

4. Reference bar (showing function-key assignments and line/column cursor position)

5. Various scroll bars and arrows

There are many wondrous ways to select menus and actions from the main screen—so many, in fact, that we call it menu navigation. The first lesson in menu navigation is to know the meaning of the term *hot key*.

▶ *Keys—Hot and Cold* ▶

A hot key is one that triggers action immediately and consistently wherever you are in the menu hierarchy, as opposed to those keys for which the function may depend on the particular mode or screen position you happen to be in. Some hot keys are single F (function) keys; others are various combinations of Alt, Ctrl, and Shift with single letters or function keys.

The bottom *reference bar* of the main screen shows the most appropriate action keys for your current situation. The main point is that little rote learning is required. The choices are usually clear from the context. Table 1.1 gives a complete list of hot keys. A tiny warning: In most error and verify conditions, the hot keys are disabled until you take the indicated recovery action. This is for your own good.

► **Table 1.1:** *QuickC hot keys*

Hot Key	Menu Selection	
Alt	Toggle activates menu bar (with menu on, single letter selects; with menu off, use Alt-letter)	
Alt-F	**F**ile	
Alt-E	**E**dit	
Alt-V	**V**iew	
Alt-S	**S**earch	
Alt-M	**M**ake	
Alt-R	**R**un	
Alt-D	**D**ebug	
Alt-U	**U**tility	
Alt-O	**O**ptions	
Alt-H	**H**elp	
Hot Key	**Function**	**Menu from Which the Function Is Also Available**
F1	Menu help	**H**elp
F2	Open last file	**F**ile
F3	Repeat last find	**S**earch
F4	Output window	**V**iew
F5	Go	**R**un
F6	Unassigned	—
F7	Continue to cursor	**R**un
F8	Trace into	**R**un
F9	Breakpoint	**D**ebug
F10	Stop over	**R**un
Shift-F1	Help on help	**H**elp

► *Table 1.1:* QuickC hot keys (continued)

Hot Key	Function	Menu from Which the Function Is Also Available
Shift-F3	Move to next error	**Search**
Shift-F4	Move to previous error	**Search**
Shift-F5	Restart (build)	**Run**
Alt-F4	Exit	**File**
Ctrl-F10	Maximize (window)	**View**
Ctrl-\	Selected text	**Search**
Alt-BS	Undo	**Edit**
Shift-Del	Cut	**Edit**
Ctrl-Ins	Copy	**Edit**
Shift-Ins	Paste	**Edit**
Del	Clear	**Edit**

Note that Esc, the escape key, is *almost* hot! Esc is a general menu-exit key that steps you up from a submenu or back from a main menu to an active window. However, Esc is not a true-blue-blooded hot key since it is inactive unless you are in a menu or help screen.

Esc and the hot keys will quickly become your close friends.

► *Help!*

The QuickC Help package is most extensive, resembling a hypertext system. I will cover just the essential features here; Appendix G gives a more detailed account. It is best learnt by browsing around on your own. Try Shift-F1 to get your first glimpse of Help—it's help on the Help system itself! The help displays are *context sensitive*—that is, the display will helpfully vary according to where you are in the system and where your cursor is situated. Esc *always* clears the help screen and restores the status quo.

Help is not confined to your context. Wherever you are, you can browse around for guidance on any other topic. While you are in the Help on Help screen, try pressing F1 to get a listing of Help topics (see Figure 1.2). Below the title bar is a set of legends showing your choices:

Help on Help

Contents

Index

Notes

Readme.doc

You can use tab to go forward or Shift-tab to go backward through the list. Notice how the selected topic is highlighted. Press Enter to display your selection.

► *Leaving Already?*

Next, try Alt-F4 to exit from QuickC to DOS, then enter QC again to recover the main menu. This early exit practice is not as bizarre as you may think! There is nothing in the whole of computerdom as frustrating as the inability to withdraw gracefully from a program. The lack of "exit standards" has driven more users insane than anything else. The many signing-off ploys in use today include logoff, logout, bye, system, end, Ctrl-C, Ctrl-D, Break,

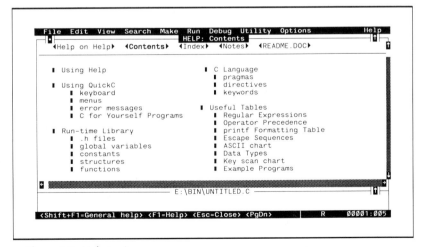

► *Figure 1.2:* Help topics

and, the last resort, turning the power off. If you forget Alt-F4, QuickC has another mnemonic for quitting—type X from the File menu.

► *Back to QC*

Entering QC invokes QC.EXE, the main QuickC Integrated Development Environment (IDE) program. Since you have not yet specified a .C file name, QuickC assumes that you are going to edit a default program called UNTITLED.C, which explains the legend appearing in the title bar. When you load a specific file into the editor, the UNTITLED.C legend will be replaced by the new file name. Later on, when you want to save your edited program, you are free to rename it.

You can load a file and invoke QC by typing QC *filename*, or QC *filename*.C, or QC *filename.ext* at the C> prompt, where *filename* may include full or partial path information. In the absence of a specific extension, QC assumes the default extension .C. If QC finds the file name, the file will be loaded for editing; otherwise you'll get a warning, as shown in Figure 1.3. You are free to create the new file, revert to UNTITLED.C, cancel the operation, or seek help. The edit window is the large upper window. When you are in edit mode, this is where the source text appears as you type. The name of the current file is always displayed in the title bar.

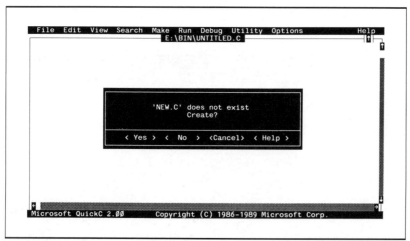

► **Figure 1.3:** *Trying to load a nonexistent file*

For much of this chapter you will be learning your way around the features of the IDE main menu screen. It allows you to load, enter, save, and edit source text, get help, switch and zoom windows, set options, then compile/link/run/debug your program. You can even return temporarily to a DOS shell, do some DOS stuff, then type exit to return to where you left off in QuickC. (While in the DOS shell, though, you must not invoke QC again or try to load any TSR [terminate and stay resident] programs.)

At various times temporary windows will appear that contain progress reports and instructions about what to do next. You'll encounter distinct window types at various times, any of which can be zoomed to cover the entire screen.

Let's now look in detail at the main menu, the key to further progress.

► *The Main Menu* ►

The essential maneuvers to learn are the following:

1. Alt by itself toggles on the menu bar. Notice how the menu bar changes in appearance as you toggle Alt.

2. With the menu bar on, a single letter—F, E, V, S, M, R, D, U, O, or H—will pull down the corresponding menu (see Table 1.1).

3. Alt-*letter* gets a main menu selection at any time, whether the menu bar is on or off.

The *main menu* is the very top bar showing the 10 main options (which are cleverly named so that each starts with a unique capital letter). This allows selection by keying the appropriate letter (together with the Alt key if the bar is inactive) or by selecting each option in turn using the left/right arrow keys. The selected option appears with a black background, whereas the unselected options remain in reverse video.

Once you have marked your choice, pressing Enter completes the selection. This convenient and contemporary method is used throughout QuickC and is easier to do than to explain. From now on, when I give an instruction such as "Select File menu," I will leave it to your own good taste which selection method you use: typing Alt then F, or Alt-F, or lowlighting the File legend and then pressing Enter. Any of these actions will pull down the File menu.

The main selections operate their own pull-down menus to offer further subselections, many of which sprout further multichoice displays. Another neat trick to remember is that while a menu option is pulled down, the left/ right arrow keys can be used to invoke the adjacent menus. When you reach Help, using a further right arrow cycles you back to File. Table 1.2 gives a brief summary of the main menu selections.

► *Table 1.2: Main menu selections*

File Menu:		
sf	**New**	
sf	**O**pen...	
f	Open Last File	F2
f	**Merge**...	
sf	**S**ave	
sf	Save **A**s...	
f	Save All	
sf	**Print**...	
f	**DOS** Shell	
sf	Exit	Alt-F4
Edit Menu:		
f	Undo	Alt-backspace
sf	Cut	Shift-Del
sf	Copy	Ctrl-Ins
sf	Paste	Shift-Ins
f	Clear	Del
f	**R**ead Only	

► **Table 1.2:** *Main menu selections (continued)*

View Menu:

f	Source...	
f	Include...	
sf	**O**utput Screen	F4
f	Maximize	Ctrl-F10
f	**W**indows...	

Search Menu:

sf	**F**ind...	
f	**S**elected Text	Ctrl-\
sf	**R**epeat Last Find	F3
sf	**C**hange...	
f	Function	
sf	Next Error	Shift-F3
sf	Previous Error	Shift-F4

Make Menu:

f	**C**ompile File	
sf	**B**uild File	
f	**R**ebuild File	
f	**S**et Program List...	
f	**E**dit Program List...	
f	Clear Program List	

Run Menu:

| sf | **R**estart | Shift-F5 |
| sf | **G**o | F5 |

► **Table 1.2:** *Main menu selections (continued)*

Run Menu (continued):

f   **C**ontinue to Cursor   F7

sf   **T**race Into   F8

sf   **S**tep Over   F10

f   **A**nimate

Debug Menu:

f   **C**alls...

sf   **B**reakpoint...   F9

f   Watch **p**oint...

sf   **W**atch Value...

f   **M**odify Value...

f   **Hi**story On (toggle)

f   **U**ndo

f   **R**eplay

f   **T**runcate User Input

Utility Menu:

sf   **R**un DOS Command...

sf   **C**ustomize Menu...

sf   **L**earn QuickC

sf   Customize **E**ditor...

Options Menu:

sf   **D**isplay

f   **M**ake

f   **R**un/Debug

► **Table 1.2:** *Main menu selections (continued)*

Options Menu (continued):

f   **E**nvironment

sf   **F**ull Menus (toggle)

► *sf—appears on both short menu and full menu*
  f—appears on full menu only

► *Short and Full Menus* ►

Before you get dazzled by the menu choices, let's see how QuickC allows you to reduce the amount of clutter in the pull-down menu windows. You can elect to go for short or full menus. The former mode removes some of the less common choices from your menus. There is no specific Short option: you get short menus simply by turning off the Full Menus option. In learning how to select and deselect full menus, you'll acquire some basic navigational skills that apply in many other situations. The written steps always make these maneuvers seem more complex than they are in practice. First we'll select full menus mode.

Select the Options menu in any one of the standard ways:

1. Press Alt to activate the menu bar, then press O (or o).

2. Press Alt to activate the menu bar, then press the right arrow until the Options menu is marked. Press Enter.

3. Press Alt-O (or Alt-o).

4. Mouse-click on the Options menu legend.

If you see a dot to the left of the Full Menus legend, then you know that full menus mode is active, and you can press Esc to return to the source window. If full menus is inactive (no dot), you can select it by typing F (or by using the down arrow to mark the Full Menus box, then pressing Enter). The Options menu will now disappear, so bring it back with Alt-O, and notice the difference that full menus mode makes. In full menus you'll see five options displayed: Display, Make, Run/Debug, Environment, and Full Menus. Note again that the capital letters D, M, R, E, and F are highlighted and are all distinct, allowing further selection by typing a unique letter.

Deselecting the Full Menus option is also done by typing F while the Options menu is pulled down. In other words, F acts as a *toggle*: If Full Menus is on, F turns it off; if it's off, F will turn it on. With Full Menus off, notice that the short Options menu offers only two of the five Full Menus selections: Display and Full Menus. Table 1.2 indicates both full and short menu options for each of the 9 main pull-down menus.

Play with this a bit to get the idea. Leave Full Menus on, pull down the Options menu, then use the left arrow to pull down each of the main pull-down menus in turn. Repeat this drill in the short menus mode and note the reduction in choices as each menu is displayed.

▶ *QC.INI Saves Your Options* ▶

An interesting twist is that QuickC remembers your last choice, so that when you exit and later return to QuickC, the full or short menus will be selected automatically to match your previous selection. Other options you'll meet are also remembered from session to session. The mechanism is a small file called QC.INI that is created or updated each time you exit QuickC. If QC.INI is not found when you start up QuickC, the system assumes certain defaults. QC.INI is not an ASCII file, by the way, so don't try to print or display it.

▶ *Active Choices* ▶

When you are browsing around the menus, notice that the initial letters of a set of menu choices are not always distinct. For example, in the File menu you'll find Save, Save As..., and Save All. Upon closer inspection, however, you'll see that these are highlighted distinctly as follows: **S**ave, Save **A**s..., and Sa**v**e All, indicating that the key, trigger letters—S, A, and V—are unique (note the selection is case insensitive).

The three dots (known as *ellipses*) indicate that when you select Save As..., for instance, you will be called upon to supply further information via some form of window, submenu, or dialog box.

A further visual clue is the highlighted letter itself. This is a dynamic signal indicating that the option is valid under the prevailing conditions. As you interact with QC, these letter highlights might appear or disappear. For example, the Edit Program List option in the Make menu will only show a highlighted E if a program list exists for that session. Attempting to call an unavailable or invalid option will invoke a discouraging rasp from the PC lo-fi system.

► *Of Mice and Trackballs* ►

If you have a Microsoft or compatible mouse (or trackball), QuickC lets you point and click in the usual way, rather than using the cursor-movement and entry keys. You can click on menu legends or on the legends shown in the reference bar at the bottom of the screen. You can also do most of the "Macintosh" tricks with the main menu scroll bars or drag the editor position marker to any part of the file being edited, thereby saving much much effort with the arrow, PgUp, PgDn, Home, and End keys.

► *WRITING AND SAVING YOUR FIRST PROGRAM* ►

Fire up QC and carefully enter the HELLO.C program by typing in the source screen as shown in Figure 1.4.

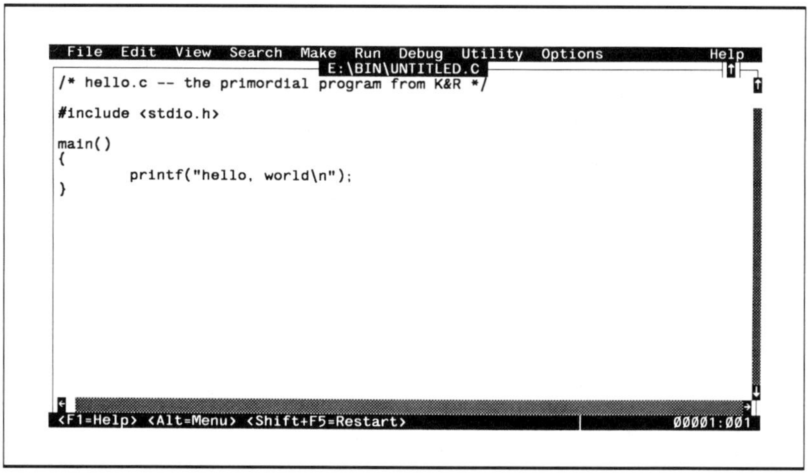

```
File  Edit  View  Search  Make  Run  Debug  Utility  Options          Help
                      E:\BIN\UNTITLED.C
/* hello.c -- the primordial program from K&R */

#include <stdio.h>

main()
{
        printf("hello, world\n");
}




<F1=Help> <Alt=Menu> <Shift+F5=Restart>                        00001:001
```

► **Figure 1.4:** *HELLO.C in source window*

I will not go into detail here on how to edit your keystrokes. The PC cursor-movement, backspace, Del, and Ins keys work in the obvious way and will suffice for this modest exercise. Later, you'll see that a whole arsenal of editing, searching, cutting, and pasting functions is available, broadly based on MicroPro's classic WordStar conventions but capable of customization to suit all your bad habits. You can even invoke your own word-processing or text editor and dispense with QC's built-in editor.

Your source code is now stored in RAM, and you could compile, link, and run it without further ado. However, RAM is notoriously volatile. Power outages and other catastrophes may nullify hours of effort, so regularly saving to disk as you enter and edit source code is a sanity-preserving habit worth developing. Whenever you select Save from the File menu, you save the current contents of the editor screen into the directory/file name shown in the title bar. Since the title bar still says UNTITLED.C, we need to use the Save As... feature, which lets you rename the saved file.

To save your source code as HELLO.C, select Save As... from the File menu using the sequence Alt-F, then A. A large window, known as a dialog box, will appear, inviting you to name the target directory/file name, as shown in Figure 1.5. Type HELLO.C to replace UNTITLED.C in the file-name box, then press Enter. Since the OK box, known as a *command button*, is highlighted, Enter means OK to save. To cancel the Save As... request, you would tab to highlight the Cancel button, then press Enter. Similarly, you can tab to

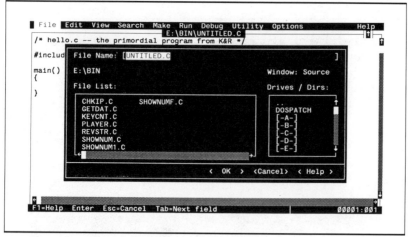

► *Figure 1.5:* The Save As... dialog box

highlight the Help button, then press Enter for Help. With command buttons, you can press Enter to trigger the highlighted action no matter where the cursor happens to be. Mousers can simply click on the command button for instant action. The Save As... display is typical of many dialog boxes used in QuickC, so I've explained the rather obvious and intuitive maneuvers in some detail. Dialog boxes such as Save As... often allow you to select a target name from the file directory listing, but for the moment this feature is not useful (mainly because HELLO.C does not yet exist!).

The title bar now shows HELLO.C, and you are almost ready to compile, link, and run this gem. First, though, a few chores to complete.

► *Checking and Setting the Environment* ►

Select Environment in the Options menu (you must be in full menus mode for this to be available). Make sure that the Include Files directory and Library File directory correspond to the places where your *.H and *.LIB files are located (typically, the procedures in SETUP will have given you X:\QC2\INCLUDE and X:\QC2\LIB, where X: is your preferred drive). Correct them if necessary, then press Enter. QC.INI will automatically save this data for subsequent sessions.

When you compile HELLO.C, the QC preprocessor will look for the include file STDIO.H in the directory specified by this Options/Environment setting. You'll get error messages such as **C1015 Cannot open include file 'filename'** if any *.H files are not found in the proper place. (Note that this message may also occur if QC runs out of file handles. If so, set a larger value of n in your **CONFIG.SYS FILES = n** line.)

Similarly, during linking, QC will expect to find any required library files (usually one of the combined libraries created during SETUP such as SLIBCE.LIB or SLIBC7.LIB) in the stated Library File directory.

► *RUNNING HELLO* ►

QC lets you compile, link, and run a program in separate stages or as a single operation. The basic idea is that if you ask QC to run HELLO, the system is smart enough to check around and decide on any prior compile/link steps needed to run HELLO.EXE. In the present situation QC determines that

HELLO.OBJ and HELLO.EXE are both missing, so a compile/link (also known as a *build*) is triggered automatically. On other occasions QC may discover that HELLO.C has been changed (edited) since the last compile/link, so although HELLO.OBJ and/or HELLO.EXE may be present, they may be out of date. If so, you will be prompted with a dialog box asking if you wish to rebuild—that is, recompile/relink. You can also force a rebuild regardless of the edit history of your source code.

When your programs consist of several modules in different *.C files, the build process is more complex because the various *.C and *.OBJ files involved may have complex dependencies and different edit histories. This is where various *Make* strategies are employed to automate the building operation. Depending on the date stamps and interdependencies of the underlying files, a Make utility will do the minimum amount of recompiling/relinking to produce a valid, updated *.EXE file.

For now, let's learn the separate build (compile/link) and run requests, remembering that run by itself will often trigger a build. Both have hot keys for immediate action:

Shift-F5   will build HELLO.C to give HELLO.OBJ and HELLO.EXE.

F5   will run HELLO.EXE.

Their menu equivalents in the Run menu are Restart (for build) and Go (for run).

► *Build and Run* ►

When you key Shift-F5, a window appears showing you QC's progress as HELLO.C is digested by the preprocessor, compiler, and linker. You'll see the number of lines and other stats flash by, then if no errors are detected the progress window will disappear. If you ran DIR HELLO.* now, you would see HELLO.OBJ and HELLO.EXE.

Any errors or warning messages will appear in a separate error window below the source screen. You can use Maximize (by typing Z) in the View menu (or hot key Ctrl-F10) to enlarge (zoom) this error window to full-screen size should you be unlucky enough to generate more than five or six error messages. This ploy, by the way, works on all of the main QC windows—whichever one is active (i.e., the one containing the cursor) can be maximized without losing data from the other windows.

Correct any errors, then type S to save your corrected file from the File menu. Because HELLO.C shows in the title bar, you do not have to enter a file name as you did with Save As.... Now rebuild with Shift-F5. (I'll have more to say on errors and debugging later.)

Now press F5 (or select Go from the Run menu). The output screen will appear as in Figure 1.6. The words *screen* and *window*, by the way, are often used interchangeably in the QC literature, without any real confusion: the output window happens to be the whole screen, whereas the other basic windows may form part or all of a screen.

```
Esc:Menu Pnum Wrap+Sp- 99% Free. 40% Thru. Edit "D:\TEMP\fig16.fig"
Mon 3-3-1989 / 12:04:09.03  :  E:\BIN
E>qc hello
  HELLO.EXE
hello, world

Elapsed time = 00:00:00.05  Program returned (13)  Press any key
```

► *Figure 1.6: Output for HELLO.EXE*

Notice that QC displays **HELLO.EXE**, the name of the program being executed, followed by whatever the program outputs, in this case the cheery **hello, world**. In a moment I'll analyze the program in some detail, but while you have QC running, here are a few more basic menu maneuvers.

► *Flipping Screens* ►

Press any key to return to the source window. Now use F4 (or the equivalent, Output Screen in the View menu) to return to the output screen. F4 flips you between the two screens at any time without losing your cursor position in the source window.

► *Loading Files* ►

Selecting New from the File menu clears HELLO.C from the editor. If you have failed to save the latest version (in spite of my pleas), QC reminds you, and you can choose Save, Not Save, or Cancel. Notice that the title bar now says UNTITLED.C; this is QC's standard way of telling you that the source editor is empty.

Now enter F2 (or the equivalent, Open Last File in the File menu). The file HELLO.C will return to the source window, being the most recent file you were editing. Type something in HELLO.C, then select Open... from the File menu. You will see a dialog box similar to the Save As... box. You can enter a target file to be loaded, or you can tab the cursor through the directory listing to select a file from your current directory. In either case, before clearing HELLO.C and loading a new file, the familiar warning will appear that HELLO.C has changed and may need saving.

► *Rerunning* ►

Now that you have HELLO.EXE, you can return to DOS and type HELLO quite independently of QC. Alternatively, you can select Run DOS Command from within QC via the Utility menu. A dialog box invites you to enter a DOS command or program, and when this has been executed, you press any key to return to QC. You can also invoke the DOS shell from the File menu and do any series of DOS work, finally typing exit to return to QC. While operating the DOS shell (which is essentially a fresh copy of COMMAND.COM in memory), you must avoid loading any TSR programs and you must not try to run QC! Doing either of these confuses the memory mapping of QC and leads to bizarre behavior.

If you have HELLO.C in the editor, you can use F5 (or Go) at any time. If nothing has changed since HELLO.EXE was formed, HELLO.EXE will run immediately; otherwise, a rebuild will be triggered, followed by a run.

► *HELLO.C—ANATOMY LESSON* ►

We leave QuickC, per se, to study line by line the text of HELLO.C (Program 1.1). It reveals several major facts about every C program.

```
/* hello.c--hello, world */
#include <stdio.h>
main()
{
    printf("hello, world\n");
}
```

► **Program 1.1:** *HELLO.C*

► *Comments (Line 1)* ►

► **/* hello.c—hello, world */** You are free, nay, encouraged, to sprinkle your source with *comments*. Any text you care to enter between **/*** and ***/** is ignored by the compiler (it is treated as white space). Like a **REM** line in BASIC, this text is there to help you and your next of kin. Since C allows many compact, unobvious expressions, commenting the obscurities is more necessary than with "verbose" languages such as Modula-2. Comments also provide a method of declaring version numbers, dates, authorship, and copyright. Remember, too, that statements that might appear crystal clear today can become obscure as time goes by.

Unlike BASIC's **REM**, C comments can straddle lines:

```
/*
    this is a comment
    so is this */
```

Standard C does not permit the *nesting* of comments. In other words, you cannot insert comments in a piece of code that already contains comments. If you added **/*** and ***/** as follows, hoping to effectively remove the **#include** line, it would not work. If you were to write

```
/*
/* hello.c—hello, world */

#include <stdio.h> */
```

the first ***/** encountered would be matched with the opening **/***, and commenting would cease prematurely. QuickC offers a nesting comment option via the Options menu, but using it can jeopardize program portability. You'll meet a safer way of *commenting out* when we discuss the **#if** directive.

► *White Space (Lines 2 and 4)* ►

The empty lines form *white space* that is ignored by the compiler. Generally speaking, carriage return, line feed, space, and tab codes, apart from serving as possible identifier separators, have no syntactic significance. In other words, if one space is needed after an identifier, then several spaces or tabs are acceptable. The physical layout of a C program can be arranged for maximum legibility without affecting its meaning. C contrasts sharply with BASIC, say, in which a new line is always syntactically significant. HELLO.C would not be compiled differently if you retyped it as

```
/* hello.c—hello, world */
#include <stdio.h>
main( ) {printf("hello, world\n");}
```

You *must* move to a new line after a directive, by the way, to prevent possible parsing problems with the preprocessor.

► *Include Directive (Line 3)* ►

► *#include <stdio.h>*   As explained earlier, the # symbol indicates that the following identifier is a preprocessor *directive*. In this instance, **#include** directs the preprocessor to add the source code of the file STDIO.H to the rest of HELLO.C prior to compilation.

You can tell the system where to find STDIO.H by using full drive/path information, or you can use angle brackets, as in **<stdio.h>**, meaning "look first in the \include directory as preset in the Options menu."

You can also write **#include "stdio.h"** using double quotes. This says, "look first in the working directory." For our purposes the *<filename>* method will suffice.

We'll return to study the contents of STDIO.H after we've looked at functions and definitions.

► *The main() Function (Line 5)* ►

► *main( )*   A C program consists of a series of *functions*. In C the word *function* is used in a wider sense than in most other languages. C functions subsume the notions of subroutine and procedure as well as the "conventional" function of BASIC or Pascal.

With C almost any block of statements can be lumped together to *define* a function to which a unique name is assigned. When that name is encountered anywhere in a program, the function is *called* or *invoked*, and the statements used to define the function are obeyed.

The block of statements defining the action of a function can include calls to other previously defined functions (including itself, *recursively*, as we say), which in turn may contain calls to other predefined functions, and so on.

Functions are therefore the heart and soul of C, and much of this book is devoted to showing how functions are built up from more primitive elements, including libraries of machine-specific functions used for I/O and memory management, for example.

When a function needs input data, referred to as *arguments* or *parameters*, they appear within parentheses after the function name and are separated by commas:

```
function_name(arg1, arg2, arg3,...);
```

You can picture the above statement as an instruction to the system to perform the previously defined function, *function_name*, using the given values *arg1*, *arg2*, and so on. Some functions take a fixed number of arguments (including none), while others can take a varying number (including none), depending on the circumstances.

A familiar example from mathematics would be the function **cube(N)**, which calculates the cube of the single argument **N**. Calling **cube(3)** would return **27**. **N** is called a *formal parameter* to distinguish it from the **3**, which is the *actual* or *real* parameter used when calling **cube( )**. Much more on this important subject anon.

The action of a function will depend entirely on the statements used in its definition and the particular values of the arguments supplied, if any. The result may be a useful *returned* value, as with conventional functions, or it may simply be an action such as displaying a message on the screen, as with conventional procedures.

You soon learn to look on functions as black boxes—you shove values in and get values or actions out. Life is too short to know exactly what goes on inside every black box. Have faith!

When a function requires no arguments, C notation still requires that you put parentheses after the function name even though there is nothing within them. In some circumstances to be discussed later, the absence of arguments is made more explicit by writing *function_name* (void). The parentheses convention makes it easier for you *and* the compiler to spot the functions in any piece of source code! Note that we will often write *name( )* without bothering to spell out the arguments to indicate that we are discussing a function rather than some other object called *name*.

You can now rightly deduce that in HELLO.C **main( )** is a function called with no arguments, whereas **printf( )** is a function called with one *string* argument. In HELLO.C the string argument happens to be a *string constant* or *string literal* for the obvious reasons that its value, **hello, world\n**, remains fixed and is expressed "literally." Later you'll meet *string variables* that can assume different string values at the whim of the programmer. The function **printf( )** can accept both kinds of string arguments and other types of arguments, by the way.

A string constant in C is any sequence of characters between double quotes, as in "**hello, world\n**". In technical parlance a string is an *array* of characters terminated by the ASCII NUL character (value 0). You don't ever "see" this NUL, but it's stored at the end of every string, or, to be more accurate, it *is* the end of every string (hence the song "Without a NUL, That String Would Never End!").

The strange looking \n provides a *newline character* and will be explained later in this chapter.

Note in passing that under different circumstances **main( )** and **printf( )** might be invoked with a different number of arguments.

The function **main( )** has a unique role to play in all C programs. Since a C program consists of sequences of functions, you may wonder which one fires up first. The answer is that **main( )**, wherever it is placed physically in the source code, is the "leader." Every complete C program must have just one **main( )** somewhere, and this is where C starts off when executing the compiled/linked code. To see what **main( )** does, you need to look at the block or body of code following it. This leads us to the next feature of HELLO.C, *block markers*.

► *Block Markers (Lines 6 and 8)* ►

► { }   Curly braces are used to signal the start and end of a block of code. They play the same role as **BEGIN** and **END** in other structured languages.

To discover what **main( )** does, you need to check out all the statements lying between the first { following **main( )** and its matching final }. This is quite simple in the case of HELLO.C since you find only the single statement

```
{
    printf("hello, world\n");
}
```

In real-world programs, **main( )** could have many other blocks *nested* inside the outer, or principal, { and } block markers. The number of {'s must always match the number of }'s, of course. There are typographical conventions to help the eye in detecting nested blocks, and these will emerge as we proceed.

The key point here is that any lump of code placed between matching pairs of curly braces represents a block that tells the compiler how to break down and process "units" of the program. In simple terms, a group of statements within { and } acts like a single, compound statement. The block concept will be clarified when you see more complex situations.

► *The printf() Function Call (Line 7)* ►

► ***printf("hello, world\n");*** As you've seen, the body of **main( )** contains the single line shown above, which is a call to the function **printf( )** with a string constant as argument.

printf( ) is a precompiled library function supplied with QuickC (and all other conforming C compilers) that displays formatted (hence the f *in* **printf**) *strings of characters on your standard output* device, which for the moment simply means your monitor screen.

The name *print* is a well-entrenched archaism dating back to those sybaritic days when output terminals were teleprinters or Flexowriters. Nowadays we have CRT's (also known as *glass teleprinters*) but the verb "print," meaning "display," still survives.

The particular version of **printf( )** supplied with the QuickC library has been written specifically for the computers in the IBM PC family (or compatibles) running under DOS. The C language achieves portability by not getting involved directly with all the machine- and OS-dependent tricks needed for device and file I/O. Your HELLO.C would compile and run on a Cray and

VAX because their libraries contain a **printf( )** written specially for their respective hardware and operating systems.

    printf( ) turns out to be quite a complex function, able to accept a variable number of parameters. Its usage in HELLO.C hides the fact that it can be used to display both numbers and strings in a wide range of formats. To display a single string like **hello, world** you can actually use a much simpler function called **puts( )**. You'll see this shortly in an exercise with the QuickC editor.

► *The Escape Sequence (Line 7)* ►

    ► **\n**   The escape character \ (familiar to UNIX users) is used to solve the problem of inserting nonprintable control codes or difficult characters into a string. For example, it's clearly impossible to plant a new line after **hello, world** by pressing Enter as in

    printf("hello, world<Enter>");

The Enter key does give a new line on the screen during input, but the compiler ignores it! To get a true new line, you type the escape sequence **\n**.

    Similarly, there is a problem if you want to display a string containing *real* double quotes. In

    printf("I am saying "Hello"");

QuickC would take the second " as an end to the string "**I am saying** ". What to do? You use the escape sequence \" for the internal double quotes as in

    printf("I am saying \"Hello\"");

which will display **I am saying** "Hello".

    The escape character \ tells the compiler to treat the following character(s) in an unusual way—i.e., *escape* from the normal interpretation. Such characters are sometimes called *metacharacters* since they have significance outside the normal set. Table 1.3 indicates how QuickC translates the escape sequences.

► *Table 1.3: Escape sequences*

Sequence	Value	ASCII	Function
\0	0	NUL	String terminator
\a	0x07	BEL	Audible bell ("attention")
\b	0x08	BS	Backspace
\f	0x0C	FF	Form feed
\n	0x0A	LF	New line (line feed)
\r	0x0D	CR	Carriage return
\t	0x09	HT	Horizontal tab
\v	0x0B	VT	Vertical tab
\\	0x5C	\	Backslash
\'	0x27	'	Single quote (apostrophe)
\"	0x22	"	Double quote
\ddd	0ddd	any	1- to 3-digit octal value
\xhhh	0xhh	any	1- to 2-digit hex value

> ► *In the Value column, octal constants start with 0 and hex constants start with 0x. This 0 is not needed after \.*

► *Escape with Special Characters*

Because the single apostrophe has the special function of designating single character constants, you can see why \' is needed to express a literal '. Similarly, \\ must be used to get a single literal \. The first \ protects the following character from being treated as a metacharacter, so '\'' means the ASCII character 047 or 0x27 (''' is illegal), and '\\' means the ASCII character 0134 or 0x5C ('\' will not work!).

► *Back to \n*

Coming back to \n, note that in place of

```
printf("hello, world\n");
```

you could achieve the same result with

```
printf("hello, ");
printf("world");
printf("\n");
```

The first statement displays **hello,** and leaves the cursor sitting after the space, waiting for something to happen. Then **world** is displayed, and, finally, **printf("\n");** provides a new line on the screen. Yes,

```
printf("\n\n\a\a");
```

would give two new lines followed by two ringy-dingies (ASCII BEL character).

Once you've mastered the QuickC editor, you can "ring" the changes on HELLO.C with such variants as

```
printf("\t\\hello\t\a\aworld\n\n");
```

This would display a tab indent followed by **hello.** You would then get two rings, and **world** followed by two new lines would be displayed.

► *A Detour into Data Types* ►

Individual character constants, as opposed to strings of them, can be expressed with single quotes: '**A**', '\101', '\x41', and '\X41' all represent the same ASCII character.

You may be wondering if there is any difference between the single character '**A**' and the one-character string "**A**". There are two differences worthy of a slight detour:

1. '**A**' and "**A**" are different *data types*. '**A**' is of type **char**, stored and treated numerically as an integer, whereas "**A**" is of type *array of* **char**. It just happens that in this example the array holds one significant character.

   As in Pascal (but unlike BASIC) C requires that the data type of each identifier be *declared* before it is used in a program.

The "why" of declarations is quite simple: The compiler can use them to efficiently allocate memory for each constant and variable and possibly check that your statements make sense (adding chalk and cheese may not be allowed). The "how" of declarations is not so easy and will be revealed as time goes by.

2. Since "**A**" is a string, it requires a final NUL, so it's stored in 2 bytes— "**A**" and NUL. Single character constants strictly need only 1 byte, but C treats them as integers as a matter of arithmetical convenience (permitting such tricks as ('A' + 1) to give '**B**'). QuickC stores **int** type integers in 2 bytes, reflecting the 16-bit registers of the IBM PC microprocessor. So, when you store a single character constant as a 2-byte integer, what happens to the other byte? In the case of '**A**', the lower byte would contain 0x41 with the upper byte usually *sign extended*—i.e., filled with 0's or 1's, depending on the value of the eighth (most significant or sign) bit of the lower byte. For characters in the standard ASCII range (decimal values 0–127), the sign bit is 0, so the upper byte is 0x00.

► *Statement Terminator (Line 7)* ►

► **;** The semicolon at the end of the **printf( )** line indicates the end of a *statement*. It is officially called a *statement terminator* in C to distinguish it from statement *separator* symbols used in other languages.

In C a line of text can contain several statements, and a statement can straddle several lines, so the ; plays a vital role in telling the compiler how to translate your code correctly. Note, however, that no ; is needed after the final } block marker. The compiler already knows the statement is ended.

You *can* legally enter a ; without having a prior statement. This represents a null or *empty* statement, which sounds rather Zen but does prove useful in situations in which the syntax demands a statement but there is no action required. (Compare this with **NOP**, the *no operation* instruction found in assembly languages.)

Note also that no semicolon is needed after the **#include** directive. The preprocessor has its own set of rules, one of which is that directives are terminated by a new line.

► *Statements and Expressions—Another Necessary Detour* ►

A C program normally runs by executing each of its statements in sequence, just as you would read them on the page. This sequential execution can be altered using various *control flow* or *conditional* statements, such as

if *(expression)* {*statement(s)*}

which says, "carry out {*statement(s)*} only if *(expression)* is true." Another example is

while *(expression)* {*statement(s)*}

which says, "keep obeying {*statement(s)*} while *(expression)* is true." There are no special Boolean data types in C, by the way. False simply means 0, and true means nonzero (usually 1).

These concepts are introduced briefly here to illustrate the use of the statement terminator. (The whole of Chapter 4 is devoted to C's armory of control flow constructs—without which, of course, programs would be confined to dull slogging through fixed sequences.) Informally, we can offer the approximate hierarchy of C language constructs shown in Table 1.4.

► *Table 1.4:* C constructs with approximate English equivalents

C	English	Examples
operands (variables & constants)	words	sum, total, flag "hello", 'A', 3
operators (arithmetic, logic, etc.)	verbs	==, =, *, +
expressions	phrases	(sum == total) flag = 1 total = sum + 3
statements	sentences	flag = 1; total = sum + 3;
complex statement	long sentence	if (sum == total) flag = 1;

The last example means, "if the values represented by **sum** and **total** are equal, then set **flag** to value 1." Note that the *assignment* operator (=) and the *equality* operator (= =) are different. In the example of a complex statement, there is no ; after the *expression* (**sum** = = **total**)—the whole statement does not terminate until after the *statement* **flag** = 1;.

Expressions in C are unusually active creatures: They not only trigger the appropriate activity according to the operands and operators found therein but are also *evaluated* in the sense that they actually acquire a value that reflects the operation.

This is so unlike BASIC and Pascal that it can be somewhat disconcerting to the beginner. The expression **flag** = 1 not only assigns the value 1 to **flag** but also "takes on" the value of **flag**, namely 1. So, you can find busy statements like

```
total = (sum = 2) + 3;                    /* set sum to 2 and total to 5 */
```

or

```
total = sum = 3;                          /* set sum and total to 3 */
```

Expressions that pack a lot of punch give C its unique flavor but can lead to over-compact, hard-to-read code if taken to extremes.

As soon as you add the magic semicolon, you complete that particular statement. QuickC will pause to digest, as it were, all the rubbish since the previous ; or }, and all the expressions in the statement will be obeyed and evaluated according to the precise rules of *precedence* and *associativity*. Depending on any conditionals encountered, execution will resume with the next or some other statement.

► *HELLO.C Summary* ►

I seem to have been continually sidetracked while trying to divine the modus operandi of my naive example, so I'll recapitulate. The key points can be summarized as follows:

1. Source code HELLO.C plus STDIO.H compiles to form HELLO.OBJ. HELLO.OBJ is linked with object code in the QuickC library to give us the executable file HELLO.EXE.

2. You learned how to set up options on the QuickC environment and load and run a program from the main menu.

3. The anatomy of HELLO.C:

   / */* for comments
   directives: **#include** <**stdio.h**>
   new line after directives—no semicolon
   white space for pretty layout
   the **main( )** function
   the function body and block markers **{ }**
   printf( ) and function arguments
   string constants: "**hello, world\n**"
   escape sequences: **\n** for a new line
   statement terminator: semicolon

► *Compile-Time Errors* ►

Unlike the BASIC interpreter you may be used to, QuickC does not immediately spot syntax errors on a line-by-line basis. Rather, being a compiler, QuickC inspects as much of your complete source code as possible before reporting your errors and inviting corrections. Such errors and warnings are referred to as *compile-time* problems.

Warnings are usually nonfatal, whereas errors must be corrected and the program recompiled and relinked before further progress is possible. The Make utility is a clever aid in such situations; using the *.MAK files and program lists mentioned earlier, it can help automate the recompiling and relinking process depending on *which* files have changed since the last compilation.

Several C interpreters or combined interpreter/compilers are now available. The trade-off is traditionally between the higher execution speed of compilers and the immediate error detection of interpreters. In fact, QuickC compiles quickly enough to settle such arguments.

Some errors may surface during linking, such as missing or misplaced .OBJ files, but these are usually corrected by telling the linker where to look. The linker may also uncover discrepancies between the modules. I'll tell you more on this when I discuss multifile programs.

► *Run-Time Errors* ►

The completed .EXE file contains all the machine code required for loading and execution by your operating system (PC-DOS or MS-DOS). Just like the many .EXE files provided with DOS, your newly created .EXE file can be invoked at any time by simply typing HELLO at the C> prompt and pressing Enter.

The fact that your code is free from syntax and other compile- and link-time errors does not guarantee that the .EXE program will run as expected or at all! *Run-time* errors come in many delicious flavors, ranging from endless loops to total system crashes, from polite error messages to getting the wrong results without a warning.

As with natural languages, you need to distinguish *syntax* (superficial conformity) from *semantics* (the deep meaning, if any). Legal statements, alas, may compile into nonsense that the system cannot usefully execute or even survive. The C language, you'll discover, is not especially mollycoddling as are Ada, Pascal, and Modula-2. In providing the power and compact notation to let you operate efficiently and close to the "machine level," the C syntax places fewer restrictions on the dumb and dangerous things you can do if you really try. C, as it were, is like assembly language in that it assumes you can handle a loaded shotgun without a safety catch. Other languages worry about your competence and make you line up for firearm permits.

Another real possibility is that your program might run to completion but fail to reflect your intentions. Either your original problem analysis, input data, or algorithms are faulty, or there are errors in your coding (or all of the above). An essential part of mastering QuickC (and any other programming language) is to develop debugging skills to track down and fix such problems. Some guidance on this vast subject will be provided in later chapters, but don't expect any magical sesames.

Finally, with software as complex as DOS and the QuickC package, you cannot entirely rule out bugs (also known as unpublished features) in the systems software. Since the latter probably have been subjected to more testing than your own programs, it is wise to double-check your work before blaming others. If you feel certain that the systems software is at fault, your report to the software vendor *must* be precisely documented with your program listings, screen printouts, hardware configuration, DOS level, and the serial numbers of your package. Unless your reported bug can be repeated under your exact configuration and environment, it will be virtually impossible to fix.

▸ *USING THE QUICKC EDITOR* ▸

Because .C and .H files are ASCII text files, you can use almost any text editor to create and modify your source files. Most word-processing packages offer a *nondocument* option that avoids peculiar formatting and typesetting codes that might upset the compiler. Since Microsoft includes a very flexible text editor with QuickC that is specially equipped to produce readable .C files, it makes sense to try it out. This editor arrives set to work almost exactly like the nondocument mode of the popular WordStar package from Micro-Pro International, but the Customizing Editor menu, detailed in Appendix B, allows you to customize the editor to suit your own bizarre prejudices.

I will not, therefore, confuse (or bore) you with a key-by-key account of the editing process itself. When I do refer to specific editor control keys, I will use the standard QuickC versions. If you are new to any form of text editing, the only way forward is constant practice and experiment with the following basic maneuvers.

▸ *Basic Editing Features* ▸

▸ *Cursor movement*   Moving right/left/up/down; moving to end/start of words, lines, screens, blocks, and files. Scrolling and paging up and down. Note that the line and column numbers are displayed dynamically on the right-hand side of the reference bar.

▸ *Insert on/off*   Toggled with the Ins key, determines whether your typing will write over (insert off) or "push" (insert on) existing text. Watch for the flashing solid cursor shape, which indicates that insert mode is on. The flashing underline cursor tells you that insert mode is off.

▸ *Deleting*   Use Del and backspace to remove a character under or to the left of the cursor. Use control combinations to erase words, whole or part lines, or blocks.

▸ *Block marking*   Use the Edit menu to move, copy, delete selected blocks.

► **Search and replace**   Use the Search menu to hunt for a target string with or without a replacement string. Many options, allowing searches with or without case sensitivity, with or without prompted replacements, with or without counted matches, with or without whole-word matching, and so on.

► *HELLO.C VARIATIONS* ►

To give you some useful practice with the built-in QuickC editor (as well as to extend your knowledge of C), make a copy of HELLO.C called HELLO1.C. Load HELLO1.C into the editor and try the following:

►   Alter the opening comments, changing **printf** to **puts** and removing the \n from the "**hello, world**" string. Use the File menu's Save option to save your changes. Your program should now look like Program 1.2.

```
/* hello1.c--hello, world variation */
#include <stdio.h>
main()
{
    puts("hello, world");
}
```

► *Program 1.2:* HELLO1.C

The function **puts( )** means, "put string." Like **printf( )**, it is declared in STDIO.H. **puts( )** is a simpler version of **printf( )**, taking only a single string argument and performing no formatting. **puts( )**, unlike **printf( )**, automatically appends a new line after displaying the string. *Put*, like *print*, is a common synonym in C for outputting *to* some device or file.

To gain familiarity with the menus, follow the procedure outlined in the following sections.

► *Compiling HELLO1.C* ►

Press Alt-M for the Make menu. Select C to produce HELLO1.OBJ. You can follow the progress of the compiler in the compiling window. If all is well, you will return to the source window without any error messages.

► *Error Correction (If Any)* ►

If you have mistyped, the error window lists the mistakes. A highlighted error message indicates your first mistake. Any other errors will be listed below the highlighted one. Use F6 to activate the error window. The arrow keys can be used to highlight each error in turn. As you move around the message window, the corresponding error in the source code is *tracked*— i.e., highlighted in the source window. Pressing F6 takes you to the offending line so you can correct it. You then press F6 to get back to the message window, select another error, and so on. Alternatively, you can press Shift-F3 (next error) or Shift-F4 (previous error) while in the edit window, and the cursor will move to the appropriate error line. When you type on the offending line, the highlight disappears.

When all the errors appear to have been corrected, you must recompile, recorrect, and re-recompile until you get it right! You will soon discover that a single source code error can often generate a host of apparently unrelated error messages. The reason for this disconcerting phenomenon will emerge as you learn more of the C syntax.

► *Linking HELLO1.C* ►

Select Alt-M, then Build. Since HELLO.OBJ is up to date, QuickC will simply link to produce HELLO1.EXE. Notice the progress window showing the linking process. QuickC is busy looking in the LIB directory for any referenced library functions. Again, success is signaled with a return to the source window. You can now select Go in the Run menu (or F5 directly). Since HELLO1.EXE exists, QuickC runs it immediately. The action of HELLO1.EXE is exactly the same as that of HELLO.EXE.

► *HELLO2.C* ►

The next variation to try is shown in HELLO2.C (Program 1.3). It introduces the **#define** directive, which is C's basic mechanism for creating *macros* and *aliases*.

```
/* hello2.c--hello, world variant */
#include <stdio.h>
#define GREETING "hello, world"
main()
{
    puts(GREETING);
}
```

► **Program 1.3:** *HELLO2.C*

The line added to HELLO1.C is

#define GREETING "hello, world"

and the argument for **puts( )** is changed to **GREETING**.

As with the **#include** directive, the # before **define** triggers action by the preprocessor. Each subsequent appearance of the *identifier* **GREETING** anywhere in your source code will be replaced by the string "**hello, world**" *before* compilation commences. So, when the preprocessor meets **puts(GREETING)**, the function call is changed to **puts("hello, world")**. We have concocted yet another way of achieving K&R's original goal!

If the preprocessor encounters the sequence **GREETING** *inside* a string, no substitution takes place. For example:

puts("GREETINGs dear friend");

will *not* be affected by the definition.

The use of **#define** here is somewhat artificial, but suppose that for some obscure reason you wanted to write a longer program peppered with occurrences of the string "**hello, world**". The one **#define** directive would eventually pay off in terms of reduced keystrokes. Before we assess the other advantages of **#define**, let's review the syntax involved. The general format for simple token substitution or aliasing is

#define *identifier string*

where you need at least one space or tab between each section and a final new line immediately after ***string***. If the string is too long to fit a single line, you can use the escape character (backslash) before the new line, then continue typing the rest of the string on the next line as in

```
#define WARNING "This is a very long warning, so I need a \
to avoid going off the screen"
```

Remember that a semicolon is a *statement* terminator, so you don't need one at the end of a directive.

▸ IDENTIFIER RULES ▸

The identifier in the **#define** line (called the *macro name*) must conform to the basic rules for all C identifiers:

1. Identifiers must start with an uppercase or lowercase letter or an underscore (_).

2. After the initial letter or underscore, you can have any number of characters from the following set: A–Z, a–z, underscore, slash (/), or the digits 0–9. QuickC actually uses only the first 31 characters of an identifier, however, so you should really show some restraint. The following two identifiers would not be distinct:

```
This_is_long_variable_numbered_1
This_is_long_variable_numbered_2
```

3. Because C is case sensitive, **Greeting** and **greeting** are distinct from **GREETING** and would not be affected by our **#define** directive.

4. It is customary but not mandatory to use all uppercase letters for macro-name identifiers simply to give a visual clue that they are not ordinary identifiers.

5. There are 40 *keywords* in QuickC that have preassigned meanings (see Table 1.5). These either cannot or should not be used as identifiers. Some reserved words may be used legitimately as macro names under special circumstances (usually to allow compatibility with pre-ANSI compilers), but the novice should accept the fact that keywords should only be used as nature intended. By the end of this book you will know the purpose of each of these keywords!

6. An initial underscore is traditionally reserved for *external* identifiers. You should avoid using such identifiers for your own internal objects.

► *SUBSTITUTION STRING RULES* ►

There are none! You can enter any sequence of characters, and they will be literally and exactly inserted in your source text, wherever the given

► **Table 1.5:** *QuickC keywords*

asm	if
auto	int
break	interrupt
case	long
cdecl	near
char	pascal
const	register
continue	return
default	short
do	signed
double	sizeof
else	static
enum	struct
extern	switch
far	typedef
float	union
for	unsigned
fortran	void
goto	volatile
huge	while

identifier is found. The only exception is the line-continuation trick using a backslash in which the backslash is not really part of the string.

Whether the substitution makes contextual sense will be determined by the compiler, not the preprocessor. This turns out to be an important issue when you meet more complex situations. A good safety-first rule is to enclose the string in parentheses to give it "syntactical" protection. The parentheses can do no harm, and they often prevent calamitous side effects due to C's precedence rules when evaluating complex expressions.

► DEFINING MACROS ►

The **#define** directive offers more than the simple substitution operation. Used as a *macro*, it allows arguments to be supplied, rather as you saw with functions. As with functions, you use (and) immediately after the macro name as in

```
#define cube(x)     ((x)*(x)*(x))     /* x is formal parameter */
/* "*" is the multiplication operator */
```

The string now defines how the formal parameters (just **x** in this case, but there may be more than one) are applied when the preprocessor encounters the token **cube** in the source text. So, **cube(3);** would be converted to **((3)*(3)*(3))** in situ before compilation, and **cube(a + b);** would become **((a + b)*(a + b)*(a + b))**, which may help you see the need for the parentheses in the **#define** line! Without them, you would get an ambiguous or erroneous result since **a + b*a + b*a + b** equals **a + (b*a) + (b*a) + b** because C places ***** higher in precedence than **+**. More on this anon.

► ON YOUR OWN ►

Write and compile Program 1.4 as a tribute to Bill Gates, the founder and CEO of Microsoft Corporation.

```
/*   GATES.C */
#include <stdio.h>
main()
{
    puts("Thanks, Bill!\n");
}
```

► **Program 1.4:** *GATES.C*

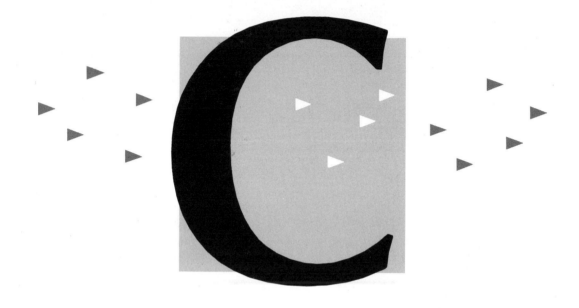

DATA TYPOLOGY

► *CHAPTER 2* ►

In Chapter 1, I introduced informally the concept of *data types*, explaining that QuickC needs to allocate appropriate amounts of memory to store different classes of objects. To keep my initial programs simple, I used only a special and rather limited class of data types known as *constants*. (I used character and string constants.) In this chapter you'll meet the arithmetical constants known as integers, but first you'll learn how to use integers as *variables*. There will be a certain amount of essential theory supported with examples before you return to the fun of QC.EXE.

To avoid repetition, many of the examples will be extracts rather than complete, compilable programs. Such snippets will not have the proper header files with a **main( )** function, and so on. Complete programs are given file names and program references—e.g., Program 2.3 is the third full program in Chapter 2.

► *WHY DATA TYPES?* ►

Now the compiler can determine the data types and memory requirements of constants from their actual typographical formats as they are encountered in the source text. However, when we use variables, the system needs some prior warning as to which data type we intend. Each data type has predetermined memory requirements and an associated range of legal values. This advanced warning is known as a data type *declaration*.

Data typing separates the identifiers used to denote variables into more or less immiscible categories, allowing the compiler to detect certain errors (like the proverbial adding of apples to pears or dividing chalk by cheese).

In *strongly typed* languages like Modula-2 and Ada, the data typing is strictly enforced so that even closely related data types cannot be intermixed without the programmer giving specific permission (or *type casting*). C is a *weakly typed* language, meaning that in many situations the compiler will quietly convert your data types to achieve compatibility within a mixed expression. It is rather like achieving *apples + pears* by first changing both to *fruit*.

Is strong typing better than weak typing? Each language has its own rationale and its own band of voluble fans. C expects you to know its internal datatype conversion policy and wastes little space or time in policing your assignments and arithmetic. The strongly typed language supporters prefer security even at the expense of compiler size and run-time efficiency.

► INTEGER VARIABLES ►

Integers, or *whole* numbers, are either positive, negative, or zero. With QuickC (and other IBM PC C implementations), integer variables (and constants) end up in 16- or 32-bit two's-complement form, which is the natural arithmetical mode of the 8088/8086/80286/80386 instruction sets. Because different computers have different register widths, though, C does not set standard bit sizes for objects like integers, nor does it dictate how numbers should be internally represented—for example, as one's complement or two's complement. (I'll explain these terms shortly.) Outside the mainframe world, 16- and 32-bit integer representations are the general rule, so QuickC will give you widely portable code provided you take a few sensible precautions.

► int and long ►

By declaring an identifier (**sum**, for example) as an **int** (integer data type) you warn the compiler ahead of time that **sum** will need 16 bits to represent its legal range of values (from − 32,768 to + 32,767 for QuickC). Exactly when the actual allocation takes place depends on factors to be discussed later.

Declaring **sum** as a **long** (or, equivalently, **long int**), tells the compiler that 32 bits will be needed, giving **sum** a legal range of − 2,147,483,648 to + 2,147,483,647.

Officially, C does not insist that **long** be longer (have more bits) than **int**—it insists only that **long** must not be shorter (have fewer bits) than **int**. For QuickC on the IBM PC, just remember that **int** is 16-bit and **long** is 32-bit. Compilers for other systems, such as the Motorola 680x0, may have both **int** and **long** as 32-bit values, so some care is needed.

► Short Integers ►

C officially recognizes a third integer data type called **short int** (or **short** for short). As with **int** and **long**, the ANSI standards leave it up to each individual implementor to choose a suitable bit size for **short**, provided only that **int** is not shorter than **short**. The rules for the three integer types can be expressed informally as **long** >= **int** >= **short** where >= means "bit size is greater than or equal to."

You'll be relieved to learn that in Turbo C **short** and **int** are indeed the same 16-bit entities. For the moment, then, we will concentrate on **int** and **long**. If you come across **short** or **short int** while reading a non-Turbo C program, make a mental note that for some systems it *may* be smaller than **int**. In the big, wide world of C, the choice of integer data types can affect program portability.

► Signed Integers ►

Note that **int** and **long** are known as *signed* data types because they are stored and manipulated using the two's-complement convention whereby the leftmost or most significant bit (MSB) acts as a sign bit. The MSB for positive integers is 0, and for negative integers it is 1.

Under this regime, the **int** value -1, for example, is written and stored as binary

1111111111111111

(hex 0xFFFF, decimal $2^{16} - 1$), while $-32,768$ is stored as

1000000000000000

(hex 0x8000, decimal 2^{15}). The **long** version of -2 would be binary

11111111111111111111111111111110

(hex 0xFFFFFFFE, decimal $2^{32} - 2$). (If this section and the following one are not absolutely clear, you should read Appendix D, "Computer Math Roundup." You need to understand signed and unsigned binary arithmetic since C assumes that you know what you are doing—there are few checks on range overflow!)

► Unsigned Integers ►

Each of the signed integer types has a corresponding *unsigned* version—**unsigned int**, **unsigned short**, and **unsigned long**. These types give nonnegative ranges: 0 to +65,535 for **unsigned int** and **unsigned short**, and 0 to +4,294,967,295 for **unsigned long**. Unsigned integers treat the MSB as 2^{15} or 2^{31}, not as a sign bit. Table 2.1 summarizes the integer data types for QuickC.

▸ *Table 2.1:* *Integer data types*

Specifier	Bit Size	Range
int short [int]	16	−32,768 to +32,767
unsigned int unsigned short [int]	16	0 to +65,535
long [int]	32	−2,147,483,648 to +2,147,483,647
unsigned long [int]	32	0 to +4,294,967,295

▸ *[int]* means *int* is optional.

▸ INTEGER DECLARATION SYNTAX ▸

If the compiler meets the identifier **sum** *before* its declaration has been made, a **'sum' undefined** error message will be generated.

The simplest integer declarations take the following forms:

```
int sum;                        /* sum is declared to be of type int */

long grand_total;               /* grand_total is of type long int */
long int salary;                /* longwinded version of long salary */

unsigned int count;             /* count is an unsigned integer */

unsigned long big_count;        /* big_count is unsigned and long */
unsigned long int Big_Count;    /* so is Big_Count */
```

For the moment, I will make no distinction between *declaring* and *defining* an identifier. Technically, a declaration simply notifies the compiler of the name and nature of the beast (size and type), while a definition actually triggers the allocation of memory. In most cases we can gloss over the distinction since the declaration also defines the variable. Later, when you start creating your own functions, you will be declaring objects that may have already been defined elsewhere.

► *Type Specifiers* ►

The keywords **short**, **int**, and **long** are known as *type specifiers*. The optional specifier **unsigned** can precede and modify these type specifiers, as shown. (**Signed** is assumed in the absence of **unsigned**.)

The general syntax of simple integer declarations is

[unsigned] *type-specifier identifier;*

where the brackets around **unsigned** indicate that it is optional. I use italics here to indicate a lexical unit that can be replaced by an appropriate set of characters in the source code.

The identifier being declared follows the rules discussed in Chapter 1 (start with a letter or underscore, follow with up to 31 letters, numbers, or underscores, and avoid reserved keywords). This identifier is called a *simple declarator* to distinguish it from more complex forms used to declare pointers and arrays.

You need some white space (at least one space or tab) between the various elements like **unsigned** and **int**, and **int** and **sum**, and a final semicolon as a terminator. Although a declaration is not, strictly speaking, a C statement, it is terminated in the usual manner.

► *Multiple Declaration* ►

You can save keystrokes by declaring several identifiers of the same type using commas as separators:

```
int sum, total;               /* sum and total are of type int */
long grand_total, bignum, X;  /* three long ints */
unsigned int a, b, c, d;      /* four unsigned ints */
```

The first line is entirely equivalent to

```
int sum;
int total;
```

Now that you know how to declare an integer variable, let's look at some of the things you can do with it in a QuickC program.

► *INTEGER VARIABLE ASSIGNMENTS* ►

Having been declared, the above identifiers are hereinafter known to the program as integer *variables*, meaning that at any time during the course of the program they can be *assigned* different values within their particular integer range. Contrast this with constants, which normally remain saddled with their original value throughout the program. In the following, **sum** is a variable:

```
sum = 1;            /* sum now holds the value 1 */
sum = - 356;        /* and now, - 356 */
sum = 269;          /* sum changed to 269 */
sum = sum + 1;      /* sum becomes 270 */
```

In C, the assignment operator (=) works from right to left. In

left-value = right-expression;

right-expression is evaluated first, then the result is assigned to the **left-value**. There are strict rules in C governing the kinds of objects you can legally use on the left and right sides of an assignment. For the moment, you need only these obvious rules:

1. The left-value must be a variable of some kind, able to "receive" the new value coming in from the right. Such variables are officially known as *lvalues* (pronounced "el-values"). Only lvalues are legal on the left, receiving end of an assignment.

2. The right-expression must be capable of providing a value compatible with the lvalue, whatever that means. In cases where right and left are of different data types, C has its own strict rules whereby

silent, internal conversions are applied to the right-expression, if possible, to make it compatible before making the assignment. Later you'll see that the programmer can intervene with *type casts* and *force* nonstandard conversions. You will also find that QuickC allows you to vary the level of warning messages emitted during compilation. At higher warning levels, QuickC will advise you of certain nonfatal, internal conversions that would remain "silent" at lower warning levels.

► *The Assignment Symbol* ►

In spite of appearances, the C assignment symbol must not be confused with that of the conventional algebraic equals sign. For example, writing the last statement of the previous example as the algebraic equation

$sum = sum + 1$

has no finite solution, while the valid algebraic lines

$5 = sum + 1$
$sum + 2 = 35$

would not make sense in C, since neither 5 nor *sum* + 2 are lvalues.

C uses two adjacent equals signs to distinguish the two concepts, equality (==) and assignment (=):

```
if (sum == total) ....
```

is read as "if **sum** equals **total** ...." whereas

```
sum = total;
```

is read as "assign the value of **total** to the variable **sum**."

A popular mental model is to picture variables as labeled boxes. To find the current value of **sum**, you open the box marked **sum**! The assignment

```
sum = sum + 1;
```

means: "Look in the **sum** box, grab the value, add one to it, and put the new value back in the box." Other readers may be more comfortable with the image of **sum** as a 16- or 32-bit word in RAM being incremented via the 8088/8086 **ADD** instruction.

► INCREMENTS AND DECREMENTS ►

Incrementing (and decrementing) by 1 is such a common computing pastime that C offers several shorthand versions of the above type of assignment. To whet your appetite:

```
total = sum++;        /* set total to sum, then inc sum by 1 */
total = sum--;        /* set total to sum, then dec sum by 1 */

total = ++sum;        /* set sum to sum + 1, then set total to new sum */
total = --sum;        /* set sum to sum - 1, then set total to new sum */
```

The double symbols ++ and -- after **sum** are called the *postincrement* and *postdecrement* operators, respectively, implying that **sum** is increased or decreased by 1 *after* the assignment to **total**. The general term *postfix* is used for such operators.

Similarly, the *prefix* operators ++ and -- appearing before **sum** are known specifically as *preincrement* and *predecrement* operators. With these, the increment or decrement by 1 is performed on **sum** *before* the assignment to **total** is made.

To illustrate these operations, consider the following snippet:

```
int sum, total;       /* declare */
total = 5; sum = 3;   /* initialize */

total = sum++;        /* total now = 3 and sum = 4 post-inc */
total = ++sum;        /* total now = 5 and sum = 5 pre-inc */
total = sum--;        /* total now = 5 and sum = 4 post-dec */
total = --sum;        /* total now = 3 and sum = 3 pre-dec */
```

If you just want to increment or decrement without any assignment, the postfix and prefix methods are effectively equivalent:

```
sum++;                /* set sum to sum + 1 */
++sum;                /* set sum to sum + 1 */
```

```
sum − − ;              /* set sum to sum − 1 */
− − sum;               /* set sum to sum − 1 */
```

What you cannot do is use **sum + +** (or the other three variants) on the left side of an assignment. **sum + +** is not an lvalue, so **sum + + = total**, for example, is not allowed.

These postfix and prefix operators, by the way, can be used with variables other than integers, but the increment or decrement produced may be other than 1.

► COMPOUND ASSIGNMENTS ►

Another useful convention in C is the *compound assignment*, which simplifies statements like **total = total + sum** as in

```
total += sum;          /* increase total by sum */
                       /* i.e. total = total + sum */

total −= sum;          /* decrease total by sum */
                       /* i.e. total = total − sum */
```

Here the operators **+=** and **−=** use the two symbols shown to form a compound assignment. These are two forms of a more general compound assignment trick:

left-value op = right-expression;

where **op** can be any one of the 10 C compoundable operators shown in Table 2.2 (these operators will all be explained in due course).

► **Table 2.2:** *Compoundable operators*

Arithmetical	+ (add), − (subtract), * (multiply), / (divide), % (integer remainder or modulus)
Shifts	<< (left shift), >> (right shift)
Bitwise	& (AND), ¦ (OR), ^ (XOR [Exclusive OR])

This general form translates into

left-value = left-value op right-expression;

assuming, of course, that **op** makes sense with the right and left sides of the assignment. For example, the following pairs of lines are equivalent:

```
sum = sum * factor;              /* multiply */
sum *= factor;

sum_of_all_sums = sum_of_all_sums / factor;        /* divide */
sum_of_all_sums /= factor;

rem = rem % divisor;             /* integer remainder or modulus */
rem %= divisor;
```

The compound assignment is one of the many features that makes C popular with programmers. If the left-value is long-winded (as in the second example above), the notation saves much typing, reducing the chance of error without obscuring the meaning.

► *ASSIGNMENT VALUES AND MULTIPLE ASSIGNMENTS* ►

C also allows you to "chain" assignments as in

```
answer = total = sum = 0;        /* clear them all */
```

The above *multiple assignment* starts at the right, setting **sum** to zero, and then assigns the value of the statement (**sum = 0**) to **total**. C is rather unusual in that assignment statements not only assign but also have a value that can be used just like a right-expression. What, then, is the value of (**sum = 0**)? It is simply the lvalue received by **sum** as a result of the assignment. So what we pass on to **total** is 0 (the new value of **sum**). Likewise, the value of (**total = (sum = 0)**) is the new value of **total**, namely 0, and this is passed to **answer**.

To cut a long story short, all three variables are set to 0, just as if we had made the three separate statements

```
sum = 0; total = 0; answer = 0;
```

In the above example, the whole multiple assignment itself has the value 0, but we make no use of this fact.

Rather than being an abstruse quirk of the language, this value property of assignments is yet another reason for C's reputation for compactness. Consider the following snippet:

```
answer = total + (sum = 4);
```

This statement is equivalent to the more verbose

```
sum = 4;
answer = total + sum;
```

► PRECEDENCE AND ASSOCIATIVITY ►

Can you guess why the parentheses are important in **(sum = 4)**? I have not yet broached the topic of operator *precedence*, mainly because only a few operators have been discussed! However, now that we have **+** and **=** rubbing shoulders, we must consider the problem.

All mathematical texts, whether for human or computer consumption, need to have conventions for grouping operands with operators and possibly for deciding the order in which they should be evaluated. For example, $2 \times 3 + 1$ is ambiguous ($6 + 1 = 7$ or $2 \times 4 = 8$?) unless you lay down a few rules. One simple rule is that operations enclosed in parentheses are completed separately: $(2 \times 3) + 1$ or $2 \times (3 + 1)$ removes the ambiguity. You may also decree that multiplication has higher precedence than addition—i.e., $2 \times 3 + 1$ means $(2 \times 3) + 1$. In this case, you needn't use parentheses, but they help the eye and do no harm. If you really want $2 \times (3 + 1)$, then parentheses are essential to override the precedence rules.

Certain commutative operators, like **+** and **−**, can have equal precedence from a purely mathematical standpoint. When calculating $x + y - z$, for example, you get the same answer, in theory, whether you do $(x + y) - z$ or $x + (y - z)$ or even $(x - z) + y$. The same is true for $x \times y/z$ (using **/** to indicate division).

However, the grouping of the operands may be relevant in practical terms since the computer may not be able to store intermediate results with complete accuracy. For example, **(x * y) / z** might lead to overflow before the division is reached, whereas the grouping **x * (y / z)** might avoid this problem. You can see that in more complex computer work both the grouping and order of evaluation can be relevant even if the pure mathematics reveals no problem.

Some C operators, like **++** and **−−**, offer a challenge in that the *sequence* of evaluation, as opposed to the grouping, can affect the result. Take, for instance:

```
total = 0;
sum = (total = 3) + (++total);    /* poor but legal code */
```

Which group, **(total = 3)** or **(++total)**, should be evaluated first? It does make a difference: **sum** will equal 7 if we evaluate **(total = 3)** first (i.e., from left to right) but 4 if we evaluate **(++total)** first (i.e., from right to left).

It is *vital* to know that the order of evaluation is *not* decreed by any C standards committee—each compiler writer is free to choose any convenient evaluation sequence (there are, though, four specific operators that require the leftmost operand to be evaluated first). For maximum sanity and portability, therefore, you must avoid code like the above example, legal though it is. A general rule is that if you assign to a variable, avoid reusing that variable in the same expression. Safer versions of the example would be

```
total = 3;
sum = total + (total + 1);
++total;
```

or

```
total = 0;
temp = ++total;              /* a temporary variable often */
                             /* solves the problem */
sum = (total = 3) + temp;
```

depending on your original intentions.

The pecking order for C's 40 or so operators is shown in full in the table inside the covers of this book. It can also be displayed at any time using the QuickC Help menu (see Appendix G). Don't rush to memorize them all just now. In fact, it pays to be more rather than less generous with your parentheses for ease of mind and legibility, though you must remember that parentheses alone will not remove the order of evaluation problem typified by the **++** example above.

► *Precedence and Association Categories* ►

There are 15 precedence categories, some of which contain several operators, while others contain just one. A lower category number indicates higher precedence.

When C is faced with a sequence of operators of the same precedence and no guiding parentheses, it follows certain grouping or *associativity* rules. These rules effectively supply default parentheses. The rules, alas, vary according to the precedence categories.

Most of the categories have left-to-right associativity, so it's easier to remember the three precedence categories that associate from right to left: categories 2, 13, and 14 in the table inside the book covers.

Category 14 contains the assignment and all the compound assignments (the most common right-to-left associative operators).

Now the example

```
answer = total = sum = 0;        /* clear them all */
```

given in the section on multiple assignments makes more sense. It is evaluated as

```
answer = (total = (sum = 0));     /* clear them all */
```

I'll point out the other right-to-left operators as they arise.

I stress again that associativity dictates how operands and operators are grouped, not necessarily the order in which each group will be evaluated. For example, the three operators *, /, and % all belong to precedence category 3, which associates from left to right. A statement such as

```
x = total * temp / price * rate % factor;
```

would be treated as though you had typed

```
x = (((((total * temp) /) price) * rate) % factor);      /* not LISP */
```

Note the low precedence of = (category 14).

Whether this is the optimum grouping, considering accuracy or overflow, is another question. Your own parentheses, of course, could force a different grouping.

On this occasion, the grouping happens to dictate a unique sequence of evaluation: **(total * temp)** must be calculated first, the result divided by **price**, and so on.

If **price** were replaced with **price + extras** without parentheses as in

    x = total * temp / price + extras * rate % factor;

you might be in for a surprise, since * (category 3) is higher precedence than + (category 4). The compiler supplied grouping would give you as step 1

    x = (total * temp / price) + (extras * rate % factor);

and as step 2

    x = ((total * temp) / price) + ((extras * rate) % factor);

We don't know which inner piece might be evaluated first.

Here again is the example that triggered the discussion on precedence:

    answer = total + (sum = 4);   /* why the parentheses? */

Let's see what happens when we remove the parentheses.

Since + has a higher precedence than = and since = associates from right to left

    answer = total + sum = 4;

would be grouped by the compiler as follows:

    answer = ((total + sum) = 4);

resulting in a *syntax error*. Why? Because **(total + sum)** is not an lvalue, so you can't assign anything to it. The error message would be **left hand operand must be lvalue**.

Summing up, the parentheses are essential to override C's natural associativity rules, since the latter would lead to a syntax error.

► *WARNING ON THE LACK OF WARNINGS* ►

Before you become complacent, here are some situations in which macho C may fail to protect you. Consider the following snippet:

```
unsigned int count, result;        /* declare */
int sum, total;

count = 0;                         /* initialize */
sum = 32767;

count − − ;                        /* decrement count? */
++sum;                             /* increment sum? */
total = count;                     /* what will total be? */
result = sum;                      /* what will result be? */
```

We have declared **count** as **unsigned**, so you might expect some complaint from the compiler when **count** is decremented by one "below" 0. In fact, C will not protect you. After going through the motions of decrement (0 − 1), the value placed in **count** is the erroneous bit pattern 0xFFFF ($2^{16} − 1$ or 65,535), which is the *largest* **unsigned** int value.

In the statement **total = count;** the erroneous bit pattern in **count** is transferred unchanged to the signed integer variable **total**. C allows such assignments between different integer types because of its weak data typing, and, as luck would have it, **total** now holds the value − 1 in signed two's-complement format! I use the word *luck* somewhat cynically, but computers not using two's-complement arithmetic would find it more difficult to preserve the correct value, − 1, from an unsigned variable.

Incrementing **sum** by one "beyond" its maximum limit of 0x7FFF (32,767 or $2^{15} − 1$) is also performed without an overflow error message. The *signed* result left in **sum** would be − 32,768 (internally represented as 0x8000 or 2^{15}). This great shift in value can produce bizarre results for the unwary.

The final assignment, **result = sum**, is made by transferring − 32,768 to an unsigned variable without flinching, so **result** ends up with an unsigned value of 2^{15}.

Similar considerations apply when assigning between **long** signed and unsigned variables. Assigning from **int** to **long** when both are signed or both are unsigned is always safe since the latter's lvalue range is greater. Going the other way, from **long** to **int**, however, must be done with care. If the value in the **long** happens to be within **int** range, the correct transfer occurs and no harm is done. On the other hand, if the **long** source exceeds the destination **int** range, you will lose the upper 16 bits of the **long**:

```
long stretch;
int sum;
stretch = 0xFFFFFFFF;
sum = stretch;                    /* sum = 0xFFFF!! */
```

These are known as *silent truncations* and must be avoided like the plague (as with clichés).

The moral is to declare integer variables according to their expected ranges.

▶ *Changing the Warning Level* ▶

QuickC lets you set a warning level from 0 to 3. In versions prior to 2, you could do this by using the dialog box in the Compile option of the Run menu. With Version 2, you must use option switches /Wn in the QCL command line to set warning level n. For example:

```
QCL /W0 MYPROG.C
```

or the equivalent:

```
QCL /w MYPROG.C
```

both turn off all warnings—so warning level 0 means no warnings at all. Similarly

```
QCL /W1 MYPROG.C
QCL /W2 MYPROG.C
QCL /W3 MYPROG.C
```

give you the other three warning levels.

The selected level determines which classes of nonfatal errors (or possible errors) will be reported during compilation. By "nonfatal" I mean those errors or near errors that do not prevent successful compilation—of course, a correctly compiled program *may* fatally direct your missile to the wrong continent.

Level 0 turns off all warning messages and should be avoided until you have achieved a higher level of competence and complacency!

At the other extreme, level 3 displays every class of warning, including any use of non-ANSI C features. Because QuickC offers several useful extensions not yet blessed by the ANSI standard, level 3 should only be used when you are aiming for strictly ANSI-conforming code (for instance, when you seek maximum portability).

Levels 1 and 2 represent intermediate levels of warning. The default when you omit the /W switch in QCL, or run within QC, is level 1. Level 1 reports most of the events that, although "legal" and nonfatal, may indicate a problem to the programmer. Level 2 includes all the level 1 warnings but adds a few more. For example, at level 2, you will be warned if automatic type conversion threatens to lose significant bits. You will also be notified that the line

```
int ;
```

has a missing identifier and similar minor transgressions.

The balance here is between being told what you already know (because you deliberately did something that might be dangerous under different circumstances) and missing an important warning. For beginners, level 1 is a reasonable default option.

► *INITIALIZATION OF VARIABLES* ►

Another time saver in C is the ability to *initialize* a variable (give it a starting value) during its declaration. For example:

```
int sum = 25;                    /* declare sum as int with initial value 25 */
```

is equivalent to

```
int sum;                    /* declare */
sum = 25;                   /* initialize */
```

You can also declare and initialize a series of variables of the same type without repeating the type specifier as in

```
short int sum = 0; total = 0; result = 0;    /* all shorts */
```

The value used to initialize is naturally known as an *initializer*. For most of the numerical variables used in this chapter, the initializer can be either a constant or a numerical expression containing previously declared and initialized variables. (Later on you'll see some restrictions depending on storage classification.) Here are some declaration and initialization examples:

```
int sum = 25;                    /* declare and initialize */
int total = sum*2;               /* declare and initialize to 50 */
long grand_total = total + sum;  /* declare and set to 75 */
```

Note that in the third line, because **total + sum** is within **int** range, a safe, silent conversion from **int** to **long** takes place before **grand_total** is initialized. Be aware of the fact that a right-expression containing only **int** values could conceivably exceed the **long** range, leading to silent truncation.

Although there are exceptions, simply declaring a variable usually will not give it an initial, predictable value such as 0. It is safer for the beginner to initialize each variable in some way before using it in the right-expression of an assignment.

► INTEGER CONSTANTS ►

In many of the previous examples we used *integer constants* like 1, −1, and 269 without much ado. Remember, though, that the compiler needs to translate the ASCII symbols, 1, 2, −, and so on, as found in the source code, into binary before expressions like **sum = 1** or **sum + 269** can be evaluated. Since we have not declared these constants explicitly as **short**, **int**, or **long**, you may wonder how the compiler knows how many bits, 16 or 32, to use in the conversion. The answer is that the compiler takes account of the value of the constant. Constants with values between 0 and 32,767 become 16-bit **int** types, while those with values between 32,768 and 2,147,483,647 take the 32-bit **long** format.

► Hexadecimal, Decimal, and Octal Constants ►

Constants can be expressed in hex (base 16), decimal (base 10), or octal (base 8) by following a few simple rules:

1. Octal constants must start with a **0** as in

   mask = 017777; sum = 012345;

   An error will occur if you use the numerals 8 or 9 in an octal integer.

2. Hex constants must start with **0x** or **0X** as in

   mask = 0XFFFFE; sum = 0x12345; tot = 0Xabcdef;

   An error will occur if you use illegal characters in a hex constant. After the **0x** or **0X**, only 0–9, A–F, or a–f are permitted.

3. Decimal constants are written conventionally with no leading **0** (otherwise they would be taken as octal).

   sum = 1; total = 269;

The number 0 presents no contradiction. Whether it is octal or decimal does not merit much angst.

The unary operator − in front of an integer constant tells the compiler to reverse the sign by subtracting the value from 0. Constants outside the upper limit will be silently truncated as we saw with integer variables. *Constant expressions*—that is, combinations such as **(1 + 3)** or **(4 − 6 * 34)**—are allowed and are evaluated according to the normal operator precedence rules.

Summing up, a constant acquires both a value and a data type from the way it appears in the source text.

The use of explicit constants as "magic numbers" should be avoided where possible. If a disk block contains 512 bytes, say, it is better to use **#define BLKSIZE 512** (as in the following snippet) than to have the source text sprinkled with references to the constant 512:

```
#define BLKSIZE 512

unsigned int rec_size = 300;
unsigned int byte_count = rec_size*BLKSIZE;
```

The resulting code is more legible and can be more quickly updated should
BLKSIZE change in value. Mnemonics such as **BLKSIZE** are often called
manifest constants.

► *DISPLAYING INTEGERS* ►

It is time to run a few programs that will help you see the various integer
types and operators in live action on your screen rather than as dry abstrac-
tions on the page. We will use SHOWNUM.C, listed in Program 2.1, as a test
bed. Later you can experiment by editing it with values and data types of
your own choice.

Fire up by typing qc SHOWNUM.C at the C> prompt and enter the text
as shown. Build SHOWNUM using Shift-F5, then run it using F5. Before you
exit QC you will be prompted to save the file SHOWNUM.C. Let's see how
SHOWNUM works.

► *printf( ) Format Control Strings* ►

Until now, **printf( )** has been used with a single string constant as an argument.
SHOWNUM uses a variation allowing you to display formatted integers.

Here, the first **printf( )** has two arguments, separated by a comma. The first
argument, ''**The value of inta is %d\n\n**'', represents a *format control
string*, the function of which is to control the conversion and formatting of

```
/* shownum.c - display various integers */

#include <stdio.h>

void main()
{
        int inta = -1, intb = 3;
        unsigned long uninta = 65535;
        printf("The value of inta is %d\n\n",inta);
        printf("Sum inta+intb = %d\n\n",inta+intb);
        printf("The value of uninta is %u\n\n",uninta);
        printf("uninta squared is %lu, (inta - uninta) is %ld\n",
                uninta*uninta, inta-uninta);
        printf("Net Profit is %d%%",intb);
}
```

► **Program 2.1:** *SHOWNUM.C*

the following argument (or arguments). This string contains two distinct classes of characters:

1. *Plain characters* such as the familiar text and newline escape characters that are displayed without change as in the HELLO.C of Chapter 1.

2. *Conversion specifications* such as **%d**. These are not displayed as part of the text but act as "templates" for the following arguments of **printf( )**.

Each conversion specification must start with a percent sign. This tells the compiler where and how to display an argument. Each argument to be displayed by **printf( )** will have an appropriate specification like **%d** embedded in the format control string. The concept is similar to the **PRINT USING MASK$** construct found in most BASICs.

There are many possible conversion specifications, offering conversions (with specified precision) from all the arithmetical data types to ASCII displays in decimal, hex, octal, and floating-point scientific (or exponential) notation, with or without left or right justification, with or without zero fill, ad nauseam. Appendix C lists all these for reference, but for now we'll concentrate on the following simpler formats used to display integers, strings, and characters with no frills:

%s	for any matching string argument
%c	for any matching single character argument
%d	for decimal **int** (signed)
%u	for decimal **unsigned int**
%o	for octal **unsigned int** (note: leading 0 not displayed)
%x	for hexadecimal **unsigned int** (note: leading 0x not displayed)
%X	for hexadecimal (as above but giving A–F rather than a–f)

Each of **d, u, o, x** or **X** can have a lowercase letter **l** prefixed to give the corresponding **long** data-type conversion or a prefixed **h** to give **short int** conversion as in

%ld	for decimal **long** (signed)
%hd	for decimal **short** (signed)

%lu   for decimal **unsigned long**

%ho   for octal **short** (unsigned)

To display a real percent symbol from a format string, you need to use two of them—that is, enter "%%" as in the old '\\' escape character trick. Only the second % will appear.

Referring back to SHOWNUM.C, the second argument in

printf("The value of inta is %d\n\n",inta);

is the **int** variable **inta**. This gets matched with the **%d** in the format string so that when you run SHOWNUM the top line should display

The value of inta is − 1

followed by two new lines. The **%d** interprets the bit pattern in **inta** as a **signed int** and converts to the ASCII pair − 1 for the display.

The next **printf( )** in SHOWNUM:

printf("Sum inta + intb = %d\n\n",inta + intb);

illustrates how the second argument can be a compound arithmetical expression. The **%d** is here replaced by the sum **inta + intb**, again interpreted as an **int** (signed, of course). However complex the expression is, it will be evaluated and *then* matched by a single conversion specification such as **%d**. The second line displayed by SHOWNUM will therefore be

Sum inta + intb = 2

followed by two new lines.

The **%u** in the third **printf( )** converts the **unsigned long** variable **uninta** to **unsigned int** and displays

The value of uninta is 65535

without error. Try changing the **%u** to **%lu** and **%d** and see if you understand the results.

The fourth **printf( )** statement shows two control specifications, **%lu** and **%ld**, embedded in the format string

```
printf("uninta squared is %lu, (inta − uninta) is %ld\n",
        uninta*uninta, inta − uninta);
```

Don't be fooled by the comma in the format string—it is inside the string, so it does not act as an argument separator. The following two arguments are arithmetical expressions, and they will be matched in turn by the **%lu** (long unsigned conversion) and **%ld** (long signed integer conversion). The display will be

```
uninta squared is 4294836225, (inta − uninta) is − 65536
```

Reversing the conversion specifications will teach you some of the quirks of mixing signed and unsigned integer types.

SHOWNUM.C ends with a simple demonstration of the "%%" trick. You should see

```
Net Profit is 3%
```

on the final line of the display.

You should play with SHOWNUM, altering values, data types, and format strings, until you are familiar with the simple conversion specifiers. Try displaying in short and long hex and octal. It will increase your knowledge of number representation as well as giving you practice with the QuickC editor and menus.

► *MAKING YOUR OWN FUNCTIONS* ►

Now that you have seen a library function in action, let's examine the problem of creating our own personal functions. Functions arise quite naturally when you find that your program is regularly doing the same or similar things. The obvious question is, Can I avoid repetitive typing in my source code? Let's take SHOWNUM as a simple example. Rather than entering several similar **printf( )** lines, we want to create a function called **dispnum( )** that can take an integer argument, say **n**, and display

```
The value of n is value
```

At the same time, we'll introduce another function called **cube( )** that takes an integer argument and returns its cube.

SHOWNUM1.C (Program 2.2) illustrates the basic mechanics of declaring, defining, and invoking these naive functions. A new type modifier called **const** is introduced and explained within comments. The topic of *storage classes* is also touched on in the comments and will be further amplified in Chapter 3.

```
/* shownum1.c - display and cube integers */

#include <stdio.h>

    const int nymph = 40;
/* this int identifier is frozen by the const modifier */
/* nymph behaves like a constant and cannot be changed */

void dispnum(n)      /* declare dispnum with dummy arg */
int n;                        /* declare dummy arg */
{                             /* body of function */
    printf("The value if n is %d\n",n);
}

int cube(n)
int n;
{
    return(n*n*n);           /* the value returned by cube() */
}

void main()
{

    int sum, inta = -1, intb = 3; /* automatic variables */

/* these variables are of storage class auto by default */
/* i.e. they are automatically created when main starts */
/* and vanish when main ends.  They are inaccessible    */
/* outside their own function.  More in Chapter 3       */

/* call dispnum with real int arguments */
    dispnum(nymph);
    dispnum(inta);
    dispnum(intb);

    dispnum(3*intb+inta); /* argument is an int expression */
    sum = cube(5);        /* call cube with real const arg */
    dispnum(sum);

    dispnum(sum++); dispnum (sum);
    dispnum(--sum); dispnum (sum);
    sum += intb; dispnum(sum *= inta);
/* can you forecast the resulting displays? */

    dispnum(cube(inta));
    dispnum(cube(intb+1));
    dispnum(cube(cube(inta)));
}
```

▸ *Program 2.2: SHOWNUM1.C*

► *Anatomy of the dispnum( ) Function* ►

There are three parts to **dispnum( )**:

1. The declaration line, **void dispnum(n)**, giving the returned data type, function name, and its argument list—the single identifier **n** in this case. If there were no arguments, the list would be empty [as in **main( )**], or you could write **dispnum(void)**. If there were two arguments we would need **dispnum(n,m)**, and so on. Note that no statement terminator is needed. The argument **n** is called a *dummy* or *formal* argument. It serves as a place marker when the function is actually called with a real argument, as you'll see presently.

   Neither **dispnum( )** nor **main( )** *return* a useful value, so we write **void** immediately before the function name. In some other languages, **dispnum( )** would be called a *procedure*—i.e., a routine that simply performs an action without returning a value. C does not make this distinction. All C functions actually return a value (**int** by default) whether you use it or not. Using **void** as the return data type simply informs the compiler that the returned value can be ignored.

2. The declaration giving the data type of the dummy argument: **int n;**. Later you'll see that this line can be incorporated in the declaration **void dispnum(int n)**.

3. The body of the function between **{** and **}**, similar to the body of **main( )**, which determines (defines) the action of the function. Here the function just performs the one action

   printf("The value if n is %d\n",n);

   and then ends because the final **}** has been reached.

► *Calling the dispnum ( ) Function* ►

The function **dispnum( )** is called (or invoked) several times from within **main( )** by simply naming it with a particular *real* or *actual* argument that matches the type of the dummy argument as in

dispnum(inta);   /* call dispnum with a real int arg */

We say that the real argument **inta** is *passed* to the function **dispnum( )**, just as the real argument "**hello, world**" was passed to **printf( )** in HELLO.C (Chapter 1). The result of the call, then, is the same as that of

```
printf("The value of n is %d\n",inta);
```

In fact, **dispnum( )** does not operate directly on **inta** but on a temporary *copy* of **inta**. In C, all function arguments are passed by *value*, so that normally a function cannot alter the real argument—it knows only the copied value of **inta**, not the memory location where **inta** resides. Even if **n**, the dummy argument, is changed by **dispnum( )**, this change cannot "get back" to **inta**.

Unlike more fussy languages, C traditionally does not engage in tedious checks to see that functions are called with matching arguments—later we'll see how ANSI C offers some help in this direction.

► *The cube( ) Function Analyzed* ►

Like **dispnum( )**, the function **cube( )** also has three parts: function declaration, argument declaration, and body, though there are a few differences: **cube( )** returns a useful value, as indicated by the presence of the return data type **int** before **cube(n)** and the keyword **return** in the function body. The expression (**n*n*n**) after **return** represents the value returned when the function is called. If a function does not return a useful value, as in the case of **dispnum( )**, then no **return** statement is needed or you can write **return;** to indicate that nothing useful is returned. A function like **cube( )** that does return a useful value can be considered as having that value when used as part of an expression in **main( )** (or anywhere else it gets called). The declaration of **cube( )**, in fact, indicates that its returned value is of type **int**. In the absence of a type specifier in a function declaration, an **int** return value is assumed, but modern practice is *always* to specify a return type for clarity.

All of this explains why **cube( )** can legally be used in assignments such as

```
sum = cube(5);
```

and the use of **cube(inta)** as a real argument to **dispnum( )** in

```
dispnum(cube(inta));
```

The latter works because **cube(inta)** is in fact an **int** derived from the evaluation of n∗n∗n using the **int** value of **inta** as the **int n**.

Similarly, **cube(inta)** is a valid **int** argument for **cube( )** itself as in

dispnum(cube(cube(inta)));

So, **cube(inta)** can be used in any situation where a non-lvalue **int** can be used.

For reasons that will emerge later, you will also encounter declarations such as

int cube (int n)

where the argument list incorporates the data-type declaration.

If you enter and run SHOWNUM1.C, your screen should look like Figure 2.1.

As with SHOWNUM, you should experiment with other values in SHOWNUM1. Note that **cube( )** can quickly exhaust the range of **int**, so try using **long** and **unsigned long** to find the maximum **n** before these ranges are exceeded. Remember to alter the format strings in **dispnum( )**!

```
 Tue  3-14-1989 / 22:20:04.22 : E:\BIN
E>shownum1
The value if n is 40
The value if n is -1
The value if n is 3
The value if n is 8
The value if n is 125
The value if n is 125
The value if n is 126
The value if n is 125
The value if n is 125
The value if n is -128
The value if n is -1
The value if n is 64
The value if n is -1

E>
```

► **Figure 2.1:** *SHOWNUM1 result screen*

► *Duplication of Variable Identifiers* ►

You may have noticed that the identifier **n** was declared twice in SHOWNUM1.C. Can you declare the same identifier more than once? A useful general answer is, "No, not for variables within the same block"; a more accurate answer for all identifiers is, "It all depends!" Take the following snippet:

```
{
    int sum;
    long sum;                    /* ERROR - sum as int still active */
}
```

sum is already declared as **int** and is still active. To understand when and where variables are active requires a discourse on the vital topics of *storage classes*, *scope*, and *visiblity*. We will introduce some of the basic concepts now, leaving a detailed study for later.

► *Storage Classes—First Steps* ►

Without realizing it, perhaps, you have been using a storage class called *automatic* in all your variable declarations so far. The keyword **auto** can be used explicitly as a storage-class specifier placed before the type specifier as in

```
auto int sum;
```

However, in the declarations used to date, **auto** has been the default, implied by the context, as it were. The comments in SHOWNUM1 indicate the flavor of automatic identifiers. They correspond to the local identifiers of languages like Pascal. The adjective *local* is perhaps more suggestive of their property than *auto* since variables like **sum** and **inta** are local to **main( )**. The **n** that is local to **dispnum( )** does not clash at all with the **n** that is local to **cube( )**. Local variables are safer in the sense that changes to them are confined to their own backyard. Imagine the chaos if the **n** being altered by **cube( )** somehow managed to infiltrate into the **n** of **dispnum( )**. Such nightmares are known as *side effects*, or rather, *unwanted* side effects. Some side effects turn out to be beneficial when used with care.

In contrast with local or automatic variables, most languages need *global* variables, which are accessible from all parts of a program and therefore at risk to the side-effects problem. In C the globals are sometimes called *external* because they "exist" outside the functions. The storage-class specifier **extern** can be used to declare a global variable as in

```
extern int sum;
```

but like **auto** it is often implied by the context and can be omitted.

C offers a rather daunting selection of storage classes and default rules that determine where a variable exists (scope) and where it is accessible (visibility). These will be gradually revealed in the following chapters as we encounter more complex function schemas.

► *SUMMARY OF CHAPTER 2* ►

Here are the main points covered in this chapter.

◄► Data typing allows the compiler to allocate the correct memory space for constants and variables and also guides the compiler as to what arithmetical operations and ranges of values are legal. C is not strongly typed: it often allows different types to be mixed in expressions and will often "silently" convert one type to another.

◄► The three basic integer data types are **short**, **int**, and **long**. They are treated by default as **signed** unless explicitly declared as **unsigned**. **short** and **int** each take 2 bytes. They are the same types in QuickC but may be different on other implementations. **long** takes 4 bytes. QuickC uses conventional two's complement arithmetic, so negative signed numbers look just like large unsigned numbers! (The sign bit is the most-significant bit.)

◄► Declarations need a data-type specifier followed by one or more identifier names:

```
int i;
int j, k;
long l, J, K;              /* or long int l, J, K; */
unsigned int m, n, o;
unsigned long salary;      /* or unsigned long int salary */
```

◄► Variables can have values assigned to them at various stages of a program; constants are fixed in value. Assignment is accomplished via the = operator:

```
i = j;                     /* assign value of j to lvalue, i */
salary = 10000;            /* assign a constant to lvalue, salary */
```

The above lines are called assignment statements. Certain objects are called lvalues because they can legally exist on the left side of an assignment. No constants are lvalues, and not every expression containing a variable is an lvalue.

◄► C may make internal conversions during assignments, either promoting an **int** before assignment to a **long** or truncating a **long** before assignment to an **int**. The latter conversions are dangerous.

◄► Multiple assignments are allowed:

    i = j = k = 20;   /* all vars now equal 20 */

This is possible because the expression **k = 20** itself takes a value equal to its left-hand member, which it then passes on to j. The expression j = **k = 20** has a value that it passes to i. The value of the whole expression is also 20, but it is not used in this example. C is unusual in having expression-statements and evaluated expressions. Any C expression can become a statement by appending a semicolon. The value of an expression is simply discarded in most cases.

◄► C has elaborate precedence and associativity rules that dictate how operators are grouped in compound expressions. The table inside the covers of this book lists the 15 categories. Parentheses can be used to override these rules—but the order in which terms are evaluated depends on the individual compiler. ANSI C allows for the unary operator **+** that gives some control over evaluation sequence.

◄► Variables can be initialized during a declaration:

    int i = 3; long L = 279;

For the moment, assume that variables contain garbage until intialized or assigned in some way.

◄► The post- and preincrement and post- and predecrement operators (**++** and **− −**) let you add or subtract 1 from all integral variables. The postfix operators return the old value before the change; the prefix operators return the changed value:

    int p = 0, q = 1;
    p = q++;   /* p = 1 and q = 2 */

```
p = ++q;                    /* p = 3 and q = 3 */
p = q--;                    /* p = 3 and q = 2 */
p = --q;                    /* p = 1 and q = 1 */
```

◄► The compound operators, += , *= , and so on, simplify assignments by combining them with some other operation:

```
i += 4;                     /* same as i = i + 4; */
j -= i;                     /* same as j = j - i; */
k *= 3;                     /* same as k = k*3; */
```

◄► Integer constants can be expressed as decimal, hex, or octal. Their size dictates their data types unless overridden with a suffix:

```
i = 34;                     /* 34 is decimal and type int */
i = 34U;                    /* 34 forced to be unsigned int */
i = 34L;                    /* 34 forced to be long int (signed) */
i = 34UL;                   /* 34 forced to be unsigned long int */
                            /* lowercase u, l also allowed */
i = 034;                    /* 034 is octal */
i = 0x34;                   /* 0x34 or 0X34 are hexadecimal */
```

◄► printf( ) can display formatted variables, expressions, and constants of different data types. A format string is used to control where and how each matching expression argument appears. Simple examples are

%d, %u, %ld, %lu

which format signed, unsigned, long, and unsigned long numbers.

◄► The declaration, definition, and calling syntax for simple functions was hinted at with examples

```
[type] func([arg1, arg2,...]); /* declaration only */

[type] func([arg1, arg2,...]) /* declaration/definition */
     [parameter declarations]
     {
/*      body of function       */
     [return] [result];
     }
```

```
main( )
{
      ...
[result =] func([real – arg1, real – arg2,...]);          /* call the function */
   ...
}
```

►► Real arguments in the function call are passed by value to the function via copies to the dummy arguments used in the definition. A function may or may not return a useful value using the **return** statement.

►► Two common storage classes were mentioned briefly: **auto** (local) and **extern** (global).

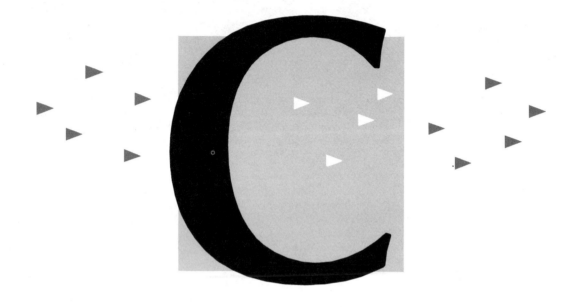

REAL NUMBERS AND
STRANGE CHARACTERS

► *CHAPTER 3* ►

This chapter introduces two more basic data types that allow you to work with *floating-point* and *character* variables. I'll explain the motivation for these types and extend the use of **printf( )** to format and display them.

Character variables lead naturally into C's unusual treatment of strings as *arrays* of characters referenced via *pointers*, so you'll get your first, gentle exposure to this central bête noire of the C language. Other languages reluctantly offer pointers in various guises and then strive to protect the programmer from the dangers of misuse. In C pointers are the primary weapons, designed to butcher both friend and foe. You'll love them!

You will also start using simple *control* structures, allowing your program to select alternative courses of action depending on the results of various conditional tests.

► *BEYOND THE INTEGERS* ►

The integer types introduced in Chapter 2 have the merit of complete, whole-number accuracy, provided that you keep within their acknowledged ranges. Although the computer works internally in binary, the conversions to and from decimal are exact for integer values. Problems can arise, though, when your calculations involve numbers or results with fractional parts. Computing, say, 3.87675×10.00234 or $1/7$ cannot be readily accomplished with integer data types unless you are happy with integer approximations such as $3.87675 \times 10.00234 = 40$ to the nearest whole number and $1/7 = 0$.

► *Integer Accuracy* ►

If you are willing and able to scale all your calculations, you can actually handle all *rational* numbers with integer data types. (A rational number is one that can be expressed as the ratio of two integers, p/q, where q is non-zero. The number 0.99 is rational since 0.99 = 99/100.) For example, it is common to treat $199.99 as 19,999 cents (scaling by 100), thereby removing the problem of decimal fractions.

Even if you need to divide or take percentages of such amounts, you can scale up again by 100 or 10,000 or whatever, depending on the accuracy needed, and keep your intermediate results as integers until the final answer is scaled back and possibly rounded as appropriate. However, the scaling is a nuisance in all but the simplest cases, and, worse still, even the **unsigned long** limit of 10 significant digits can easily be exceeded.

Accuracy in all types of computation boils down to how many significant figures you can retain at each step. The position of a decimal (or binary) point is irrelevant.

Note that you can concoct programs that can achieve any given degree of precision, subject only to storage limitations. For example, the extended multiply equation

$$(10 \times a + b) \times (10 \times c + d) = 100 \times a \times c + 10 \times a \times d + 10 \times b \times c + b \times d$$

is an example of how you can multiply two extra long numbers without overflow by using the proper software gymnastics. There is also the BCD (Binary Coded Decimal) approach that allows exact arithmetic on strings of digits of arbitary length.

► THE FLOATING-POINT SOLUTION ►

C, and most other languages, offers a more compact solution: the *floating-point* or *FP* data types. In the following sections, you will see how they let you handle fractions, such as 3.14159 and – 0.00001, as well as integers outside the **long int** range. Internally, FP does a form of scaling for you automatically. (Appendix D explains the basic rules for FP notation and manipulation.)

FP is not a general panacea. Even though FP operations extend enormously the range of values you can handle, there are inherent problems of precision that require constant attention. As a simple example, the fraction 1/3 (= 0.3333... recurring) cannot be exactly represented in FP format using a finite number of binary bits. Even if there are clever ways of storing such rational numbers, transcendental numbers such as pi can only be stored as approximations. Long before the electronic computer arrived, the branch of mathematics called numerical analysis had evolved to study the problems of reducing the errors that accumulate when you are forced to round off and approximate at various stages of a long calculation.

Let's review the basic arithmetical operators and, in particular, study the quirks of / (division) and % (integer remainder)—these are relevant to a proper understanding of floating-point operations.

► ARITHMETICAL OPERATIONS ►

You have already met the arithmetical operators + (add), – (subtract and also unary minus), * (multiply), / (divide), and % (integer remainder) as applied to integers (variables and constants).

We call % the integer remainder operator to remind you of the fact that it can be used only with integer types. The other operators can be used with both integer and FP numbers (variables and constants).

There are no problems with precision or rounding when you add, subtract, and multiply positive or negative integers unless the results go out of range. Integer division and its associated operation, integer remainder, though, have some anomalies to be discussed in the next section.

► *Integer Division, Remainder and Modulus* ►

Dividing an integer by an integer in C using / gives you only a whole number quotient (usually truncated and therefore incorrect), while the % operator does not always give the expected integer remainder. The normal classroom paradigm for integer division is

dividend/divisor = quotient with remainder

or

dividend = quotient×divisor + remainder

where the absolute value of the remainder is less than the absolute value of the divisor. If the latter is not true, you have clearly not completed the division process! The absolute value of *x* is written abs(*x*) or | *x* | and is defined as follows:

If $x \geqslant 0$ abs(x) = x

If $x < 0$ abs(x) = $-x$

In other words, if x is signed and negative, just reverse the sign to get abs(x); otherwise x and abs(x) are the same. (C provides such a routine, **abs( )**, in STDLIB.H.)

We must also rule that the divisor is nonzero. For a zero divisor, the operation is simply *undefined* (so forget all that 1/0 = infinity nonsense).

In C notation, with integers **a** and **b** (**b** being nonzero), this equation can be written

a divided by b = (a/b) with remainder (a%b)

so you would expect that

a = (a/b)*b + (a%b) with abs(a%b) < abs(b)

would always be true (excluding overflow problems). Unfortunately, if either **a** or **b** or both are signed, you have ambiguities if either or both go negative. Unsigned **a**s and **b**s, by definition, of course, cannot go negative, and no problems arise. Look at the following examples:

1/0 illegal	1%0 illegal
0/1 = 0	0%1 = 0 check: 0 = 0*0 + 0 and 0 < 1 OK
4/2 = 2	4%2 = 0 check: 4 = 2*2 + 0 and 0 < 2 OK
3/2 = 1	3%2 = 1 check: 3 = 1*2 + 1 and 1 < 2 OK
1/2 = 0	1%2 = 1 check: 1 = 0*2 + 1 and 1 < 2 OK
10/3 = 3	10%3 = 1 check: 10 = 3*3 + 1 and 1 < 3 OK

So far, with both **a** and **b** positive, there are no surprises. The **%** gives you the conventional *mod* (or *modulo*) operation, which yields the remainder of a division process. Let's see what happens if **a** goes negative:

−12/3 = − 4 −12%3 = 0 check: −12 = (− 4*3) + 0 and 0 < 3 OK

No problem here, but perhaps we were lucky since −12 is divisible exactly by 3. Let's try again:

$$-10/3 = -3 \quad -10\%3 = -1 \text{ check: } -10 = (-3*3) + (-1)$$

and

$$\text{abs}(-1) < 3 \text{ OK}$$

Note that the unary – has higher precedence than / and %, so **–10/3** means **(–10)/3** not **–(10/3)**.

This seems fine, but what if we write

$$-10/3 = -4 \quad -10\%3 = 2 \text{ check: } -10 = (-4*3) + 2 \text{ and } 2 < 3 \text{ ALSO OK!}$$

Both answers for **–10/3** and **–10%3** meet the mathematical tests, so which set is correct? And what will C do? C officially says that the result is machine dependent, so for true portability you should avoid division and remainder operations with negative integers.

Most C compilers, including QuickC, opt for the values in the first example by always taking as **a/b** the value nearer to zero and the **a%b** with the same sign as **a**.

For QuickC then, –10/3 = –3 because –3 is nearer to zero than –4. This makes –10%3 = –1. Another way of looking at QuickC's value for –10/3 is to think of the full answer –3.3333... and discard the fractional part (with no rounding).

The plot thickens if **b** is negative. Again, the official C reaction is that the results are implementation dependent. QuickC gives the following result:

$$10/-3 = -3 \quad 10\%-3 = -1 \text{ check: } 10 <> (-3*-3) + (-1)?? \text{ NOT OK}$$

but

$$\text{abs}(-1) < \text{abs}(-3) \text{ OK}$$

So here we meet a potentially dangerous violation of the basic rule that **a = (a/b) × b + (a%b)**.

There is a similar problem with

$$-10/-3 = 3 \quad -10\%-3 = 1 \text{ check: } -10 <> (3*-3) + 1?? \text{ NOT OK}$$

but

    abs(1) < abs(–3) OK

The ambiguity stems from two distinct approaches to integer arithmetic: *Eulerian arithmetic*, as in C, and *modulo arithmetic*, as in many computer contexts. Fortunately, the two arithmetics agree for nonnegative integral dividends (the **a**s) and positive integral divisors (the **b**s). The moral is to use unsigned and/or positive signed integers when using **%**.

C uses the one divide operator **/** for integers and floating-point numbers, but with the latter there is no ambiguity regarding sign or meaning. When both **a** and **b** are integer types, the quotient of **a/b** is also an integer type, with possible truncation. But if one or both of **a** and **b** are FP, **a/b** becomes FP. This is an example of a general rule in C that is invoked when expressions have mixed types: internal, silent conversions are made whenever necessary (and possible).

The function **fmod(x,y)** is provided in the QuickC math library to calculate *(x mod y)* for floating-point **x** and **y**.

▶ *FLOATING-POINT DATA TYPES* ▶

C offers three FP data types to handle numbers with fractional or decimal parts. They also permit the use of numbers, both integral and fractional, outside the maximum **long int** range.

The three types, **float**, **double**, and **long double**, correspond to the *single*, *double*, and *extended* precision formats available on many current computers and math coprocessors. Table 3.1 shows their bit allocations and legal ranges as assigned in QuickC.

▶ *Table 3.1:* Floating-point data types

Type Specifier	Bit Size	Range
float	32	–3.4e–38 to + 3.4e+ 38
double	64	–1.7e–308 to + 1.7e+ 308
long double	64	–1.7e–308 to + 1.7e+ 308

► *Floating-Point Declarations* ►

You declare FP variables in the usual way, using a type specifier:

```
float x, y, z = 2.0;        /* 3 floats – one initialized */
double pi, eps;             /* 2 doubles */
long double scotch;         /* 1 long double */
```

As with integers, ANSI C leaves it to the implementor to decide exactly how these FP types should be internally represented, provided only that

```
long double > = double > = float
```

where $>=$ is used informally to indicate "greater than or equal precision."

Just as you saw with **short** and **int**, QuickC's **double** and **long double** turn out to be identical in format and range. Other C systems might have an 80- or 128-bit **long double**, so some care is needed to ensure complete portability. We will use only **float** and **double** in this book.

Note that there are no **signed** or **unsigned** versions of the FP data types— they are all implicitly **signed** by definition.

The ranges shown in Table 3.1 use *scientific* notation (also called *E* or *signed exponent* notation). Symbolically

$$Me^X = M \times 10^X$$

where *M* is the fixed-point part or *mantissa* and ^{X} is the *exponent*. The e can also be written as *E*.

A positive exponent shifts the decimal point to the right (multiplying by a power of 10), and a negative exponent shifts the decimal point to the left (dividing by a power of 10). A zero exponent does not affect the mantissa, since $10^0 = 1$ by definition. Some examples of scientific notation are shown in Table 3.2. As you can see, there can be many different FP expressions (and internal bit patterns) representing the same number. (Zero is an exception because it has a unique FP bit pattern.)

► *Floating-Point Pros and Cons* ►

The FP format is most economical. For instance, the maximum number of type **double** would take 309 decimal digits to write out in full and over 1000

► **Table 3.2:** *Scientific notation examples*

120.0e+0	=	120×10^0	=	120
12.0e+1	=	12×10^1	=	120
1200.0E–1	=	1200×10^{-1}	=	120
1.2e+2	=	1.2×10^2	=	120

bits if stored in conventional binary. This enormous range, however, does not indicate the true precision available with **double**. Precision is a function of the mantissa width (52 bits), which gives "only" 15 or 16 significant digits. (Appendix D explains this in detail.)

Among the quirks of FP arithmetic are the following:

1. Adding a small number to a large one may have no effect. The significant bits of the small number may be lost when it is aligned prior to addition to the larger number.

2. It can be misleading to test for equality between two FP numbers. Rather than testing for equality as in

    if (fp1 == fp2) { ... }

    it is better to test their difference as in

    if (fabs(fp1 – fp2) <= delta) { ... }

    where **delta** is a small constant reflecting the precision of the FP type, such as 1.0e–15. **fabs( )** is a standard library function giving the absolute value of an FP argument.

► *More Internal Conversions* ►

Because of the limited precision of **float**, the system always converts **float** to **double** internally, temporarily, and silently, before evaluating any expression containing **float**s. If the final result has to be assigned to a **float** or **int** variable, another silent conversion from **double** to **float** or from **double** to **int** takes place before the assignment, with possible loss of accuracy.

You may ask why **float** is used at all. The answer is memory conservation: each **float** variable uses only 32 bits compared with 64 bits for a **double**. If speed and precision are more important than RAM, use **double** variables to reduce the conversion time.

► *Speeding FP with Math Coprocessors* ►

All FP arithmetic performed by software is quite heavy on CPU cycles. This fact has motivated the invention of *math coprocessors*, chips specially designed to handle the FP chores faster by hardware. As the name implies, a coprocessor works in conjunction, and often in parallel, with the main CPU.

For the IBM PC range, the Intel 8087, 80287, and 80387 are a family of math coprocessors compatible with the 8088/6, 80286, and 80386, respectively. The improvement in performance is well worth the modest investment.

You can write FP routines without knowing in advance if the target system is equipped with an 8087/80287/80387 coprocessor. During compilation (using QCL switches or SETUP options), you can determine whether compilation code or special coprocessor code will be generated. Note that emulated code will still run OK even if an 8087/80287/80387 is installed.

► *Floating-Point Constants* ►

Unless followed by an **F**, floating-point constants are always interpreted as **double** even if the value would fit in a **float**.

FP constants can be written in two different ways: normal decimal-point notation or scientific:

```
float w, x, y;                /* declare three floats */
double z;                     /* declare one double */

w = 3.14159; x = 4e + 5;      /* x = 400000.00 */


/* internal conversions: constant converted to double, then to float
   before assignment */
```

```
y = 1.0F                          /* F inhibits conversion to double */

z = –2.5e–12;                     /* z = –0.0000000000025 */
/* no conversions: constant and lvalue are both double */
```

You can use **e** or **E**, and the + signs are optional. Notice that if you use scientific notation, the decimal point is not essential: **4e + 5**, **4.e + 5** and **4.0e + 5** are identical.

For decimal-point (unscientific) notation of FP constants, the decimal point *is* needed: **4.**, **4.0**, **.0**, and **0.** are all FP, but **4** and **0** would be taken as **int**s.

The exponent must be a whole number and may be negative: **2.4e3.8** is illegal.

▸ *Floating-Point in Action with printf( )* ▸

You may recall using the format-conversion code **%d** with **printf( )** to display signed integers. The corresponding trick for both **float** and **double** is to use **%f**. For example:

```
float height   = 2500.35;
double depth = 3.12e5;
printf("Height is %f and Depth is %f\n",height,depth);
```

will display

```
Height is 2500.349854 and Depth is 312000.000000
```

(I'll cover the chief variants on **%f** in the following sections, but see Appendix C for the whole story.)

All values are converted to **double**, if necessary, before the **%f** conversion to ASCII takes place. This explains the slight error in the display of **height**. You'll see how to control the precision of the conversion shortly.

Using **%e** or **%E** in place of **%f** in the previous example

```
printf("Height is %e and Depth is %E\n",height,depth);
```

will give

```
Height is 2.500350e + 003 and Depth is 3.120000E + 005
```

Note the choice between **e** and **E** on display. The exponent is always signed + or − and displayed with three decimal digits (padded with zeroes as required). The mantissa is always scaled to give **d.ddd...** but you can control the layout and precision, as you'll see anon.

Another useful variant is **%g**, which will display the shorter of the two versions **%f** and **%e**. (**%G** does the same but displays **E** rather than **e**.) The **%f** version is used if both formats take the same space. The **%g** variant is useful when you have no idea of the range of the results.

► The Precision Specifier

The default conversion for **%f** is rounded to six decimal places, whatever the argument type. You can vary this precision using a decimal point and a *precision specifier* as shown in Table 3.3.

► **Table 3.3:** *Precision specifier examples*

Example	Displays Height As...
%f	2500.349854 (default = %.6f)
%.0f	2500
%.1f	2500.3
%.2f	2500.35
%.3f	2500.350
Example	**Displays Depth As...**
%e	3.120000e + 005 (default = %.6e)
%.3e	3.120e + 005

► The Width Specifier

Whether or not you have a precision specifier, you may supply a *width specifier*, **%wf** or **%w.pf**, where **w** is a number indicating the **minimum** number of columns to be allocated to the display and **p** is the precision number just described.

Leading spaces will normally be used to pad the display, but you can pad with leading zeroes by using **%0wf** or **%0w.pf**. Padding with leading spaces and zeroes is known as *right justification* since it effectively lines up columns of numbers to a flush right-hand margin. To indicate the layouts more clearly in the following examples, I will use the symbol *s* for space.

Using too small a width value will not lead to the loss of any characters— **printf( )** will simply override and take the space it needs. Examples are easier than descriptions—see Table 3.4.

► *Table 3.4: Width specifier examples*

Example	Displays Height As...
%.2f	2500.35 (no width specified)
%6.2f	2500.35 (width ignored—too small)
%9.2f	s s 2500.35 (pad blanks to 9 columns)
%09.2f	002500.35 (pad zeroes to 9 columns)
%14f	s s s 2500.349854 (same as %14.6f)
%14.0f	s s s s s s s s s s 2500 (note no decimal point)
%#14.0f	s s s s s s s s s s 2500. (unless you add a #)

The last example shows one use of the # modifier flag. In other situations it can modify the appearance of leading or trailing zeroes.

Width and precision specifiers work in a similar way with **%e**, **%E**, **%g**, and **%G**. With the integer conversion specifiers like **%d** and **%u**, of course, precision is not relevant (there are no decimal places), but you can use the width specifier to pad the field as shown above.

I have by no means exhausted the formatting possibilities, but I will conclude with just one more tweak—the use of – to force left justification within a given field width by padding with spaces (never zeroes) on the right. The – here can be confusing unless you think of it as reversing the normal right-justification! It has nothing to do with displaying a minus sign for negative values. Examples are shown in Table 3.5. (See Appendix C for much more.)

► **Table 3.5:** Left justification

Example	Displays Height As...
%.2f	2500.35 (no width specified)
%–6.2f	2500.35 (width ignored—too small)
%–9.2f	2500.35 *s s* (pad right blanks to 9 columns)
%–09.2f	2500.35*s s* (same! The zero is ignored)
%–14f	2500.349854*s s* (same as **%–14.6f**)
%–14.0f	2500*s s s s s s s s s* (note no decimal point)
%–#14.0f	2500.*s s s s s s s s s* (unless you add a #)

► *SHOWNUMF.C* ►

To try out some of these **printf( )** variations, enter SHOWNUMF.C as listed in Program 3.1. The entry **%%f** is needed to display **%f**—it is not a format specifier. SHOWNUMF.C also introduces the simple function **fsquare( )** to advance your understanding of function declarations and definitions.

Check your results against Figure 3.1.

► *fsquare( ) Declaration and Definition* ►

The line

```
double fsquare( );
```

in **main( )** is a function *declaration*, warning **main( )** that **fsquare( )** will return a **double**. The actual function *definition* comes later, spelling out in detail what arguments **fsquare( )** needs (just one **double** argument, **n**, in this case) and how the function calculates its returned value.

Note that this particular style of function declaration, known as the classical C style, has empty parentheses—it is not concerned with function arguments, only with the data type of the returned value. Later you will meet the modern variant, in which the function declaration also indicates the argument types.

```
/* shownumf.c - display fp numbers */

#include <stdio.h>

void main()
{
        double fsquare();   /* declare a function */

        float height = 2500.35;
        double depth = 3.12e5;

        printf("%%f      height is %f\n",     height);
        printf("%%.2f    height is %.2f\n",   height);
        printf("%%9.2f   height is %9.2f\n",  height);
        printf("%%-9.2f  height is %-9.2f\n", height);
        printf("%%09.2f  height is %09.2f\n", height);
        printf("%%14.0f  height is %14.0f\n", height);
        printf("%%-14.0f height is %-14.0f\n",height);
        printf("%%#14.0f height is %#14.0f\n",height);

        printf("%%e      height is %e\n",     height);
        printf("%%.3e    height is %.3e\n",   height);
        printf("%%g      height is %g\n",     height);

        printf("%%f      depth  is %f\n",depth);
        printf("%%E      depth  is %E\n",depth);
/* try your own format variants here, e.g. %10.4g etc. */

        printf("%%f depth squared is %f\n",  fsquare(depth));
        printf("%%e depth squared is %e\n",  fsquare(depth));
        printf("%%g depth squared is %g\n",  fsquare(depth));
}

double fsquare(n)   /* define the function */
double n;
{
     return(n*n);         /* the value returned by fsquare() */
```

► **Program 3.1:** *SHOWNUMF.C*

```
 Mon  3-13-1989 / 11:51:04.69 : E:\BIN
E>shownumf
%f        height is 2500.350098
%.2f      height is 2500.35
%9.2f   height is   2500.35
%-9.2f  height is 2500.35
%09.2f  height is 002500.35
%14.0f  height is           2500
%-14.0f height is 2500
%#14.0f height is          2500.
%e        height is 2.500350e+003
%.3e      height is 2.500e+003
%g        height is 2500.35
%f        depth  is 312000.000000
%E        depth  is 3.120000E+005
%f depth squared is 97344000000.000000
%e depth squared is 9.734400e+010
%g depth squared is 9.7344e+010

E>
```

► **Figure 3.1:** *SHOWNUMF.C screen output*

In the absence of such a declaration, **main( )** will assume that **fsquare( )** returns an **int**. In other words, unless told otherwise, **int** is the default data type returned by a function. Try omitting the **fsquare( )** declaration from **main( )**—you will get an instructive error message. QuickC finds a clash between the implied **int** returned by its first encounter with **fsquare( )** and the **double** value called for in the subsequent definition.

Next, try moving the **double fsquare(n)** definition ahead of **main( )** using QC's cut and paste features. You'll find that the **fsquare( )** declaration within **main( )** can now be omitted.

This explains why you often see programs with no function declarations within **main( )**: Either the function is defined first, or the nondeclared function encountered before its definition can be safely treated as though it returned an **int**. (I'll get deeper into this subject in Chapter 7.)

► *Conversion of Arguments* ►

As a further experiment, try calling **fsquare( )** with the **float** variable **height** in place of the **double** variable **depth**. Although **fsquare( )** officially asks for a **double** argument, you'll find it works equally well with a **float**. This is part of the grand internal conversion plan already discussed—passing real to formal arguments during function calls triggers promotions and conversions like those found in assignments and mixed-expression evaluations.

To return to more mundane matters, we next consider another basic data type called **char**, so far encountered only in constant forms.

► *DATA TYPE char* ►

The type specifier **char** is used to declare variables in the now familiar manner:

```
char c, ch, flag;    /* three char variables declared – not initialized */
```

The variables **c**, **ch**, and **flag** are each allotted 1 byte in memory and can be assigned values within this range at any point in the program from which they are visible.

► *The Hidden Truth About char* ►

Despite its name, the data type **char** is best considered as a special integer type representing the whole number values assigned internally to the computer's character set, in our case the ASCII set (see Appendix A). The ASCII set consists of 128 printable characters (0–9, A–Z, a–z, and punctuation marks) and nonprintable control characters encoded in 7 bits. Hence the natural bit width for storing such characters is the 8-bit byte.

The IBM PC extends the ASCII set, providing printable characters for the control codes and taking advantage of the additional 128 bit patterns by assigning special symbols that use the eighth bit. This is the *IBM PC extended ASCII character set*, full of hearts, clubs, sharps, flats, and happy faces. Some of my examples will refer to this enlarged set.

When I describe **char** as a numeric type, I mean that **char** variables can be manipulated just like integers:

```
c = 'a'; ch = c + 1;
```

will increase the bit value in **c** by 1 and move the resulting sum to **ch**. The ASCII code chart tells us that **ch** now holds the bit pattern for 'b'. A common example is the conversion of characters from lowercase to uppercase or vice versa:

```
c = 'Z'; c = c + 'a' – 'A';      /* c now equals 'z' */
ch = c – 'a' + 'A';              /* ch equals 'Z' */
```

This trick works because the values of the uppercase and lowercase ASCII characters differ by a constant: 32 (decimal) = 'a' – 'A' = 'b' – 'B' and so on. You could write

```
c = c + 32;                      /* lowercase shift – possibly! */
ch = ch – 32;                    /* uppercase shift – with due caution! */
```

but this obscures the underlying logic and will reduce portability. 'a' – 'A' = 'b' – 'B' is true for most character sets, but the value of the constant difference may not be 32.

You can multiply and divide **char**s even if the results defy any character logic ('!' times 2 equals 'B' for instance). C will go through the motions without complaint, possibly truncating in the process.

► *The Sign of a char* ►

The question immediately arises whether **c** and **ch** in the above example will behave like **signed** or **unsigned** integers. If **c** reaches the value 127 (01111111 in binary), would **(c + 1)** represent 128 (unsigned) or −128 (signed)? The answer is that, as with **int**, you have control over which interpretation the system will make. You can use the optional type modifiers **signed** and **unsigned**:

```
signed char c;              /* c has the range −128 to +127 */
unsigned char ch;           /* ch has the range 0 to +255 */
```

► *More Arithmetic with char* ►

Thinking of **char**s as numbers makes sense of the following type of manipulation you'll frequently encounter:

```
if (ch >= 'A' && ch <= 'Z') ch = ch + 'a' − 'A';
/* convert ch to lowercase ONLY if ch is an uppercase letter */
/* The parentheses around the if (condition) are essential */
```

► *BRIEF LOGICAL DETOUR* ►

The **&&** is C's logical AND operator, so **if** is testing to see if **ch** is both greater than or equal to 'A' AND less than or equal to 'Z'.

Expressions like **ch >= 'A'** are called *Boolean* to honor the English mathematician George "Kelly"-Boole (1815–64). Boolean expressions are two-valued, either true or false, and can be combined with the Boolean logical operators ! (NOT), **&&** (AND), and ¦¦ (OR) as listed in Table 3.6.

Simple and compound Boolean expressions are regularly tested in C to determine which course of action the program should take. Without such *program control* mechanisms, of course, programs would be reduced to predetermined, inflexible sequences. The **if** clause is just one method of setting up a control structure. You can also perform blocks of statements **while** a certain condition holds or iterate blocks with a **for** loop until a certain condition is false. These and other constructs will be explained as we progress.

► *Table 3.6: Boolean operators*

Operator	Meaning	Examples
!	NOT	If **X** is true then *!X* is false.
		If **X** is false then *!X* is true.
¦¦	OR	If either **X** is true or **Y** is true (or both) then (**X ¦¦ Y**) is true, otherwise (**X ¦¦ Y**) is false.
&&	AND	If **X** is true and **Y** is true then (**X && Y**) is true, otherwise (**X && Y**) is false.

► *The Truth About C* ►

C demands no profound wrestling with the real meanings of *true* and *false*. Mundanely, any expression that evaluates to zero is considered *false*, while any expression that evaluates to a nonzero value is taken as *true*. Unlike Modula-2, there is no specific **BOOLEAN** data type. You can legally write **if (X)** where **X** is any data type, variable, or constant that can legally be compared with zero. (Parentheses *must* surround the conditional portions of control statements.)

        if (3) {....}   / * legal but pointless */

means *always* perform the following block, since (**3**) is true (nonzero). More useful is

        if (ch) {...}   /* if ch is non-NUL */

where **ch** is a **char**. The ASCII NUL character is value zero, so the block after the **if** is performed only for non-NUL characters. More long-winded equivalents would be

        if (ch ! = '\0') {...}   /* if ch is non-NUL */

or

        if (ch ! = 0) {...}   /* if ch is non-NUL */

since **ch** is promoted to an **int**. You can reverse the logic with

if (!ch) {...}   /* if ch is NUL */

If **ch** is non-NUL, **!ch** becomes zero (false), but if **ch** is NUL, **!ch** becomes one (true).

Here is the character test example again:

if (ch >= 'A' && ch <= 'Z') ch = ch + 'a' – 'A';
/* convert ch to lowercase ONLY if ch is an uppercase letter */

If the first condition fails, C does not bother to test the second one since the compound expression must be false. If the first condition succeeds, the second one is tested. Only if both conditions hold will the statement

ch = ch + 'a' – 'A';

be executed. The two conditions ensure that **ch** is indeed an uppercase letter. Note that >= and <= work with characters in a purely numerical way, just like the other *relational* operators listed in Table 3.7. For the ASCII set, you need to remember that 'a' > 'A' and that all the control codes are less than ' ' (a blank space).

► **Table 3.7:** *Relational operators*

Operator	Meaning	Examples
==	Equals	if (x == 1) {....}
!=	Not equals	while (ch != EOF) {...}
<	Less than	if (ch < 'z') {...}
<=	Less than or equals	while (i <= maxi) {...}
>	Greater than	if (j > blk*siz) {...}
>=	Greater than or equals	if (i%j >= k%l) {...}

► BACK TO DATA TYPE char ►

The next piece of the **char** jigsaw is knowing what C actually does when performing arithmetic on **char**s.

► From char to int and Back ►

Before evaluating expressions, any **char** encountered is quietly *promoted* to an **int**, and this is where the sign of the **char** comes into the picture.

For signed character types, the upper byte of the **int** will be *sign-extended*, thereby maintaining the sign and value of the 8-bit **char** in the 16-bit **int**. With unsigned character types, the upper byte of the **int** is cleared to zero. For example, the letter 'a' (hex 0x61) is promoted to hex 0x0061 regardless of whether it is initially represented as a signed or unsigned **char**. On the other hand, the Greek beta (hex 0xE1) is promoted to 0x00E1 if it is unsigned but becomes 0xFFE1 if it is signed.

Note that inner conversions and promotions are made in temporary registers or RAM before the evaluation. The actual sizes of the variables are unaffected.

► Using int for Characters

A more common requirement is using **int** when you might feel that **char** is more natural. This twist of fate occurs because of C's EOF (end of file) convention. When your program is pulling characters from a text file using a function such as **fgetc( )** (a popular maneuver that you'll learn in Chapter 8), you need to know when the end of the file is reached. And, preferably, you would like to detect this condition from the value returned by **fgetc( )** since the program is usually engaged in perusing each of these "character" values anyhow. The alternative would be having to test some other flag or condition before each **fgetc( )** call ("Are we there yet?"). What you need is some unique value from **fgetc( )** that says, "This is *not* a character because there are no more characters available!" It is clear that no unique character from the ASCII or extended ASCII set can meet this requirement. For portability, such a character would have to be universally agreed upon, and it would then be taboo except as an end of file marker. (You may know that the Ctrl-Z [ASCII value 26] EOF convention for DOS text files causes many headaches when handling non-DOS files.)

The conundrum is solved in C by having **fgetc( )** and similar file and stream I/O functions return an **int** rather than a **char**. The choice of a unique, non-clashing, readily detectable EOF value suddenly becomes easy. That value is traditionally −1, but any noncharacter value would work. The price paid is that the variable receiving characters and EOFs must be of type **int**, not of type **char**. The price is not really high since most manipulations of the returned value would incur a promotion to **int** in any case. **EOF** is defined as −1 in STDIO.H, so you will often find the following snippet:

```
#include <stdio.h>
      ...
      int ch;                          /* the char is really an int! */
      ...
      while ((ch = fgetc(stream)) != EOF)
      {
/* while ch is not equal to EOF...do something with ch */
/* Its bottom byte is a character from the file since you have
   not reached the end of file */
      ...
      }
/* end of file here */
```

Generally speaking, library functions that require a **char** argument are written to accept an **int** argument. You saw a similar philosophy of silent promotion with functions taking **float** and **double** arguments.

► *Precanned char Aids* ►

The QuickC library contains a set of useful routines declared in CTYPE.H (whether they are functions or macros need not bother us—the end result is the same) that help you classify a **char** variable. In fact, the test we examined earlier:

```
if (ch >= 'A' && ch <= 'Z') {...}
```

can be written succinctly as

```
#include <ctype.h>
      ...
      if (isupper(ch)) {...}
```

The macro **isupper( )** behaves very much like a function taking an **int** argument: when you "call" it with a **char** argument, an **int** within ASCII range, or an **int** with value EOF, **isupper( )** returns nonzero (true) if the argument is an uppercase letter. Otherwise it returns zero (false). I will use the expression *ASCII + EOF* to indicate the set of ASCII characters and equivalent ASCII integers (0–127), supplemented by the EOF value (–1).

There are 12 such **is**... *predicates* or properties returning true or false. One of them, **isascii( )**, can be called with *any* integer value—it tells you if the argument is a valid ASCII value (0–127). The others work with ASCII + EOF arguments only. Table 3.8 lists them and their properties.

► **Table 3.8:** *Character tests*

Predicate	Argument	Tests True If...
isascii(ch)	int	$0 < ch < 127$
isalnum(ch)	ASCII + EOF	ch is a letter or digit
isalpha(ch)	ASCII + EOF	ch is a letter
iscntrl(ch)	ASCII + EOF	ch is control character or DEL (0x00–0x1F or 0x7F)
isdigit(ch)	ASCII + EOF	ch is a digit
isgraph(ch)	ASCII + EOF	ch is printable nonspace character (0x21–0x7E)
islower(ch)	ASCII + EOF	ch is lowercase letter
isupper(ch)	ASCII + EOF	ch is uppercase letter
isprint(ch)	ASCII + EOF	ch is printable character or space (0x20–0x7E)
ispunct(ch)	ASCII + EOF	ch is punctuation symbol (all printable characters, excluding alphanumeric, spacing, and control characters)
isspace(ch)	ASCII + EOF	ch is white space, i.e., space, tab, CR, LF, or FF
isxdigit(ch)	ASCII + EOF	ch is hex digit (0–9, A–F or a–f)

► *ARRAYS* ►

There are many instances where you want to handle a number of related variables of the same type. Suppose you wanted to manipulate a group of eight characters with a view to creating anagrams. You could start by declaring them with individual identifiers as in

```
char ch0, ch1, ch2, ch3, ch4, ch5, ch6, ch7;
```

but before long this would prove quite restrictive and time consuming. A more convenient approach is to declare a single entity, called an *array*, with eight elements:

```
char ch[8];                    /* ch is an array of char with 8 elements */
```

The syntax is simple and suggestive if you have ever used vector notation. The **[N]** immediately following the identifier tells the compiler that you are calling for an array of N elements where **N** must be a positive integer. You can now refer to the eight **char** elements of the array **ch** by using an *index* from 0 to 7:

```
unsigned int i; char ch[8];

ch[0] = 'a'; ch[1] = 'b';      /* initialize 1st two chars */
ch[6] = 'g'; ch[7] = 'h';      /* and last two chars of array */
i = 2; ch[i] = 'c';            /* set third char to 'c' */
ch[i + 2] = ch[0];             /* set fifth char to 'a' */
```

You can treat each of the elements from **ch[0]** through **ch[7]** exactly as if you had declared them individually as type **char**. Also, as you can see, it is possible to use constants or integer variables and expressions as your indices (or indexes, if you prefer the modern, dubious spelling). In fact, you can use a type **char** as an index simply because **char** has the basic integral properties needed for counting 0, 1, 2,.... Indices can never be **float** or **double** unless you first force them into **int**s. **ch[2.3]**, for instance, is verboten.

The first element of an array is *always* indexed with 0, *never* with 1. This simple fact is often overlooked, much to the amusement of the compiler. The Nth element of an array is **array_name[N–1]**.

You can set up arrays for any of the data types discussed so far:

```
#define MAXVEC 1000

    float grid[100];              /* grid[0] to grid[99] are all floats */
    double vector[MAXVEC];        /* 1000 doubles */
    long salary[MAXVEC*2];        /* 2000 longs */
    vector[MAXVEC−1] = 3.14159;   /* set last element of vector */
```

For the moment, we'll confine our attention to arrays of **char**. As I hinted earlier, arrays of **char** provide us with a natural and powerful mechanism for handling string variables.

► *Initializing Arrays* ►

In the earlier examples we declared an array and then set individual members of it using separate assignments. C allows a more concise way of declaring and initializing arrays:

```
    char ch[8] = {'a','b','c','d','e','f','g','h'};
/* declare and initialize: ch[0] = 'a', ch[1] = 'b'.... */
```

The sequence of constants, with commas as dividers, is enclosed in curly braces. The resulting object is called an *initializer*. Each constant in the initializer is assigned in turn to the elements in the array. If you have fewer constants than array elements, the extra array elements are set to zero. Having more constants than array elements will trigger an error.

If you are exceptionally lazy, you can omit the number of elements inside the [ ]. C will then calculate this number for you from the number of constants in the initializer.

```
    char name[ ] = {'S','t','a','n','\0'};
/* name becomes an array of 5 elements i.e. name[5] */
```

In the above example you can see that **name** is looking suspiciously like a string holding "**Stan**" with the final NUL that we discussed back in Chapter 1. In fact, the above initialization can also be achieved with either

```
char name[5] = "Stan";
```

or

```
char name[ ] = "Stan";          /* name[ ] becomes a name[5] */
```

using a string constant in place of an initializer. "**Stan**" as a string constant is stored with a final, invisible NUL automatically appended, so **name[]** receives five characters not four.

Quick quiz: What is the value of **name[4]**? Yes, it is NUL ('\0') because **name[4]** is the fifth, final character of the array **name**.

► *The Name of the Pointer* ►

Each of the expressions **name[i]**, as i ranges from 0 to 4, is of type **char**. However, the identifier **name** by itself (which you'll see used shortly) is *not* treated by C as either a string or as a **char** but as a special data type known as a pointer to **char**.

Unlike **name[0]**, which is of type **char** because it is the first byte of the array, **name** itself represents the memory address of the byte **name[0]**. We say that **name** *points* to **name[0]**. You could find the address held in **name**, peek into the byte at that address, and confirm that is was indeed 0x53 (the ASCII character 'S') as placed in **name[0]** by our initialization. The actual value of **name** is seldom of importance.

► *Pointer Size and Memory Models* ►

For most of the programs we'll be considering, the pointer types can be considered to be simple unsigned 16-bit values that can address up to 64KB of memory.

The 8088/8086/80286 has a complicated segmented memory-addressing scheme that is beyond our immediate scope (see Appendix E). Briefly, QuickC allows you to choose between five different *memory models*: small, medium, compact, large, and huge. This choice dictates the pointer size, 16-bit or 32-bit, the compiler will use, and this in turn determines the number and maximum sizes of your program and data segments.

It turns out to be wasteful to use a larger model than you actually need since the pointer arithmetic becomes progressively more complex. The normal QC default is the small memory model, which uses 16-bit pointers (known as **near** pointers, in contrast to the 32-bit **far** pointers). The small model allows you one 64KB segment for data and one 64KB segment for program code. Chapter 5 will develop this theme in more detail.

► *Pointer Awareness* ►

We will be returning regularly to the topic of pointers because they play a central role in C. Strangely enough, they can be used and enjoyed without an intimate knowledge of how RAM is addressed.

The symbolism employed by C allows you to manipulate pointers in an abstract, algebraic way, much as you get used to writing **a*b/c** without fretting unduly about how the machine is multiplying and dividing, provided that **c** is nonzero!

The two key symbols are **&**, meaning *address of*, and *****, meaning *pointed at by*. The two are complementary, as illustrated by the following informal definitions:

&var is the address in memory of the identifier **var**.

*ptr is the object found in memory at address **ptr** provided only that **ptr** is not the *NULL pointer*. If **ptr** has the value NULL (effectively zero, or false), ***ptr** is *undefined*.

So you can say that **&var** points to **var** and **ptr** points to ***ptr**.

The NULL exception for ***ptr** is extremely important (it corresponds to the "never divide by zero" injunction). Zero or NULL pointers are perfectly valid and legal; indeed they are as indispensible as the number 0 in arithmetic. However, NULL pointers do not point at anything, so you cannot use the ***** operator with them. Later you'll see a typical use of the NULL pointer as the terminator of a chain of linked lists rather as ASCII NUL is used to terminate a string.

& is known as the *address* operator. * is called the *indirection* operator because it expresses the idea that you get an operand indirectly by first getting its address and then accessing that address.

What data types are pointers? Well, if **var** is of type **int**, we naturally say that **&var** is of type pointer to **int**. Likewise, if **ptr** is of type, say, pointer to **float**, then ***ptr** must be of type **float** (unless **ptr** is NULL, of course).

► *The Big BUT...* ►

But, and herein lies the danger, in one sense all pointers are simply unsigned 16-bit (we confine our attention to **near** pointers) addresses with no distinguishing birthmarks. Some programmers get into the habit of using unsigned **int** or **long** variables as pointers. C does not always object, but portability suffers since there are computers with larger addressing ranges.

Pointers can be painlessly "corrupted" to point to places they shouldn't! You can take **&var**, do some pointer arithmetic, obtain a **ptr**, and then rashly assign something to ***ptr**:

```
int var, *ptr;              /* declare an int and a pointer to int */
                            /* this is explained below */
ptr = &var;                 /* ptr points to var */
{play around with ptr}
if (ptr) *ptr = 96          /* assign only if ptr is not NULL */
```

The **if (ptr)** screens out NULL pointers since NULL evaluates to zero (false).

But ***ptr** may, without due care, turn out to be part of your program or QuickC or even DOS rather than part of your data. A crash or something worse may result!

► *Pointer Declarations* ►

I've said that when you declare an array **name[5]**, the identifier **name** is actually **&name[0]**, a pointer to the first element of the array. You do not have to declare **name** as a pointer to **char**—C does that for you as part of the array declaration.

C does allow you to explicitly declare pointers to any data type (except **void**) as in

```
int *int_ptr; char *char_ptr;
float *float_ptr; unsigned long *ul_ptr;
```

The presence of the * is sufficient warning to the compiler that the identifier following is a pointer to the type specified.

Although **int_ptr** now exists as a variable of type pointer to **int**, all you have is a 16-bit uninitialized allocation of RAM; **int_ptr** is not yet pointing to anything in particular, and no **int** variable has been created. As you saw with all the earlier declarations, it is possible to initialize during a pointer declaration. Consider the following snippet:

```
int i = 1, j = 2, *int_ptr = &i;
/* initialize int_ptr with the address of int i */
    printf("int_ptr points at %d/n",*int_ptr);
    int_ptr = &j;      /* reset pointer */
    printf("int_ptr now points at %d/n",*int_ptr);
/* what will display? */
```

► *Pointer Power* ►

In spite of the dangers, pointers provide C with a certain grace and power. One of the chief applications is when you want a function to change the value of one or more of its arguments. I explained that C passes all arguments by *value*—in other words, the function receives a copy of the argument and cannot normally alter the original argument variable. (Refer back to **cube( )** in Chapter 2 to refresh your memory on this.)

However, if you pass a pointer argument, **ptr** say, to a function, the function makes a local copy of **ptr** as it does with all arguments. Using this copy pointer, the function can actually access and alter *****ptr** (unless **ptr** is NULL). So we effectively achieve what is known as *calling by reference*. This mechanism allows functions to return values in the usual way (as in **x** = **cube(y)**) and also alter the actual arguments passed to the function when desired.

The library routine **scanf( )** is a good illustration and one I have been dying to introduce since it allows you to get input from the keyboard. Its introduction has been delayed until now because it uses pointer arguments.

► KEYBOARD INPUT ►

printf( ) and **puts( )** allow you to display data on your screen (**stdout**, or *standard output device*). So far these data have been embedded in the programs themselves, which hardly leads to realistic applications! We need to explore another, rather obvious source of data—your keyboard, also known as the *standard input device*, or **stdin**.

► *Keyboard Input Using scanf( )* ►

scanf( ) uses a similar format control string to **printf( )**. Each element of this string determines how the elements read from the input device will be interpreted and where they will be stored. Take the following simple case:

```
int i;
char name[30];
printf("\n Enter your number and name:");
scanf("%d %s", &i, name);
```

If you respond to this by keying in the line

```
35 Stan
```

with any amount of white space between the two fields, the control string matches the **35** with the pair **%d** and pointer **&i** and then matches the string "**Stan**" with the pair **%s** and pointer **name**. As with **printf( )** the conversion specification **%d** causes a conversion of the ASCII characters "**35**" to **int**. The resulting number is stored at the address of **i**, namely **&i**. This is a fancy way of saying that the variable **i** is assigned the value 35. As explained in the previous section, C functions cannot alter **i** directly. Passing **i** rather than **&i** to **scanf( )** would not work: **scanf( )** would receive only a copy of **i**, and no change to **i** itself could be made.

Similarly, **%s** tells **scanf( )** to expect a string pointer, **name**, and the input string "**Stan**" is moved (with an appended NUL) to the array **name[30]**. Recall that **name** is a pointer to the first element of the array **name[30]**.

As with **printf( )**, **scanf( )** has wide choice of control specifiers, and they are best learned by osmotic exposure. Appendix C lists them all for reference.

The most common conversions are **%f** (floating point), **%u** (unsigned integer), and **%c** (single character). **scanf( )** trudges along until all the conversion specifications in the control string have been matched by input items.

The key to **scanf( )**, and the cause of most frustration, is the need to pass pointers to the target identifiers. With **&i** this is visually obvious. The puzzle for beginners is that **name**, which looks like a normal identifier, is in fact a pointer to **char**   that is, **name** is an address. It therefore doesn't need a preceding **&** to turn it into an address. You do not write **&name** (illegal), but you can write **&name[0]** (which is the same as **name**—both are pointers to **char**. From my definitions of **&** and ***** it should also be clear that ***name** would be a synonym for **name[0]** since **name** is the pointer and ***name** is the *pointee*, to coin a word.

I'll end this varied chapter with GETDAT.C (Program 3.2). The comments explain what is going on, and Figure 3.2 shows a typical screen that would result from running GETDAT.EXE.

```
/* getdat.c - simple keyboard input and outpt */

#include <stdio.h>

void main()
{
    int i, j;
    char name[31]; /* declare array of char - 30 + NUL */

    printf("Enter your Name and Number!: ");
    j = scanf("%s %d", name, %i);
/* scanf also returns a value! The number of successfully */
/* matched input items */
    printf("Well, hello %s!\n",name);
    if (i > 99)
        printf("Your number is greater than 99!/n");
    else
        printf("Your number is less than 100!/n");
    printf("PS: You entered %d items\n",j);

}
```

► *Program 3.2:* GETDAT.C

```
 Mon  3-13-1989 / 11:52:28.78 : E:\BIN
E>getdat
Enter your Name and Number!: Rudolf 200
Well, hello Rudolf!
Your number is greater than 99!
PS: You entered 2 items

E>
```

► *Figure 3.2:* GETDAT.C screen output

► SUMMARY OF CHAPTER 3 ►

Here are the main topics covered in Chapter 3:

◄► Integer data types cannot handle decimal fractions or large numbers. Division and remainder with integers may lead to erroneous results.

◄► The FP (floating-point) data types extend the range and numerical precision available by storing numbers in two parts—a mantissa and an exponent.

◄► Three FP types are provided: **float**, **double**, and **long double** (although **long double** happens to be the same as **double** in QuickC). These type specifiers are used in declarations in the same way as is **int**.

◄► **float**s are promoted to **double** internally during all FP calculations.

◄► The considerable software overhead in floating-point arithmetic can be reduced with a math coprocessor such as the 8087 or 80287. If there is no coprocessor, QuickC performs floating-point calculations with software (emulation with EM.LIB).

◄► **printf( )** can format FP numbers with precision and width specifiers in conjunction with %f, %e, and %g.

◄► I provided more information about function declarations and function definitions—where they can be placed and what happens if they are missing. This big subject will occupy much of Chapter 7.

◄► The **char** data type is really a small integer—it can be signed or unsigned by default and later specified either way with an explicit **unsigned char** or **signed char** declaration. All **char**s are promoted to **int** (signed or unsigned as appropriate) during arithmetic. You can add 1 to 'A' to get 'B', subtract 2 from 'c' to get 'a', and so on.

◄► I introduced C's simple approach to logic: false is zero, true is nonzero. Almost any variable or constant can therefore be used in Boolean expressions. Typical conditionals such as **if** and **while** simply test the following expression for zero or nonzero.

◄► Compound Boolean expressions use ! (NOT), ¦¦ (OR), and && (AND) in any logical combination. Booleans can also be generated using the relational operators == (equals), != = (not equals), < (less than), <= (less than or equals), and so on.

◄► Character constants take up 1 byte. Character constants can be expressed in various formats: 'A', '\t', '\007' (octal), or '\x1F' (hex).

◄► You should declare as **int** any characters read from streams and files since the EOF signal received at end of file is the non-**char** –1.

◄► CTYPE.H contains many precanned **char** testing routines such as **isupper( )** and **isascci( )**.

◄► Arrays are collections of variables sharing the same base data type. They are declared as **base_type array_name[size];** where each variable **array_name**[i] is of type **base_type** for i = 0 to **size**–1. The index i must be an integral type.

◄► Arrays can be initialized with **= {val1, val2,...valn}**; as part of their declaration.

◄► The identifier **array_name** is of type pointer to **base_type**. Hence, **array_name** is a constant pointer to the first element of the array, **array_name[0]**.

◄► I presented pointer notation: **&var** is a pointer to **var**, and ***ptr** is the object being pointed at by **ptr** unless **ptr** is NULL, in which case ***ptr** is undefined.

◄► Variable pointers to any nonvoid **data_type** can be declared and optionally initialized using

```
data_type *ptr_to_data_type [ = &data_type_var];.
```

◄► Pointers are powerful and dangerous. QuickC does its best to warn you by checking pointer and pointee types, but you can poke yourself to death if you wish. Pointers have their own arithmetical rules (which are covered in Chapter 4).

◄► Pointers allow functions to alter their real arguments (via a simulated "call by reference"), which is not otherwise possible with C's "call by value" regimen.

◄► Data from the keyboard (and other sources, as you'll see later) can be formatted and passed to variables using **scanf( )**. **scanf( )** uses format strings in the same way as **printf( )**. The arguments must be pointers to the variables receiving the keyboard input:

```
int number; char name[30];
scanf("%d %s",&number, name);
```

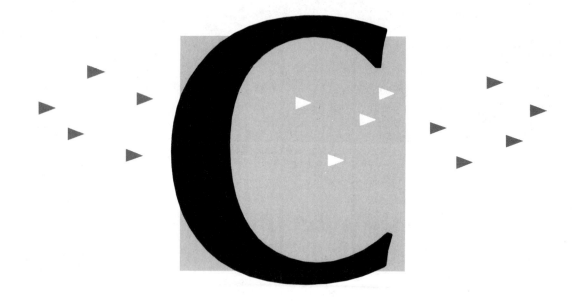

CONTROLLING THE FLOW

► *CHAPTER 4* ►

The main topic in this chapter is the use of *control flow* statements, entailing a brief homily on *structure*. The program examples, en passant, will reveal other aspects of C, such as *type casting*, *conditional expressions*, *string manipulation*, and *pointer arithmetic*.

► *CONTROL FLOW STATEMENTS* ►

You have already seen some simple control flow examples using **if, else,** and **while.** These use the simple fact that an expression can be tested for true (nonzero) or false (zero), and, depending upon the result of the test, the flow of the program execution can be varied—blocks can be bypassed or performed repeatedly (looped).

In theory, you can get by with the plain vanilla **if,** from which the other control effects can be derived, howbeit at the expense of clarity and code size.

C offers many control flow variants and extensions: **goto, else if, do...while, continue, break,** the **case/switch** statement, and the **for** loop.

All of these except **goto** enforce the expression of algorithms in a logical and legible way—the approach now generally burdened by the name *structured* programming.

► *THE IMPORTANCE OF BEING STRUCTURED* ►

In a properly structured program, sets of actions are grouped together in units that are, in a certain sense, self-contained syntactically for the compiler and visually for the human reader.

At the top level, C encourages the division of a program into many small routines, called functions, with well-defined interfaces and an efficient calling mechanism. Functions can call other functions (including themselves).

Unlike structured languages such as Ada and Modula-2, however, C does not allow you to *define* a function within another function.

Within each function, the code is structured into blocks using { and } as block markers. Blocks can be nested to any level, but if you concentrate your attention on any given block, however large or small, the ideal is that control enters only at the start of the block and emerges eventually only at the bottom. I say "eventually" because sections of code within the block may be iterated many times via various looping constructs.

What is frowned upon is the anarchy of, say, BASIC (excluding the more recent structured versions) or assembly languages, in which a conditional or unconditional **GOTO** or branch instruction can pass control to or from any part of the program regardless of block structure, creating what is commonly known as spaghetti coding. Consider the following simple pseudo-code with an outer and inner (nested) block:

```
block A   label A1: initialize block A variables
          label A2: process them
            block B
              label B1: initialize block B variables
              label B2: process them
              label B3: exit block B
          label A3: more processing
          label A4: exit block A
```

For block A to work safely, it is essential that control starts at **label A1:**. It should be impossible to branch directly to **label A2:**, say, from outside A, bypassing the initialization code at **label A1:**. The nested block B, which is used in processing block A, should be completely inaccessible from outside A. Even from within A, B should be entered only via **label B1:**. Once control is in B, we should be free to iterate via **B1:** and **B2:** but forced to exit via **B3:**. Similarly, we should not be able to jump out of A except via **A4:**.

Hard-earned experience in programming has proved that accuracy and maintainability are greatly improved if these rules are either followed voluntarily or enforced by the language specification.

Summing up the structured paradigm: From outside of A only **A1:** is accessible. Within A, all A labels and **B1:** are accessible. Within B, only B labels are accessible.

Most of C's control flow statements enforce this regime, but there are some minor loopholes and one major one!

► *THE goto STATEMENT* ►

C (like BASIC and Pascal) has a **goto** and **label** control flow mechanism. The C **goto** can only transfer control within a function, but it can still violate the rules for a strictly structured programming language by allowing jumps in and out of blocks. The programmer, therefore, must use **goto** with extreme caution. Accidentally bypassing initializations and branching into and out of other control loops are the chief dangers.

In practice, **goto** is used sparingly, usually to exit from a deeply nested block when some calamity is detected that would be difficult to handle by a succession of exits from each enclosing block. Adding a **goto** to our earlier example illustrates this situation:

```
block A   label A1: initialize block A variables
          label A2: process them
            block B
             label B1: initialize block B variables
             label B2: process them
              if (ERROR) goto A4;
             label B3: exit block B
            label A3: more processing
            label A4: exit block A
```

► *The goto Syntax* ►

The **goto** syntax is rather like BASIC's:

    goto *label*;

Anywhere in the current function, you can label the target statement as follows:

    label: *statement*;

The net result is that if and when the **goto** is executed, control passes to the (possibly empty) statement appearing alongside the matching label. *label* can be any identifier unique within the scope of the function. Labels can never appear without a real or empty statement, so

    goto error;
    ...
    error: /* illegal – hanging label */

is illegal, but

```
goto error;
...
error:;                              /* OK – empty statement at label */
```

is legal.

In view of the **goto**, we can say that, in general, the constructs offered by C encourage structured programming but do not guarantee it!

We now goto the well-behaved control flow statements.

► *THE if, else, AND else if STATEMENTS* ►

Any expression that can be legally evaluated (with internal conversion when necessary) to give an integer or pointer value (zero or nonzero) can be used as the condition-expression in the following schema:

```
if (condition-expression) T-statement
[else F-statement]
TF-statement
```

(Recall that [ ] surround an optional element.)

As in plain English, the **if** suggests a testing of the following expression in order to determine a course of action. Many computer languages use the format **IF...THEN** to stress the idea of consequence, but in C the **THEN** is implied (as it often is in English: "If that's true, [then] I quit!"). Also, as you saw in Chapter 3, C takes a purely numeric view of Boolean variables, converting the conditions (3 >= 2) to 1 (true) and (3 == 2) to 0 (false). Any nonzero condition-expression will be interpreted as true, which is reflected in the object code with the branch-not-zero instruction found in all machine languages.

T-statement represents the piece of code (possibly the empty statement ;) that will be followed (obeyed) *only* if **condition-expression** is true (nonzero). If this code contains more than one statement, it will need block marker braces to distinguish it from any following code sequences. Curly braces are optional if the T-statement consists of just one statement as in

```
if (x == 1) y = 2*x;          /* T is a single statement */
if (z >= 5.1) { x = 0; y = 3; }   /* T is a multiple statement so braces
                                 are needed */
if (n < *ptr) {ch[n+1] = '\0';}  /* braces harmless – not really needed */
```

If your condition-expression is false (zero), the whole T-statement is bypassed, ignored and forsaken. The layout of your source code should therefore make it as clear as possible exactly where T-statements start and end. This is by no means a trivial problem since T-statements often contain many lines (and possibly pages) of complex code with embedded (nested) conditions. In such cases, indents and comments should be used to indicate the different nesting levels. (Examples will follow shortly.)

Returning to the basic schema

```
if (condition-expression) T-statement
[else F-statement]
TF-statement
```

if *T-statement* is executed, control passes to **TF-statement** whether there is an **else** clause or not, and we are back into the main program sequence again.

If *condition-expression* evaluates to false, *T-statement* is ignored, and if there is an **else** clause, *F-statement* will be executed. After *F-statement*, which may be empty, single, or multiple, we continue normal service with *TF-statement*. In summary

- ► A T-statement is obeyed only if the condition-expression is true.

- ► An F-statement (if any) is obeyed only if the condition-expression is false.

- ► A TF-statement is obeyed if condition-expression is true or false.

(To be super pedantic, of course, the program may actually terminate rather than meet a TF-statement.)

► *Poor Dangling Else—The if...else Pitfall* ►

Since the T- and F-statements may contain further **if** and **else** clauses, great care is needed to avoid faulty logic. The problem is in deciding which **else** belongs with which **if**.

The golden rule is that an **else** matches the previous innermost unmatched **if** that is nearest. This matching may not always be immediately apparent. Take the following snippet:

```
if (x == 1)
    if (y == 1) puts("x = 1 and y = 1");
else puts("x != 1");              /* wrong conclusion */

/* reminder: puts( ) displays arg string plus newline */
```

At first sight you might be misled by the indentation to think that the **else** branch is taken only if **x** is not equal to 1. However, the **else** syntactically "belongs" to if **(y == 1)**.

Recall that the C compiler is unaware of your pretty (but possibly pretty wrong) indents. Correct versions, both logically and typographically, are

```
if (x == 1)
    if (y == 1) puts("x = 1 and y = 1");
    else ;                        /* an empty F-statement is
                                     legal but wasteful */
else puts("x != 1 and y = don't care");   /* correct conclusion */
```

or

```
if (x == 1)
    if (y == 1) puts("x = 1 and y = 1");
    else puts("x = 1 and y != 1");        /* good conclusion */
else puts("x != 1 and y = don't care");   /* also good */
```

or

```
if (x == 1) {
    if (y == 1) puts("x = 1 and y = 1");
}                                 /* note: the added braces
                                     make a difference here */
else puts("x != 1 and y = don't care");   /* correct conclusion */
```

depending on your intentions.

In the third version, if **(y == 1)**... is surrounded with braces and becomes a complete block with no **else** option. C therefore matches the **else** with the if **(x == 1)**... condition. Curly braces are optional in the second version since the T- and F-statements are both single statements.

Mismatched or dangling **else**s often occur when a piece of good code is patched up with some additional nested **if** tests, disturbing the previous indentations or block markers.

Another common and frustrating error is putting a spurious semicolon after the condition-expression:

```
if (x == 1); y = 2*x;        /* T is now the empty statement */
                             /* y = 2*x becomes the TF-statement */
```

The syntax is impeccable, but the results may not be as intended.

► *The else if Format* ►

The **else if** is really a combination already covered by the foregoing syntax. In this case the F-statement happens to start with an **if** that may sprout further **else**s and **if**s!

Because this is a common construction, though, it deserves a special note. You often need a series of **if...else if** to cover a multichoice situation:

```
int x;
...
if
   (x == 1) puts("x = 1");
else if
   (x == 2) puts("x = 2");
else if
   (x == 3) puts("x = 3");
else if
   (x == 4) puts("x = 4");
else
   puts("x is none of the above!");
/* resume here for all cases */
```

Note the optional final **else** that traps any value of **x** not already matched by the chain of tests. Also observe that the layout clearly reveals the program's intention. Unless you had multiple T-statements, spurious braces would simply obscure matters.

► ANALYSIS OF CHKIP.C WITH EXPERIMENTS ►

Program 4.1, CHKIP.C, will give you some practice with **if** and **else**, as well as introducing you to **getche( )**, a standard library I/O routine declared in CONIO.H. The program also illustrates the use of a type cast in a typical situation. Figure 4.1 shows the screen output from a typical session with CHKIP.

► Type Casting ►

In the statement

    ratio = (float) i / j;

we force (or *coerce*) the compiler to *cast* or convert (internally and temporarily) the **int** i to type **float** before the division by **int** j is attempted. Type casting allows you to do this conversion trick between variables of *most* data types by using the target type specifier in parentheses followed by the variable to be converted.

    (type specifier T) var;

will internally and temporarily convert **var** to data type **T**.

The type specifier, considered as an operator, is in precedence category 2, so it has higher precedence than *****, **/**, and **%**, which are in category 3. This explains why **(float)** i /j is interpreted as **((float)** i)/j rather than **(float)** (i/j).

Casting can be used to influence the result of an arithmetic expression or to avoid type-mismatching errors, when passing arguments to functions, for example.

The following is a mixed bag of examples that are mostly legal but are not all equally useful:

```
int i, *int_ptr;
char c; *char_ptr;
unsigned long ul;
double d;
float f;

c = (char) i;                    /* cast int to char */
```

```
/* chkip.c - simple conditional flow control */
#include <stdio.h>
#include <ctype.h>
#include <conio.h>
/* conio.h defines getche() */

main()
{
    int i = 0, j = 0;
    double ratio = 0.0;
    char ch, *cp;
/* we could also use int ch, see text */

    printf("\tEnter two smallish numbers: ");
    scanf("%d %d", &i ,&j);
    if (j != 0) {
        ratio = (float) i / j;
/* force conversion of int i to float before division */
/* further silent conversions occur - see text         */
        printf("%d / %d equals %f\n", i, j, ratio);
    } /* end if (j != 0) */
    else printf("%d / %d is undefined\n", i, j);

    if (i == j)
        puts("Your two numbers are equal");
    else if (i > j)
        puts("First number is larger");
    else
        puts("Second number is larger");

    printf("\tEnter a character: ");
    ch = getche();

/* getche() is "get char with echo"                    */
/* It waits for a keystroke, echoes it and returns its
   char value, which is then assigned to ch            */
/* No <enter> is needed with getche()                  */

 cp = &ch; /* assign the pointer &ch to cp
              which is a char pointer */

/* *cp now is the same as ch - so the maneuver serves only
   to illustrate pointer manipulation. You could replace
   *cp with ch in each of the following statements      */

        printf("\nYou entered \"%c\"\n",*cp);
    if (isalpha(*cp))
        printf("'%c' is alpha\n",*cp);
    else if (isdigit(*cp))
        printf("'%c' is a digit\n",*cp);
    else if (ispunct(*cp))
        printf("'%c' is punctuation\n",*cp);

    if (isalnum(*cp) && !isdigit(*cp) && !islower(*cp))
        printf("'%c' is uppercase letter\n",*cp);
    if (isgraph(*cp) || *cp == 040)
        printf("'%c' is printable or space\n",*cp);
}
```

► *Program 4.1:* CHKIP.C

```
  File  Edit  View  Search  Make  Run  Debug  Utility  Options        Help
                         E:\BIN\CHKIP.C
            puts("First number is larger");
      else
            puts("Second number is larger");

      printf("\tEnter a character: ");
      ch = getche(); cp = &ch; /* assign the pointer &ch to cp
                                  which is a char pointer */
          printf("\nYou entered \"%c\"\n",*cp);
      if (isalpha(*cp))
            printf("'%c' is alpha\n",*cp);
      else if (isdigit(*cp))
            printf("'%c' is a digit\n",*cp);
      else if (ispunct(*cp))
            printf("'%c' is punctuation\n",*cp);

      if (isalnum(*cp) && !isdigit(*cp) && !islower(*cp))
            printf("'%c' is uppercase letter\n",*cp);
      if (isgraph(*cp) || *cp == 040)
            printf("'%c' is printable or space\n",*cp);
  };

 <F1=Help> <F5=Run> <F8=Trace> <F10=Step> <F9=Brkpt>              00032:006
```

► **Figure 4.1:** CHKIP screen output

```
/*    (char) i = c; NO, NO - (char) i is not an lvalue */

      i = (int) *char_ptr             /* cast char to int */
/* assuming char_ptr points somewhere */

      int_ptr = (int *) char_ptr;
      char_ptr = (char *) int_ptr;
/* convert a char pointer to an int pointer and vice versa */
/* note the syntax */

      i = (int) f + (int) c;          /* cast float,char to int */
      i = (int) (f + c);              /* cast the float sum to int */
      f = (float) d;                  /* cast double to float */
      d = (double) i;                 /* cast int to double */
      ul = (unsigned long) i;         /* cast int to unsigned long */
      (void) func( );                 /* the value returned by
                                         func( ) is discarded */
```

The data type **void** was introduced in ANSI C to remove some potential trouble spots in K&R. The default return value of a function is **int** even if the definition does not explicitly return a value. Further, all functions, technically speaking, do return values of some kind whether you use them or not. **void** allows you and the complier to distinguish between a declaration such as func( ); [which is the lazy way or writing **int func( )**] and **void func( );**. The latter says "discard the returned value of **func( )**." Objects of type **void** do not have values like the other types (even NULL is excluded as a value). A similar problem in K&R is distinguishing between functions taking arguments and those taking no arguments. A K&R declaration such as **char func( );** can be legally followed by definitions such as **char func( )** or **char func(arg1,arg2)**. The ANSI C prototype declaration format removes this ambiguity by allowing **char func(void);** when declaring a function with no arguments or **char func(type1 arg1,type2 arg2);** when declaring a function with two arguments. The complier can now check that the function definitions and calls match the declarations.

Now some of the above examples of type casting are wasteful insofar as C already implicitly performs certain internal conversions (promotions and truncations) when evaluating expressions and making assignments.

For example, **c = i;** will eventually truncate the **int i** from 16 to 8 bits in order to make the assignment to **char c**. The type cast **c = (char) i** simply makes this conversion explicit without altering the net result. So when are type casts essential?

Try omitting the **(float)** coercion in CHKIP.C. C will first perform the integer division **i/j** and then internally convert the integer quotient to **double** in order to make the assignment **ratio = i/j**. The result will be **nnnn.000000**, correct only to the nearest whole number. With **(float) i** you get a dramatic change. **int i** is converted to **float** and immediately promoted to **double** (since all FP calculations in C are performed with double precision). Next, **int j** is automatically promoted to **double** to match the data type of the dividend. The quotient is therefore a **double** before the assignment to **ratio**. **printf( )** will therefore show the answer correct to six decimal places (the default precision of **%f**).

Now try replacing **(float) i/j** with **(double) i/j**. If you have followed the previous discussion, you will realize that this will not alter the actual result; in fact, using **(double) i** is more logical and slightly faster. I had you use **(float) i** to illustrate the underlying theory.

Note carefully the difference between

```
i = (int) f + (int) c;            /* cast float,char to int */
```

and

```
i = (int) (f + c);                /* cast the FP sum to int */
```

The answers might be different. In the second line, **char c** and **float f** will each be converted to **double** before the addition, then the sum will be rounded and truncated to **int**. The first line converts each to **int** and then performs an integer addition.

► *DETOUR TO FORMAL CONVERSION RULES* ►

It is time to list C's conversion policy during arithmetic evaluation a little more formally. There are rules for *unary* conversion (in which just a single operand is involved) and rules for *binary* conversion (in which two operands need to conform before the operation is carried out). We can combine these rules as follows:

1.   Any operands of type **short** or **char** are converted to **int**.

2.   Any operands of **unsigned char** or **unsigned short** are converted to **unsigned int**.

3.   All **float**s are promoted to **double**s.

4.   Types "array of T" are converted to types "pointer to T."

5.   If either operand is **double**, the other is converted to **double**, giving a **double** result.

6.   Else if either operand is **unsigned long [int]**, the other is converted to **unsigned long [int]**, giving an **unsigned long [int]** result.

7.   Else if one operand is **long [int]** and the other is **unsigned [int]**, they are both converted to **unsigned long [int]**, giving an **unsigned long [int]** result.

8.   Else if either operand is **long [int]**, the other (which must by now be an **int**) is converted to **long [int]**, giving a **long [int]** result.

9.   Else if either operand is **unsigned [int]**, the other is converted to **unsigned [int]**, giving an **unsigned [int]** result.

10.   Else both operands must be **int**, and the result is **int**.

This seems a formidable list to remember, but most of the conversions are logical when you consider the internal representations of each data type.

With a complex right-expression made up of mixed data types, variables, or constants, you can picture the above rules being applied successively to pairs of operands according to the precedence and associativity rules. It is quite easy to simulate the compiler with pencil and paper, and often there is one dominating type, such as **double**, that simplifies the process of deciding the type of the final result.

► *Assignment Conversions* ►

For assignment conversions the rules are much simpler. If the lvalue has the same type as the evaluated right-expression, the assignment is trivial. If the types differ, C attempts to convert the type of the right-expression to match that of the lvalue. With arithmetic types, this can always be done either by extension, as in **int** to **long** (safe), or by truncation, as in **double** to **long** (probably dangerous). Later you'll meet more complex data types that just refuse to be mixed or assigned. Following are examples of conversion of arithmetic types:

```
char c; unsigned char uc;
short s; unsigned short us;
int i; unsigned u;
long l; unsigned long ul;
float f; double d;
    ...

    d = (c + ul)*(c − s + f)/(uc + l);
/* using a shorthand notation:
    Conversion rules for right-hand expression:

    rules 1 and 2: c and s −> int; uc −> ui
        d = (i + ul)*(i − i + f)/(ui + l)

    rule 3: f −> d
        d = (i + ul)*(i − i + d)/(ui + l)

    rule 5: d and x −> d
        d = (i + ul)*(d)/(ui + l)

    rule 6: ul and x −> ul
        d = (ul)*(d)/(ui + l)
```

rule 7: l and ui -> ul
    d = (ul)*(d)/(ul)

rule 5: d and x -> d
    d = (d)*(d)/(d)

Assignment is double to double, no conversion */

/* Note: the order of evaluation is compiler dependent */

```
i = d;          /* truncation */
d = i;          /* int converted to double - safe */
d = f;          /* float converted to double - safe */
f = d;          /* f converted to double, double
                   assigned to double, then double
                   truncated to float */
```

► BACK TO CHKIP.C— PROTOTYPES AND getche( ) ►

Rather than use **scanf( )** with a %c conversion string, CHKIP.C (Program 4.1) uses a useful standard library facility, **getche( )**. This is declared in CONIO.H as

    int getche(void);

This form of declaration is known as a *function prototype*—it provides both the user and the compiler with a clear indication of what arguments (if any) are legal and what value is returned (if any).

The prototype concept is one of the many important additions made to C as a result of the new ANSI standards. It allows the compiler writer greater scope to check that function calls are made with the correct number and types of arguments. There are special prototype formats to indicate when a variable number of arguments is allowed. For example:

    int printf(char *format,...);

in STDIO.H shows that **printf( )** has one string argument (pointer to **char**). The comma and three periods indicate that any number of arguments (including none) can follow.

The traditional (classic) pre-ANSI method of declaring and defining functions will still work, but it offers less protection. Pre-ANSI declarations of **printf( )** and **getche( )** might have looked thus:

```
printf( );                    /* returns int by default */
getche( );                    /* returns int by default */
```

giving no indication that their argument requirements were widely different.

QuickC, of course, allows both approaches, and I used the classic style in earlier chapters to avoid digressions. There may be some temporary portability problems with non-ANSI systems, so you need to know both styles. You will still encounter the classic style in much of the literature and published C source code.

You are free (and encouraged) to browse around the *.H files to see the prototypes of the various functions together with macro definitions and conditional compilation directives. The definition and working code for **getche( )**, however, is buried within the QuickC libraries—out of sight, out of mind, and beyond tamperage!

The **int getche(void)** prototype tells you that it takes no arguments and returns an **int** value. You might have expected a **char** value, since the role of **getche( )** is to capture and display a keyboard character. Even though **getche( )** cannot return the **EOF** (– 1) that we discussed in Chapter 3, nevertheless it does return an **int**. In CHKIP.C, it is quite safe to assign

```
ch = getche( );
```

where **ch** is type **char**, in view of the assignment rules just covered. The zero upper byte of the **int** is discarded in any case—so it's no big loss.

CONIO.H, derived from the DOS abbreviation CON (for console), contains several related routines for console I/O. They overlap the I/O routines in STDIO.H to some extent, reflecting the separate historical strands of UNIX and MS-DOS. For now, notice that many of the **get** variants work with input from files or streams, of which **stdin** (your keyboard) is just one particular example. This will become clearer when we tackle file I/O in Chapter 8.

Try replacing **getche( )** in CHKIP.C with **getch( )**. The only difference is that **getch( )** does not echo your keystroke on the screen. This is useful in many situations, such as selecting from a menu—you want to capture the chosen key without disturbing the menu layout.

It is instructive to add the following line after **getche( )**:

```
printf("The ASCII value is %d\n",ch);
```

Now try keying some control-key combinations and see if you understand the results. Ctrl-R will display **18** (i.e., 82 − 64), confirming that pressing Ctrl subtracts 64 from the corresponding letter code. You will also see some of the IBM extended ASCII symbols. Ctrl-C, by the way, will interrupt your program prematurely. The Alt-key combinations will give bizarre results since they emit special scan codes giving pairs of characters.

► CONDITIONAL EXPRESSIONS— SHORTHAND USING ? AND : ►

Ever searching for compact notation, C offers the *conditional expression* as a shorthand way of writing the commonly occurring **if** (X) {Y} **else** {Z} type of statement. It is well worth mastering its peculiar syntax since it can simplify your source code in many situations. In

```
max = (x > y) ? x : y;
```

the right side of the assignment is a conditional expression, signaled by the *conditional operator* symbols **?** and **:**. The complete statement is equivalent to

```
if (x > y)
   max = x;
else
   max = y;
```

which results in **max** being set to the larger of **x** and **y** (or to **y** if they are the same). The conditional expression consists of three expressions separated by **?** and **:** (plus optional white space):

test-expression ? *T-expression* : *F-expression*;

This ternary (three-part) form is evaluated as follows:

1. If the test-expression evaluates to nonzero (true), the T-expression is evaluated, and this becomes the value of the conditional expression.

2. If the test-expression evaluates to zero (false), the F-expression is evaluated, and this becomes the value of the conditional expression.

Since the whole conditional expression ends up with a value, it can be used just like any other non-lvalue C expression. You can use it as the right-expression in an assignment as we did with **max**, or it can be part of a compound expression as in

    i = ((x > y) ? x : y)*(j >= 0 ? j : −j)/3;

This highlights the advantage of the conditional expression. The above line would take two **if**s, two **else**s, four assignments, and possibly additional temporary variables. Do you lose too much in legibility? This is a subjective issue. Once the conditional expression is familiar to you, you quickly spot that the expression

    j >= 0 ? j : −j

evaluates to the absolute value of j since it evaluates to −j only if j is negative.

A few details need attention. The precedence of **?** and **:** is very low (category 13), just above the assignment operators (category 14), and well below the relational operators (categories 6 and 7). This means that parentheses are not strictly needed in

    max = (x > y) ? x : y;

as they would be in

    if (x > y) {...}

You should go with what the bible says: "...they [parentheses] are advisable anyway, however, since they make the condition part of the expression easier to see." (*The C Programming Language*, page 48).

Since the conditional expression is a single entity, C performs the usual conversions and promotions during evaluation, taking note of both the T-expression and the F-expression. There is a potential pitfall here. Take the following snippet:

```
int i;
double d;
...
i = (i > 0) ? i : d;
```

You might expect that if **i** were greater than zero, the right-expression would evaluate to type **int** with value i, which could then be assigned to the **int** lvalue without conversion. In fact, the presence of the **double d**, even when it is not directly involved in the i-positive case, forces the right-expression to **double** under all conditions. In this example, of course, the assignment immediately triggers a conversion back from **double** to **int**, so error-prone truncation only occurs in the i < 0 case. You can see that care is needed if conditional expressions are embedded in more complex code—remember to watch the data types of all three components.

Here are a few more examples of ?...: in action:

```
#define MAX(x,y)     ( (x) > (y) ? (x) : (y) )
#define MIN(x,y)     ( (x) > (y) ? (y) : (x) )
#define MY_DIV(x,y)  ( (y) ? ((x)/(y)) : BIG_QUO)
```

The compactness of the conditional expression is especially useful in *para-metrized macro* definitions, as shown above. The parenthetical profusion is absolutely essential, allowing the macros to be called with complex arguments as in

```
d = MAX( a + 2*b, (n − m)/(k + MIN(4*p,q(r − 1))) );
```

Here the *formal parameters* **x** and **y** in **MIN(x,y)** would be replaced in situ by the *actual parameters* as follows:

```
( (4*p) > (q(r − 1)) ? (q(r − 1)) : (4*p) )
```

This is known as *token replacement*. In many cases, the parentheses may prove to be redundant, but it is better to use them since we have no advance knowledge of the relative precedences of the operators used in the actual parameters and the macro definition. Omitting the parentheses in a macro is extremely hazardous—bugs can lie dormant for years.

Macros are often used in libraries as alternatives to functions. They avoid the overhead of function calls but are less flexible since you cannot take the address of a macro. Pointers to functions, on the other hand, allow you to pass functions as arguments to other functions.

► *THE while LOOP* ►

Like **if**, **while** corresponds to normal English usage. You can repeatedly execute a statement or block of statements while a certain condition is true:

```
while (condition-expression)
    T-statement
TF-statement
```

First of all, ***condition-expression*** is evaluated. If it is zero (false) control passes immediately to ***TF-statement***. If ***condition-expression*** is nonzero (true), ***T-statement***, consisting of one or more possibly empty statements, is executed.

If a **break** statement is executed during the T-statement, control immediately passes to the TF-statement, and you *exit* the loop.

If a **continue** statement is executed during the T-statement, control moves back to the **while** condition, which is retested to determine whether the loop will repeat (if true) or terminate (if false).

If neither **break** nor **continue** are encountered, the T sequence is completed normally, and the **while** condition-expression is reevaluated. Again depending on this test, you either reexecute the T sequence or drop through to the TF-statement.

In less fancy verbiage, we say that T is looped until the **while** condition is false or a **break** is made.

Note that there is one exceptional situation in which looping ends regardless of condition tests: within a function definition the **return** statement always terminates execution and returns control to the calling routine. I will exclude this possibility for the moment to simplify the exposition.

If there is no **break** and the condition remains true forever, the loop is *endless*—your needle is stuck in the groove until you interrupt manually, reboot, or lose power.

Normally, though, some action within the loop or within the condition itself is geared to render the condition false or induce a **break** sooner or later. When that occurs, you exit the loop and resume normal, sequential execution. Take the following simple case:

```
int count = 10;

while (count >= 0) {
    printf("Countdown is %d\n",count);
    count = count − 1;
}
puts("BLAST OFF!");
```

As you saw with **if**, a compound T-statement requires block markers. The above snippet will display

```
Countdown is 10
Countdown is 9
...
Countdown is 0
BLAST OFF!
```

Within the T-statement, we are reducing the value of **count**, ensuring that when **count** reaches − 1 the **while** condition will fail. Let's make this program more like real C:

```
int count = 10;

while (count >= 0)
    printf("Countdown is %d\n",count − −);
puts("BLAST OFF!");
```

The postdecrement saves a line, saves a pair of braces, and incidentally saves a little time since **count − −** translates into a faster machine code instruction than **count = count − 1** or **count −= 1**. Consider also the following:

```
int count = 11;
while ( − −count + 1)
    printf("Countdown is %d\n",count);
puts("BLAST OFF!");
```

Here the countdown loop will end when − − **count** + 1 reaches 0 (false), i.e., after **Countdown is 0** has been displayed.

An artificial variant to show how **break** works might be

```
int count = 10;

while (count >= 0)
   if (count = 3) {
      puts("ABORT!");
      break;
   }
   printf("Countdown is %d\n",count − − );
puts("BLAST OFF!");
```

The loop exits when **count** reaches 3. Usually, though, **break** is used to exit upon some abnormal or error condition not immediately involved in the **while** condition being tested.

Often you will find deliberate endless loops that rely on internal tests or events to exit or abort. Rather than construct a complex **while** condition, some loops start with **while(1)** or **while(true)**, which clearly mean loop forever. Within such loops you are bound to find some terminating mechanism! In addition to the built-in **break** and **return** statements, the C library offers the **exit( )** and **abort( )** facilities in PROCESS.H. These are machine-dependent functions or macros that terminate not only the loop but also the whole program. **exit( )** is the more graceful termination—it will close files, flush buffers, and perform similar *housekeeping* chores. **exit( )** takes an integer argument that indicates the status of the exit as in

```
if (calamity) exit (n);
...
```

The status number, **n**, is transmitted to DOS as the reason for program termination. A status of 0 indicates normal termination. A variant of **exit( )**, written **_exit( )**, exits without any prior housekeeping. The **abort( )** facility also terminates without housekeeping but writes an error message to a designated device called **stderr** (usually your screen) before calling **_exit( )** to perform the emergency termination.

exit( ), unlike **abort( )**, allows you to invoke your own *exit functions*. You set up a pointer to the first exit function using **atexit( )** in STDLIB.H. Each call to an exit function can chain to another up to a total of 32 functions. These allow you to perform your own "cleaning up" operations before the standard ones are invoked by **exit( )**.

These program termination facilities are essential in the real world, where a disk-full or printer-not-ready condition can occur at precisely the wrong time.

Since **while** loops can be nested, you have to watch your indents, braces, and the scope of any **break** statements. Just like the nested **if...else** situation outlined earlier, **break** will terminate the innermost, enclosing **while**. KEYCNT.C (Program 4.2) offers a simple test bed to try out nested **while**s.

```
/* keycnt.c -- test nested while loops */
#include <stdio.h>
#include <conio.h>

main ()
{
        int count = 3;
        char ch = '\0';

        while (count-- >= 0) {
            while ((ch = (char) getch()) != 'q') {
                printf("ch = %c\n",ch);
                if (ch == 'x') break;
            }
            puts("Inner loop ends!");
        }
        puts("Outer loop ends!");
}
```

► *Program 4.2: KEYCNT.C*

► ANALYSIS OF KEYCNT.C ►

The outer loop can be invoked only four times since **count** decrements from 3 to −1 before the outer **while** condition becomes zero. The inner loop cycles until either a q or x is keyed. Avoiding these two characters keeps you forever in the inner loop. So, to exit the outer loop and thence the program, you need to type four qs or xs in any combination (e.g., three qs and one x). You might find this useful one day!

KEYCNT.C illustrates again the power of C's expressions. The function **getch( )** is invoked, converted to **char**, assigned to **ch**, and compared with 'q' all within the second **while** condition. Try replacing the **printf( )** line with

```
printf("ch = %c\n",ch = (char) getch( ));
```

and remove the **getch( )** from the **while** condition expression to get

```
while (ch != 'q')
```

The second argument in **printf( )** is an assignment expression and function call neatly rolled into one.

► *The Busy while* ►

Since you can pack a lot of action inside the **while** condition-expression, you often see examples of code where the **while** T-statement is empty:

```
while ((ch = getche( )) == SPACE);
```

will simply ignore any keystrokes giving **ch** equal to **SPACE** (a predefined value). Notice that one ; after the) is all you need to indicate an empty statement. Beginners are sometimes tempted to write

```
while ((ch = getche( )) == SPACE);;                    /* surplus ; */
```

This is legal but wasteful since it gives you two empty statements, one within the **while** loop and one outside it.

Another instructive example is

```
int count;
char *ch_ptr;                    /* pointer to char */
char name[ ] = "Microsoft";      /* initialize array of char */
ch_ptr = &name[0];               /* or ch_ptr = name;! */
...
count = 0;
while (*ch_ptr++)
   count++;
/* advance pointer to end of string, count the number of chars
   excluding final NUL */
```

The intriguing condition-expression (***ch_ptr++**) will evaluate to false only when the final ASCII NUL is reached in the string "**Microsoft\0**". Or will it?

Astute readers may notice that the operators * (indirection) and ++ (post-increment) have equal precedence (both in category 2). So do we take

   (*ch_ptr)++

to mean "add 1 to the **char** at address **ch_ptr**" or do we interpret it as

   *(ch_ptr++)

meaning "take the **char** at the pointer given by **ch_ptr++**"? Clearly, it makes a difference, and we need to be told!

The answer lies in the associativity rules for category 2 operators like * and ++. They associate from right to left, so *(ch_ptr++) is the correct interpretation. But does the indirection occur before or after the pointer is incremented? You need to note very carefully how the postdecrement works. Although ++ increments **ch_ptr** as a side effect, the expression **ch_ptr++** returns the old, nonincremented value. So the sequence of events for *(ch_ptr++) is as follows:

1.   **ch_ptr++** is evaluated first, returning old value of **ch_ptr**.

2.   The variable **ch_ptr** is incremented.

3.   The * operator "grabs" the **char** at old **ch_ptr**.

I spell out this example in detail because it is the source of much confusion.

The convolutions are not yet over. What increment does **ch_ptr++** actually achieve? Pointers in C have their own special arithmetical rules.

► POINTER ARITHMETIC
AND THE sizeof OPERATOR ►

When we write **ch_ptr++** or __ch_ptr or **ch_ptr + 3**, we are certainly changing the value of the pointer variable **ch_ptr**. C helpfully (some say unhelpfully) takes into account the size of what the pointer is pointing at before doing the arithmetic.

Each data type and variable in C has an associated size, expressed as a number of basic storage units. This basic unit is machine dependent, but in most systems, including IBM PC QuickC, data-type size is measured in bytes. Thus **char** is of size 1, **int** and **short** are size 2, **float** is size 4, and so on.

Furthermore, larger objects like arrays (and structures and unions to be seen later) have sizes that depend on their particular declarations and assignments. Remember, too, that all these sizes may differ between different C implementations. We therefore need some mechanism to ease the writing of portable code.

The solution is the operator **sizeof**, which determines the size of any data type or object:

```
int i, size, *int_ptr, table[10];
char ch, *chr_ptr, name[30];
double d, grid[20];
...
size = sizeof(int);          /* size now = 2 */
size = sizeof(ch);           /* size now = 1 */
size = sizeof(size);         /* size now = 2 since size is int */
size = sizeof(ch_ptr);       /* size = 2 or 4 depending on memory
                                 model */
size = sizeof(float);        /* size now = 4 (32 bits) */
size = sizeof(d);            /* size now = 8 (64 bits) */

size = sizeof(name);         /* size now = 30 */
/* NOTE: sizeof treats name as a 30-byte array NOT as the pointer
         to an array */
size = sizeof(&name[0]);     /* size = 2 or 4 depending on memory
                                 model */
/* above gets the pointer size */

size = sizeof(table);        /* size now = 10*2 = 20 */
size = sizeof(grid);         /* size now = 20*8 = 160 */
```

► *Portability and sizeof* ►

You are sometimes tempted to use the "fact" that **int** is 16 bits. For example, the function **malloc(N)** in MALLOC.H allocates **N** bytes of memory (the details are not important), so to allocate enough memory for 12 integers you could write **malloc(24);**. This works fine with QuickC, but you have unnecessarily constrained your program. By writing **malloc(12 * sizeof(int));** you achieve portability to systems that may have 32-bit **int**s.

► Pointer Sums with sizeof ►

When you add 1 to a pointer, you are really adding **(sizeof)** storage units, so the actual increment depends on the size of the object being pointed at. The same logic applies to subtraction:

```
i = *int_ptr++;          /* int_ptr incremented by sizeof(int) = 2 */
ch = * − −_chr_ptr;      /* chr_ptr decremented by sizeof(char) = 1 */
j = *(int_ptr + 2);      /* int_ptr incremented by 2*2 = 4 */
```

The general idea behind pointer arithmetic can be summarized in the following manner: for

```
T *ptr_to_T;             /* T is a type specifier. Declare a pointer to T */
```

(ptr_to_T + i) evaluates as (ptr_to_T + i*(sizeof(T)))

(ptr_to_T ++) evaluates to (ptr_to_T + sizeof(T))

(ptr_to_T __) evaluates to (ptr_to_T _ sizeof(T))

► PHILOSOPHICAL INTERLUDE ►

Some people complain that C encourages opaque code, while others praise the language for offering compact notation. The truth is that C's powerful expression/statement approach can be misused. Theoretically, you might be able to cram most of your program into one C statement, but there is a commonsense limit beyond which your intentions become clouded and your code becomes not just illegible but also impossible to alter without painful side effects. C's philosophy is to break problems down into a large number of simple, easy-to-analyze functions. Within each function, your statements should also be kept as simple and clear as possible.

Meanwhile, back in the loop....

► THE do...while LOOP ►

A normal **while** loop is only entered if the leading condition turns out to be true. It is useful to have another construct, called **REPEAT...UNTIL** in other languages, in which the loop condition is tested at the end of the loop. This approach ensures that the loop is always performed at least once. The C syntax is

```
do
    loop-statement
while (loop-condition)
```

A loop-statement can be empty, single, or multiple with braces. It is always executed before the **while** loop-condition is evaluated. Remember that parentheses are mandatory around the loop-condition. If this is zero (false) the loop is over; otherwise control returns to the keyword **do**, and we loop again.

If a **break** statement is executed during a **do...while** loop, a premature exit occurs, and control passes to the statement beyond the matching **while**.

A **continue** statement will send control forward to retest the condition.

Although less common than the normal **while** loop, the **do...while** is convenient when some input or event must be established at least once and then possibly repeated. For example:

```
int choice;
...
do {
    puts("Enter Menu item# 1 – 8 (9 to exit): ");
    scanf("%d",&choice);
    if (choice == 9) break;
    if (choice == 1) {
        /* process choice 1 */
        ...
        break;
    }
    /* handle other valid choices */
    ...
    ...
} while (choice < 1 || choice > 9);
```

Here the menu prompt always appears at least once and keeps appearing if an invalid choice is made. Within the loop we can **break** as soon as a good choice has been processed.

The above sequence of **if**s to process choices is effective enough but is considered somewhat inelegant in C, which provides a specific **switch... case...break...default** construct for multiway branches.

► *THE switch STATEMENT* ►

Before discussing the formal syntax of the **switch** statement, let's revamp
the above menu example:

```
int choice;
...
do {
    puts("Enter Menu item# 1_8 (9 to exit): ");
    scanf("%d",&choice);
    switch (choice) {
        case 9: break;
/* choice 9 will exit switch _ no action */
        case 1: func_1( );
            break;
/* choice 1 will invoke func_1( ) then exit */
        case 2: func_2( );
            break;
        case 3: func_3( );
        case 4: func_4( );
            break;
/* choice 3 will invoke func_3( ) followed by func_4( ) */
/* choice 4 will invoke just func_4( ) */
        case 5:
        case 6:
        case 7:
        case 8: func_x( );
            break;
/* choices 5 - 8 will invoke func_x( ) */
        default: puts("Bad choice!);
            break;
    } /* end of switch */
} while (choice < 1 || choice > 9);
/* repeat menu display for bad choices */
/* reach here after a good choice 1 - 9 has been processed */
```

There are several new keywords at work here.

First, the **switch (choice)** statement establishes the integer variable **choice**
as the *control* expression for the following multiway choices. C evaluates the
current value of **choice** and searches sequentially for a match in the list of
case n: labels.

Each **case n:** line acts like the named label you saw in the **goto** syntax at
the beginning of this chapter. You can picture the machine performing a

goto label **case n:** whenever **choice** equals the integer value **n**. The statement or statements following the **case n:** label will be executed until a **break** is encountered or until we reach the end of the whole **switch** sequence, signaled by the final matching, enclosing }.

Note that there is no need to list the **case n:** labels in any particular order apart from grouping common-action cases like 5–8. Each **case n:** will be found no matter where it is positioned. On the other hand, you must avoid **case** label duplications within the same **switch** sequence.

If **choice** is 9, a match is made at the line **case 9:**, and execution of the **break** statement occurs—leading to an instant exit from the **switch** sequence down to the **while** statement. The **while** condition is false, so we also exit the **do...while** loop. Note carefully that **break** is now terminating the **switch**, not the **do...while** as in the previous menu example.

Suppose you entered **choice** as 1. It would then match the **case 1:** label and obey whatever statements are found there, namely a call to **func_1( )** (assumed to be declared and defined elsewhere) followed by a **switch-break** and thence a **do** loop exit as with **case 9:**.

The choice 3 is especially instructive. After the **case 3:** label we find **func_3( );**, so this function will be called. Since there is no **break** statement following, the program carries on and obeys the statements for **case 4:**. As in BASIC, control passes by intervening labels, picking up all instructions in its path. So, a choice of 3 will perform **func_3( )** followed by **func_4( )** and then meet a **break** to exit. Choice 4, of course, invokes only **func_4( )**.

I cannot overstress the action of choice 3—it is the source of many bugs. Unless you want a choice to trigger the work for other, later choices, you must put in **break**s to prevent the code from *running on*.

Now look at choices 5–8. Here we have the situation where the same action, **func_x( )**, is needed for different choices. Hence the labels **case 5:** to **case 7:** are empty. Control will end up at **case 8:** for all choices in the range 5–8.

The special label **default:** is optional. If it is used, it will attract the attention of any case not covered by specific **case n:** labels. In my example, any integer entered as **choice** outside the range 1 <= **choice** <= 9 will be trapped by **default:**, giving a warning display. When control exits to the **while** condition test, the **do** loop will be reinvoked, and the menu prompt will reappear.

In the absence of a **default:** label, any unmatched cases will simply filter down to the final } of the **switch** sequence with no particular action being triggered.

The final **break** after the **puts("Bad choice!)"** is not actually needed—the end has been reached already! However, it is considered good style: if you ever go back and enlarge the **switch** choices, that final **break** serves as a *sentinel*.

After that informal breeze through a fairly complex construction, let's recap **switch**, giving the syntax with more precise notation:

```
switch (control-expression) {
    case constant-expression-1:
        statement-sequence-1;
        [break];

    case constant-expression-2:
        statement-sequence-2;
        [break];
    ...
    ...

    [default:]
        default-statement-sequence;
        [break];
    }
```

The value of the control-expression must be integer compatible, i.e., of type **int**, **char**, or any of the **int** variants (**short**, **long**, **signed**, or **unsigned**). Later you will meet a data type called **enum** that is also integer compatible. **float** and **double** are absolutely verboten.

The control-expression itself can be any constant (not too useful!), variable, or function returning an **int**-like value.

The **case** labels, though, must be constants or constant-expressions. **case 'A':** and **case (1 + 4):** are valid, but **case choice:** and **case (2*i):** are not. The colon is C's standard way of indicating a label, as you saw earlier.

► *switch Caveats* ►

Note that **continue**, unlike **break**, has no impact on the **switch** sequence. If you have a **switch** embedded in some other control loop, however, a rashly used **continue** might cause strange aberrations. It will affect only the nearest enclosing control loop, not the **switch**.

Because **switch** is really a multiple **goto**, it is possible to write code that violates the structured rules presented earlier in the section on **goto**. The **case n:** labels can be legally positioned alongside any statement in the **switch** body, just as **goto** labels can go anywhere within a function. If your **case n:** labels are badly placed, they can result in initialization code being bypassed or branches into or out of nested control loops.

I have saved the best control loop to the end. The **for** loop, well known to BASIC and Pascal users, provides a powerful and concise method of loop iteration under a wide variety of conditions.

► *THE for LOOP* ►

Let's start with a simple example before the laying on of the syntax:

```
int count;
...
for (count = 0; count < = 10; count + +)

    printf("Countup is %d\n",count);        /* body of loop */

    puts("That's all!");                     /* first statement after loop */
```

This will display the fascinating sequence

```
Countup is 0
Countup is 1
Countup is 2
...
Countup is 10
That's all!
```

After the keyword **for** there are always three expression statements within the parentheses (some or all of which may be empty), representing in order of appearance:

1. The **for** loop counter initialization (**count = 0** in the above example). You can also have multiple initialization expressions separated by commas as in

    for (count = 0, i = 100; count <= 10; count + +)

    (See the section on *comma expressions* below.)

2. The **for** loop test condition (**count <= 10**). Unlike **while (count <= 10)**, the parentheses are optional.

3. The **for** loop modifier (**count + +**), sometimes called the *reinitializer*. This may also contain multiple expressions separated by commas as in

    for (count = 0, i = 100; count <= 10; count + + , i − −)

    Following the **for** line is the body of the loop, which comprises a single- or multiple-statement block (possibly empty). In the above example the body consists of the single statement

    printf("Countup is %d\n",count);   /* body of loop */

    so no curly braces are required.

▸ *The for Loop—Step by Step* ▸

When the **for** in my example is encountered, the following sequence of events occurs:

1. The initialization statement is executed (**count** is initialized to zero). This step occurs only once.

2. The loop condition (**count < = 10**) is evaluated.

    If loop condition is zero (false),

    > exit the **for** loop and resume control after the last statement in the loop, displaying **That's all!**.

    If loop condition is nonzero (true),

    > the body of the **for** loop is executed, displaying the current value of **count**. Then execute the loop modifier, expression statement 3, to reinitialize the loop. **count** is postincremented by 1. The loop now repeats from step 2 and the test condition is reevaluated.

If you trace this sequence in the example, it is clear that count <= 10 is true until **count** has been incremented from 0 to 11. After 11 iterations of the **for** loop body, the condition test gives false, and the looping ends. Hence you get a simple counted loop, just one of the many applications of the **for** loop.

The **for** loop flow can always be simulated with a long-winded **while**:

```
int count;
...
count = 0;                              /* initialize */
while (count < = 10) {                  /* loop condition */
    printf("Countup is %d\n",count);    /* body of loop */
    count + + ;                         /* loop modifier */
}
puts("That's all!");                    /* first statement after loop */
```

Note carefully the position of the loop-modifer statement—it follows the loop body.

► *The Endless Loop Revisited* ►

As with **while** loops, the **break** and **continue** statements can be used to exit a **for** loop or force an early reevaluation of the **for** loop-modify expression. Recall, too, that within a function definition, a **return** always preempts a loop of any kind, sending control back to the statement after the function call. The dreaded **goto** may also be used to exit the loop.

In the absence of such abnormal exits, it is important that the loop condition contains variables that are altered either in the modifier statement, in the loop body, or both. Iterations that do not somehow *converge* to a false loop condition will loop forever:

```
for( i = 0; i <= 20; j ++)          /* ??? */
    puts("This show will run and run!");
```

Since i remains at 0, the test i <= 20 is forever true.

The body of the loop often provides the loop modifier and/or the exit condition. In fact, you can have a **for** with one or more empty statements. Here are three examples:

```
int j = 0;
...
for (;j <= 3;)                    /* no init, no modifier */
    printf("j = %d\n",j++);

int j;
for (j = 0;;j++)                  /* no condition means true */
    if (j <= 3) printf("j = %d\n",j);
    else break;

int j = 0;
for (;;)                          /* no init, no condition, no modifier */
    printf("j = %d\n",j++);
    if (j >= 3) break;
```

An empty loop condition is taken as being always true. The last snippet is similar to the deliberate **while (1)** you saw earlier. It deliberately sets up an endless loop condition and relies (hopefully) on a **break** or **return** to terminate. In fact, a common macro in the C world is **#define forever for (;;)**.

► *Nested for Loops* ►

By now you will be unsurprised to learn that **for** loops can be, and often are, nested.

```
int i, j;
for (i = 0; i <= 10; i++)
    for (j = 0; j <= 10, j++)
        printf("i = %d, j = %d\n",i,j);
puts("All done!");
```

will display the following 121 lines:

```
i = 0, j = 0
i = 0, j = 1
...
i = 1, j = 0
i = 1, j = 1
...
```

```
...
i = 10, j = 0
i = 10, j = 1
...
i = 10, j = 10
```

It is easy to add unwanted semicolons after the **for(...)**. If you write

```
int i, j;
for (i = 0; i <= 10; i++);                    /* ????? semicolon ????? */
    for (j = 0; j <= 10, j++)
        printf("i = %d, j = %d\n",i,j);
puts("All done!");
```

the syntax is good, but the first **for** loop body is now an empty statement that will be pointlessly "obeyed" 11 times. The **printf( )** will be invoked only 11 times, not 11×11 as intended.

An interesting point arises: what will be the value of i when the first loop ends? In Modula-2 there is no guarantee that **FOR** loop counters preserve useful values outside the loop. C, on the other hand, imposes no such limitations, so i has the usable value 11 when the loops ends.

► COMMA EXPRESSIONS ►

I mentioned earlier that a **for** loop could start with multiple expressions in the initializer and modifier (reinitializer) sections.

```
for (count = 0, i = 100; count <= 10; count++, i--)
```

would initialize **count** and i as shown, and each iteration would increment **count** and decrement i. These are particular cases of a construct called the *comma expression*. Generally, you can have any number of expressions separated by commas as in

```
exp1, exp2, exp3,...expn
```

C always evaluates these one by one, from left to right, but only the data type and value of the final, rightmost evaluation are preserved and returned as the type and value of the whole comma expression. The comma in this context has the *lowest* precedence of all the C operators (see group 15 in the table inside the covers of this book), so parentheses are only rarely needed to avoid ambiguity with function-argument commas. For example:

    k = j++,i--;

would increment j, decrement i, and then assign the old value of i to k. In the above **for** loop, the two comma expressions are used purely for their side effects—their resulting values are discarded. This is a common situation in C. Unless the resulting value of an expression evaluation is assigned to an lvalue, it simply disappears. i-- certainly decrements the variable i in the **for** loop above, but the value of the comma expression, namely the value of i--, is discarded.

► ANALYSIS OF REVSTR.C ►

The comma expression can pack a lot of punch into a **for** loop. You can often avoid nested loops by processing several indices together. Try REVSTR.C (Program 4.3) as an exercise in using **for** to reverse the characters in a string. The **for** loop here is typical of many array-manipulating loops. In this particular case, the array is a character string.

```
/* revstr.c - reverse a string using for loop */

#include <stdio.h>
#include <string.h>
/* get prototype declaration of strlen() */

main () {

    unsigned i, j;
    int ch;
    char name[] = "aibohphobia"; /* the fear of palindromes */

    for (i = 0, j = strlen(name) -- 1; i < j; i++, j--) {
/* i selects chars from start to middle, j selects them from end
   to middle. Loop stops when i >= j */
        ch = name[i];
        name[i] = name[j];
        name[j] = ch;
    }
    printf("\'aibophobia\' spelled backwards is %s\n",name);
}
```

► *Program 4.3: REVSTR.C*

► *A Peep at STRING.H* ►

The library function **strlen( )** is introduced in REVSTR.C to obtain the length of the string **name**. **strlen( )** is one of 30 or so string-handling functions defined in STRING.H. You should locate this in \c\include and print out the prototype declarations. Most of these functions take arguments of type pointer to **char**—for example:

```
unsigned strlen(char *str);
/* returns length of string as unsigned int excluding the final NUL */

char * strcpy(char *destin, char *source);
/* copies source string to destination string. Returns a pointer
   value = destin */

int strcmp(char *str1, char *str2);
/* compare the two strings str1 and str2 */
/* returns an int < 0 if str1 < str2
              = 0 if str1 = str2
              > 0 if str1 > str2
   where the comparison is made lexicographically as in a
   dictionary sequence */
```

As you can see the returned values vary according to function.

C does not have a data type **string** per se, like BASIC, but when you get acquainted with the STRING library, you'll find that you can do anything with strings just as easily as in BASIC. You can't copy strings with **A\$ = B\$** as in BASIC, but you simply write **strcpy(a,b)** where **a** and **b** are array names or pointers to **char**.

For the moment we'll need only **strlen( )**, which returns an **unsigned int**, namely the length of the string excluding the final NUL. Because I set j to **strlen(name) − 1** in the **for** loop initialization expression, j indexes the *last* character in **name**. **ch** is used as a temporary variable while **name[i]** and **name[j]** are swapped.

The chief lesson of REVSTR.C is the use of i + + and j − − in the **for** loop— they allow a single loop to pick out characters from either end of the string.

Once you have mastered the logic of REVSTR.C, enter and run PALIN.C (Program 4.4). It defines a function, **rev( )**, based on the **for** loop in REVSTR.C. You can use this to experiment further with reversing strings and finding palindromes (words or phrases that read the same in both directions). With **rev( )** you should

```
/* palin.c  - reverse a string */
#include <stdio.h>
#include <string.h>
/* get prototype declaration of strlen() */

#define MAXLEN 80

void rev(char *str);
/* function declaration */

      char name[] = "able was i ere i saw elba";
      char copy[MAXLEN];
/* these are global variables declared outside main() */

main () {

      strcpy(copy,name);
      rev(copy);
      printf("\'%s\' spelled backwards is \'%s\'\n",name,copy);
}

void rev(char *str)
{
      unsigned i, j;
      int ch;

      for (i = 0, j = strlen(str) -- 1; i < j; i++, j--) {
/* i selects chars from start to middle, j selects them from end
   to middle. Loop stops when i >= j */
      ch = str[i];
      str[i] = str[j];
      str[j] = ch;
      }
}
```

► **Program 4.4:** *PALIN.C*

be able to modify the program so that any string entered via the keyboard using **scanf( )** can be displayed in both directions. Then you could use **strcmp( )** to compare the two.

Note that the definition of **rev( )** uses the ANSI prototype style, with the formal argument declared within the parentheses. The logic of PALIN.C should be plain sailing, apart (possibly) from the use of global variables. In Chapter 7 we'll be looking at these and other storage classes in more detail.

► *SUMMARY OF CHAPTER 4* ►

Summing up, the key point of Chapter 4 is how to control the flow of program execution while maintaining legible, structured source code. The **goto** with named labels (**label_name:**) should be used with care to avoid the traditional problems of unstructured programs.

◄► You met the conditional tests of **if** and **else**, which select alternative blocks of statements depending on C's purely arithmetic evaluation of Boolean expressions (true is nonzero, false is zero or NULL). Nested **if** and **else** clauses demand clear logic and matching indentations to avoid the dangling-**else** pitfall. The **else if** form allows a legible sequence of multichoice selections.

◄► Two of the basic library I/O routines from CONIO.H, **getche( )** and **getch( )**, were introduced as alternatives to **scanf( )** when you want to grab a single **char** from the keyboard. A detour on type casting showed how you can coerce variables from one data type to another, overriding C's standard rules for internal arithmetical and assignment conversion. The latter were listed and their dangers analyzed.

◄► The new **void** data type lets you override the normal **int** default return value of a function. **void** also distinguished functions declared with *no* arguments—e.g., **func(void);**—from K&R functions with *unspecified* arguments—e.g., **func( );**.

◄► The rationale and syntax of function prototyping was illustrated with **int getch(void)** and **int printf(char ∗format,...)**, and I stressed the importance of studying the prototypes in the various header files supplied with QuickC.

◄► The ternary conditional expression, **lval = X ? Y ; Z;**, offers a compact alternative to **if (X) (lval = Y;) else (lval = Z;)**.

◄► Parametrized macros behave rather like functions without the calling overheads, but, unlike functions, macros cannot be passed via pointers as arguments to other, generic functions. The formal arguments in macros are replaced in situ, token by token, with the corresponding real arguments, so protecting parentheses are *de riguer* to avoid diabolical bugs.

◄► **while** (*condition*){*loop*} loops until (*condition*) becomes false or until some abnormal exit statement, such as **break**, **goto**, **exit( )**, **abort( )**, or **return** is encountered. **continue** forces a premature reevaluation of (*condition*). **while(1)** is used to generate an endless loop that relies on abnormal termination, **while** loops can be nested, and (*condition*) often packs in many expression statements for their side effects.

◄► C interprets ∗**ptr++** as ∗**(ptr++)** because of the right-to-left associativity of the equal-precedence operators ∗ and ++.

◂▸ Pointer arithmetic is based on the size of the pointee. Expressions like **ptr + +** and **ptr − 3** can only be understood if you know how many bytes are used to store ***ptr**. **sizeof( )** ensures portability. **ptr + N** evaluates to **ptr + N*sizeof(T)** where ***ptr** is of type *T*.

◂▸ **do {***loop***} while (***condition***);** is a variant of **while** that guarantees at least one attempt to execute **{***loop***}** before **(***condition***)** is tested. Premature termination is possible, as with the **while** loop.

◂▸ The **switch (n)** statement offers a concise, legible multiway choice mechanism, using **case n: labels**. **n** is restricted to integral values. **break** must be used to prevent unwanted running-on from a matching label to the next label. **default:** is used to trap any unmatched **switch**es.

◂▸ The **for** loop offers flexible "counted" loops sensitive to many different termination criteria. The generic form is **for (***init***;** *condition***;** *reinit***) {loop_body}**. Theoretically, a C program can be packed into a **for** loop with an empty body since each of the three expression statements can be as complex as you wish, using comma expressions with side effects.

◂▸ Comma expressions are evaluated left to right and evaluate to their rightmost expression.

◂▸ All the control flow structures can be internested to any depth. Nested **for** loops are common for scanning multidimensional arrays.

◂▸ C does not have a specific string data type like BASIC's. Strings are realized as arrays of **char**, and a suite of library functions declared in STRING.H allows all the usual string and substring manipulations found in other languages.

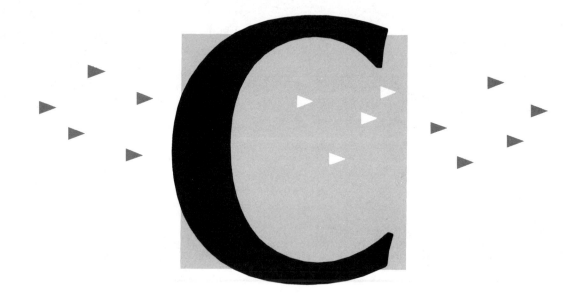

COMPLEX DATA TYPES:
TAPPING THE POWER OF C

► *CHAPTER 5* ►

The data types used so far have been either simple, atomic types like **int**, **float**, and **char**, or pointers to them. You also met the one-dimensional array based on these types. C allows more complex data types based on arbitrary combinations of the basic types, and you can even define your own personal data types using the keyword **typedef**.

In this chapter you'll meet *multidimensional* arrays, *enumerated* types, **typedef**s, and conditional directives.

Before I discuss higher-dimensional arrays, there are some new facts about the relationship between arrays and pointers to be mastered.

► *ARRAYS AND POINTERS—A FRESH LOOK* ►

The one-dimensional array **x[n]** defined in Chapter 4 lets you reference a series of **n** variables **x[0]** to **x[n-1]** (all of the same data type) by means of a single integer-type index or subscript:

```
int vec[100], i, sum;
    ...
/* here you set values in vec */
    ...
    for ( i = 0, sum = 0; i < 100; i++)
        sum += vec[i];
/* total the elements vec[0] to vec[99] */
```

Whenever C encounters the identifier **vec** without a subscript, it is interpreted as a pointer to **int** (as a pointer to the first **int** of the array **vec[100]**, in particular).

The major advantage of treating arrays as pointers shows up when you want to pass an array as an argument to a function. By passing a pointer to the first array element rather than passing the whole array, the function can be written without prior knowledge of the size of the array. In the program VECSUM.C (Program 5.1), I establish a function **intvecsum(n,array)** that will sum the first **n** elements of any integer array.

```
/* VECSUM.C - calling a function with an array argument */
/* Program 5.1 */

long intvecsum(unsigned long n, int int_array[]);
/* use modern style function declaration */

/* declaration needed because function is encountered (in main)
   before its definition _and_ it returns a non-int */

  int vec[8] = {0, 1, 2, 3, 4, 5, 6, 7};
  int arr[6] = {23, 27, 24, 0, 8, 123};
/* define/declare and initialize two external arrays */

void main()
{
    long vecsum;
    unsigned long siz;
    printf("\n\tSize of vec array is %u bytes",sizeof(vec));
    siz = sizeof(vec)/sizeof(int);
    printf("\n\tNumber of elements in vec = %u\n",siz);
    vecsum = intvecsum(siz, vec);
    printf("\n\tThe vec elements total = %ld\n", vecsum);
    printf("\n\tFirst 3 arr elements total = %ld\n",intvecsum(3,arr));
}

/* define intvecsum() */

long intvecsum(unsigned long n, int int_array[])
/* use modern style function definition format */

/* intvecsum() takes two args:
                number of elements to be summed
                an 'open' array of int
   intvecsum() returns a long int value */
{
    long sum = 0;
    unsigned long i;
/* vars local to function */

    for (i = 0; i < n; i++)
        sum += int_array[i];
/* total the elements int_array[0] to int_array[n-1] */
    return sum;
}
```

► *Program 5.1:* VECSUM.C

► *Analysis of VECSUM.C* ►

The function **intvecsum( )** has **int_array[ ]** as its second dummy argument, and there is no specific reference to the array dimension. The empty brackets indicate an *open* array—the number of elements is left open, as it were.

The **array[ ]** form is allowed when declaring formal arguments and also when a declaration is immediately followed by an initializer. The compiler can fill in the array size from the number of elements in the initializer.

As you can see, the function has been invoked with **vec** (an eight-element array) and **arr** (a six-element array), proving that **intvecsum( )** will work with variable-length arrays. You may wish to test this for yourself by setting up other arrays.

What really gets passed to **intvecsum( )** is a pointer value, namely a *copy* of **vec (&vec[0])** or **arr (&arr[0])**. The function then blindly sums a certain number of elements, counting up from this base. Try invoking **intvecsum(10,arr)**. You will probably get a spurious answer with no warning that **arr** only has six elements. You will be adding to the true sum of **arr[6]** whatever lies in memory at the addresses **(arr + 6)**, **(arr + 7)**,...,**(arr + 9)**.

Keep in mind that by receiving a copy of the constant pointer **vec** as an argument, the function has direct access to the array elements. **intvecsum( )** simply reads the array elements, but there is nothing to stop you from changing the function so that it writes new values into any part of the array. Such side effects can be exploited or they can be a nuisance. Passing pointers, then, is a mixed blessing. It allows you to handle open arrays, but it exposes the array to side effects. Since C always passes arguments by value, you have to pass a copy of a pointer if you want to simulate passing by *reference* in order to change the real argument.

The **sizeof( )** operator is used to derive the actual number of elements in an array. The general strategy for any type **T** is

```
number_of_array_elements = sizeof(array_of_T)/sizeof(T);
```

Using **unsigned long** for these variables is a possible overkill! I used it as a reminder that arrays *can* exceed 65,535 elements.

sizeof(array_of_T), you should notice, provides a quirky exception to the rule that array names are interpreted as pointers. When used with **sizeof( )**, an array argument is taken as the whole array, not as the pointer. Otherwise **sizeof(array_name)** would be interpreted as **sizeof(&array_name[0])**, which would always return the size of a pointer (2 or 4 bytes)!

In VECSUM.C, try replacing **int int_array[ ]** with **int *int_array** in both the declaration and definition of **intvecsum( )**. You will find no difference in operation, providing another illustration that **intvecsum( )** is actually treating the argument as a pointer.

► *Arrays and Pointers—The Differences* ►

In spite of the intimate relation between pointers and arrays, there are subtle differences that can undoubtedly be a source of confusion. At the risk of boring the cognoscenti, let's delve deeper into this subject. Take the following declarations:

```
        int vec[100], *ip, **ih;
   /* an array of ints, a pointer to an int, and a pointer to a pointer to an int */
        double table[50], *dp, **dh;
   /* an array of doubles, a pointer to a double, and a pointer to a pointer
     to a double */
```

Both **vec** and **ip** are pointers to **int**. However, **vec[100]** has 200 bytes of contiguous storage allocated at a memory location that is fixed at run time, so during execution **vec** is effectively a pointer constant, namely the fixed address **&vec[0]**. In spite of appearances, **vec** is not an lvalue; it cannot be changed or assigned to. Each of the **vec[i]** *are* int lvalues, though—otherwise the array would hardly be useful! When you initialize **vec[100]** you are setting values in each **vec[i]**, but the pointer **vec** is unchanged. Keep in mind that whether you initialize **vec[100]** or not, **vec** receives a real pointer value as a result of the declaration, and 200 bytes are definitely allocated.

The pointer **ip**, on the other hand, is a variable awaiting some assignment before it becomes useful. Potentially, **ip** can address any byte in the system (subject only to the pointer constraints of the memory model in force). But immediately after the declaration, **ip** is not pointing anywhere in particular— it may contain some (possibly legal) old garbage, or it may have a 0 (NULL) value, which is C's way of saying that **ip** is definitely not pointing at anything.

If C meets the expression ***ip**, it tries to access the **int** at address **ip**. This attempt will be illegal if **ip** is NULL or outside the legal addressing range, and you will get a run-time error message. If **ip** holds residual rubbish, so will ***ip**, and you may not get any warning. A very high proportion of programming errors turn out to be due to misdirected pointers, and they are often quite difficult to trace. The lesson is clear: avoid using ***ip** until **ip** is assigned a valid address. How to do this will now be considered.

► *Setting Pointers* ►

There are two common ways of setting a useful address in a virgin pointer: dynamic memory allocation and assignment from an existing address. Let's look at each in turn.

► *Dynamic Memory Allocation*

You can dynamically allocate some contiguous memory, using **calloc( )** or **malloc( )**. These library functions in MALLOC.H or STDLIB.H grab and clear (set to 0) the number of bytes requested, provided there is sufficient free memory in the *heap*.

The heap is a section of RAM set aside for such allocations. In fact, the heap is what's left of your 640KB when all the other memory demands, such as the OS, TSR (terminate and stay resident) programs and data, and the current program code, data, and stack have been met.

During execution there may be many **malloc( )** and **calloc( )** calls requesting memory for a variety of reasons. Allocations are made in multiples of 16-byte paragraphs. They can sometimes fail because of *fragmentation* even if the total of free memory in the heap exceeds your request, so you should always check for success after each call.

The key to **malloc( )** and **calloc( )** is that they return a *generic* pointer value that represents either the address of the first byte of the region allocated or NULL if the heap cannot meet the demand. By casting this returned value to type pointer to **int**, say, then testing for NULL and assigning it to **ip**, you have a definite target to point at—just as if you had declared an array of **int**, in fact.

Using expressions such as **ip[N]** or ***(ip + N)**, you can write and read the (N + 1)th integer in the allocated memory. Dare I stress that if you make N too large (plus or minus), you can recklessly intrude outside the allocated region with bizarre results?

To free a **malloc( )** or **calloc( )** memory allocation and return it to the heap, you call the **free( )** function using the original pointer as the argument: **free(ip);**. This ability to grab and return blocks of RAM of variable sizes during a program explains the term *dynamic* memory allocation (in contrast to *static* memory allocations determined by the compiler/linker and maintained until the program exits).

An example of **malloc( )** in action follows:

```
#include <stdio.h>
#include <malloc.h>
#include <stdlib.h>
/* exit( ) and malloc( ) are in STDLIB.H.  malloc( ) is also in MALLOC.H.
   calloc( ) is in MALLOC.H.  puts( ) is in STDIO.H */
    ...
    int *ip, ints_req = 100;
    ...
    ip = (int *) malloc(ints_req*sizeof(int));
```

```
/* try to allocate 100*2 bytes in memory heap. A NULL (zero) pointer is
   returned if allocation fails, else a pointer to the allocated
   memory is returned */

/* malloc returns a generic 'pointer to void' so the (int *) is an essential
   type cast forcing malloc's pointer to be a 'pointer to int' before the
   assignment to ip */

    if (ip == NULL) {
        puts("Insufficient memory for allocation!");
        exit (1);

/* exit (n) terminates the program, telling DOS the reason, e.g. exit (0) for
   normal termination, exit (1) for error type 1. */
    }

/* The same effect with calloc( ) would require:

    ip = (int *) calloc(ints_req,sizeof(int));

*/
    ...
/* now you can use ip as a valid pointer to a 100 int block */
/* Note that all 200 bytes are cleared to 0 */
```

This example introduces two new constructs briefly explained in the comments: type casting of pointers and the **exit( )** function. For the moment, just note the general concepts and syntax—they will be covered in more detail later.

The prototype declarations for **malloc( )** and **calloc( )** follow, together with those of two related memory-management functions:

```
    void *malloc(unsigned memsiz_chars);
/* malloc returns a 'pointer to void' value. You have to type cast this to
   'pointer to T' before assignment, where T is the data type of the
   target block contents. Pre-ANSI systems use char *malloc( ), so
   watch for possible portability snags */

    void *calloc(unsigned number_elements,
                         unsigned element_size);
/* as for malloc, except that two args are required. Their product gives the
   memory size allocated in bytes */
```

```
                void free(void *original_ptr);
        /* return the original malloc or calloc allocation to the heap */

                void *realloc(void *original_ptr, unsigned newsize);
        /* used after malloc or calloc, realloc expands or shrinks the original
           block, copying the previous contents if possible. Returns a
           pointer to new block _ this may be a different value from
           the original allocation*/
        /* There are far versions: _fmalloc( ) and _ffree( ) for handling
           allocations over 64KB in the larger memory models with 32_bit
           far pointers and a far heap. See Appendix E.*/
```

Now you can look at the second, more direct method of setting pointer values.

► *Direct Pointer Assignment*

You can simply assign an existing, initialized, valid pointer to **ip** during or after its declaration as in

```
        int vec[100], *ip = vec;              /* equivalent to ip = &vec[0] */
        /* *ip and vec[0] now represent the same integer */
```

The assignment *ip = vec; can be rather puzzling at first sight. If this were a normal assignment statement rather than part of a declaration initializer, you would appear to be trying to assign a pointer value to the *ip (an int)! What, in fact, is happening is

```
        int vec[100];
        int *ip = vec;
```

Written this way, you can take the second line to be equivalent to (int *)ip = vec, where (int *) plays the role of the type specifier, pointer to int. The assignment is now seen in its true light: ip = vec—you *are* assigning pointer to pointer. I'll have more to say on C's declaration syntax quite soon.

► *Type Casting with Pointers*

The idea of (int *) as a type specifier has already cropped up as the type cast applied to the pointer (void *) returned by malloc( ).

Generally speaking, QuickC will warn you without aborting if you try to assign **ptr_to_T1** to **ptr_to_T2** where **T1** and **T2** are incompatible types. The onus is on the programmer to heed or ignore the warnings. The problems can be quite subtle, depending on the legal address boundaries for different data types. For example, **ptr_to_char** can legally take any odd or even number within the memory model limits, but more complex types may be constrained to byte addresses that are multiples of 2, 4, or 8. The safest course is to type cast the right-hand pointer:

```
int *ip;
char *cp;
...
ip = (int *)cp;
cp = (char *)ip;
```

The **malloc( )** and **calloc( )** pointers to **void** must always be type cast before assignment, as shown in the earlier examples. Similarly, when passing pointer arguments to a function, you must ensure that they match the pointer types in the function prototype.

► *The Pointer Having Been Set...* ►

Once you have assigned an address to **ip**, *ip will be interpreted as an **int** even if **ip** has been wrongly made to point at a **float** or **double**. Also, arithmetic on **ip** will be automatically based on **sizeof(int)** = 2, so (**ip** + 1) will advance the pointer by 2 bytes to point to the next integer (or whatever lies ahead!). Similarly, with pointer to **double**, once **dp** is given an address *dp will be taken as the 8 bytes at address **dp**, with bizarre results if these are not in fact in double-precision FP format. Also, −−**dp** will predecrement **dp** by the **sizeof(double)**, namely 8. All of which underlines the importance of getting the pointer type correct.

► *Handles or Pointers to Pointers* ►

The declaration int **ih; means

```
(int *) *ih;
```

so *ih is a pointer to **int**. Therefore, ih is a pointer to a pointer to an **int**. **ih represents an **int**, but before using it as such you now have to check that both ih and *ih are non-NULL.

Multiple indirection like this can be extended to any depth (until RAM or paper or reason runneth out).

It is often useful to have a *master* pointer or *handle* pointing to a table of pointers that, in turn, point to objects of interest. As the objects move about in memory, the table of pointers is updated, but access is guaranteed via the fixed handle. (The word *handle* has acquired other meanings in the computer world, so take care. Some handles are simply integers or channel numbers, not pointers to pointers.)

You'll shortly meet another application for **ih as I pursue the relationship between pointers and arrays.

► *The Pointer as an Array* ►

Now that you've seen the array as a pointer, you are ready for the obverse of the coin—the concept of the pointer as an array. Consider again the familiar snippet

```
char ch, *cp, name[30] = "Microsoft";
/* a char, a pointer to char and an array of char */
       cp = name;              /* same as cp = &name[0] */
       ch = name[4];           /* ch now = 'o' */
```

When you write ch = name[4], some internal pointer arithmetic is generated to evaluate the right-expression:

name[4] → *(name + 4*sizeof(char)) → *(name + 4) → 'o' → ch

where **name** is the pointer **&name[0]** and → indicates the direction of the evaluation. The **name** pointer is advanced 4 bytes, then dereferenced to give the fifth character of "**Microsoft**". This process is a simple example of the *storage mapping function* that C uses to evaluate all array subscripts. Now the same result arises if you write

ch = *(cp + 4*sizeof(char));   /* ch now = 'o' */

since you have assigned **cp = name**.

As you may guess from this, C allows you to treat the pointer **cp** as an array identifier and write

```
        ch = cp[4];              /* ch again = 'o' */
  /* if you think this should be ch = *cp[4], reread the previous
     paragraph. Note that x[4] implies indirection on x after
     the pointer addition */
```

In other words, the notation **x[i]**, whether **x** is considered an array of **T** or a pointer to **T**, really means ***(x + i*sizeof(T))**. As always, the onus is on you, the programmer, to ensure that **x** and **i** are meaningfully defined. In the above example, **name[31]** and **cp[69]** may well return rubbish without complaint from memory locations beyond the region allocated to **name**.

► *More Pointer Arithmetic* ►

You've seen that

```
  ptr2_to_T = (ptr1_to_T + int_value);
```

and

```
  ptr2_to_T = (ptr1_to_T _ int_value);
```

give new pointer values depending on the size of the underlying type, **T**. You may correctly guess from this that it is also legal and useful to subtract pointer values if they share the same underlying type:

```
      int_lvalue = ptr2_to_T _ ptr1_to_T;
  /* assuming ptr2_to_T >= ptr1_to_T */
      int_lvalue = ptr1_to_T _ ptr2_to_T;
  /* assuming ptr1_to_T >= ptr2_to_T */
```

Provided that the noted inequalities hold, the difference between two compatible pointers represents the number of *elements* of type **T** (each of **sizeof(T)**) that lie between the pointers. Watch out for this potential stumbling block: If you picture the two pointers merely as byte addresses, you can be deceived into thinking that their "numeric" difference represents the number of bytes between them. Nothing could be further from the truth unless **sizeof(T)** is 1 byte!

Adding, multiplying, and dividing two pointers is not a fruitful exercise, so avoid it.

► *Pointers to Functions* ►

The pointer arithmetic covered so far does not apply to all pointer types. For example, C allows pointers to functions but these are excluded from the pointer arithmetic you've seen with arrays. A pointer to a function is best viewed as the address in memory where control jumps to when the function is called. It usually makes no sense to add or subtract integers to such addresses, and, incidentally, it is illegal to apply **sizeof( )** to a function. The main application of pointers to functions arises when you want to pass a function as an argument to another function—as with arrays, C achieves this with a pointer argument.

► *Pointers—Near and Far* ►

Pointer arithmetic with **far** pointers has some quirks that I'll cover in the next few sections. (You may wish to skip these first time round and proceed to the section entitled "Arrays of Pointers and Pointers to Arrays.")

QuickC offers three classes of pointers to cope with the vagaries of the 8088/6 segmented addressing scheme. These are **near** (16-bit), **far** (32-bit), and **huge** (also 32-bit).

The default classes of pointer you get when you write **T *ptr_to_T**, (declare a pointer to data type **T**) depend on the prevailing memory model, which is *small, medium, compact, large,* or *huge.* These are selected during setup or via command-line options.

The default model is small, which automatically provides **near** pointers stored in 16 bits (sufficient to address 64KB of code and 64KB of data without overlap). All the example programs so far have assumed this small model default, so your pointer declarations were **near** by default. You could have used the addressing modifier **near** as follows:

```
      int near *ip;
      char near *ch_ptr;
  /* explicitly declare near pointers */
```

without affecting the pointers generated.

Regardless of the memory model in force, you are allowed (with due care) to override the default pointer class by using the modifiers **near**, **far**, or **huge** in the pointer declaration (and in certain function declarations also). The reason you need to know something about these different pointer classes is that the pointer manipulations I have been discussing are radically affected.

Appendix E gives a brief technical summary of the 8088/6 registers and explains why these three pointer variants and five memory models are needed.

► *The Four Segments*

The key point is that the 8088/6 uses four 16-bit registers, known as *segment* registers: CS (code segment), DS (data segment), SS (stack segment), and ES (extra segment). These registers hold the base addresses of their respective segments. Without further support, a 16-bit segment register could only access a 64KB address space, but the IBM PC can actually address 1 megabyte via a 20-bit address bus.

The trick works like this. Imagine the segment register shifted left by 4, giving a 20-bit value. The "shifted" register can be envisaged as addressing 64KB distinct *paragraphs* of 16 bytes each. If the contents of a 16-bit *offset* register are added to the 20-bit segment address, the 8088/6 can now access any byte in the full 1-megabyte address space. (The address calculation, by the way, is done internally by the chip.) We often refer to the address *segment:offset* as a shorthand for the byte address *(segment*16) + offset*.

You are actually using 32 bits to obtain a 20-bit addressing space; the extra addressing capacity is lost because many different segment:offset pairs can represent the same byte address. For example, Table 5.1 shows that there are 17 valid representations of the given byte address. Obviously, before you start using conditionals like (**ptr1** == **ptr2**) or (**ptr1** >= **ptr2**), you need to know exactly how your pointers relate to segment:offset pairs. Similarly, adding integers to pointers can become problematical close to segment boundaries. QuickC's memory models and pointer classes offer the most reasonable solution short of switching to the linear addressing mode of the 80386 (protected mode) or any of the Motorola M68000 family!

► *Small Memory Models*

The four segment registers can keep track of four 64KB segments, each of which must start on a paragraph (16-byte) boundary. With the 16-bit **near**

► **Table 5.1:** *Hex representations of a single byte address*

Segment:Offset	Real Address
0000:0100	0100
0001:00F0	0100
0002:00E0	0100
...	...
0010:0000	0100

pointer you can consider, say, the DS register fixed while the pointer supplies the offset, giving a 64KB upper limit to the program's data. You can see that pointer arithmetic and comparisons are simplified with this arrangement: you manipulate only the 16-bit offset from 0000 to FFFF (just like an **unsigned int**), and all is well provided you don't overflow. (Overflow will not affect the segment.)

Likewise, if the CS register is fixed, a **near** function pointer can cope with programs not exceeding 64KB of code. In fact, by restricting both code and data to 64KB each (without overlap), the default small memory model can operate with **near** pointers throughout. With the small model, three of the segment registers—DS, SS, and ES—all start at the same address, while the CS is set so that the code segment cannot clash with the common data/stack/extra segment.

The total size of a small memory model program, therefore, cannot exceed 128KB: 64KB data and 64KB code. You will not find this limit irksome until your projects become more ambitious.

► *The Larger Memory Models*

The other models vary in having **far** pointers for some or all of their segments, allowing either data or code, or both, to beat the 64KB barrier—but the pointer arithmetic required is more complex.

The **far** pointer is the default for all pointers in the large and huge models. In the intermediate models, you get the following mixed defaults: medium gives **far** for code, **near** for data; compact gives **near** for code, **far** for data. Table 5.2 summarizes the model-pointer defaults.

► **Table 5.2:** *Memory models and default pointer classes*

Model	Data Segments pointer size		Code Segment pointer size	
Small	near	64KB	near	64KB
Medium	far	1MB	near	64KB
Compact	near	64KB	far	1MB
Large	far	1MB	far	1MB
Huge	far	1MB	far	1MB

► The far Pointer

The 32-bit **far** pointer contains both the segment:offset values, but because of the address ambiguities mentioned above, the test if (far_ptr1 == far_ptr2) may fail even when the same effective address is being compared—e.g., 0000:0100 does not equal 0001:00F0, although both represent address 0100.

The == and !== operators are applied to the 32-bit segment:offset as though it were an **unsigned long**. The reason for testing all 32 bits for equality and inequality stems from the essential need to correctly compare pointers with NULL, the pointer represented as 0000:0000. As you have seen, non-NULL addresses may well have their offsets zero.

On the other hand, **far**-pointer arithmetic and the comparisons >, >=, <, and <= are applied only to the offsets. If you add or subtract too much to a **far** pointer, then, you simply overflow the offset without affecting the segment: (0000:FFFF + 2) will give you 0000:0001 with possibly unfortunate results and no forewarning!

► The huge Pointer

The **huge** pointer comes to the rescue! Although stored as segment:offset in 32 bits like **far**, the **huge** pointers are automatically *normalized* to allow safe comparisons and arithmetic. The secret is to convert each segment:offset in such a way that the offset lies in the range 0 to F (hex, of course). If you followed the derivation of a real address from a segment:offset pair, you will see that for each real address there can be only one normalized segment:offset. For example, real address 100 is uniquely normalized as 0100:0000 because none of the other pairs has an offset between 0 and F.

When you increment a **huge** pointer offset past a 16-byte paragraph, it is automatically renormalized, updating the segment part. You can now safely move your pointers around data structures exceeding 64KB. Likewise, comparisons are applied to the full 32 bits, giving a true test of equality, inequality, and relative size.

I leave you to verify that arithmetic on **huge** pointers is well behaved. You can safely compare **if (huge_ptr1 >= huge_ptr2)** and so on, without worrying about segments and offsets. But as you can imagine, the price paid for this ease of pointer manipulation is some CPU overhead for the normalizations.

Note the default pointer is **far** even in the **huge** model, so you always have to ask for **huge** pointers if you want them, as in

```
int huge *ip;                          /* ip is a huge pointer to int */
```

Since pointer arithmetic is never (hardly ever!) done on function pointers, the **huge** pointer is not allowed for function pointers. The **far** pointer is quite adequate for functions.

► Modules and the 64KB Limit

You should keep in mind that the larger memory models can only beat the 64KB *total* code and data limits when you break your programs into suitable *modules* or source files. Regardless of memory model, each compilable module is limited to one code segment and one data segment. By definition, these are each limited to 64KB. However, if you divide a big program into smaller source files, compile them separately, and then link them, you can have many distinct segments. What the larger models with 32-bit pointers allow is the resetting of CS and DS so that these separate 64KB segments can be accessed from anywhere in the program.

I now return to the pleasant world of small models and nice, normal, **near** pointers.

► ARRAYS OF POINTERS AND POINTERS TO ARRAYS ►

The base type of an array can be any type, excluding **void** and functions. When the base type is a pointer, some interesting situations arise. An *array of* *pointers* is declared as follows:

    char *ptr[30];   /* ptr[0]...ptr[29] are pointers to char */

The C syntax for such declarations is rather opaque compared with, say, Modula-2's

        ptr: ARRAY[0..29] OF POINTER TO CHAR;
    (* or more legibly, with intermediate types:
        PointerToChar = POINTER TO CHAR;
        ArrayOfPointers = ARRAY[0..29] OF PointerToChar;
        ptr: ArrayOfPointers; *)

In C, the type of **ptr** is indicated "indirectly" by a *declarator* showing *how* **ptr** is used, preceded by a type specifier showing the data type being pointed at. As you saw earlier with **int *ip**, you can look on **char *ptr[30]** as **(char *)ptr[30]**, which stresses the fact that **ptr[30]** is an array with base type **(char *)**, namely pointer to **char**. To get a better feel for C declarators, compare the following declarations:

        int x;   /* x is an int */

        int *x;   /* x is pointer to int − *x indicates usage */

        int x[20];   /* x is an array of 20 ints */
        int x[ ];   /* x is an open array of ints */
    /* the number of elements is left 'open' − used in prototype declarations
        of formal arguments */

        int *x[ ];   /* x is an array of pointers to ints */
    /* above could be written int *(x[ ]) or (int*)x[ ] but [ ] is higher precedence
        than '*' so parentheses are optional */

        int (*x)[ ];   /* x is a pointer to an array of ints */
    /* these parentheses are essential − see next paragraph */

        int x( );   /* x is a function returning an int */

        int *x( );   /* x is a function returning a pointer to an int */
    /* above could be written (int *)(x( )), but the function call ( ) is
        higher precedence than '*' so extra parentheses are optional */

```
int (*x)( );      /* x is a pointer to a function returning an int */
/* The parentheses (*x) are essential here */

int (*x[ ])( );   /* x is an array of pointers to functions returning ints */
```

Not all of these declarations will be of immediate significance; they are listed together to indicate the variety of declarators allowed in C. The two declarations I will concentrate on are those for *arrays of pointers* and *pointers to arrays*.

Returning to the declaration

```
char *ptr[30];                          /* ptr[0]...ptr[29] are pointers to char */
```

note first that the precedence of the array brackets is higher (category 1) than that of the indirection operator (category 2), so **char *ptr[30]** is taken as **(char *)(ptr[30])**, whence **ptr** is an array of pointers to **char**.

Each variable **ptr[i]** is a pointer to **char**, but remember that the declaration simply allocates space for 30 pointers—they cannot be used until useful addresses have been assigned to them:

```
char name[25] = "Microsoft";
char *ptr[30];              /* array of pointers to char */
ptr[3] = name;             /* or = &name[0] */
/* ptr[3] can now be used – the other ptr[i] not yet defined */

/* or using malloc: */
     for (i = 0; i < 30; i++) {
         ptr[i] = (char *) malloc(sizeof(name)*sizeof(char));
         if (ptr[i] == NULL) exit (1);
     }
/* give each ptr[i] 25 chars (bytes) to point at */
```

A common use for arrays of pointers is storing a set of variable-length messages. Rather than waste space using fixed-length arrays of characters to match the longest string, the array of pointers approach allows each string to be just as long as needed. The following snippet illustrates this:

```
        char *err_ptr[ ] = {
/* 0 */      "All's Well!",
/* 1 */      "Insufficient Memory",
/* 2 */      "Drive A not Fitted" ,
```

```
/* 3 */        "Power Off",
/* 4 */        "Wrong Version",
/* 5 */        "Read the Manual" };
```

/* the declaration could have been written char *err_ptr[6], but
     the [ ] notation is sufficient, and allows future addition
     of more error messages. The array will be set to [n] if
     you supply n string constant initializers. */

```
    int err_code = 0;
    ...
```
/* some event here may set err_code */

```
    if (err_code < 0 || err_code > 5) {
        puts("\n\tUnknown Error Code\n");
        exit(9); }

    else { puts(err_ptr[err_code]);
            exit(err_code); }
```

Each **err_ptr[i]** receives the address of the start of a particular string constant, and this is exactly the type of argument that **puts( )** expects. The final ASCII NUL for each string is quietly supplied by the compiler when the string constants are stored. To perform more complex operations that depend on the value of **err_code**, the **case...switch** construct would be a natural choice. For simple string selection, as illustrated above, the array of pointers to **char** is ideal.

► *Pointers to Arrays* ►

Next, contrast char *(ptr[30]), an array of pointers, with

```
char (*ptr_a)[30];        /* pointer to array of char */
```

The parentheses here dictate that **ptr_a** is a *pointer to an array* of 30 **chars**, not *ever* to be confused with an array of 30 pointers to **char**!

Once **ptr_a** has been properly initialized, you can dereference it with (*ptr_a) to give you an array of 30 characters. Then you can access individual **chars** with (*ptr_a)[0], (*ptr_a)[1], and so on. Since the array is really a pointer to **char**, the real nature of **ptr_a** is "pointer to pointer to **char**." This explains the assignment **ptr_a = &name** in the following snippet illustrating the differences between arrays of pointers and pointers to arrays:

```
            char name[30] = "Microsoft";      /* initialize an array of 30 chars */
/* name[0] = 'M'; name[1] = 'i',..., name[9] = '\0' final NUL */
/* The identifier name is interpreted as &name[0], a pointer */
/* to the first char of name[ ] */
     char *ptr_c;                   /* pointer to a char */
     char *(a_ptr[30]);             /* array of 30 pointers */
     char (*ptr_a)[30];             /* pointer to array of 30 chars */
     char **cpp;                    /* pointer to pointer of char */

     ptr_c = name;                  /* set pointer to start of name[30] */
     a_ptr[0] = ptr_c;              /* set first pointer of array */
     cpp = &ptr_c;                  /* both sides are 'ptr to ptr to char' */
     ptr_a = &name;                 /* both sides are 'ptr to array' */

/* NOT ptr_a = &name[0] since right-hand is only 'ptr to char' */

     ch = (*ptr_a)[0];              /* ch now = "M" */
/* since name is array of 30 char, &name is ptr to array of 30 char, just like
     ptr_a. (*ptr_a)[0] is same as name[0] */

         puts(name);
         puts(ptr_c);
         puts(a_ptr[0]);
         puts(*ptr_a);
         puts(*cpp);

/* all five statements will display Microsoft */

         ptr_c++;                   /* advance ptr_c by 1 byte */
         cpp++;                     /* advance cpp by 2 or 4 bytes
                                       depending on pointer size */
         ptr_a++;                   /* advance ptr_a by 30 bytes! */
/* Note that ptr_T++ increments ptr_T by sizeof(T) */
```

Until you hit the last three statements and comments, you may have been lulled into thinking that **ptr_c**, **cpp**, and **ptr_a** were pretty much the same kind of beast! They do happen to get you to the "**Microsoft**" string in their own fashion, but their underlying data types are different:

ptr_c is a pointer to **char**, sizeof(*ptr_c) = 1
cpp is a pointer to (**char ***), sizeof(*cpp) = 2 or 4

ptr_a is a pointer to array of **char**, sizeof(*ptr_a) = 30

The implications should be digested before proceeding.

► MULTIDIMENSIONAL ARRAYS ►

You have seen the array base type as simple (**char**, **int**, and so on) and as "pointer to simple." The next step is to see that the base type of an array can itself be an array. The *array of arrays* provides the basic mechanism for handling multidimensional data. For example, you can declare a two-dimensional *matrix* by writing

```
int mat[4][3];                      /* mat is a 4 x 3 matrix of integers */
```

Each of the 12 elements of **mat[4][3]** can be referenced via the **int** variables **mat[i][j]**, where the *row* subscript i ranges from 0 to 3 and the *column* subscript j ranges from 0 to 2.

► Matrices in Action ►

Nested **for** loops are commonly used for processes that need to access all the elements of a matrix, for example:

```
        int max, row, col, sum, mat[4][3];
        ...
/* program here sets the values for mat[i][j] */
        ...
        max = mat[0][0];
        for (row = 0, sum = 0; row < 4; row++)
            for (col = 0; col < 3; col++) {
                if (mat[row][col] > max) max = mat[row][col];
                sum += mat(row,col);
            }
/* find max element and get total of all 12 elements */
```

Exactly how the elements of **mat[4][3]** are stored in RAM is rarely of interest to the programmer—you just set up the subscripts and use **mat[i][j]** like any other **int** variable. In fact, C stores multidimensional arrays in *row-column* sequence as follows, with **mat[0][0]** at the lowest memory location:

```
mat[0][0], mat [0][1], mat [0][2], mat[0][3]
mat[1][0], mat [1][1], mat [1][2], mat[1][3]
mat[2][0], mat [2][1], mat [2][2], mat[2][3]
```

Occasionally, you can make use of this fact, by treating **mat[4][3]** as a linear array of 12 elements:

```
int mat[4][3], *pm, i;
pm = &mat[0][0];              /* point to first row, first col */
pm[1] = 0;                    /* mat[0][1] now zero */
i = pm[2];                    /* i now = mat[0][2] */
/* You can now use a single, faster 'for' loop to initialize the elements
   of mat[4][3] */
       for (i = 0; i < 12, i++)
           pm[i] = 0;
```

You can also initialize a matrix during its declaration as in:

```
int mat[4][3] = { {11, 10, 9},
                  { 8,  7, 6},
                  { 5,  4, 3},
                  { 2,  1, 0} };
```

This sets **mat[0][0]** to 11, **mat[0][1]** to 10, and so on. If you omit the **[4][3]** ranges by writing **[ ][ ]**, C will set the ranges for you according to the initializer list.

As with single array initialization, the number of initializers may be less than the stated number of elements—if so, the unassigned elements are set to 0. Having too many initializers will trigger an error message. Note how the curly braces are used to group the rows and columns of the initializer matrix.

► *Dimensions Unlimited* ►

Higher dimensional arrays are defined by a simple extension of the above scheme:

```
float galactic_temp[100][100][100];
/* the temperature measured at each of the 1,000,000 cartesian test
   points (x,y,z) in the galaxy */
```

```
    unsigned int hits[10][24][30][24][100];
  /* the number of hits in season 0 – 9, for club 0 – 23, by player 0 – 29,
    at stadium 0 – 23, against pitcher 0 – 99 */
```

Before declaring such arrays, you should make sure that you have enough RAM (for example, 34MB for the baseball database!). In fact, when you study disk file I/O in Chapter 8, you'll see that there are more practical ways of handling large amounts of data.

► Multidimensional Arrays as Function Arguments ►

As with simple arrays, you can pass multidimensional array arguments to functions by passing a base pointer to the first element. However, to permit the compiler to compute element addresses, you must supply additional information in the formal argument definition. In VECSUM.C, **intvecsum( )** was declared as

```
long intvecsum(unsigned long n, int int_array[ ]);
```

which allowed any size of array to be passed. But if you want a function to operate on matrices, you cannot get away with

```
long intmatsum(unsigned long n, int int_mat[ ][ ]);                /* NO */
```

It is necessary to specify the second dimension range, for example:

```
long int3matsum(unsigned long n, int int_mat[ ][3]);               /* OK */
```

This would allow you to pass any **[x][3]** matrix to a suitably coded function. Similarly, for a three-dimensional array, you need to spell out the second and third dimension bounds—for example, **[ ][4][5]**. The first dimension range can vary in the actual array argument, but subsequent dimension ranges must be fixed and matched in both actual and formal arguments. There are several ways around this restriction—using **int *ptr** arguments for the start of the array and passing the array bounds as separate arguments. I will not pursue them here. Rather, I want to quickly cover enumerations, one of the remaining data types that C offers. I'll give you the flavor with some example programs and defer the formal definition until later.

► *ENUMERATIONS* ►

The basic idea behind enumerations is to increase source code legibility by providing mnemonic identifiers for small classes of related objects, for example:

```
enum days { mon, tue, wed, thu, fri, sat, sun }
            today, holiday;
```

```
/* declare a new enumeration type: 'enum days' and also declare two
   variables of type 'enum days' viz. today and holiday */
```

```
enum days workday;
/* later, declare another variable, workday, as type 'enum days' */
```

You can now assign any of the enumerated *values*, **mon**, **tue**, and so on, to variables of **enum** type **days**:

```
today = tue;
holiday = sun;
```

You can now test and compare values and/or variables in many obvious ways:

```
if (holiday == wed)
    puts("Wednesday is a holiday");
if (sun > sat)
    puts("Sunday follows Saturday");
```

Notice first that the values **mon, tue,...,** **sun** resulting from the above declaration are treated internally as **int** constants 0 to 6, the values being assigned in the sequence entered. You are allowed to vary this natural assignment at the time of declaration, but the values are fixed thereafter:

```
enum days {mon = 1, tue = 2, wed = 3, thu = 4, fri = 5, sat = 6,
           sun = 0} deadline, freeday;
```

Once they are declared and given integer values, the enumerated value identifiers are not lvalues, so you cannot assign values to them later in the program. The variables of **enum** type **days** can also be considered as internally taking any of the declared **int** values, so with the previous declaration you could write either **deadline = 1** or **deadline = mon** with the same result. However, the whole point of enumeration types is to increase legibility:

```
long total_expenses = 0, expenses[7];
enum days { mon, tue, wed, thu, fri, sat, sun }
                    today, special;
special = sun;
...
/* set the expenses here for each day */
...
/* now total them for whole week */
for (today = mon; today <= sun; today++) {
    if (today == special)
        expenses[today] *= 2;        /* up a notch! */
    total_expenses += expenses[today];
}
printf("\n\tTotal expenses for week =
                %ld\n",total_expenses);
```

Other popular enumerations are the names of months, the graphics modes and colors of your monitor, file error states, and so on. The original K&R C did not offer enumeration types—they were added later to "keep up with the Wirths." You still find C programs that use the **#define** method of creating mnemonics—i.e.:

```
#define MON 1
#define TUE 2
...
```

where an enumeration would offer more flexibility. The above **#define** does not create a data type, which would allow dedicated **days** type variables, but simply replaces occurrences of **MON** with the constant 1. Without **enum**, your day variables would be **int** or perhaps **unsigned char**. It is largely a matter of personal taste and style.

► *Enumeration Tags* ►

In the declaration

```
enum days { mon, tue, wed, thu, fri, sat, sun } today, holiday;
```

the identifier **days** is known as the enumeration *tag*—a word that will crop up again when you meet structures and unions. The tag turns out to be optional. If **today** and **holiday** are the only **enum** variables you'll ever need to declare, there is no strict need to declare a tag:

```
enum { mon, tue, wed, thu, fri, sat, sun }
            today, holiday;
/* no tag, so all vars must be listed here */
```

In this case, you could not declare further variables later in the program because **enum tag var1, var2** is required. Tag names and enumeration value identifiers follow the same rules as normal variable identifiers regarding duplications. They need only be unique within their scope.

► TYPE DEFINITION AND CONDITIONAL COMPILATION ►

I'll conclude this chapter with a brief look at two related topics: **typedef**, the useful *type definition* facility for creating your own names for data types, and *conditional compilation* operators. Both facilities can increase the portability of your programs.

► The typedef Mechanism ►

Consider the declarations

```
unsigned char ch;           /* ch is a variable */
typedef  unsigned char BYTE;  /* BYTE is a data type */
```

The presence of the keyword **typedef** alters the interpretation of the following declaration. The identifier **BYTE** is not a variable like **ch**, but rather a synonym for the type specifier **unsigned char**. In subsequent lines you can write, for example:

```
BYTE flag, marker;          /* declare two vars of type BYTE */
BYTE *byte_ptr;             /* declare a pointer to BYTE */
byte_ptr = (BYTE *)malloc(n*sizeof(BYTE));
/* type cast (void *) to pointer to BYTE */
```

with exactly the same effect as writing

```
unsigned char flag, marker;
unsigned char *byte_ptr;
byte_ptr =
     (unsigned char *)malloc(n*sizeof(unsigned char));
```

The use of uppercase letters for the data-type synonym is not mandatory, but it does improve legibility.

Note that **typedef** cannot create new data types; it simply adds new names as aliases for existing types. With the simple examples shown so far, I could have used the **#define** directive as in

```
#define   BYTE (unsigned char)
```

which, you'll recall from Chapter 1, causes the preprocessor to replace all occurrences of **BYTE** with **unsigned char**. **typedef**, on the other hand, is a compile-time construct, so **BYTE** actually joins the "list" of data types. This difference shows up when you use **typedef** with more complex declarations beyond the scope of simple textual substitutions.

Consider

```
typedef   char *STRING;
typedef   double (*PTR_FUNC_D)( );
```

Here we have created a mnemonic synonym, **STRING**, for the type pointer to **char**. The second line gives us the single data type name **PTR_FUNC_D** for the type "pointer to function returning **double**." The new names greatly simplify declarations. Rather than write

```
char *menu_heading, *buffer;
double (*func_p1)(char *), (*func_p2)(unsigned char), (*array_fp[10])( );
```

you can use the more intuitive declarations

```
STRING menu_heading, buffer;
PTR_FUNC_D func_p1(STRING), func_p2(BYTE), array_fp[10];
```

Here, **func_p1** is a pointer to a function taking a "pointer to **char**" as an argument and returning a **double**. **func_p2** is a pointer to a function taking an

unsigned char as an argument and returning a **double**. In the final example, you have an array of 10 pointers to functions (with unspecified arguments), each returning a **double**. The **typedef** version eases the undoubted pain of deciphering complicated declarators like (***array_fp[10]**)( )—and you can readily concoct even worse cases. If the data type calls for additional modifiers such as **far**, the source text clutter can be reduced even more.

► *Portability and typedef*

In addition to simplifying complex declarations, **typedef** is a wonderful aid in improving portability. Suppose you have a Motorola M68000-based C program using many 32-bit **int** variables. (Recall that C mandates only the relative sizes of **short**, **int**, and **long**.) Moving this program unchanged to QuickC, where **int** is 16-bit, could prove hazardous. You might be reduced to replacing several hundred **int** declarations with **long** to preserve the program's precision and prevent overflow. It is therefore common practice to start programs with some **typedef**s (or tuck them in a header file). In a program with

```
typdef int M_INT;
typedef long M_LONG;
typedef short M_SHORT;
```

all **int**s would be declared as **M_INT i, j, k;**, while pointers to **int** would be **M_INT *ip, *iq;**, and so on. Porting is now simplified by changing some or all of these three type definitions to match the target system:

```
typedef long M_INT;
```

All the **M_INT** declarations would be magically transformed from **int** to **long**, as would any type casts you may have used:

```
M_INT *ip;
char *cp;
ip = (M_INT *)cp;
/* cast cp from "pointer to char" to "pointer M_INT" */
```

Of course, there may be other tweaks required. Each C implementation has its private quirks, pace the ANSI committees. Even within a complex package like QuickC, there are options that might require subtle changes in the source code. For example, running a program in a different memory model might call for different pointer declarations. C offers a flexible mechanism called *conditional compilation* that allows you to write one version of your source code that can respond to different situations.

► *Conditional Compilation Commands* ►

C offers several *preprocessor conditional commands* that can help to automate the changes mentioned in the previous section. The compiler can be made to conditionally bypass any portion of the source code by using #if, #else, #elif, #endif, #ifdef, or #ifndef.

These directives work rather like the familiar if...else if...else conditional statements, but there are important differences. In the following schema, the *process-sections* can represent any sequence of source code, including other preprocessor lines. They need not be statements or blocks as with if...else if...else (although they usually are).

```
#if constant-expression-1
      process-section-1
[#elif constant-expression-2
      process-section-2]
[#elif ...
      ...]
[#else
      process-section-n]
#endif
      normal-compilation-section
```

As might be obvious from the layout, you are telling the preprocessor to bypass **process-section-1** if **constant-expression-1** evaluates to zero (false)—in which case, each optional #elif (note the spelling) is evaluated in turn until a nonzero (true) expression is encountered or the optional #else is reached. Once a "true" section is processed, "control" passes to the #endif line and normal preprocessing resumes. The net result is that only one of the sections will be processed and the rest will be ignored. The impact of all this is that the preprocessor passes on to the compiler only those sections of your source code that meet your various #if...#elif...#else conditions. You can spread these tests all over your source text, and they can be nested just like normal program conditionals. When nesting, you need a matching #endif for each **#if** loop. Since the process-sections are quite arbitrary (not necessarily block structured with { }), the **#endif** is an essential sign to the preprocessor that the matching **#if** condition is ended:

```
#if x
        section – x – true
#if y
        section – x – true – y – true
#else
        section – x – true – y – false
#endif
/* ends if y */
#else
        section – x – false
#endif
/* ends if x */
```

The **#if**...**#endif** sequence cannot straddle different files. You cannot, for instance, pull in parts of the sequence from **#include** files.

► *The #if...#elif Constant Expression*

The various *constant expressions* shown in the **#if**...**#elif** tests must obviously consist of constants or calculable combinations of constants that evaluate to zero or nonzero integer-compatible values. To form such expressions, you can use any or all of the following binary operators:

```
* / % + – << >> == != < <= > >= & ^ ¦ && ¦¦
```

together with the unary operators

```
– ˜ !
```

and the ternary, conditional operator

```
x ? y : z
```

QuickC will give you a fatal error—**C1017: invalid integer constant expression**—if the expression following **#if**...**#elif** does not evaluate to an integer constant.

▶ *The #ifdef and #ifndef Directives*

#ifdef (if defined) and #ifndef (if not defined) test whether an identifier has been previously defined as a preprocessor macro name. **#ifdef name** is exactly the same as **#if 1** (true) provided that **name** is already known to the preprocessor from some earlier, current **#define name xxxx** directive. If **name** is not currently defined, then **#ifdef name** is treated exactly like **#if 0** (false). Because of this translation, **#ifdef** can be used with **#elif** and **#else**, and it must be terminated with a matching **#endif**.

#ifndef works the other way round: If **name** is currently undefined, then **#ifndef name** behaves like **#if 1** (true). If **name** is defined, then **#ifndef name** is the same as **#if 0** (false).

▶ *The defined Operator*

You can also use the new ANSI C keyword **defined** as follows:

```
#if defined name
        compile – if – name – defined
#else
        compile – if – name – undefined
#endif
```

where **#defined name** evaluates to 1 (true) if **name** is currently defined; otherwise it evaluates to 0 (false).

At first sight, **#if defined** seems to be a superfluous duplication of the **#ifdef** directive. However, you can combine Boolean expressions with **#defined name** in ways not possible with **#ifdef** and **#ifndef**:

```
#if defined name ¦¦ defined(tag) ¦¦ defined title
        section – if – either – name – or – tag – or – title – defined
#elif defined unix && defined !msdos
        section – if – unix – defined – AND – msdos – NOT – defined
#endif
```

▶ *The #undef Directive* ▶

To add to the merriment, you can *undefine* any macro (whether previously defined or not) by using the directive **#undef name**. You are free to *redefine* **name** later if you so desire. Undefining an undefined **name**, by the by, is pointless but legal.

You must distinguish carefully between an undefined macro name and an empty macro name. For example:

```
#define name xxxx
#undef name
#ifdef name
    this – section – bypassed
#endif
#ifndef name
    this – section – compiled
#endif
#define name
#ifdef name
    this – section – is – processed
#endif
#ifndef name
    this – section – bypassed
#endif
```

At this point, **name** is defined but empty (not to be confused with ASCII NUL or pointer NULL). Any subsequent occurrence of **name** will be ignored (replaced by nothing at all):

```
#define name "Stan"
    puts(name);                 /* display "Stan" and new line */
#undefine name
    puts(name);                 /* error – undefined identifier */
#define name
    puts(name);                 /* puts( ) will display a new line */
```

► *Conditional Compilation in Action* ►

You may be wondering what you can do with all this defining, undefining, and testing for defined macros. Here are some practical examples.

► *Default Macro Values*

When you have a large collection of .H include files together with **#define**s scattered around your program files (modules), which macro names are defined or what values have been assigned to them often may be uncertain. The actual order in which include files are **#include**d can clearly be significant. Some discipline is called for. A typical plan may use a special include file called LOCAL.H or DEFAULT.H with lines, such as

```
#ifndef BUFF_SIZE
#define BUFF_SIZE 512
#endif
```

The idea here is that if no earlier .H file has defined **BUFF_SIZE**, then the default value of 512 is supplied. If any earlier definition is current, the above **#define** is safely ignored. This widely used example illustrates the important point that conditional compilation should more correctly be called "conditional preprocessing and/or conditional compilation." If you browse around the QuickC .H files, you will meet many instructive applications of the conditional directives.

► *Commenting Out the Comments*

Another simple application is to "comment out" a whole section of source code that may already include comments. Since you cannot normally nest comments in C, you cannot simply surround arbitrary sections of code with /* and */. The following snippet illustrates the problem in trying to comment-out two lines that include a comment:

```
/*
/* messages.c */
    printf("hello, world!\n"); */
    printf("how are you?\n");
```

The first */ pair terminates the attempt prematurely. Now look at this solution:

```
#if 0
/* messages.c */
    printf("hello, world!\n");
#endif
    printf("how are you?\n");
```

I deliberately entered a false expression so that everything between **#if 0** and **#endif** will be ignored by the compiler.

► *Optional Debugging Aids*

A similar ploy can be used when you have optional sections of code to display debugging data during program development. Once the program is running well, you want to suspend these displays but keep the debugging code around just in case!

```
#define DEBUG 1
/* change this to 0 to suspend debugging code */
    ...
#if DEBUG
    printf("ptr1 = %p, name = %s\n",ptr1,name);
#endif
    ...
```

► *Setting Macros Externally*

In fact, you could switch debugging on and off without touching the source code. QCL.EXE (the freestanding compiler linker) allows you to define macro names and optionally pass their values to your program at compile time. You use the /D option in the QCL command line as follows:

```
QCL /DDEBUG = 1 FILENAME.C
```

or

```
QCL /DDEBUG = 0 FILENAME.C
```

With this strategy, your program would not need a **#define DEBUG 1** or **0** directive—you would just retain the **#if DEBUG** test.

► *Selecting Pascal, FORTRAN, and C Function Declarations*

For a more exciting application of conditional compilation, here is an extract from the QuickC header file, MALLOC.H:

```
/***
* malloc.h - declarations and definitions for memory allocation functions
*
* Copyright (c) 1985-1989, Microsoft Corporation. All rights
* reserved.
*
```

```
* Purpose:
* Contains the function declarations for memory allocation
* functions; also defines manifest constants and types used by
* the heap routines. [System V]
*
****/

...
#ifndef _SIZE_T_DEFINED
typedef unsigned int size_t;
#define _SIZE_T_DEFINED
#endif

...
#ifndef NO_EXT_KEYS              /* extensions enabled */
      #define _CDECL cdecl
      #define _NEAR near
#else /* extensions not enabled */
      #define _CDECL
      #define _NEAR
#endif                                /* NO_EXT_KEYS */

...
/* external variable declarations */
extern unsigned int _NEAR _CDECL _amblksiz;

/* function prototypes */
...
void * _CDECL malloc(size_t);
...
#ifndef NO_EXT_KEYS              /* extensions enabled */
...
void huge * cdecl halloc(long, size_t);
...
...
#endif                                /* NO_EXT_KEYS */
```

Consider the first conditional section:

```
#ifndef _SIZE_T_DEFINED
typedef unsigned int size_t;
#define _SIZE_T_DEFINED
#endif
```

This code defines **size_t** as an alias for **unsigned int** provided only that
_SIZE_T_DEFINED has not been previously defined. The reason for this

trick should be clear from my earlier discussion of **typedef** and portability. To avoid changing every occurrence of **unsigned int** to **unsigned long**, for example, in programs destined for a system with different data sizes, you can simply change the **typedef** of **size_t** in the header file(s). Note how the condition "protects" itself against repeated invocations: Once **size_t** has been established, **_SIZE_T_DEFINED** is defined (as NULL, but it is defined!) in order to bypass any further, unnecessary **typedef**s.

To understand the **cdecl** sections, you need to know that QuickC allows you to compile and run C programs that contain some or all of their functions written with the naming and calling conventions of Pascal and FORTRAN. Also, you can link object code derived from a mix of these (and other) languages. I will initially restrict my discussion to Pascal for the sake of brevity, but note that FORTRAN's calling conventions are very similar (at least as far as they impact this lesson).

To allow C's functions to handle a variable number of arguments (**printf( )** being a familiar example), the arguments are passed to the stack from *right to left*. When **func(arg1, arg2,...argn);** is called, **argn** gets pushed first, followed by **argn-1**, and so on until **arg1** is pushed last, arriving at the top of the stack. The function is then executed by accessing the arguments on the stack, with **arg1** first, and so on. This method clearly allows a crisper argument-passing arrangement in that advanced knowledge of the number of arguments is not needed. One snag, though, is that the *calling* function rather than the *called* function has to tidy up the stack. So, to get the flexibility of variable argument lists, there is usually a code-size overhead to be paid, since there are typically more function calls (each lumbered with code to clean the stack) than functions in a program.

Each Pascal function, however, allows only a predetermined, fixed number of arguments. Pascal therefore chooses to pass its arguments from *left to right*, the opposite direction to C, and this allows the called function to tidy the stack before returning to the caller. Pascal functions, therefore, are slightly more efficient at the expense of flexibility.

QuickC lets you control the calling conventions in several ways, so you can call Pascal and/or FORTRAN programs from C or let Pascal and/or FORTRAN call programs written in C. First of all, if you compile with QCL using the /Gc switch, *all* your functions will be taken as following the Pascal/FORTRAN conventions unless you take special steps to individually override the /Gc influence. You do this using the **cdecl** keyword when declaring a function for which you want to retain the C argument-passing conventions. The declarations

```
int cdecl func1(arg1, arg2);
void func2(arg3, arg4);
```

tell QuickC that **func1( )** must be treated as a C function, regardless of whether the /Gc option is in force or not, whereas **func2( )** will be treated as Pascal/ FORTRAN or as C depending on the /Gc switch.

Similarly, there are keywords **pascal** and **fortran** that are used just like **cdecl** to override the prevailing /Gc mode:

```
int pascal func1(arg1, arg2);
void fortran func2(arg3, arg4);
```

If you compile with /Gc, of course, the extra keywords would be ignored as superfluous. Strictly speaking, **pascal** and **fortran** do exactly the same thing, so you can use whichever seems appropriate.

The **cdecl**, **pascal**, and **fortran** specifiers also affect the way identifier names are stored internally, since Pascal and FORTRAN are not case sensitive as is C. With /Gc active, all identifiers are converted internally to uppercase. Alternatively, you can apply the keywords to individual data and pointer identifiers when /Gc is not being used.

All the standard QuickC library functions default to the **cdecl** type, so you are free to call them in the usual C manner even when using the /Gc option. But, here we hit a snag. The **cdecl** specifier is not an official ANSI C keyword but belongs to the class of QuickC *extension words*. The other extension words are **fortran**, **pascal**, **near**, **far**, and **huge**.

If you compile with the /Za option of QCL, you disable all the extension words (and also disable several other non-ANSI C features). You use /Ze, by the way, to enable the extensions, but this is the default in the absence of any contrary command. The compiler automatically defines the identifier **NO_EXT_KEYS** when the /Za option is detected.

Returning to the MALLOC.C code (at last), you can see the significance of the following conditional directives:

```
#ifndef NO_EXT_KEYS          /* extensions enabled */
  #define _CDECL cdecl
  #define _NEAR  near
```

```
#else                          /* extensions not enabled */
  #define _CDECL
  #define _NEAR
#endif                         /* NO_EXT_KEYS */
```

If **NO_EXT_KEYS** is not defined (/Za is not used), **_CDECL** is defined as
cdecl; otherwise **_CDECL** is set to NULL. Hence the declaration

```
void * _CDECL malloc(size_t);
```

becomes either

```
void * cdecl malloc(size_t);        /* non-ANSI OK */
```

or

```
void * malloc(size_t);              /* non-ANSI suppressed */
```

(also, **size_t** will usually be replaced by **unsigned int**).

Further on in MALLOC.H, all the declarations with **huge** pointers will be
bypassed if extension words are disabled:

```
#ifndef NO_EXT_KEYS            /* extensions enabled */
...
void huge * cdecl halloc(long, size_t);
...
#endif                         /* NO_EXT_KEYS */
```

Whenever you want to be certain that your code conforms with the ANSI
C standards, use the /Za option when compiling. Any nonstandard tricks or
keywords will be disabled, possibly with errors or warnings.

▶ SUMMARY OF CHAPTER 5 ▶

Here are the key points covered in Chapter 5:

◄▶ The array **int vec[10]** consists of 10 **int** elements, **vec[0]** to **vec[9]**. The
identifier **vec** is the base pointer **&vec[0]**.

◄► A function can take an open array, **vec[ ]**, as a dummy argument without prior knowledge of the size of the real array argument used in the function call. Arrays are passed to functions via their base pointers.

◄► **sizeof(array_T)** gives the total number of bytes in the array, while **(sizeof(array_T)/sizeof(T))** gives the total number of elements of type **T** in **array_T**.

◄► The declarations **int vec[10];** and **int *ip;** both create integer pointers, **vec** and **ip**. However, the constant pointer **vec** points to a definite, fixed memory location, whereas the variable pointer **ip** points "nowhere," and ***ip** cannot be used until **ip** is initialized.

◄► You can initialize a pointer using the dynamic memory allocation functions **malloc(mem_size)** and **calloc(elem_number, elem_size)**. Before assignment, you must type cast the generic **(void *)** pointers returned by **malloc( )** and **calloc( )**: **ip = (int *)malloc (mem_size)**, then test **(ip == NULL)**.

◄► Pointer assignments such as **ip = vec;** require that the pointer types are compatible; otherwise you get a **Doubtful pointer conversions in function...** warning. Type casting allows incompatible pointer assignments: **ptr_T1 = (T1 *)ptr_T2.**

◄► **int **ih;** declares a pointer to a pointer to integer, sometimes called a handle.

◄► A pointer can be indexed like an array: **t = ptr_T[i];**, which is the same as **t = *(ptr_T + i*sizeof(T))**.

◄► All sums on pointers depend on the size of the pointer type. Pointers of the same type can be subtracted but cannot be usefully added: **num_elems_ptr2_ptr1 = (ptr1_T _ ptr2_T);**.

◄► The declaration **int *x( );** declares a function, **x( )**, returning a pointer to integer. By contrast, the declaration **int (*x)( );** declares that **x** is a pointer to a function returning an integer. Functions can be passed as arguments to functions by means of pointers (rather like passing arrays to functions).

◄► QuickC pointers come in three flavors: **near**, **far**, and **huge**. Unless explicitly specified, the pointer class is defaulted according to the memory model set up by SETUP options or QCL.EXE switches. The five models are small, medium, compact, large, and huge. They determine the sizes of the code and data segments available.

◄► **near** pointers are 16-bit offsets with fixed segments. **far** and **huge** pointers are 32-bit with variable segment:offset values. **huge** pointers have normalized offsets, allowing safer pointer arithmetic.

◄► int *ip[10]; declares an array of 10 pointers to int, while int (*ip)[10]; is a pointer to an array of 10 **ints**.

◄► Multidimensional arrays are declared int mat[3][4], hype[3][4][5];.

◄► Pass multidimensional array arguments to functions via base pointers. You need to specify every dimension except the first.

◄► Enumerations are declared by enum [tag] {e1, e2, e3} x1, x2;. The listed identifiers, e1, e2,..., behave like integers, 0, 1,.... The enum variables x1, x2,... can be assigned any of the e1, e2,... values. Enum variables can also be declared by enum tag v1, v2;.

◄► **typedef** gives you synonyms for any existing data type:

```
typedef char *STRING;
typedef int *PTR_FUNC_INT( );
```

◄► Conditional compilation is controlled by the directives #if, #elif, #else, #endif, #ifdef, #ifndef, #if defined *xxx* in conjunction with #define *xxxx*, #undef *xxxx*, and constant expressions. External macro names can be defined and assigned values via the QCL.EXE command line.

◄► The **cdecl** modifier with variables or functions overrides the Pascal/ FORTRAN conversion and argument-passing conventions when running in Pascal/FORTRAN mode. **pascal** and **fortran** overrride the C conventions when running in C mode. The /Gc option gives compilation in the Pascal/ FORTRAN mode.

◄► Use the /Za option to disable the QuickC non-ANSI extension words and features.

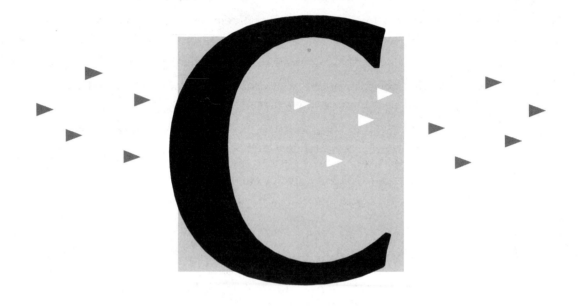

STRUCTURES AND UNIONS: ADAPTING DATA TYPES TO YOUR APPLICATIONS

► *CHAPTER 6* ►

C's most versatile data type is the *structure*. It allows you to create and manipulate sets of objects of mixed types, including other structures and pointers of any kind. If you have used the *records* of Pascal or Modula-2, you will already be familiar with the general concept, although the details differ.

As you grapple with the syntax for declaring and manipulating structures, keep in mind that *data structures* form one of the two basic abstract elements of contemporary computer science. As Niklaus Wirth puts it, "Programs = Algorithms + Data Structures." In C language terms, this could be restated as, "Programs = Functions + Pointers to Structures." Being able to assign single identifiers to complex collections of data and then compose functions that operate on them was a major step forward in software engineering. Learning which data structures to employ is as least as important as knowing which algorithms to use. In fact, the two often appear as inextricably bound together as the chicken and the egg.

► *THE STRUCTURE DECLARED* ►

Until now your arrays have been restricted to holding elements of any one base type: integers, characters, pointers, and other arrays of a fixed base type. The structure lifts this restriction. You declare a structure using the keyword **struct** followed by a list declaring each of the *components* (also known as *members* or *fields*) required in the structure.

The layout of the declaration aims at legibility. For smaller structures, you often find the following one-line format:

```
struct employer { char name[MAXN]; int id, ext; } emp;
/* structure has 3 fields: one array, two ints */
/* one variable, emp, declared */
```

For larger structures use the following layout:

```
#define NAME_SIZE 30

    struct player {                    /* optional tag */
        char name[NAME_SIZE];          /* field 1 */
        unsigned char player_number;   /* field 2 */
        float batting_average;         /* field 3 */
        BOOL active;                   /* field 4 */
    } pl1, pl2;                        /* struct vars */
    /* pl1 and pl2 are two variables of type 'struct player' */
```

The components listed between the curly braces can be as numerous as you like and of any data type except **void** and function. The component types can be the basic ones like **char** and **float**, user-named types from earlier **typedef**s, pointers to any of these, or arrays of any of these. The type **BOOL**, for example, comes from an earlier **typedef unsigned char BOOL**, as explained in Chapter 5.

The variables **pl1** and **pl2**, once initialized, can be envisaged as each holding values for each of the four component variables. Before I explain how these four members are set up and accessed, let's explore the implications of the **struct** declaration.

The user-supplied *tag* **player**, appearing after **struct**, can be used later in your program to declare more variables of type **struct player**:

```
    struct player pl3, pinch_hitter;
    /* declare two more player structures */
```

In other words, **struct player** represents a type specifier that acts just like **int** or **unsigned long** when declaring variables of the type specified.

As with **enum**, the tag can be omitted when you want to declare all your structure variables in one fell swoop:

```
#define NAME_SIZE 30

    struct {
        char name[NAME_SIZE];
        unsigned char player_number;
        float batting_average;
        BOOL active;
    } pl1, pl2, pl3, pinch_hitter;
    /* four variables of this 'struct' type — no more needed */
```

The above declaration is effectively the same as the two previous declarations combined, but you won't be able to declare more variables with this structure type because you don't have a type specifier called **struct player**. You could, of course, edit your program to add some variables after pinch_hitter.

Even when you have no more structure variables in mind, though, a mnemonic tag identifier such as **player** is often useful as an aid to documentation and discussion.

Another common alternative is to use **typedef** to create a synonym for **struct player**. Consider the following snippet:

```
typedef struct {
    char name[NAME_SIZE];
    unsigned char player_number;
    float batting_average;
    BOOL active;
} PLAYER_REC;
/* no memory allocated yet! */

/* now we can declare structure variables */
    PLAYER_REC pl1, pl2, outfielder;
/* memory now reserved */

/* or declare pointers to structure variables */
    PLAYER_REC *player_ptr;
/* no structure memory allocated here */

/* and arrays of pointers to player structures */
#define TEAM_SIZE 45

    PLAYER_REC *team[TEAM_SIZE];
/* TEAM_SIZE pointers only - no structures created.
    Each team[i], i = 0 to i = 44, is a pointer to a PLAYER_REC */

/* and arrays of player structures */
    PLAYER_REC squad[TEAM_SIZE];
/* each squad[i], i = 0 to i = 44, represents a player structure */

/* perhaps arrays of arrays of PLAYER_REC structures */
#define LEAGUE_SIZE 28

    PLAYER_REC league[LEAGUE_SIZE][TEAM_SIZE];
/* declares LEAGUE_SIZE x TEAM_SIZE separate players */
```

A tag such as **player** can still be inserted after **typedef struct** but is now less useful since **PLAYER_REC** plays the role of **struct player**. If you do use a tag, you simply have two equivalent ways of declaring further variables:

```
typedef struct player {
    char name[NAME_SIZE];
    unsigned char player_number;
    float batting_average;
    BOOL active;
} PLAYER_REC;

    struct player pl1;
/* same as PLAYER_REC pl1; */
    struct player *player_ptr;
/* same as PLAYER_REC *player_ptr */
```

In the early days of C, before **typedef** was introduced, the structure tag played a more important role. Nowadays, as you can guess, it is often omitted in favor of the more economical and legible **typedef**s.

Confusing tags with **typedef** names is a common source of bugs, so make sure you understand the examples. I have used the uppercase convention for my **typedef** name, but you'll encounter code in which tags and type names look very similar.

I have introduced pointers to structures and some more exotic variants to whet your appetite. You'll see them in action shortly.

► *THE STRUCTURE ANALYZED* ►

Let's see what the various **struct player** and **PLAYER_REC** declarations have achieved. First of all, for each variable of this structure type, C reserves enough memory to hold the listed components. (The actual timing of this memory allocation need not concern you for the moment.) How much memory is enough? Well, you can simply add up the bytes for each component, or you can use **sizeof(struct player)** to determine the total allocation more accurately. The total for **PLAYER_REC** is 30 + 1 + 4 + 1 = 36 bytes.

So far you have seen how to declare structures and how to determine their size. It is time to examine the vital process of accessing the member variables within the structure.

► *ACCESSING THE STRUCTURE COMPONENTS* ►

The variable **pl1** of type **PLAYER_REC** (or equivalently, of type **struct player**) represents a set of four variables of the types declared in the **struct** list. You can access these individually using the *member*, or *selection*, operator (a period) as follows:

```
pl1.player_number = 29;
pl1.batting_average = 0.335;
pl1.active = TRUE;
/* TRUE is #defined earlier as 1 */

strcpy(pl1.name,"Clark");
/* remember that pl1.name is an array name, i.e., a constant pointer. So
   pl1.name = "Clark" is illegal; you must use the string copy function */
```

The general format is **struct_var.member_var**. You use this joint identifier just as if it were a variable of the type of **member_var** as declared in the structure's member list, and you can therefore do anything that's legal for that type. Here are a few examples:

```
strcpy(pinch_hitter.name,pl1.name);
/* copy pl1.name to pinch_hitter.name */

pl2.batting_average += 0.001;
/* notch up pl2's average */
fptr = &pl1.batting_average
/* get a pointer to a component */
pl2.player_number = pl3.player_number++;
/* assign pl3's old number to pl2, then increment */

pinch_hitter.active = FALSE;
/* deactivate the PH */

pl2.active = !date_sick;
/* right – hand evaluates to TRUE if date_sick is 0 */

printf("Player #%d is hitting %f\n",
    pl1.player_number,pl1.batting_average);
if (pl2.active) printf("Player %s is active\n",
    pl2.name);
```

(Pascal and Modula-2 programmers should note the absence of a **with** construct in C. You must write out the **struct_var.member_var** in full each time.)

► STRUCTURE ASSIGNMENTS ►

A major convenience for the programmer is the ability to assign all the component values of one structure variable to those of another structure variable of the same type. For example:

```
pinch_hitter = pl1;
```

will move the four component values sitting in **pl1** over to the corresponding four members of **pinch_hitter**. This single structure assignment is the equivalent of the four separate assignments

```
    strcpy(pinch_hitter.name,pl1.name);
/* this is effectively an assignment of one array to another */
    pinch_hitter.player_number = pl1.player_number;
    pinch_hitter.batting_average = pl1.batting_average;
    pinch_hitter.active = pl1.active;
```

Observe that this structure assignment has achieved the "assignment" of one array to another—a feat that cannot be accomplished outside of a structure without the **strcpy( )** function (or some equivalent character-copying code).

This economical structure-assignment maneuver is only possible if the left and right structures are declared as the same type. If you declare two structures with exactly the same size and format but different types, you lose structure assignment compatibility:

```
struct giant {
    char g_name[NAME_SIZE];
    unsigned char g_player_number;
    float g_batting_average;
    BOOL g_active;
} g_pl1, g_pl2, g_pl3, g_pinch_hitter;
...
...
g_pinch_hitter = g – pl3;        /* OK – same struct types */
pl1 = g_pl2;                     /* ILLEGAL – different struct types */
pl1.active = g_pl2.active        /* OK – members are compatible */
```

As this example shows, however, the individual components of different structures can be assigned just like any other compatible variables. To achieve **pl1 = g_pl2;**, therefore, you would need to make four separate assignments. Better still, ask yourself if you really need a separate **struct giant**. Since the data formats are identical, you could save time and trouble by declaring

PLAYER_REC g_pl1, g_pl2, g_pl3, g_pinch_hitter;

Before we relinquish **struct giant**, there is a useful observation to make. Within **struct giant** I went to the trouble of naming each component differently from **PLAYER_REC**. In fact, component names need only be unique within a structure. It is legal to have

```
struct player {
    char name[30];
    unsigned char player_number;
    float batting_average;
    BOOL active;
} pl1, pl2, pl3, pinch_hitter;

struct giant {
    BOOL active;
    unsigned char player_number;
    float batting_average;
    char name[30];
} g_pl1, g_pl2, g_pl3, g_pinch_hitter;
```

At first sight it would appear unseemly to have two variables called **name**, two named **active**, and so on, in adjacent declarations. Indeed, the K&R 1978 C specification expressly forbade the above kind of component-name duplications. (This restriction was relaxed, though, if the components had the same types and relative positions within the two structures.) Nowadays it is legal to duplicate component names in different structures since the **struct_var.member_var** format ensures uniqueness.

▶ *STRUCTURE INITIALIZERS* ▶

As with arrays, you can initialize structure variables during their declaration:

PLAYER_REC mays = { "Willie Mays", 45, 0.333, FALSE };

(Some compilers are less tolerant than QuickC and will not initialize automatic arrays or structures.) The now-familiar rules for initializers apply. Each constant expression within the curly braces is assigned in turn to each component of the structure. If there are too many initializers, or if they are not assignment compatible, you get an error. If there are insufficient initializers, the unmatched components are cleared to zero. (I use the word *zero* to cover all the possible internal forms that C can generate to clear different component data types, including **int 0**, **char '\x0'**, **long int 0L**, **double 0.0**, and pointer NULL.)

► *NESTING STRUCTURES* ►

Once a structure is declared, variables of that type can be used within another structure. Take the following simple example:

```
typedef struct {                 /* no tag */
    unsigned char month, day; /* fields 1 & 2 */
    unsigned int year;           /* field 3 */
} DATE;                          /* structure type name */

DATE signing_date = { 9, 15, 1929 };
                                 /* declare & initialize a DATE variable */
/* sizeof(DATE) is 4 */

typedef struct {
    char name[NAME_SIZE];
    unsigned char player_number;
    float batting_average;
    BOOL active;
    DATE date_joined;            /* new field 5 is a struct */
} PLAYER_REC;
/* sizeof(PLAYER_REC) now = 40 (byte aligned) or 42 (word aligned) */

PLAYER_REC pl1, pinch_hitter;
/* pl1 and pinch_hitter are two PLAYER_REC variables */
```

First I **typedef**ed a simple structure type called **DATE**. Then I declared and initialized a variable, **signing_date**. Next I added a new variable of type **DATE**, **date_joined**, to the player record. Within **date_joined** the components are referenced via the variable names **date_joined.month**, date_joined.day, and date_joined.year. Within pl1, the new components must now be accessed using

```
pl1.date_joined.month
pl1.date_joined.day
pl1.date_joined.year
```

Note the positions of the two member operators. This format arises quite naturally whenever the struct1_member in struct1_var.struct1_member is itself of the form struct2_var.struct2_member. Substituting the latter value gives

```
struct1_var.struct2_var.struct2_member
```

This nesting of structures can be continued to any depth, and the rules for accessing the lower level components are obvious extensions of our two-level example. You can end up with as many member operators as the nesting depth as in

```
struct1_var.struct2_var.struct3_var.struct3_member
```

In spite of the length and complexity of such constructs, the simple fact to remember is that the the whole expression behaves exactly like a variable of the type of the last named member. Using our new **PLAYER_REC**, here are some valid statements:

```
pl1.date_joined.month = 3;
pl1.date_joined.day = 25;
if (pl1.date_joined.year <= 1950 && pl1.active) {
    pl1.active = FALSE;
    ...
}
pinch_hitter.date_joined.month += 2;
signing_date.year = pl1.date_joined.year;
...
switch (pl1.date_joined.month) {
    case 1: puts("January"); break;
    case 2: puts("February"); break;
    ...
    default:
        puts("Month error");
        exit(1);
}
```

Nested structures can be initialized using nested initializers! If we add

```
PLAYER_REC ruth = {"Babe Ruth", 1, 0.389, FALSE,
                    { 10, 18, 1925 } };
```

the three fields of the **date_joined** structure are initialized with the nested expression **{ 10, 18, 1925 }**. Having too many initializers at any level will give you an error signal. Having too few initializers results in the surplus members being cleared to zero.

▸ Restrictions on Nested Structures ▸

There is one important restriction on nested structures: you cannot include a structure variable within its own structure. For example:

```
/* ILLEGAL declaration */
    struct bad {
        int a;
        struct bad no_no;    /* NOT ALLOWED */
        double c;
    } none_such;
```

is illegal because it could lead to an infinite sequence of memory allocations! If this limitation depresses you, you will be pleased to hear that C does allow a structure to hold a pointer to variables of its own type:

```
/* This declaration is LEGAL */
    struct good {
        int a;
        struct good *yes_yes;    /* pointer to struct is ALLOWED */
        double c;
    } any_such;
```

The compiler can make sense of this. The component **yes_yes** is a fixed-length pointer (16 or 32 bits depending on the memory model) of type pointer to **struct good**. The memory allocation is therefore predetermined.

It turns out that many important abstract data structures can be realized in C using this mechanism. *Linked lists* and *trees*, for example, require structure elements to contain one or more pointers to other structure elements of the same type.

► A SIMPLE LINKED LIST ►

To give you the flavor of this approach, let's revamp the **PLAYER_REC** structure as follows:

```
typedef struct player {
    char name[NAME_SIZE];
    unsigned char player_number;
    float batting_average;
    BOOL active;
    DATE date_joined;
    struct player *next;          /* new field 6 is pointer to next record */
} PLAYER_REC;

PLAYER_REC clark, ruth, mays;
```

The new field **next** is of type pointer to **struct player**. By setting various addresses in this field for different **PLAYER_REC** variables, we can create a linked list of player records. I'll fill in the details later, but for now assume that the variable **mays** has been initialized with appropriate values for **mays.name, mays.player_number**, and so on. We set **mays.next** to NULL to indicate that this record does not point anywhere. This is the normal convention for indicating that there is no **next**—in other words, **mays** is the last player in the linked list. We now enter Babe Ruth's data into the structure variable **ruth**, ending with the assignment

```
ruth.next = &mays;
```

Informally, you can say that **ruth** points to **mays**. Using the **next** field as a pointer or *link* explains the term *linked list*. To complete our list, we put Jack Clark's data into **clark** and set

```
clark.next = &ruth;
```

What we now have is a very simple linked list of three players. Starting with **clark**, we can scan the list by picking up pointers to the next player record until a NULL pointer is reached. For example, from **clark.next** we can access **ruth** as *clark.next provided that **clark.next** is not NULL. You can even access **mays** directly using the construct *(*clark.next).next since this is equivalent to *ruth.next (we know that **ruth.next** isn't NULL).

▶ *THE STRUCTURE POINTER MEMBER OPERATOR (–>)* ▶

Note that the member operator (.) has higher precedence (category 1) than the indirection operator (*, category 2). (See the table inside the covers of this book for a complete listing.) Therefore, *clark.next is treated as *(clark.next), which is precisely what we seek—i.e., the structure being pointed at by clark.next. In the case of *(*clark.next).next, the parentheses are needed. The member operators associate left to right, while direction operators associate right to left. To make the code even more legible, you may want to write

        ((clark.next).next)

which highlights the sequence of events.

Now suppose you have a pointer to PLAYER_REC called player_ptr. To access the components of *player_ptr, the structure being pointed at, you would need expressions like

        (*player_ptr).name
        (*player_ptr).player_number
        (*player_ptr).batting_average

and so on. The parentheses here are essential in view of the previous remarks about precedence. Because this method of component access is so common in C, K&R wisely provided a special operator called *structure pointer member*, or *right arrow*, to simplify your typing. The two symbols – (minus) and > (greater than) are combined (with no white space) to give the operator –>. This has the same category 1 precedence as the normal member operator. The previous three expressions can be written more concisely as

        player_ptr –>name   (*player_pointer).name
        player_ptr –>player_number   (*player_pointer).player_number
        player_ptr –>batting_average   (*player_pointer).batting_average

Parentheses are not required with –> since the compiler dereferences player_ptr first as part of the –> operation. When you mix –> with more complex expressions, of course, parentheses may be needed.

Using our linked-list declarations, here are some examples of –> in action:

```
(clark.next) –>batting_average = 0.450;

/* since "clark.next = &ruth" and "*clark.next = ruth"
   the above is the same as (&ruth) –>batting_average = 0.450;
   which is the same as ruth.batting_average = 0.450; */

((clark.next –>next) –>active = FALSE;

/* since "(*clark.next).next = ruth.next = &mays"
   the above is the same as
      ((*clark.next).next) –>active = FALSE;
   which is the same as
      (*(*clark.next).next).active = FALSE;
   which is the same as
      mays.active = FALSE */

/* since "." and "–>" are equal precedence and associate left to
   right, you can also write:
      clark.next –>next –>active = FALSE;
   with no parentheses! */
```

► ADVANTAGES OF LINKED LISTS ►

The neat thing about this type of data structure is that you can easily insert and delete records. Changing **clark.next** to **&mays**, for example, effectively strikes out **ruth**! Changing **ruth.next** to **&aaron** and then setting **aaron.next** to **&mays** adds **aaron** to the list.

For more complex manipulations such as forward and reverse scanning of a list, the *double-linked list* is often used. This adds another pointer to point to the previous record:

```
typedef struct player {
    char name[NAME_SIZE];
    unsigned char player_number;
    float batting_average;
    BOOL active;
    DATE date_joined;
```

```
        struct player *next;        /* field 6 is pointer to next record */
        struct player *prev;        /* new field 7 is pointer to previous
                                        record */

    } PLAYER_REC;

    PLAYER_REC clark, ruth, mays;
```

Under this dispensation **clark.prev** would be NULL, indicating that this is the first record in the list, while **mays.prev** would be set to **&ruth**.

My examples are hardly realistic, of course. Since the three player records have known identifiers, we can access them directly without scanning the linked list. I've used these examples to establish the general technique and terminology that we'll use later with more realistic applications employing arrays of pointers to structures.

► POINTERS TO STRUCTURES ►

Pointers, as you can see, play a central role in C. This role is underlined when you consider pointers to structures and pointers to functions. The previous section showed how structure elements can be linked together in various ways by means of pointers embedded in the structure itself. A further use of pointers arises because structures are usually passed to functions *indirectly as pointers* just as you saw with array and function arguments to functions. At one time, in fact, structures could only be passed to functions as pointers, but this restriction is now lifted. Although you can have a **func(PLAYER_REC pl)** in QuickC taking a structure argument, only a copy of the structure is passed (C always passes by value), so **func( )** cannot change the actual argument. Also, it can put a strain on available memory if the structure is a large one.

Similarly, although a function defined as **PLAYER_REC func( )** can return a structure value directly, it is more common to return a pointer to a structure as with **PLAYER_REC *func( )**.

You will recall that an array identifier like **name** is actually a pointer to the first element of the array **name[ ]**. In the same way, a function identifier **func** used without the ( ) is taken as a pointer to **func( )**. This is not the case with structure variables. The variable **pl1**, declared to be of type **PLAYER_REC**, is *not* a pointer to anything. You must apply the address operator to get **&pl1**, the address of **pl1**, as with simple variables. You can also declare variables of type pointer to structure X as well as arrays of structures and arrays of pointers to structures. A few examples will help clarify these distinct objects:

```
typedef struct player {
    char name[NAME_SIZE];
    unsigned char player_number;
    float batting_average;
    BOOL active;
    DATE date_joined;
    PLAYER_REC *next;
} PLAYER_REC;
/* PLAYER_REC is type 'struct player' */

/* sizeof(PLAYER_REC) is now 42 */

    PLAYER_REC pl1, pl2, outfielder;

    PLAYER_REC *player_ptr;
/* declare a pointer to struct player */

    player_ptr = &pl1;
    pl2.next = player_ptr;
/* assign pointer values */
    player_ptr -> active = TRUE;
/* assign a component value */
    PLAYER_REC *team[TEAM_SIZE];
/* declare an array of 'pointers to struct player'*/

    if (&out_fielder) team[0] = &out_fielder;
/* the first pointer of this array now points to the struct
    variable outfielder - if not-NULL */
    team[0] -> player_number = 39;
/* assign a component value */
    PLAYER_REC squad[TEAM_SIZE];
/* declare an 'array of type struct player' */

    squad[2] = pl2;
/* the third element of squad is now pl2
    complete assignment of all fields */

    PLAYER_REC *trade(PLAYER_REC *pl_ptr);
/* declare a function, trade, that takes as argument a 'pointer
    to struct player' and returns a value 'pointer to struct player'*/
```

▶ ALLOCATING DYNAMIC MEMORY FOR STRUCTURES ▶

When I declared **pl1**, C established a fixed amount of RAM to hold the member variables of **PLAYER_REC**. Declaring a pointer to a structure, however, does not allocate any memory for that structure, nor is the pointer set to point at anything in particular! As you saw in Chapter 5, pointers need to be initialized in some way before they are usable. In my previous examples, I did this with assignments of known addresses of existing structure variables such as **&ruth**.

Using **malloc( )** is another way of creating real space for a structure and at the same time establishing a pointer to that space.

When allocating dynamic memory for structures with **malloc( )**, using **sizeof( )** is always safer, easier, and more portable than "manually" counting bytes. Writing **malloc(42)** to get one **PLAYER_REC** allocation is clearly dangerous in view of my earlier comments on alignment boundaries.

The argument for **sizeof( )** should be the data type **struct player**, or its **typedef** synonym **PLAYER_REC**, or another variable of that type. So **sizeof(PLAYER_REC)** or **sizeof(pinch_hitter)** will each give you the right structure size, but **sizeof(player)** is illegal since **player** is a tag not a type or variable. Examine the following snippet:

```
PLAYER_REC *player_ptr;          /* declare a pointer to struct player */
    ...
    if ((player_ptr = (PLAYER_REC *)malloc(sizeof(PLAYER_REC)))
                                == NULL) {
        puts("\n\tInsufficient memory for player allocation\n");
        exit(1);
    }
/* here we have player_ptr pointing to first byte of allocated
    memory – all ready to 'take in' player values */
    ...
```

Here we have a typically "busy" piece of C code. The **if** statement first invokes **malloc( )**, then type casts its **(void *)** returned value to type pointer to **PLAYER_REC**, assigns that pointer to **player_ptr**, and finally tests for NULL! Remember that the value being tested is the value of the assignment statement, namely the lvalue resulting from the assignment.

You should now read through PLAYER.C (Program 6.1). It's a somewhat longer example than usual, so don't expect to digest it all at once. A detailed analysis appears in Chapter 7 since PLAYER.C relies on the **static** storage specifier to control scope and visibility.

```
/* PLAYER.C - a simple, volatile player database */
/* Program 6.1 */
/* overall strategy due to N. Gehani, AT&T Bell Labs */

#include <stdio.h>
#include <malloc.h>
#include <ctype.h>
#include <string.h>

#define FOUND 1
#define MISSING 0

#define PL_MAX 2        /* max number of player */
#define NAME_MAX 25     /* max name + 1 null */
#define HDG "Pl# Name                      Posn  RBI ERA    DATE Active"

        typedef struct {
                unsigned char month, day;
                unsigned int year;
        } DATE;

        typedef unsigned char BOOL;

        typedef enum {
           X, P, C, I, S, O, D
        } POSITION;

        typedef struct player {

                char name[NAME_MAX];
                unsigned char player_number;
                POSITION player_position;
                unsigned int rbi;
                double era;
                DATE date_joined;
                BOOL active;
        } PLAYER_REC;


        static PLAYER_REC *pptr[PL_MAX];
/* global to all functions in this file,
   but not accessible elsewhere.
   Declares an array of 'pointers to PLAYER_REC structure' */

        static int pind;
/* player index used with pptr[] */

        static int db_size;
/* number of players in database */


/*---------------------------------------*/
/* INIT_PLAY - set up player database    */
/* data in memory only - until Chapter 8! */


/*---------------------------------------*/
void init_play(void)
{
     int dbind;    /* local var - scans the database */
     char pos;     /* ASCII player position */

  for (dbind = 0; dbind < PL_MAX; dbind++) {
     if ((pptr[dbind]=(PLAYER_REC *)malloc(sizeof(PLAYER_REC)))
                           ==NULL) {
```

► **Program 6.1:** PLAYER.C

```
                 puts("Memory Allocation Failure");
                 exit(1);
         }

/* here pptr[dbind] points to an allocated record awaiting input */

         printf("\n#%3d Enter Player Number <99=exit>: ",dbind);
         scanf( "%d",&(pptr[dbind]->player_number) );

         if (pptr[dbind]->player_number == 99) return;

         printf("\n      Enter Player Name: ");
         scanf( "%s",pptr[dbind]->name );
/* Next item could be entered with getch() but I want to */
/* show scanf() with %s                                  */
         printf("\n      Enter Player Position: ");
         scanf("%s",&pos);
         pos = toupper(pos);
         switch (pos) {
             case 'P': pptr[dbind]->player_position = P; break;
             case 'C': pptr[dbind]->player_position = C; break;
             case 'I': pptr[dbind]->player_position = I; break;
             case 'S': pptr[dbind]->player_position = S; break;
             case 'O': pptr[dbind]->player_position = O; break;
             case 'D': pptr[dbind]->player_position = D; break;
             default:  pptr[dbind]->player_position = X;
         }
         if (pptr[dbind]->player_position != P) {
             pptr[dbind]->era = 0.0;
             printf("\n      Enter Runs Batted In: ");
             scanf( "%d",&(pptr[dbind]->rbi) );
         }
         else {
             pptr[dbind]->rbi = 0;
             printf("\n      Enter Earned Run Average: ");
             scanf( "%lf",&(pptr[dbind]->era) );
         }
         printf("\n      Enter Date Joined (mm/dd/yyyy): ");
         scanf( "%2d/%2d/%4d", &((pptr[dbind]->date_joined).month),
                        &((pptr[dbind]->date_joined).day),
                        &((pptr[dbind]->date_joined).year) );

         printf("\n      Active=Y or N? :");
         scanf( "%s",&pos);


         pptr[dbind]->active = ('Y' == toupper(pos));
         } /* end for loop */
         db_size = dbind;          /* set current size of database */
}
/*-------------end init_player--------------------*/


/*----------------------------------------*/
/* ASC_POS() coverts position code to ASCII */
/*----------------------------------------*/

char *asc_pos(POSITION x)
{
         switch (x) {
             case P: return "P";
             case C: return "C";
             case I: return "I";
             case S: return "S";
             case O: return "O";
             case D: return "D";
```

► *Program 6.1:* PLAYER.C *(continued)*

```
                    default:  return "X";
              }
}
/*-------------------end asc_pos----------------*/


/*-------------------------------*/
/* LIST_PLAYER - lists the database */
/*-------------------------------*/

void list_play(int start)
{
 int dbind;

 puts  (HDG);
    for (dbind = (start>=0 ? start : 0);
         dbind < db_size;
         dbind++) {
      printf
      ("\n%3d %-26s %1s       %3d      %7.3f  %2d/%2d/%4d %s\n",
       pptr[dbind]->player_number, pptr[dbind]->name,
       asc_pos(pptr[dbind]->player_position), pptr[dbind]->rbi,
       pptr[dbind]->era, pptr[dbind]->date_joined.month,
       pptr[dbind]->date_joined.day, pptr[dbind]->date_joined.year,
       (pptr[dbind]->active) ? "Y":"N");
    }
}
/*-------------------end list_player-----------------*/


/*-----------------------------------------------*/
/* GET_STR returns a pointer to a copy of arg string */
/*-----------------------------------------------*/

char *get_str(char str[])

{
        char *ptr;

        if ((ptr = (char *)malloc(strlen(str)+1)) == NULL) {
            puts("Insufficient Memory for get_str");
            exit(1);
        }
        else
            strcpy(ptr, str);
        return ptr;
}
/*--------------------- end get_str ------------------*/


/*------------------------------------------------------*/
/* GET_NAME() sets global index pind to pptr[] array    */
/* such that pptr[pind] points at record with target name */
/* Returns FOUND or MISSING                             */
/*------------------------------------------------------*/

static int get_name(char target_name[])
{
        if (strcmp(target_name, pptr[pind]->name) == 0)
            return FOUND;
/* first test if previous find is still useful */

        for (pind = 0; pind < db_size; pind++)
           if (strcmp(target_name, pptr[pind]->name) == 0)
              return FOUND;
        pind = 0;
        return MISSING;
}
/*---------------------end get_name-----------------------*/
```

► **Program 6.1:** *PLAYER.C (continued)*

```
/*---------------------------------------------------------*/
/* GET_NUMBER() sets global index pind to pptr[] array     */
/* such that pptr[pind] points at record with target number */
/* Returns FOUND with good pind or MISSING with pind=0      */
/*---------------------------------------------------------*/
static int get_number(unsigned char target_number)
{
        if (target_number == pptr[pind]->player_number)
           return FOUND;
/* first test if previous find is still useful */

        for (pind = 0; pind < db_size; pind++)
        if (target_number == pptr[pind]->player_number)
               return FOUND;
        pind = 0;
        return MISSING;
}
/*-------------------end get_number------------------------*/


/* ---------------*/
/* NUMBER_TO_NAME */
/*----------------*/
char *number_to_name(unsigned char tn)
{
        return get_number(tn) ? get_str(pptr[pind]->name) : NULL;
}
/*----------------*/
/* NAME_TO_NUMBER */
/*----------------*/
unsigned char name_to_number(char tname[])
{
        return get_name(tname) ? pptr[pind]->player_number : MISSING;
}

void main()
{
    char *tname = "S";
    unsigned char tnumber = 0;

    init_play();
    list_play(0);

  while (tnumber != 99) {
      printf("\nEnter Target Number <99=Exit>: ");
      scanf("%d",&tnumber);
      if (tnumber == 99) break;
      if ((tname = number_to_name(tnumber)) != NULL)
          printf("\tName is %s\n",tname);
      else puts("\tNo such Player Number");
  }
  while (strcmp(tname,"X") != 0) {
      printf("\nEnter Target Name: <X to Exit>");
      scanf("%s",tname);
      if (strcmp(tname,"X") == 0) break;
      if ((tnumber = name_to_number(tname)) != NULL)
          printf("\tNumber is %d\n",tnumber);
      else puts("\tNo such Player Name");
  }
}
```

► **Program 6.1:** PLAYER.C (continued)

► UNIONS ►

A *union* in C corresponds to the *variant record* of Pascal and Modula-2. The basic idea is to create a structurelike object in which only one set of components is active at any particular moment. Unions are declared using the keyword **union** with a similar syntax to **struct**:

```
union stats {
    unsigned int rbi;          /* runs batted in */
    float era;                 /* earned-run average */
} player_stats;
/* declare player_stats a variable of type 'union stats.' */
```

The first point to realize is that the variable **player_stats** does not occupy 6 bytes (2 for **unsigned int** and 4 for **float**). Unlike a structure, a **union** allocates only enough memory for the largest component—in this case 4 bytes for the **float era**. The **union** variable **player_stats** can hold either **rbi** or **era** but not both simultaneously. If you assign, say, **player_stats.rbi = 120;**, only 2 of the 4 bytes will be occupied, so, if you tried to display the variable **player_stats.era** before some other assignment came along, you would get bizarre results. Similarly, after **player_stats.era = 4.70;**, accessing **player-_stats.rbi** would give you nonsense. The moral is to use only the active variable of the two.

There are two main reasons for using unions. First, you can save memory since two (or more) fields are effectly overlaid. If the program is such that only one component is active at any given time, the system does not have to allocate space for each individual component. The **PLAYER_REC** example hardly justifies a union on this basis, but consider

```
union results {
    int grid[2000];
    double test[500];
} lab_test;
```

If **lab_test.grid** and **lab_test.test** results are never processed at the same time, you save 4KB.

► *Unions in Action* ►

The second reason for unions is that they allow you to change the interpretation of a group of bits, rather like a supercharged type-casting operation.

A major application for this is writing portable libraries. If you have a union such as

```
union x {
     type1 a;
     type2 b;
} combo;
```

you can load **combo.a** with a value and then read it as **combo.b**. Depending on the particular types of **type1** and **type2**, you can perform many advanced tricks such as fooling functions as to the real nature of your arguments. Remember that unions are manipulated like structures, so you can use pointers to unions for argument passing, arrays of pointers, and so on. The – > operator works in the same way. Look at the following snippet:

```
          type1 rval;
          type2 lval;
   /* type1 and type2 are previously defined types */
          typedef union x {
               type1 a;
               type2 b;
          } COMBO;

          COMBO *combo_ptr;
   /* declare a 'pointer to type union x' */
          combo_ptr – >a = rval;
          lval = combo_ptr – >b;
```

Without worrying about the deep meaning of this, observe the use of – > and how the bit patterns for **rval** have been coerced into an entirely different format. The types involved will often be structures. A good example of this appears in DOS.H in the QuickC \include subdirectory:

```
/***
* dos.h - definitions for MS-DOS interface routines
*
* Copyright (c) 1985-1989, Microsoft Corporation.  All rights * reserved.
*
***/

/* word registers */
```

```
struct WORDREGS {
        unsigned int ax;
        unsigned int bx;
        unsigned int cx;
        unsigned int dx;
        unsigned int si;
        unsigned int di;
        unsigned int cflag;
        };

/* byte registers */
struct BYTEREGS {
        unsigned char al, ah;
        unsigned char bl, bh;
        unsigned char cl, ch;
        unsigned char dl, dh;
        };

/* general purpose registers union -
 * overlays the corresponding word and byte registers.
 */

union REGS {
        struct WORDREGS x;
        struct BYTEREGS h;
        };
```

(Appendix E outlines the 8088/6 register model, but to follow this next section you need some technical DOS background.)

You can declare variables of type **union REGS** and then set values in either the 16-bit registers (AX, BX, ...) or in their upper or lower halves (AH, AL, ...).

QuickC offers several functions for direct access to DOS. For example, **intdos( )** can call any of about 80 DOS "universal" functions using interrupt 33 (0x21). You set a function number in register AH, set various values in other registers, and call **intdos( )**. After the particular action is invoked, which can range from setting the time to creating a file, back comes a set of register values as a result of the call. **union REGS** allows considerable flexibility in handling the many function-call variations. The **intdos( )** prototype

```
int intdos(union REGS *inregs, union REGS *outregs);
```

indicates that you send **intdos( )** a pointer to union argument, **inregs,** and get one (**outregs**) back. The **outregs** set of values includes the carry flag **cflag** that you can test for errors. In addition, the **int** returned by **intdos( )** is the value DOS puts in register AX (usually an error number). MYTAB.C (Program 6.2) offers a brief example as a test bed for further experiments with other DOS functions. It would not normally be necessary to check the carry flag after such a simple call—I do so merely to show how **union REGS** is used.

► *Analysis of MYTAB.C* ►

DOS function 2 of interrupt 0x21 will display whatever single ASCII character is placed in DL before the call. Since **regs** is the union of two structures, you need two member operators, **regs.h.ah**, to access the **ah** component of the **h** structure. You pass a pointer to union, **&regs**, as the **inregs** argument. The **outregs** argument is passed via the same pointer—although you could have declared a separate **union REGS** variable for this. In this trivial example, once the **inregs** registers are set using the **regs.h**

```
Program 6.2

/* MYTAB.C - using DOS 0x21 interruppts */

#include <dos.h>
#include <stdio.h>

#define FAIL 0
#define OK 1

/* mytab() displays one tab on screen; returns nonzero for
   success */

int mytab()
{
    union REGS regs;

    regs.h.ah = 0x02;      /* DOS function 2 is display a char */
    regs.h.dl = '\t';      /* set DL to Horizontal Tab */
    intdos(&regs, &regs);  /* call the function */
    return(regs.x.cflag ? FAIL : OK);
}

void main()
{
    puts("It's mytab, I believe!");
    mytab() ? puts("Waiter!") : puts("Error!");
}
```

► *Program 6.2:* MYTAB.C

member of the union, you have no further use for them. Remember that **&regs** is essential for **outregs** because the function actually alters **regs** (C simulates "passing by reference" by using "passing by pointer value").

Note especially that **outregs** uses the **x** structure of the union from which we pick up **cflag**. The value returned by **mytab( )** is either **FAIL** or **OK** depending on **regs.x.cflag**:

```
return(regs.x.cflag ? FAIL : OK);
```

This is a good illustration of the economical **a ? b : c** operator. Achieving this returned value using **if (regs.x.cflag == 0) {...} else {...}** would be awkward and not in the best C traditions!

Similarly

```
mytab( ) ? puts("Waiter!") : puts("Error!");
```

relies on the fact that **mytab( )** not only invokes the function but also returns **FAIL** (0) or **OK** (1).

► Caveats About Unions ►

Unlike the variant records of Pascal and Modula-2, the unions in C do not have a **CASE tag** mechanism for distinguishing the components. In C, therefore, you must take care that any writing or reading of union variables is done using the appropriate component variants—unless, of course, you are deliberately coercing the two fields. In other words, you must remember which component is currently active. If I revamp **PLAYER_REC** to be

```
typedef struct player {
    char name[30];
    unsigned char player_number;
    union {
        unsigned int rbi;
        float era; } stats;
    BOOL active;
} PLAYER_REC;

PLAYER_REC pitcher, dh, player;
```

the intent is to store either **era** (earned-run average) for pitchers or **rbi** (runs batted in) for **dh**s (designated hitters). You've already seen structures inside unions. Here you have unions inside structures! Assuming that a given player (in the American League, presumably) never needs both statistics, the above structure simplifies the creation of a player database. C will allocate memory for the worst case, namely 4 bytes for a pitcher's **era** variant. For **dh**s, only 2 of these bytes will be occupied. You can write and read values as follows:

```
pitcher.stats.era = 5.21;
dh.stats.rbi = 56;
tot_rbi += dh.stats.rbi;
team_era = (pitcher.stats.era * inns + x)/tot_inns;
```

without danger. If you have a general variable such as **player**, however, you may have no a priori knowledge of which component is active. One obvious answer to this is to add a player-position field to **PLAYER_REC**. One way of doing this uses an enumeration type:

```
typedef enum {
    X, P, C, B1, B2, B3, SS, LF, CF, RF, DH } POSITION;
typedef struct player {
    char name[30];
    unsigned char player_number;
    POSITION player_position;
    union {
        unsigned int rbi;
        float era; } stats;
    DATE date_joined;
    BOOL active;
} PLAYER_REC;

PLAYER_REC pitcher, dh, player;
...
if (player.player_position == P) {
    /* use the era field here */
}
else if (player.player_position == DH) {
    /* use the rbi field here */
}
...
```

Before leaving unions, I should mention that they share most of the syntactical rules of structures. You can omit the tag identifier, you can use **typedef**, you can pass unions or pointers to unions as function parameters, and functions can return unions or pointers to unions.

► *GOING DOWN TO THE BIT LEVEL* ►

Since C is a systems programming language, it has features for manipulating at the bit level not usually found in high-level languages. In application programs you are primarily concerned with bytes (characters) or groups of bytes (strings, integers, floating-point numbers, pointers, or addresses). You are seldom interested in the individual bits that make up these variables.

When you tackle the problems of writing compilers, operating systems, communications packages, or device drivers (to name but a few possibilities), the need to set, clear, or test a particular bit within a field or register arises in many contexts. To give two concrete examples, a stored sequence of 0's and 1's, called a *bit map*, is often used to represent the state of a disk. Each free sector is mapped to a 0 in the bit map, while an occupied sector is signaled by a 1. The operating system must constantly monitor and update the bit map as files are created and deleted. A simpler example is the use of a byte as a status flag, where groups of bits indicate some property—for example, bit 7 ON equals "read-only"; bit 6 ON equals "busy"; bits 0–2 equal "interrupt level 0–7"; and so on. C has a set of *bitwise* operators and a means of defining *bit fields*.

► *Bitwise Operators* ►

The bitwise operators work only on integerlike objects such as **int** and **char**. Table 6.1 lists their names, symbols, and operation. What is probably the most common mistake in using these operators stems from a confusion between the bitwise operators **&** and ¦ and their *logical* operator twins **&&** and ¦¦. Also, ˜ is often confused with ! (logical negation). A few examples are worth pages of exposition. I'll use 8-bit **char** variables for simplicity—the 16- and 32-bit extensions follow naturally. Table 6.2 shows examples based on **a** and **b** with the following bit patterns:

a = 00010110 = 18 decimal
b = 10011010 = 158 decimal

► **Table 6.1:** *Bitwise operators*

Symbol	Name	Operation
&	Bitwise AND	c = a & b. Each bit in c is the bitwise AND of the corresponding bits in a and b.
¦	Bitwise OR	c = a ¦ b. Each bit in c is the bitwise OR of the corresponding bits in a and b.
^	Bitwise XOR	c = a ^ b. Each bit in c is the bitwise XOR of the corresponding bits in a and b.
~	Bitwise negate	c = ~ a. Each bit in c is the bitwise negation of the corresponding bit in a.
>>	Bitwise right shift	c >> n. The bit pattern in c is shifted to the right by n places.
<<	Bitwise left shift	c << n. The bit pattern in c is shifted to the left by n places.

► **Table 6.2:** *Illustrations of bitwise operations*

	a & b = 00010010	
	a ¦ b = 10011110	
	a ^ b = 10001100	
	~ a = 11101001	
	~ b = 01100101	
Left shift	a << 1 = 00101100	(1 overspill discarded on left)
	a << 2 = 01011000	
	a << 3 = 10110000	
	a << 4 = 01100000	(0 pushed in at right)
Right shift	a >> 1 = 00001011	
	a >> 2 = 00000101	(1 overspill discarded on right)
	a >> 3 = 00000010	
If b is unsigned	b >> 1 = 01001101	(0 pushed in at left)
If b is signed	b >> 1 = 11001101	(sign bit = 1 pushed in at left)

► *a = 00010110, b = 10011010*

The rules for each bit-by-bit composition are shown in Table 6.3.

► **Table 6.3:** *Rules for bit-by-bit composition*

AND (&)	0 & 0 = 0; 1 & 0 = 0; 0 & 1 = 0; 1 & 1 = 1; (i.e., both must be 1 to give 1)
OR (¦)	0 ¦ 0 = 0; 1 ¦ 0 = 1; 0 ¦ 1 = 1; 1 ¦ 1 = 1; (i.e., either or both must be 1 to give 1)
XOR (^)	0 ^ 0 = 0; 1 ^ 1 = 0; 1 ^ 0 = 1; 0 ^ 1 = 1; (i.e., either but not both must be 1 to give 1, hence the name eXclusive OR)
NEGATE (˜)	˜0 = 1; ˜1 = 0 (i.e., reverse or invert each bit)

Right shifts vary with signed and unsigned variables. To maintain the correct sign when shifting signed values, the sign bit is pushed in from the left as the bits are shifted right. In all cases, any bits that spill out from either end during a shift are discarded and lost.

Now look at **a** and **b** as decimal values (18 and 158, respectively) rather than as bit patterns. The logical, non-bitwise operators give the following results:

(a && b) is equivalent to 1 (true) since **a** is true (nonzero) AND **b** is true (nonzero).

(a ¦¦ b) is also 1 (true) while !a = !b = 0 (false).

The logical parallel to the bitwise XOR is **!=** , since **(a != b)** evaluates to 1 if either **a** is zero and **b** is nonzero or **a** is nonzero and **b** is zero but evaluates to 0 if both **a** and **b** are zero or if both are nonzero.

► *Bitwise Applications* ►

The bitwise operators are often used to clear, set, or invert individual bits within a flag or bit map. The idea here is to create a certain constant bit pattern called a *mask* and then perform operations such as **(a = a & mask)**, **(a = a ¦ mask)**, or **(a = a ^ mask)** in order to update the bit pattern in **a**.

These manipulations are so commonplace that the shorthand **op =** , as you saw with **+ =** , is available:

a &= mask; a |= mask; a ^ = mask;

The choice of masks requires some practice, but once you are familiar with the following rules, things are quite logical:

1. Use **&** with mask-bit = 0 to clear a bit to 0.

2. Use **&** with mask-bit = 1 to leave a bit unchanged.

3. Use ¦ with mask-bit = 1 to set a bit to 1.

4. Use ¦ with mask-bit = 0 to leave a bit unchanged.

5. Use ^ with mask-bit = 1 to invert a bit.

6. Use ^ with mask-bit = 0 to leave a bit unchanged.

Suppose **char status** has the bit flags defined as shown in Table 6.4. To create legible masks, you can start with some **#define**s:

```
#define OPEN_CLOSED     1
#define READ_WRITE      (1 << 1)
#define RAND_SEQ        (1 << 2)
#define PRIV_PUB        (1 << 3)
#define FLOP_HARD       (1 << 7)
/* these give you a 1 in each bit position.
    You can build masks from them as follows */

    status |= (RAND_SEQ ¦ PRIV_PUB);
/* set bits 2 and 3, leaving the others unchanged */
    status & = (~OPEN_CLOSED);
/* clear bit-0, leaving others unchanged */
    status ^= (FLOP_HARD ¦ OPEN_CLOSED);
/* reverse bits 0 and 7, leaving others unchanged */
    if (status & OPEN_CLOSED)    { /* do something if bit-0 set */ }
}
```

► *Shifts in Action* ►

The shifts offer a faster alternative to multiplication and division by powers of 2. For example, a << 2 is equivalent to a * 4, while a >> 3 gives the same

► **Table 6.4:** *Sample status byte*

Bit Number	Meaning
0	0 = file closed; 1 = file open
1	0 = read-only; 1 = read/write
2	0 = random; 1 = sequential
3	0 = private; 1 = public
4	reserved
5	reserved
6	reserved
7	0 = floppy; 1 = hard disk

result as **a/8**. The same care over truncation and overflow is needed, and you should note that >> and << have lower precedence (category 5) than + and − (category 4). Shifts associate from left to right, so you sometimes find strange expressions like

```
int i;
i << 4 >> 8;
```

used to extract the middle 8 bits from a 16-bit integer. Note also that **a = a << 2** can be shortened to **a << = 2**, and so on.

► *BIT FIELDS* ►

The bit-field facility allows you to name structure components as individual groups of bits within a 16-bit field (maximum). As with the status byte listed above, bit fields allow you to pack a lot of information in a small space. The syntax is as follows:

```
struct status {
    unsigned open        :1;    /* width of bit field */
    unsigned read        :2;
    unsigned random      :1;
```

```
            int permit              :4;    /* int is allowed */
            unsigned                :3;    /* unused – so no name */
            unsigned pointer        :5;
         } freg, greg, *reg_ptr;
```

The above 16-bit structure allocates six groups of bits and names five of them. Apart from the bit width specifier (**:n**) the usual rules for structure declaration apply. There are a few minor quirks, as you'll see soon. The member selection operators are used to access structure components.

The component **freg.open** would occupy bit 0, the first, low-memory bit of the structure. The **reg_ptr –>read** component would be 2 bits in bit positions 1–2, and so on. The **:n;** after each declaration indicates the width of that field. A zero bit width (**:0**) is legal—it tells C to align the next field on an even address (padding, if necessary). Identifiers are optional, as shown in the fifth, unused field above.

Although bit fields can occupy odd or even bit positions within a structure, they cannot straddle integer boundaries. You can form arrays of structures containing bit fields, but arrays of bit-field variables are not allowed. It is also illegal to form the address of a bit-field variable with **&** since there is no guarantee that it has a byte address.

Only **signed** and **unsigned int**s are allowed, but note carefully that the actual valid range of each identifier is dictated by its bit width. One consequence of this is that a bit field of width 1 must be declared as **unsigned** since it can never hold a negative value! When you extract and manipulate a bit-field component, it will be treated as declared (**signed** or **unsigned int**) in the obvious way. For example, a bit field of width 2 holding the binary value 11 would be taken as 3 if **unsigned** but as – 1 if **signed**. The sign bit is always taken as the leftmost bit of the field. Bizarre results can occur if you overflow the real bit-field range:

```
         greg.read = 3;
         greg.read *= 2;
   /* the 2-bit field now holds 4 (binary 10), not 6 */
```

Bit fields are commonly used to match the peculiar storage layouts of hardware devices—a communications interface, for instance, may provide signals and data via groups of bits within a 16-bit register. With memory-mapped I/O, such registers are actual memory locations. Rather than use bitwise operators to extract these values, bit fields can be used for elegance and legibility.

Portability of such code may be a problem, though, mainly because different systems have different conventions with respect to how bytes are stored within words in memory. The "low-byte/low-address" scheme, favored by DEC and National Semiconductor, contrasts with the "high-byte/low-address" convention of Motorola. (The fierce proponents of each approach have been labeled "little endians" and "big endians" in honor of Swift's *Gulliver's Travels*.) The following program by Samuel P. Harbison and Guy L. Steele, Jr., in *C: A Reference Manual* (Englewood Cliffs, New Jersey: Prentice-Hall, 1987) is worth knowing if you plan to port your code to alien machines. It also provides an excellent insight into unions.

```c
#include <stdio.h>

union { long Long; char Char[sizeof(long)]; } u;
/* u can be viewed as a long or as a sequence of byte */

int main( )
{
    u.Long = 1;                    /* low-order byte of long set to 1 */
    if (u.Char[0] == 1)            /* check which char has the 1 */
        puts("Addressing is right – to – left (little – endian)");
    else if (u.Char[sizeof(long) – 1]) == 1)
        puts("Addressing is left – to – right (big – endian)");
    else puts("Addressing is strange");
    return (0);
}
```

The byte order will affect how bit fields exceeding 8 bits are organized. Another machine-dependent factor can be the maximum bit fields allowed—this is normally dictated by the word size of the CPU.

Finally, it is perfectly legal to mix bit fields with normal variables within a structure or union. If file size was a critical factor, for example, you could pack three fields into one byte of the **PLAYER_REC** structure:

```c
typedef struct player {
    char name[29];
    unsigned char player_number;
    unsigned position      :4;   /* 16 positions 0-15 */
    unsigned doctor        :3;   /* 8 doctor codes 0-7 */
    unsigned active        :1;   /* 0 = inactive 1 = active */
    union {
```

```
        unsigned int rbi;
        float era; } stats;
    DATE date_joined;
} PLAYER_REC;
```

► *SUMMARY OF CHAPTER 6* ►

◄► A structure is a record containing a list of arbitrary variables. The declaration syntax is

```
struct [tag] {
    type1 var1;
    type2 var2;
    ...
    typen varn;
} [struct_var1, struct_var2,...];
```

This allows you to declare structure variables immediately as above or later with

```
struct tag struct_var3, struct_var4,...;
```

if a tag has been named.

◄► Components are referenced as **struct_var.member_var**. If **struct_ptr** is a pointer to a structure, the components can be referenced as

```
(*struct_ptr).member_var)
```

or more economically as

```
struct_ptr ->member_var
```

◄► Structures of the same type can be assigned:

```
struct_var1 = struct_var2;
```

This transfers all components, including any arrays within the structure.

◄► Structures cannot contain themselves as a member, but they can contain nested structures and pointers to themselves. This opens the door to interlinked data structures of all kinds.

```
struct node {
    type1 data;
    struct facts {
        type2 data2;
        type3 data3;
    }
    struct node *next;
    struct node *previous;
} list1, list2,...;

struct tree {
    type1 data;
    struct tree *left;
    struct tree *right;
} tree1, *tree_ptr1,...;
```

◄► C allows certain forward references to "pointers to structures" before the structure has been declared:

```
        struct s1 { type1 data1; struct s2 *s2_ptr;} struct_s1;
/* forward reference to (struct2 *) - struct2 not yet declared */
        struct s2 { type2 data2; struct s1 *s1_ptr;} struct_s2;
```

◄► The size of a structure can depend on the word- or byte-alignment option chosen. Dynamic memory for structures can be allocated using struct_ptr = (struct *)malloc(sizeof(struct)).

◄► Unions are a special form of structure. (They are similar to the variant records of Pascal.) The two components of a union "share" the same memory allocation, but only one of them can be accessed at any moment. Unions are declared and accessed using the same syntax as for structures:

```
union [tag] {
    type1 member_var1;
    type1 member_var2;
} [union_var1, union_var2, *union_ptr1,...];

union tag another_one;          /* if tag available */
```

```
union_var1.member_var1 = x;
union_var2.member_var2 = union_var1.member_var1;
union_ptr_>member_var1 = y;
```

sizeof(union tag) is the maximum of **sizeof(type1)** and **sizeof(type2)**. Unions can be nested in structures and vice versa.

◄► Bitwise operators perform bit-by-bit, Boolean operations on integer types. The bitwise AND (**&**) must not be confused with the logical AND (**&&**). Likewise, bitwise OR (¦) is not the same as logical OR (¦¦). The bitwise XOR does not have a logical ^ sibling (you use **!=** for logical XOR). The two shift operators, << and >>, can be used to multiply, divide, and extract bit patterns.

◄► Bit fields are special structure components that allow you to have **int** variables of specified bit width (0–16). They enable you to access device-dependent bit positions within bytes or words; they can also reduce record sizes by using bits as flags or small numeric fields.

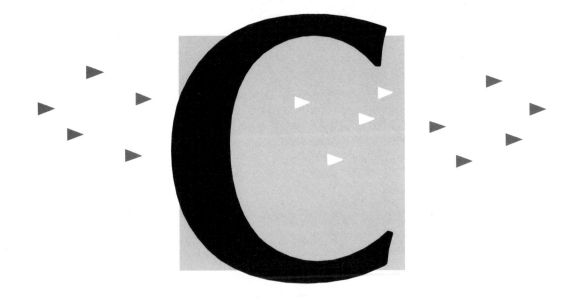

STORAGE CLASSES:
STRATEGIES FOR DATA INTEGRITY

CHAPTER 7

I have touched on the subject of storage classes several times, hinting that they govern the accessibility and life span of the objects you declare and define in C. In this short chapter, I will knit together the various strands of this important subject and introduce some new storage classes. I will then analyze PLAYER.C (from Chapter 6), in which storage classes play a leading role.

Before attempting to establish a formal terminology and syntax, I will show you some of the storage classes in action. Be aware of the fact that prior to ANSI C there were several ambiguities in this area, and different implementors still use different interpretations of K&R. The use of terms such as *scope*, *external*, and *extent* is also inconsistent in the C literature. I plan to converge to the truth by a series of approximations!

Every variable and function in C has an associated type and storage class. You have already seen how the type of an object establishes its memory requirements and its range of legal operations. The storage class determines other essential properties of the object such as *scope* (where is its declaration active?), *visibility*, (from which parts of the program is it accessible?), and *extent* (when is it created, initialized, and destroyed?). In addition, the storage class can indicate whether selected integral variables should be stored in registers (if any are available) to improve execution speed. As you'll see, these properties are not exclusive—they overlap in various ways.

► *STORAGE CLASS SPECIFIERS* ►

A single storage class specifier can be used when you declare or define an object in order to establish (or request) certain storage class properties for that object. In most cases these properties have defaults that depend on whether the object is a variable or function and on where the declaration or definition is made. Explicit storage class specifiers are relatively rare, but don't be fooled! Storage classes, whether specified up front or not, are always assigned and always play a vital role in how your program behaves.

For those important occasions when you do need to alter the defaults, the storage class specifier goes in front of the data-type specifier and modifier(s), if any. Here are some typical declarations/definitions that use the four basic storage class specifiers, **auto**, **static**, **extern**, and **register**. The comments will be expanded as I proceed.

```
    {
    auto long sum = 3;
    ...
    }
/* sum is defined long int, storage class automatic.
   sum will be created and reinitialized each time this
   block is executed.  sum disappears outside the block.
   The specifier auto is the default and can be omitted
   in this context */

    ...
    static char ch = '\0';
/* ch is defined/initialized as a char with static extent.
   ch is 'private' to a block, function, or file */

    ...
    static int func(void);
/* func( ) declared: it returns an int and will be defined
   as static later in this file –– see below */

    ...
    static int func(void)
    { /* function body */ }
/* func( ) defined, but will not be exported to linker.
   func( ) is therefore 'private' to this file */

    ...
    extern int count;
/* count is declared int, storage class external.
   No storage allocated –– count will be
   defined in another file */

    ...
    extern void func2(double d);
/* func2( ) is declared external; its returned value is discarded;
   its name will be passed to the linker.  func2( ) is
   accessible from other files */

/* NOTE: extern is always assumed with function declarations
   in the absence of the static specifier */

    ...
    {
    register unsigned i;
    ...
    }
```

```
/* i is unsigned int; same as auto except that if possible
   i will be stored in a register rather than RAM */
   ...
```

(This selection should be considered as isolated examples rather than as a contiguous sequence you might expect to find in a legal program. It is intended to illustrate the variety of combinations available.)

Technically speaking, the keyword **typedef** is also a storage class specifier, but I will confine my discussion to the four classes listed above for the time being.

The word *default* in relation to storage classes must be treated with caution. With type specifiers it makes no difference whether you write **unsigned** or **unsigned int** since **int** is the true default. But you'll meet situations in which a variable "defaults" to external because of the placement of its declaration, and yet the apparently innocent, superfluous use of the **extern** specifier materially affects the situation! In other words, there are occasions when you must omit the default storage specifier. I'll point out these quirks as we continue.

To appreciate the differences between the four storage classes, you need to carefully distinguish the related concepts of scope, visibility, and extent.

► *SCOPE* ►

The declaration of an identifier is *active* over a certain region of the source code text, known as its scope. With one major and two minor exceptions, an identifier cannot be legally referenced outside its scope. These exceptions allow what are known as *forward references*.

The two minor anomalies are

1. **goto label** is valid before **label:** is encountered.

2. **struct**, **union**, and **enum** tags can be forward-referenced under some circumstances (see Chapter 6).

The major exception is that the C compiler will supply the *implicit declaration* **int func( );** if you call **func( )** before its explicit declaration. The use of prototype declarations, encouraged under ANSI C and QuickC, can eliminate this potentially dangerous situation.

So, in the majority of cases, the scope starts with the declaration. Where the scope ends depends on where the declaration is made in relation to the source text—i.e., outside or inside a function definition.

► *Scope of Top-Level Declarations* ►

Declarations made at the head of a program file, before any of the function definitions, are called *top-level* declarations. The scope of these is from the point of declaration until the end of the source file. This is often called *global* scope (but there are some caveats about this description that I'll explain later).

► *Scope of Declarations Within Functions* ►

Declarations made within a function definition fall into two categories. They can occur as *formal parameter declarations*, in which case their scope is from the point of declaration to the end of the function definition, or they can occur at the start (or head) of any block within a function definition. A *head-of-block* declaration has a scope from the point of declaration to the end of that block.

Both formal parameters and head-of-block variables are said to have *local* scope. The scope of a formal parameter is local to the function, while the scope of a head-of-block variable is local to its block. (Be careful not to misuse the term *local*—it has different meanings when applied to scope and extent. You will see later that a variable with local scope need not have local extent. Unless the context is absolutely clear, avoid statements such as "**x** is local." The correct usage is, "**x** has local scope," or, "**x** has local extent.")

Program 7.1 is a generic C source file to illustrate how scope is affected by the location of the declaration.

Note the absence of storage class specifiers! In GENERIC.C the scope has been determined completely by the placement of the declarations. The variables **global_int** and **global_ch_ptr** can be used freely within **main( )** and any of the functions.

```
/* GENERIC.C */

/* top--level ---- outside any function definitions */

/*-------------------------------------------*/
/* include header files */
/*-------------------------------------------*/

#include <any.h>
/* any declarations pulled in here are top--level with scope
   extending to the end of the file GENERIC.C */

/*----------------*/
/* macros */
/*----------------*/

#define X Y
/* any macro names here have scope until end of file or until an
   #undef undefines them */

/* #includes and #defines can be placed anywhere, but they are
   usually safer as shown to give maximum scoping */

/*-----------------------------------------------------*/
/* func2 prototype declaration */
/*-----------------------------------------------------*/
    void func2(int a, char *b);    /* note the ; for a func
                                      declaration */

/* vars a and b are not formally declared here -- they provide a
   'template' so that calls to func2() made before its definition
   can be checked for valid arg types and numbers */

/* you are still at top--level! */

    int global_int;       /* two top--level declarations */
    char *global_ch_ptr;  /* scope is the whole source file */

/*---------------------------------------*/
/* func1() definition */
/*---------------------------------------*/

int func1(a,b,c)              /* no ; after a func definition */
/* now inside func1() definition */
/* formal parameters classic style declarations */
    int a,b,c;
/* scope of a,b,c is local ---- from here until the end of the
   function definition */
/* a and b have no connection with the prototype args of
   func2() */
{
/* head--of--block A */
    int local_int_A;         /* scope is block A */
    ...
    {
    /* head--of--inner--block B */
    int local_int_B;       /* scope is block B */
    ...
/* scopes of local_int_A and local_int_B overlap here */
    ...
    } /* end block B */
    ...
} /* end block A, also end func1() definition
```

► **Program 7.1:** *GENERIC.C*

```
/*-----------------------------------end of func1() definition----------------------
-----------*/

/*------------------------------------*/
/* main() starts here */
/*------------------------------------*/

void main (void)
{
/* head--of--block */
     int local_int_main;      /* 2 local--scope vars */
     char *local_ch_ptr_main; /* scope is main() */
     ...
     func2(local_int_main, local_ch_ptr_main); /* call func2() */
     func2(global_var, global_ch_ptr);         /* call func2() */
/* both calls valid, since actual args are assignment compatible with those of the
   prototype; also, the actual args are used within scope */
     ...
     int_local_main = func3(local_int_main);
/* call to an undeclared function, func3()!
   The compiler will make an implicit declaration:
   extern int func(); hoping that func3 will be defined eventually ---- see note on
   implicit declarations above.
   If func3() is not defined elsewhere, a link--time error occurs.  If func3() is
   defined as returning a non--int results may be bizarre */
     ...
}
/*--------------------------------------end of main()--------------------------
-----------------*/

/*-------------------------------------*/
/* func2()  definition */
/*-------------------------------------*/

void func2(int a, char *b) /* modern style formal parameter declaration */
/* scope of a and b is whole of func2() body ---- unrelated to earlier a's and b's */
{
...
/* global_int and global_ch_ptr could be used here, as well as a
and b */
...
}
/*-----------------------------end of func2() definition-----------------------
*/

/*********************/
/* end of source file */
/*********************/
```

▶ **Program 7.1:** *GENERIC.C (continued)*

▶ *VISIBILITY* ▶

Normally an identifier is *visible* throughout its scope—that is, references to that identifier will be related by the compiler to the original declaration in order to determine data type and current value. The annoying exceptions occur when the same name is legally used to declare a new identifier within the scope of the original identifier. If duplicate identifier names were ruthlessly banned, scope and visibility would coincide!

Visibility therefore relates to the region of a source text in which an identifier reference refers to the object as originally declared or defined. An identifier is never visible outside its scope, but it may become invisible during its scope!

As you read through a source text, you will see identifiers coming in and out of scope according to the scoping rules outlined above. If all the identifiers are uniquely named, then scope and visibility coincide throughout. When identifier names in the same *name space* are duplicated, however, one declaration may *hide* a previously declared identifier.

ANSI C specifies five name spaces: macros, labels, tags (for **struct**, **union**, and **enum**), components (of **struct** and **union**), and all others (variables, functions, **typedef** names, and **enum** constants). Name spaces are also called *overloading classes*. C keeps a separate table of names for each of these, so the five objects called **same** in the following bizarre snippet are all distinct and can share the same scope level without clashing:

```
#define same ==                 /* macro name */
    if ((x) same (y)) {...}
...
#undef same
...
int same;                       /* variable name */
struct same {                   /* tag */
    int same;                   /* component */
} Same;                         /* 'same' here would be illegal */
same:                           /* label */
Same.same = same;               /* ! */
```

Pre-ANSI C compilers may have different name spaces, so for maximum portability (and common sense) you should avoid excessive duplications regardless of class.

An illegal duplication occurs if you try to redeclare an identifier belonging to the same name space while still at the same scope level as the original identifier. Replacing **Same** with **same** in the previous snippet would result in an error since the **int** variable **same** is still in scope and **struct** variables share the same name space as other variables.

Once you move into a distinct scoping level, though, the same identifier can be legally redeclared. The original identifier is hidden until the new declaration's scope ends. Rather than attempting a rigorous definition of scope levels, I offer an example that should clarify the situation:

```
            int  i = 9;              /* top – level */
main( )
{
            float i;
            char ch;
            i = 3.141;               /* i is a float throughout main( ) */
            ...                      /* int i is now hidden but still in
                                         scope with value 9 */

}

void func1(void)
{
            i = 3;                   /* i reverts to int */
            ...                      /* float i is out – of – scope and
                                         therefore invisible */
            ch = 'A';                /* ILLEGAL reference! ch not visible */
}

void func2(void)
{
            char i;                  /* i is a char throughout func2( ) */
            ...                      /* int i is hidden again but still in
                                         scope with value 3 */
}
/* char i is now out – of – scope and therefore inaccessible */
/* More on this when extent of variables is dicussed */
/* i reverts to int here if any further references */
```

Since QuickC supports identifiers that comprise as many as 31 characters (allowing more choices than there are atoms in the solar system), you may wonder why programmers cannot avoid such confusing duplications. I wonder too. It may be that certain small "temporary" identifiers such as i, **sum**, and **count** are irresistible. It is also the case that individual functions are often developed in isolation, so hiding does serve as a useful protection against unplanned duplications.

The key point is that a reference to an identifier must be interpreted as applying to the currently visible declaration.

► EXTENT ►

The extent of an object refers to the period of time during which the object is allocated storage. Extent is therefore a run-time property. As with scope, though, your source code controls extent by means of storage classes and the placement of declarations and definitions. Extent applies only to variables and functions since other objects, like data types and **typedef** names, are not run-time entities.

There are three classes of extent:

1. *Static* extent applies to those objects that are allocated fixed memory locations when the program executes and retain those allocations until the program ends. All functions have static extent, as do variables declared at the top level. Variables declared elsewhere are not normally of static extent, but some can be made so with the **static** and **extern** storage class specifiers. A static-extent variable is initialized only when it is first created. If no explicit initializer accompanies its declaration/definition, a static-extent variable is cleared to zero.

    The two key properties of static-extent variables are that they endure throughout the program and they retain their values between function calls regardless of their scope and visibility. (In addition to this correlation between **static** and the property of "permanence," you'll meet in C a less obvious connotation, namely "private." This will be clarified when I explain the **static** storage class.)

2. *Local* or *automatic* extent applies only to variables, never to functions. Local-extent variables are allocated memory (and given values, if initialized) as their local function or block is executed. At the end of this execution, local-extent variables are destroyed, their memory is deallocated, and their values are lost. If the function or block is reexecuted, local-extent variables are automatically recreated at the point of declaration and any initializers are reapplied. This explains the term *automatic extent*. In the absence of explicit initializers, automatic variables will contain garbage when created. Contrast this with static-extent variables, which are always initialized either to zero or to your specific instructions.

    Formal parameters are always of local extent, but other variables can have either static or local extent depending on the declaration format and placement. The general rule is that top-level variables have static extent and head-of-block variables have local extent. You can vary these defaults only by using storage class specifiers.

3. *Dynamic* extent applies only to temporary, user-generated objects allocated with **malloc( )** (or a similar dynamic memory-allocation library function) and deallocated using **free( )**. The dynamic classification is not strictly a part of C's scoping or extent rules. Keep in mind that although **malloc**ed objects are created and destroyed at arbitrary moments in your program, the pointers you use to access them are represented by variables subject to the scoping and extent rules under discussion.

► *Extent and the Memory Map* ►

From a RAM point of view, it is useful to picture three areas of user memory defined at run time: the *text* or *code* area holding the machine instructions, the *data* area storing all the static objects, and the *dynamic* area holding the automatic and dynamic variables.

The layout of the text and data areas depends on the memory model. The small model limits you to two 64KB segments, one for text and one for static data. With the larger memory models, the text and data areas may each occupy several distinct 64KB segments.

The dynamic area contains both the stack and the heap. The stack is a constantly changing LIFO (last in, first out) data structure in which automatic variables (including any local parameters being passed to functions) are temporarily created, accessed, and discarded. The heap is the area from which **malloc( )** grabs its memory allocations. Its size will vary with memory model, the amount of user RAM, and the size of your program and data areas.

You should now have a feel for scope, visibility, and extent. Their properties are as summarized in Table 7.1.

► *SCOPE AND EXTENT RELATIONSHIPS* ►

Now I come to the tricky parts: how do these properties affect programming strategies, and how do you establish each property for any given object in a C program?

► **Table 7.1:** *Scope, visibility, and extent*

Declaration Point	Scope/Visibility* (from declaration to end of...)	Extent
Outside Function (top-level)	File	Static
Inside Function		
Formal parameter	Function	Local
Head-of-block	Block	Local or Static**

> ► ** Scope equals visibility unless hidden by duplicate name.*
> *** All functions have static extent. Extent of variables depends on storage class specifier.*

Though extent and scope are closely related, they are distinct properties. C allows you to have objects with static extent that are not accessible from all parts of the program. In other words, although scope cannot "exceed" extent (there's nothing there to access), extent can "exceed" scope (it's there but you can't access it). To explain the implications of this, I need to discuss how C programs are constructed from several files.

► *Scope and Separately Compilable Files* ►

I mentioned earlier that top-level and inside-function scopes are often called *global* and *local* scopes, respectively. As in Pascal, top-level declarations extend to the end of the file, while the inside-function declarations are confined to their local function or block.

In C, however, the word *global* has somewhat different connotations than in Pascal. As in Pascal, a global C identifier is certainly "available" to all following sections of its file, but, unlike standard Pascal, a C program may consist of several separately compilable files (often referred to as modules). Indeed, unless you want to forgo the assistance of the C library functions, your final programs will definitely contain code pulled in from many files.

Apart from the fact that you supply a unique file holding the function **main( )**, all the component files are technically equal—there is no built-in priority scheme for modules.

main( ) always starts the ball rolling. It can process any visible data and call any accessible function. A called function in turn can process its own visible data and call any of its accessible functions. The process continues until the final statement, which is usually back in **main( )**, is reached.

Four types of data are available to a function: local parameters (copies of actual arguments passed to the function); local "working" variables declared within the function; dynamic variables created with **malloc( )**; and, finally, any visible global variables. The latter may be top-level-declared/defined objects global to a particular file, or they may be set up to be global to several files. Some authors use the term *semiglobal* for identifiers limited to a particular file, reserving *global* for identifiers that can straddle several files.

How do scope and extent fit into this grand plan? The answer lies with the interaction between storage classes and the linking process.

► *The Role of the Linker* ►

The linker combines the various .OBJ files (some of which may be embedded in standard or user-supplied libraries) to produce the final executable .EXE file.

You can see immediately that this complicates the simple division of identifiers into local and global scopes. Some objects may be global for a particular file, and others may need to be accessed from several files. You may also wish to hide the details of a data structure but allow its manipulation via certain functions. (This is known as *data abstraction* and has the further merit that the data can be restructured without the user being bothered.) Conversely, selected functions within the same module may need to be hidden while some variables are freely exported. (These problems do not arise with standard Pascals, which do not support separate compilability, but Modula-2 and Ada programmers will recognize the situation.)

For these and other reasons, C lets you vary the accessibility of objects with the **extern** and **static** storage class specifiers. During separate compilations you'll want to suspend the **identifier unknown** message by explicitly or implicitly tagging certain objects as *external*, thereby exporting their names to the linker.

► *EXTERNAL IDENTIFIERS* ►

C uses the physical file as a basic mechanism to establish the scoping of objects, but objects within any file can be made external (explicitly or by default). Now automatic variables come and go with no fixed abode, so we certainly exclude these from being external. Only static-extent objects can be sensibly passed to the linker, thereby allowing other files to access them.

Remember that all functions have static extent (you cannot alter this property), so they are obvious candidates for exporting to the linker. In fact, unless you take special action, a function defaults to external, meaning that functions in any file are usually callable from any file linked to it. As you'll see, you can select which static-extent identifiers, functions, or variables, are exported, but there are complications if the same object is declared in several files.

Summing up, whatever scope an object may enjoy within its own file, it can only be referenced by other files if it has static extent and if its identifier is known to the linker. The function of the **extern** storage class specifier (whether explicit or implied) is to give a variable static extent and to export its identifier to the linker. By contrast, the **static** specifier (which must always be stated explicitly) conveys static extent but witholds the identifier from the linker, thereby reducing its accessibility to a particular file, function, or block (depending on the scope). This is the "private" connotation of **static** that I mentioned earlier.

(This terminology, already suffering from two connotations for the word *static*, has become further confused because some books refer to top-level **static** declarations as *external* or *external static* [meaning that they are external to the functions in a file], as opposed to *internal static* [which would mean **static** declarations made at head-of-block within a function]. I will reserve the designation *external* for those **extern**ed objects available to several files.)

The same external object can be declared (no storage allocated) in several files but must be defined (storage allocated) in only one of the .OBJ files presented to the linker. The linker first has to check for consistency among these independent declarations of the object and its unique definition and then make sure that all references in the component .OBJ files are made to the defined object (the "real" one—i.e., the one with memory allocated at a known run-time location).

Even with our simple HELLO.C, these machinations have been involved behind the scenes! The **#include** directive in HELLO.C brought into your source code various function and variable declarations. The compiler passed the external function name **printf** to HELLO.OBJ, and the linker checked it against the appropriate precompiled definition in one of the .LIB collections of .OBJ files.

► *Referencing and Defining Declarations* ►

It will become increasingly important to keep in mind the fundamental difference between *referencing declarations* and *defining declarations* of identifiers.

With functions it is easy to spot the difference. Function definitions have bodies containing the necessary code, whereas function declarations have no bodies. Functions can be declared at the top level or at head-of-block within another function's definition, but it is illegal to define a function within a function definition. (Pascal users may consider this a strange limitation since Pascal allows the nesting of procedure definitions.) Remember, though, that a function can be called recursively from within its own defining body. This is a direct result of the scoping rules stated earlier—the scope of a function stretches from its definition or declaration point to the end of its containing file.

► *EXTERNAL FUNCTIONS* ►

All C functions are external by default no matter where they are declared or defined. The storage class specifier **extern** is assumed unless you use **static**, which is the only other legal specifier for a function. When you declare an external function, you are telling the compiler/linker that somewhere, in this file or in another to be linked, this external function will be defined just once. A function is made external simply by omitting the storage class specifier. You are allowed to add a redundant **extern** to a declaration or definition of an external function.

By passing all the external function names (including possible duplicate declarations) to the linker, you ensure that all calls to **func( )** will be associated with the unique definition of **func( )**. This simply means that the externally defined **func( )** becomes freely accessible by linking its .OBJ file with your own .OBJ files. By *accessible*, of course, I mean callable—the source code for **func( )** may well be under lock and key beyond your reach, and you may just have the minimum written explanation of what the function does and how to call it.

► *STATIC FUNCTIONS* ►

What the **static** specifier does with functions is to limit this accessibility by withholding the function name from the linker. If you create the file MYPROG.C as follows:

```
/* MYPROG.C */
...
static int secret(char ch)              /* function defined as static */
/* ch is local scope, local extent */
{ /* body of secret( ) */
    int i = 0;
    ...
    return i;
}

int public(char ch)                     /* function defined as external */
/* extern storage class specifier by default */
/* ch is local scope, local extent */
{ /* body of public( ) */
    ...
    return 2*secret(char ch);
/* Legal call to secret( ) since scope of secret( ) is from definition point
   to end of MYPROG.C */
}
/* end of file MYPROG.C */
```

you can compile it to MYPROG.OBJ and let other programmers link it to their .OBJ files. You offer them MYPROG.H, which contains the prototype declaration **int public(char ch);** with some comments on how to call it and what it does. The **secret( )** function cannot be called directly by other users even if they know of its existence. When they write THEIRPRG.C, compile it to THEIRPRG.OBJ, and then link it with MYPROG.OBJ to get THEIRPRG.EXE, any attempted calls on **secret( )** other than the ones made within MYPROG.OBJ would result in a link-time error. The **static** specifier has prevented the export of the name **secret** to the linker. The function **public( )** was declared as external (by default) in MYPROG.H and defined as external in MYPROG.C with matching arguments and returned values. The compilation of THEIRPRG.C would "warn" the linker that an externally defined function called **public( )** is expected somewhere, and this expectation would be eventually fulfilled.

The following snippet recaps the syntax of **extern** and **static** with function declarations and definitions:

```
[extern] [type] func1([arglist]);
/* the declared function is known to the linker – it will be
    defined as external elsewhere */

/* WARNING: you cannot omit both extern and type */
/* [type] will default to int and storage class will default to
    extern – BUT you cannot omit BOTH lest the resulting
    declaration looks like the func1 call: func1( ); ! */

static [type] func2([arglist]);
/* the declared function will be defined later in this file with
    storage class static and matching type and arglist */

[extern] [type] func1([arglist])
            [parameter declarations]
{ function_body
  [return var;]
}
/* define an external function – NO storage class specifier
    implies extern; other files can reference this function */

/* [type] defaults to int */
/* NOTE: extern and type can BOTH be omitted in a definition –
    there is no possible confusion with a call to func1( ); */

static [type] func2([arglist])
            [parameter declarations]
{ function_body
    [return var;]
}
/* define a static function – explicit storage class specifier
    is required; this function can be referenced within current
    file only – name not exported to linker */
/* [type] defaults to int safely, because the storage class is explicit. */
```

The first example above carries a warning. Consider the following variants:

```
/* classical declarations */
    extern int myfunc( );
    extern myfunc( );          /* [type] defaults to int OK */
    int myfunc( );             /* defaults to extern OK */

    myfunc( );                 /* NOT a declaration but a CALL */
```

In other words, you cannot default both the storage class and the returned type. I recommend that you always supply both storage class and type to provide increased legibility and peace of mind.

As I mentioned earlier, the keyword **static** is often a source of confusion. All defined functions, whether **extern** or **static**, have static extent. Both **func1( )** and **func2( )** (above) are assigned storage throughout the run life of the linked program, and the defining names **func1** and **func2** are pointer constants that hold the addresses of their respective implementation codes. Their scopes differ as stated, however. **func2( )** can only be called from within its own file, and **func1( )** can be called from any file that declares **func1( )** consistently and is linked to the defining file.

► *EXTERNAL VARIABLES* ►

As with functions, you can control whether variable identifiers names are passed to the linker or not. The basic principle is the same: If a variable is to be accessible from other files, it must have static extent. It must also be declared external in each client file and defined as external somewhere just once. Unlike functions, variables only default to external when declared/ defined at the top level, outside the functions. Elsewhere, the explicit specifier **extern** is needed with the declaration to request linkage with the variable's definition in some other file.

The definition of the external variable is distinguished from any of its declarations by the *absence* of the specifier **extern**! Also, to avoid chaos, only the defining declaration can have an optional initializer attached. When you think about it, initialization only makes sense for a static-extent variable at the time it is created—that is, at run time when the definition is encountered. Keep in mind that static-extent variables are initialized only once, either to zero in the absence of an explicit initializer or to the constants of the evaluated initializer.

Before ANSI C clarified the distinction between external-variable referencing declarations (no storage allocated, no initializer) and defining declarations (storage allocated, optional initializer), different compilers used different strategies. Fortunately, QuickC follows the ANSI C proposal that external variables be declared and defined as follows:

```
/* start of file A */
    ...
    extern int x;                   /* this is a referencing declaration */
/* compiler knows that x is an external int to be defined
    elsewhere. No memory yet, so no initializer */
/* location of this declaration will determine its scope in file
    A. Regardless of scope, x will have static extent */
    ...
    x++;                            /* reference to x is OK if visible in A */
    ...
/* end of file A */
/****************/


/* start of file B */

/* top – level only */
    int x = 3;                      /* this is the defining declaration */
/* Note absence of extern. Note optional initializer */
/* Scope of x is whole of file B */
    ...
/* end of file B */
/****************/
```

The variable **x** defined in file B is truly global in the sense that any function in any file like A that declares **extern int x;** can access **x** within that declaration's scope. As with external functions, the linker must check that any external variable declarations encountered are consistent with the unique variable definition. Such global variables are clearly exposed to inadvertent changes in unexpected places that can make debugging even more painful.

► *STATIC VARIABLES* ►

You can protect a variable from abuse by using the **static** specifier, just as you saw with functions. **static int x;** tells the compiler not to pass the name **x** to the linker. **static** also performs the important task of giving **x** static extent, no matter whether the declaration occurs at the top level or head-of-block. Note that formal parameters cannot be declared as **static** since they exist only for argument passing and must clearly be of local scope and extent.

The presence of **static** in a declaration also indicates that it is a defining declaration, so memory is allocated. Any explicit initialization is performed just once—when the declaration is encountered. In the absence of an explicit initializer, **static** variables are cleared to zero. It is important to note that static variables can only be initialized with constants or constant expressions, whereas **auto** variables can be initialized using constants or other previously declared variables.

The once-only **static** initialization must be understood—it contrasts fundamentally with the reinitializations that occur each time an **auto** (or local-extent) declaration is executed. Consider the following snippet:

```
{ int i = 1;                          /* auto implied */
  static int j = 6;
  ...
  i++; j++;
  printf("i = %d, j = %d\n", i, j);
}
```

If the above block were executed three times in succession, the resulting display would be

```
i = 2,  j = 7
i = 2,  j = 8
i = 2,  j = 9
```

You can see that i is set to one each time round, while j retains its previous value once it has been initialized.

► *Static Variables in Action* ►

This example highlights a common application for **static** variables: Often you simply want to preserve a value between function calls or block executions, and the other implications of **static** (nonexport and privacy) are incidental. An oft-used illustration is that of calculating a seed for a random-number generator. Each call calculates a new seed based on the previous value, so either a global variable or an internal static variable must be used. The latter is safer, as explained earlier.

Although QuickC contains the library functions **rand( )** and **srand( )** in STDLIB.H, it is instructive to write your own pseudorandom-number generator. LOTTERY.C (Program 7.2) keeps picking three lucky numbers until you enter a Q to quit.

► *Analysis of LOTTERY.C*

I refer you to Donald Knuth's definitive text on random-number generators, *The Art of Computer Programming* (*Volume 2: Seminumerical Algorithms.* 2d ed. Reading, Mass.: Addison-Wesley, 1981). My extremely naive

```
/* lottery.c - picks three lucky numbers */

#include <stdio.h>
#include <stdlib.h>
#include <time.h>

#define FIRST_SEED 17
#define MULTIPLIER 5
#define INCREMENT 1
#define MODULUS 4096

int randy(void);
void show3rand(void);

void main(void)
{
    do {
      show3rand();
      printf("\nHit a key for more - Q to Quit: ");
    }
    while (getche() != 'Q');
}

int randy(void)
{
    static int seed = FIRST_SEED;
    seed = (seed*MULTIPLIER + INCREMENT) % MODULUS;
    return seed;
}

void show3rand(void)
{
   printf("\n\tLucky Numbers are %d,%d,%d\n",randy(),randy(),randy());
}
```

► *Program 7.2:* LOTTERY.C

example is a linear congruential formula explained on page 170 of that book. The key point is that the first time **randy( )** is called, **seed** is initialized with the constant **FIRST_SEED**. Subsequent calls bypass the initializer, and **seed** retains the same value it had when **randy( )** was last exited.

Because **randy( )** itself is **extern** by default, other files could access it by declaring **int randy(void);**. On the other hand, the variable **seed** cannot be accessed or altered except via calls to **randy( )**. Even **main( )** and **show3rand( )** cannot access **seed** directly even though they are in the same file as **randy( )**. By defining **randy( )** as **static**, you could block access to **seed** from any function outside LOTTERY.C.

► SUMMARY— IMPORTANCE OF SCOPE AND EXTENT ►

The key to program security and robustness is local and global scope. Local variables are protected from deliberate or accidental change by functions or blocks of code outside their own bailiwick. Global variables are more at risk in that they can be legally changed by any statement in any function within their scope. Globals must therefore be used sparingly and only where functions need to share and modify the same variables.

I have some bad news and some less bad news on how a function can access a global variable. First, the bad news: the global variable might appear in the body of the function. If so, it is possible for the function to modify the variable quite independently of the normal argument-passing mechanism. This reduces the modularity of the program and should be avoided.

The less bad news is that you can pass a global variable as an argument to the function. In this case, remember that the formal parameters of a function have local scope so that the function acts on a local copy of the real argument. Any side effects are therefore confined to the called function, but you may be able to make use of the returned value back in the calling function. The only other way to directly change a global is to pass a pointer as argument. This has its dangers, but at least the format of the function indicates what is going on. The following snippet shows the three possibilities:

```
/* how functions can attack a global variable */
        ...
        int i = 0;              /* top – level global */

void inci(void);
int inc1(int i);
void inc2(int *i);
```

```
void main( )
{
        inci( );
        printf("\ni = %d",i);   /* i now = 1 */
        i = inc1(i);
        printf("\ni = %d",i);   /* i now = 2 */
        inc2(&i);
        printf("\ni = %d",i);   /* i now = 3 */
}

void inci(void)                 /* increments i in body – not a good idea */
{
        ++i;
}
int inc1(int j)                 /* increments a copy of i & returns value */
{
        return ++j;
}

void inc2(int *j)               /* takes &i as arg and increments i */
{
        ++(*j);
}
```

► THE register STORAGE CLASS ►

The final storage class specifier to consider is **register**. It is applicable only to automatic variables (both head-of-block and formal parameters) of integer type, such as **int, unsigned, short, char,** and 16-bit pointers. Unlike the other specifiers I have discussed, **register** is entirely a suggestion to the compiler. The suggestion in

```
{ register int i;              /* set to auto if no register free */
      for (i = 0; i < 10000; i++)
      { ... }
}                              /* i no longer exists here */
```

is that since i is heavily used it should be allocated to a register, if possible, rather than to the usual RAM of the stack. If there is no spare register, the declaration is taken as **auto int i;**.

All data movements and arithmetical operations are much faster with data in registers than when memory has to be accessed. Using registers, then, is a good thing, and the more frequently a candidate variable is accessed during its lifetime, the more the savings will show.

On the other hand, the 8088/86 family is not excessively endowed with registers! Because of all the other jobs that registers have to do during execution (holding temporary values, keeping track of segments and stacks, and so on), SI and DI are usually the only ones available for holding **register** variables. Recall that SI and DI are each 16-bit, which explains the restriction to integer and **near**-pointer data types. These two registers will be assigned on a first-come, first-served basis, so you should position your **register** declarations accordingly.

The scope of a register variable is exactly the same as that of the corresponding **auto** variable. In the above example, i ceases to be a **register** variable as soon as the **for** loop ends. The register, if one was assigned, is then free for any subsequent **register** requests.

Under some unusual circumstances it is possible that the same **register** declaration could be encountered a second time with a different register allocation prevailing, so your variable could be **register** on one occasion and **auto** on another.

One important limitation applies to **register** variables. You cannot apply the address operator (**&**) since a register variable does not have a memory address. Even if a register is not found, QuickC would signal an error after processing the following snippet:

```
int *kp;
register int k;
kp = &k;                          /* ILLEGAL even if k is nonregister */
```

This makes sense portability-wise in view of the fact that you can never be certain whether a register would be found for **k** on any particular system or invocation.

► ANALYSIS OF PLAYER.C ►

Now that you have a better understanding of storage classes, you can look at PLAYER.C in Chapter 6 with more comprehension. Note first that the main( ) function is set up simply to test the basic functions:

init_play( ) enters the player data.

list_play( ) lists the database.

number_to_name( ) finds the name of a given player's number.

name_to_number( ) finds the number of a given player's name.

These and several other functions are all **extern** by default, so you can envisage them being collected together, compiled, and set up as a library to be incorporated into application programs.

Other variables and functions, including the database array of pointers to the **PLAYER_REC** structure, have been declared as **static**:

```
         static PLAYER_REC *pptr[PL_MAX];
/* global to all functions in this file,
     but not accessible elsewhere.
     Declares an array of 'pointers to PLAYER_REC structure' */

          static int pind;
/* player index used with pptr[ ] */

          static int db_size;
/* number of players in database */

static int get_name(char target_name[ ])
      { /* body */}

static int get_number(unsigned char target_number)
      { /* body */ }
```

This division between external and static objects is a simple example of data abstraction. You provide a set of primitive functions to initialize, access, list, and maintain the database. Other programmers can build up application programs based on these primitives without any knowledge of how the database is implemented. One obvious advantage is that the application programmer cannot accidentally or maliciously violate the abstract data structure's integrity; less obvious is the flexibility you enjoy in changing the structure. If the function names are unaltered, the application programs can run with minimum disturbance. (Often relinking is all that's needed.)

The global variable **pind** is directly changed in the bodies of **get_number( )** and **get_name( )**, apparently disregarding my earlier warnings. However, **pind** and these two functions are **static**, which confines the danger. **pind** also plays an important role in reducing the amount of searching required. Assuming that successive inquiries often apply to the same player, I preserve that last-found index and check a match there before embarking on the admittedly inelegant **for**-loop search. A larger database, of course, would call for either a binary search on a sorted array or some form of indexing. Remember that the data abstraction approach allows such enhancements without affecting the application software.

► *Miscellaneous Notes on PLAYER.C* ►

- ► The function **toupper(pos)** declared in CTYPE.H returns the upper-case of **pos** if **pos** is a lowercase ASCII letter; otherwise it returns the argument unchanged. There is a slightly faster macro version, **_toupper( )**, which works correctly only when the argument is a lowercase letter. In the present context, the function is safer—I trap non-matching entries as position *X*. Note that CTYPE.H also contains **tolower( )**, **_tolower( )**, and **toascii( )**. The latter simply clears all but the bottom 7 bits from an integer argument to guarantee that you have a valid ASCII code, 0–127.

- ► The machinations between the **enum** values **P**, **C**, etc., and the ASCII symbols "**P**", "**C**", etc., should drive home the point that enumerations are simply synonyms for integers. Displaying **P** directly would give a misleading **0**.

- ► The format **scanf("%2d/%2d/%4d", ...);** is best understood by reading Appendix C, but I'll cover it briefly here. The characters "**/**" in the format string are set to match the same character in the input date. The **%2d** indicates that a *maximum* of two digits is expected. A proper program would test for sensible date input. There is an official MS-DOS **date** structure defined in DOS.H:

```
struct date {
int da_year;
char da_day;
char da_mon;
};
```

with many functions for capturing and converting the current time and date to strings and UNIX formats.

► The expression **(pptr[dbind] – >active) ? "Y" : "N"** as an argument in **printf( )** is another illustration of C's compact notation.

► **get_str( )** is another security mechanism. Database queries are given pointers to a copy of the answer string, rather than as pointers into the database itself. Corruption of the database is made more difficult.

► BASIC users need to get used to **strcmp( )** and **strcpy( )** for comparing and copying strings!

► The fact that a function like **number_to_name( )** is defined in one line as in

```
char *number_to_name(unsigned char tn)
{
        return get_number(tn) ? get_str(pptr[pind] – >name) : NULL;
}
```

highlights the general principle that C favors a large number of simple functions rather than a small number of complex functions. There are no magic rules for the ideal division of a program into functions, but one clue here is that **number_to_name( )** is **extern**, while **get_number( )** is **static.**

► SUMMARY OF CHAPTER 7 ►

◄► The most succinct summary of Chapter 7 is Table 7.1 coupled with Table 7.2, below. Together they provide an overall picture of C's scoping, visibility, and extent rules and how they are related to the storage class specifiers.

◄► You also saw how **static** and **extern** were used to control the modularity of programs in conjunction with separately compilable source files and the linkage operation.

► **Table 7.2:** *Storage class specifier summary*

Storage Class	Where	What	Default	Action
auto	head-block	vars	yes	defining; local extent
[auto]	formal-parms	vars	[omit]	defining; local extent
extern	top-level, head-block	vars funcs	no yes	declaring; static extent, export to linker
[extern]	top-level, head-block	vars funcs	[omit] [omit]	defining; static extent, export to linker
static	top-level, head-block	vars funcs	no no	defining; static extent, no export to linker
register	func parms, head-block	vars	no	defining; local extent, **register** if possible, else **auto**

◄► The difference between **static** and **auto** variables can be summed up as follows:

> Static-extent variables, scalar or array, can only be initialized during declaration/definition with constants or constant expressions. In the absence of explicit initializers, static variables are cleared to zero. Such initializations are applied *only once*, prior to program execution. A static variable retains its value between function calls.
>
> Automatic scalar variables must be initialized explicitly, using any assignment-compatible expression, constant, or variable. These initializations will be applied each time the automatic variable is created. An automatic variable loses it value between function calls.

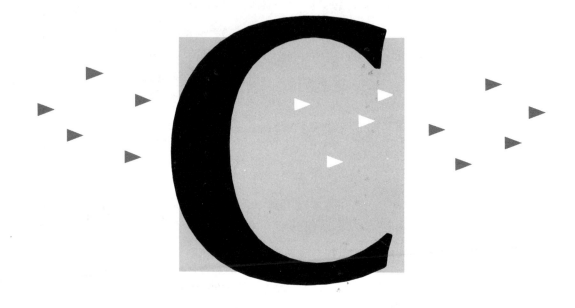

FILE I/O:
FULL STREAM AHEAD

► *CHAPTER 8* ►

So far you have been communicating with the computer via the screen and keyboard. Both your input data and the output results of your programs have disappeared after each session. No great loss, to be sure, with the possible exception of the PLAYER.C database!

QuickC, of course, has been busy saving your programs in permanent disk files, and it's time to show you how you can do the same for your data. I was tempted to do this earlier, but until I had covered structures and storage classes, I felt that a reasonable exposition of C's file input/output (I/O) operations would leave too much unexplained and "on trust."

► *C, ANSI C, AND I/O* ►

Languages such as BASIC and Pascal provide predefined, built-in I/O operations invoked with **SAVE**, **PRINT**, and **WRITELN**, for example. The C language proper has no such keywords, but ANSI C has specified a complete set of standard library routines that all conforming implementations must offer.

In the K&R bible similar libraries were implied, mainly based on the UNIX concepts of device files and hierarchical directories, but they were never, strictly speaking, an integral part of the language definition. Over the years, library routines have tended to diverge in name, number, and functionality in spite of efforts by various groups to standardize. (This has been especially true of I/O routines.) The ANSI C committee has decreed a set of library functions, weeding out some of the less portable UNIX-only routines.

The names of these functions and macros (and to a large extent, the names of the libraries themselves) are reserved in principle. Further, ANSI C allows any library function to be additionally implemented as a "safe" macro (one that evaluates each argument just once), possibly allowing the direct generation of assembly-language code by the compiler. This approach removes the function-calling overhead and further blurs the distinction between built-in and library routines.

So, one could say that C is as at least as well endowed with I/O and similar operations as any other language. Whether **getche( )** or some equivalent is "inside" C or in an approved linkable library might be counted as irrelevant from a practical point of view as long as the function performs efficiently and as specified. It is source code portability that matters—no one expects object code to run unchanged on widely disparate systems!

Implementors can add to the library to their heart's content, but **printf( )**, **getche( )**, and all the old favorites must be available and perform according to the book in order to qualify as ANSI C conformists. Programs using only the standard library routines are as portable as anyone can expect in this mad, mad world. The ANSI C standard is not yet engraved in stone, but Microsoft has taken great pains to provide routines that conform to the latest draft and has also retained some of the older functions that may be useful during the interregnum.

This chapter will concentrate on the most useful, MS-DOS-oriented I/O functions found in QuickC's STDIO.H, but first I'll briefly review the basic vocabulary.

► *WHEN IS A FILE NOT A FILE?* ►

What is a file? As with most questions in computerdom, there is no single answer for all seasons. At the average end-user level, a computer file is the electronic version of the eponymous manila folders that refuse to go away. Files are simply collections of data given a unique name by which the data can be referenced and updated. Files are usually stored on disks or tapes from which particular characters, blocks, or records can be transferred temporarily to RAM for display, updates, and subsequent rewrites to permanent mass storage.

The type of access available is often used to characterize a file or the file storage medium. *Sequential* files require byte-by-byte scanning to reach any given record, while *random* files allow some mechanism for moving directly to the target byte on record. Disks can handle both sequential and random files, but tapes are by nature confined to sequential access.

► *The Logical and the Physical* ►

Users are not usually concerned with a file's physical disposition—i.e., how the data is encoded (ASCII or EBCDIC), the sectors and tracks allocated, and so on. The task of translating from the "logical" (file name) to the "physical" (a set of bytes residing on some mysterious surfaces) is given to the operating system. (I will use the terms *file name* or *file specification* to indicate the drive, path, name, and extension, unless any of these are specifically excluded.)

This translation process is extremely machine and OS dependent, not to mention OS-version dependent! (Although I will not get too involved with MS-DOS technicalities, I will assume that you are working with MS-DOS/PC-DOS Version 2.00 or later since this version marked a significant turning point in MS-DOS file organization.)

DOS has to locate a directory entry that matches the file name, check its file size and attributes (read-only, hidden, etc.), and find the starting cluster number from the FAT (file allocation table). Then it has to allocate a *file handle*, which is a pointer to an FCB (file control block). From this point onward, the operating system can perform most of the basic operations (such as reading and writing) in terms of the file handle.

► *UNIX and Device Files* ►

The UNIX operating system, developed with, by, and for C, extended the traditional concept of a file to almost anything that can be treated as a data source (input) and/or as a data sink (output or destination). From this philosophy emerged the idea of device files, which allow programmers to treat devices such as keyboards and screens as though they were files. Files and devices are effectively treated as abstract *streams* or unstructured sequences of bytes, regardless of contents, origin, or destination.

► *Illegitimate Son of UNIX?* ►

MS-DOS gradually adopted the file-directory structure, the device file, and the stream from UNIX. These allow a wide range of generalized stream I/O commands that work if the data is being input from keyboards, joysticks, communications ports, or conventional disk files, or if it's being output to screens, printers, modems, or disk files. You can even fool the system into thinking that a designated region of RAM is a disk with directories and files.

Clearly, all these "files" have their individual physical quirks and buffering requirements, but the beauty of the device-file concept is that both UNIX and MS-DOS let you write code that is largely device independent, leaving the user to *redirect* and *pipeline* input and output as required.

For example, A>DIR *.C will display the directory listing by sending data to the standard output "file" (the screen), while

A>DIR *.C > FILENAME.EXT

redirects the data to the disk file called FILENAME.EXT. Similarly, you can send the output of one command to the input of another using the pipe operator ¦, as in A>DIR *.C¦SORT > DIRECT.LST. Here, the output of DIR is sent to SORT, and the sorted output is written to the disk. Pipes can be chained as in

A>TYPE FILENAME.EXT ¦ SCRUB ¦ NOPARITY > PRN

Programs in these chains are often called *filters* for obvious reasons. The multitasking UNIX and single-tasking MS-DOS pipeline mechanisms differ considerably, but the overall effects are the same.

▸ Text and Binary Files ▸

In one important respect, MS-DOS deviates from UNIX in its treatment of files. UNIX takes the view that the content and format of a file is not the concern of the operating system but should be entirely determined by the individual programs using the file. The files created by UNIX utilities are "flat" sequences of bytes that start at the beginning and end at the end! There is no special byte placed at the end of a file as a flag since this would violate the notion that all 0–255 byte values are democratically equal.

A UNIX programmer is free to create formatted files using special byte values as delimiters, fixed fields, or whatever—this is a private matter between the programmer and the file. The UNIX kernel keeps track of each file's length, so as you read these bytes it can signal when there are no more left. This signal is the EOF discussed in Chapter 3. EOF must be a value impossible to find by reading any byte. The value is defined in STDIO.H:

```
#define EOF ( − 1)                              / * end of file indicator */
```

MS-DOS, on the other hand, uses Ctrl-Z (decimal 26) as a unique text-file terminator, and this raises the problem of how to handle binary files (such as object code files) that may contain this value at any point. The net result is that, unlike UNIX, MS-DOS has to make a distinction between binary files (anything goes) and text files (ASCII plus terminator). This and other differences led to various extensions to the C file I/O library routines. I'll point these out as we proceed.

The difference between DOS text and binary files shows up in the treatment of newline characters. In text mode the CR/LF pair, generated by many devices when Enter is keyed, is internally translated into a single LF or newline character '\n' (octal 012) with a converse translation in the other direction. With binary files, no such translation is made—you have a simple one-to-one transmission of each byte.

► *Buffering* ►

When you have streams of data moving to and from diverse devices in a system, matching speeds becomes a major headache. As a naive example, it would not be sensible to transfer to a disk file each of my keystrokes one by one as I peck at the keyboard. An area of memory called a *buffer* is used, and my typed characters rest there until a suitable moment when they can be economically transferred to disk.

The optimum size of a buffer depends on the relative speeds of the two devices and how they respond to each other. You don't want the buffer filling up too often, forcing frequent writes, nor should it be so large that a power failure wipes out eight hours of work. *Flushing* a buffer, by the way, is the essential final operation that you use to write out what's left before moving on to other things, possibly reassigning the buffer to some other purpose.

A similar situation occurs when you're reading from a disk. You could certainly display a text file by grabbing one byte at a time from the disk and sending it to the screen, but it is more rational to fill a buffer (typically by reading a disk sector) and then pull from the buffer as required. Note that in multiuser systems great care is needed since your buffer data will be out of date if the disk file is changed by some other action. Note also that the same buffer can often be used for transfers in either direction, depending on the nature of the two devices. Further, there are many situations where a hierarchy of buffers is needed. For example, you might need to have a disk buffer feeding a printer buffer.

You'll also meet different buffering strategies. Should you flush a buffer only when full, after each newline character, or on demand? The C libraries provide the tools for setting buffer behavior if the default strategies are unacceptable.

Throughout an I/O system there are a myriad of buffering needs, the exact forms of which will vary with the source and destination. You need to have a general feel for what a buffer is (a first-in, first-out queue), but the C functions covered in this chapter, with help from DOS, usually take care of the details.

When you write something to a file, you can safely picture it as going straight there. In the current jargon we say that the buffering is *transparent*. For advanced programming, you can dig down nearer to the operating system and forgo the luxury of the power tools provided.

► STREAMS ►

I defined a stream as a potentially endless sequence of bytes that you can associate with a particular physical device or file. Once a stream is established, you interface with it in a uniform way whether it represents a disk file or some I/O device. For your added convenience, as they say, all streams can be treated identically even though the associated device might vary from a keyboard to a plotter not yet invented.

I can now show you the C code needed to create streams, attach them to a device file, and perform I/O.

► File Pointers and the FILE Structure ►

In C a stream is represented by a *file pointer* of type **FILE *** where **FILE** is a structure defined in STDIO.H. **FILE** defines five fields that represent the current status of a stream.

```
/*** Edited/simplified extract from STDIO.H ***/
/* Copyright (c) 1985-1989, Microsoft Corporation.
   All rights reserved.
*/

/* define file control block */

#define FILE struct _iobuf
```

```
extern FILE {
        char    *_ptr;
        int     _cnt;
        char    *_base;
        char    _flag;
        char    _file;
        }       _iob[ ];
/* iob[ ] is an array of structures of type FILE */
```

You can see from this simplified extract that **FILE** actually means struct_iobuf and _iob[ ] represents an open array of such structures. The significance of each structure component will emerge as I proceed. For now it is sufficient to get a feel for how streams are set up.

► *Opening and Closing Streams* ►

A variable of type **FILE**∗ is given a value by *opening* a stream. The usual method is to use **fopen( )**. This associates a stream with a named file by initializing a structure of type **FILE** and returning a pointer to it (known as a *file pointer*). All of C's stream I/O is performed with file pointers. **fopen( )** takes two arguments, a file name and a stream type, as follows:

```
char *filename;          /* string representing full file name */
char *type;              /* string controls type of stream */
FILE *fp;                /* declare a pointer to FILE structure */

/* set up filename and file type here before calling fopen( ) */

fp = fopen(filename, type);
/* open filename according to value of type and return fp.
   type can be "r" (read – only), "w" (write – only), "a" (append),
   – see Table 8.1 for full list */
   ...
   fclose(fp);
/* close filename – see text */

   ...
   fp = fopen("hello,c","r");
/* open hello.c for reading only (input) */

   ...
   fclose(fp);
/* close hello.c */
```

► *Table 8.1:* Stream types in fopen

Text or Binary Files

Type	Stream
"r"	Read only (input)—existing file
"w"	Write only (output)—create new file
"a"	Append mode (output)—write at end of existing file or create new file
"r + "	Update. Read/Write (input/output)—existing file
"w + "	Update. Read/Write (input/output)—create new file
"a + "	Update. Append mode (input/output)—update at end of existing file or create new file.

► Where **x** represents one of the types above, **"x"**

defaults to **"xt"** (text file) if **_fmode** equals **O_TEXT**.
defaults to **"xb"** (binary file) if **_fmode** equals **O_BINARY**.

► **_fmode** is the file-translation global variable, normally set to **O_TEXT**.

► **O_TEXT** and **O_BINARY** are defined in FCNTL.H

Text Only Files

Type	Stream
"rt"	Read only (input)—existing file
"wt"	Write only (output)—create new file
"at"	Append mode (output)—write at end of existing file or create new file
"r + t"	Update. Read/Write (input/output)—existing file
"w + t"	Update. Read/Write (input/output)—create new file
"a + t"	Update. Append mode (input/output)—update at end of existing file or create new file.

► the **"xt"** forms give text file modes regardless of **_fmode** settings.

► **Table 8.1:** *Stream types in* **fopen** *(continued)*

	Binary Only Files
Type	**Stream**
"rb"	Read only (input)—existing file
"wb"	Write only (output)—create new file
"ab"	Append mode (output)—write at end of existing file or create new file
"r + b"	Update. Read/Write (input/output)—existing file
"w + b"	Update. Read/Write (input/output)—create new file
"a + b"	Update. Append mode (input/output)—update at end of existing file or create new file.

►   the *"xb"* forms give binary file modes regardless of *_fmode* settings.

Once a stream is attached to a real file, it becomes a little pedantic to distinguish the two, so you can talk about reading a file or reading a stream interchangeably. Note that **type** is a string, so "r" is essential. A common error is to use "r", which is a **char** constant, not a string.

► fopen( ) Failures

If the **fopen( )** call is unsuccessful, a NULL pointer will be returned, and an error code is placed in the global variable **errno**. The following snippet will crop up frequently in various guises and is definitely worth remembering:

```
if ((fp = fopen(filename, type)) == NULL) {
        printf("/nCannot open %s/n",filename);
   /* or use perror(errmsg); to get a more specific error message
     based on value of errno */
          exit (1);
      }
```

Apart from when it encounters illegal file names, inactive drives, and missing files, **fopen( )** can also fail because MS-DOS sets an upper limit on

the number of streams that can be open at any given moment. The CON-
FIG.SYS file determines this upper limit with **FILES = <*number*>**, where
<*number*> defaults to 8 and must not exceed **FOPEN_MAX** in STDIO.H
(usually 20).

► *fclose( ) and fcloseall( )*

Because of the limit on the number of streams that can be open simultaneously, it is important to *close* streams when you've finished with them. This
frees up various system resources and reduces the risk of exceeding the
limit. Closing a stream also flushes out any associated buffers, an important
operation that prevents loss of data. You close a stream as follows:

```
fclose(fp);                        /* close the stream with file pointer fp */
```

fclose( ) returns an **int** value; 0 for successful closure, EOF if the closure
failed for any reason. The non-ANSI function **fcloseall( )** is worth knowing
when you want to exit a program with many open streams:

```
int i;
...
i = fcloseall( );
/* flush and close all open streams except stdin, stdout.
   Return the number of streams closed */
      printf("\nWe had %d files open\n",i);
```

► *Stream Types* ►

The **type** variable or constant in **fopen( )** can be any of 18 strings. These
strings determine the mode and type of stream you want, as shown in
Table 8.1. Cutting through the morass, you can see that there are really three
basic stream types, "**r**" (read), "**w**" (write), and "**a**" (append). The variants
are formed by tagging on " **+** ", "**t**", or "**b**".

Since text mode is the default, the most common types you'll encounter
are the following:

"r"— Open an existing text file for reading only. Signals an error if the file
doesn't exist.

"w"—Erase file if existing one found; create and open a file for writing only.

"a"— Open a text file for appending (write at the end) or create a new file if one with the given name does not exist.

The dangers of "w" should be familiar to BASIC users—**OPEN #3** *FILE-NAME*, **OUTPUT** will erase an existing file with the name *FILENAME* before creating a new, empty file of that name.

The **filename** in **fopen( )** can be any string constant or variable that evaluates to a legal DOS file specification. A quirk to note is that the \ character used in DOS pathnames must be doubled to overcome the C conventions:

directory\\filename.ext

The pleasant news is that once you have your file pointer from **fopen( )**, the file name is no longer needed for subsequent I/O.

► *fflush( ) and flushall( )*

You saw that **fclose( )** and **fcloseall( )** performed any necessary buffer flushing. There are two functions that will flush without closing the stream—**fflush( )** and **flushall( )**. The action of flushing depends on the file type—a file open for reading will have its input buffer cleared, while a file open for writing gets its output buffer written out to the file.

```
        fflush(fp);                    /* flush buffer but leave stream open */
   /* returns int = 0 for success, EOF for failure */
        flushall( );                   /* flush all buffers of all open files but
                                          leave them open */
   /* returns int = number of buffers flushed */
```

Note that **flushall( )**, like **fcloseall( )** is non-ANSI C.

► *The Standard Streams* ►

There are five special streams that you never have to open or close since the system does it for you. Looking again at STDIO.H, observe the identifiers stdin, stdout, and stderr (ignore stdaux and stdprn for now).

```
#define stdin          (&_iob[0])
#define stdout         (&_iob[1])
#define stderr         (&_iob[2])
#define stdaux         (&_iob[3])
#define stdprn         (&_iob[4])
```

Since _iob [ ] is an array of **FILE** structures, each **&_iob[n]** is a fixed pointer of type **FILE ***. They therefore fit the bill as far as defining streams is concerned. Whenever a QuickC program runs, these pointers are internally initialized so that **stdin** is associated with your standard input device (the keyboard), and **stdout** and **stderr** are both associated with the standard output device (your screen). Not only can you use these identifiers wherever a file pointer is legal (and sensible, of course—you can't write a file to your keyboard), but these pointers can also be effectively transferred to other streams or device files whenever redirection or piping is invoked (typically from a DOS command). And that, briefly, is how redirection is achieved.

The reason for **stderr** (standard error output) is that you normally want error messages from functions such as **perror( )** to appear on your screen. If such messages were sent out on **stdout**, they would run the risk of being redirected to a disk file. Of course, there are situations where you may want error messages in a file—if so, you can always redirect **stderr** to another stream.

► *Console and Stream I/O Functions* ►

Although any stream I/O can be directed to the three standard streams, the C libraries contain a mix of functions. Some of these are general stream I/O functions (for files or the console) and others are dedicated to console I/O. Recognizing this fact can simplify your mastery of the somewhat daunting list of I/O routines. For example:

printf( ) sends formatted output to **stdout** (wherever that is pointing).
cprintf( ) always sends formatted output to the console (screen).
fprintf( ) sends formatted output to any stream.
vprintf( ) works like **printf( )** with a variable argument list.
vfprintf( ) works like **fprint( )** with a variable argument list.

The **scanf( )** family that gets formatted input from a keyboard or file shows a similar pattern:

> **scanf( )** gets formatted data from **stdin** (wherever that is).
> **cscanf( )** always gets formatted data from the console (keyboard).
> **fscanf( )** gets formatted data from any stream.
> **vscanf( )** works like **scanf( )** with a variable argument list.
> **vfscanf( )** works like **fscanf( )** with a variable argument list.

The **f** suffix in many I/O functions indicates that you will find a file-pointer argument in addition to the normal arguments. Here is an example:

```
int   fprintf  (FILE *fp, const char *format, ...);
int   printf   ( const char *format, ...);
```

Sometimes, however, the **f** indicates the function version of a macro—for example, **fgetc( )** is the function version of the macro **getc**.

Once you have mastered **printf( )** and **scanf( )**, the other variants follow quite readily.

To get some useful work out of this preamble, I will introduce two simple buffered I/O routines, **getc( )** and **putc( )**. These handle only one byte at a time, but you can do a lot of fruitful work despite that limitation.

► *The getc( ) Routine* ►

Given the declarations

```
#include <stdio.h>              /* essential for macros */

    int ch;                     /* treated as a char but allow for EOF */
    FILE *fp;                   /* file pointer */
```

the statement

```
    ch = getc(fp);              /* read a byte and return it as int */
```

simply reads a byte from the stream given by the file pointer **fp**, assuming that the stream is open for reading or update. The word *simply* is perhaps an exaggeration! There are a number of subtleties in getting a single byte from a stream. There may not be such a byte, or there could be a byte in the stream that for some reason is reluctant to be read. So let's discuss EOF conditions (no more bytes to read) and real error conditions (the byte cannot be read).

► *Testing for EOF and File Errors* ►

As explained in Chapter 3, I declare **ch** as an **int** because if **getc( )** tries to read beyond the last byte in the stream, it will return the special value EOF, defined as − 1 in STDIO.H. Normally, **getc( )** returns a byte representing the character read (whether the stream is text or binary) into the lower byte of the **int ch** with no sign extension.

Declaring **ch** as a **char** is fairly safe with text files but dangerous with binary files. Meeting the byte 0xFF, which is quite legal and not unusual in a binary file, would signal a spurious EOF.

You need a useful macro called **feof( )**, which can be used under any conditions to test if a true end-of-file condition occurred on the last input operation. The **char _flag** component in the **FILE** structure holds the following status flags, defined mnemonically in STDIO.H:

```
#define   _IOREAD     0x01
#define   _IOWRT      0x02

#define   _IOFBF      0x0
#define   _IOLBF      0x40
#define   _IONBF      0x04

#define   _IOMYBUF    0x08
#define   _IOEOF      0x10
#define   _IOERR      0x20
#define   _IOSTRG     0x40
#define   _IORW       0x80
```

These flags are best left for the I/O functions to manipulate. I show them to indicate the range of data stored in the **FILE** structure and to explain the EOF and file-error macros.

The **flag** bits of each active stream are being constantly monitored internally using expressions such as

```
        if (fp −>_flag & _IOREAD) {...}
/* test READ flag with bitwise AND */
```

```
           ...
                (fp –>_flag) |= _IOWRT;
   /* set WRITE flag with bitwise OR */
```

The **feof( )** macro is defined as

```
   #define feof(f)                      ((f) –>_flag & _IOEOF)
```

so if the **_IOEOF** flag (bit 4) is set (indicating a genuine end-of-file situation), **feof( )** returns 1 (true). The following snippet shows **feof( )** in action:

```
   /* assume fp open stream for input */
         ch = getc(fp);                /* grab a char – int */
         if (feof(fp)) {
   /* macro expands to if (((fp) –>_flag & _IOEOF)) */
            puts("No more! Fini!");
            fcloseall( );
            exit (1);
      }
   /* returns TRUE if nonspurious end-of-file was
      detected on the last input from stream fp */
```

Note that the **_IOEOF** flag remains set until the stream is closed or rewound (I'll explain **rewind( )** in a minute), so further attempts with **getc( )** are blocked.

The macro **ferror( )** works similarly but tests the **_IOERR** flag, which gets set for a host of hardware- and software-related reasons:

```
   #define ferror(f)                    ((f) –>_flag & _IOERR)
```

I strongly urge you to test **ferror(fp)** after each stream I/O operation, but, to be honest, it is a "custom more honored in the breach...."

```
   /* after each read or write: */
      if (ferror(fp)) {
         puts("File read or write error!");
         fcloseall( );
         exit (1);
      }
```

The **_IOERR** flag remains set until **clearerr( )** or **rewind( )** is called or the stream closed. If you want to program repeats after a file error, you should call **clearerr(fp);** first.

► *The Current Pointer Moves...* ►

Each call to **getc( )** advances a pointer in the ***fp FILE** structure called **_ptr**, the *current active pointer*. You can picture **_ptr** as tracking progress in the stream—the next I/O operation will usually take place at the current active pointer.

Most I/O functions refer to **_ptr** for some reason or other, and many update it after reading or writing to the stream. In terms of the given file pointer, **fp**, the I/O routine accesses **fp – >_ptr**. You should never idly fool around with this member!

The simple function **ftell( )** will return the **long int** value of **_ptr** as follows:

```
long file_pos = 0L;
file_pos = ftell(fp);          /* where are we in stream fp? */
/* if ftell fails it returns – 1L and sets errno */
```

If you have awfully long streams, you get **_ptr** mod 2^{32}!

There are two functions that allow you to alter **_ptr** without you having to access **fp – >_ptr**. You can use them to get random access to certain streams (usually binary and on disk) provided that you know how they are formatted. I am more concerned now with sequential streams, in which **_ptr** soldiers on from byte to byte, but let me show you briefly how **_ptr** can be made to point at arbitrary bytes in a stream.

► *Setting the Current Active Position*

Immediately after opening a stream, the current active pointer is zero and points to the first byte of the stream. **rewind(fp)** winds **_ptr** back to the start of the stream and always returns **void**. **rewind( )** also clears the **_IOEOF** and **_IOERR** flags, as noted in the **feof( )** discourse.

For more exotic **_ptr** changes, you use **fseek( )** on an opened stream as shown in the following snippet:

```
#include <stdio.h>
/* defines SEEK_SET = 0; SEEK_CUR = 1; SEEK_END = 3
   as possible values for 'fromwhere' */

        long recsiz = 30L, offset = 0L;
        int fromwhere, seek_fail;      /* 0 = success */
        FILE *fp;
```

```
        ...
/* open the stream here */
        ...
        offset = recsiz;
        fromwhere = SEEK_CUR;          /*set value of offset*/
        seek_fail = fseek(fp, offset, fromwhere);
/* move _ptr offset bytes from current position */
        if (seek_fail) {
                puts("\nSeek Failure!");
                fcloseall( );
                exit (1)
        }
        ...
```

fseek( ) repositions _ptr by **offset** bytes from either the start, the current position, or the end of the stream, depending on the value of **fromwhere** (0, 1, or 2, respectively). You can use the mnemonics defined in STDIO.H as shown. Note that **rewind(fp)** has the same effect as **fseek(fp, 0L, SEEK_SET)**. Note carefully that **fseek( )** returns zero for success. This unnatural reversal, viz. "false equals success" and "true equals failure" is quite common in I/O functions. Using **seek_fail**, as above, is one way to restore some logic to the situation: you test if **seek_fail** is true for failure or false for success.

► *The putc( ) Routine* ►

The call

```
putc(ch, fp);                      /* write the lower byte of ch to stream */
```

will output **ch** to the stream at the current position with the same declarations I used for **getc( )**:

```
#include <stdio.h>                 /* essential for macros */

        int ch;                    /* treated as a char but allow for EOF */
        FILE *fp;                  /* file pointer */
```

but with the stream opened for write, append, or update modes. The macro **putc( )** also returns an **int** value—either the byte just written (top byte cleared) if the write was successful or an EOF if an error occurred. Writing to an output stream cannot cause a normal end-of-file error since sequential files usually just grow on you. However, many possible hazards such as device-full, write-protect, and parity-fail problems can interfere with progress. The **ferror( )** macro can be usefully called, or you can test the value of **putc( )** after each call.

► *Variants fgetc( ) and fputc( )*

Note that STDIO.H also defines **fgetc( )** and **fputc( )**. These are operationally equivalent to **getc( )** and **putc( )** but are true functions not macros. The difference is only important if you ever want to pass these as arguments to another function. Remember that the identifier **fgetc**, unlike **getc**, is a pointer to a function type and can be used as an argument.

► *STREAMS IN ACTION* ►

Here is KOPY.C (Program 8.1), a simple program that will copy the file HELLO.C to HELLO.CBK. Later on this will be generalized to allow each file name to be entered on the command line from the DOS prompt.

► *Analysis of KOPY.C* ►

I declare two file pointers with the suggestive names **infile** and **outfile**. The **fopen( )**s are combined with the test for success. Note the literal strings for the file names and modes. HELLO.C is opened for "rb" (read-only binary), while HELLO.CBK is opened for "wb" (write-only binary). If a file called HELLO.CBK is found in the current directory, KOPY.C will erase it. If HELLO.C is not found, **perror("Sorry about HELLO.C");** will display

    Sorry about HELLO.C : No such file or directory

The second part of the above message is triggered by the value set in the global variable called **errno**. A colon is displayed after your optional message string argument to **perror( )**. Using **perror( )** is a neat way of letting QuickC do the error analysis.

```
/* kopy.c -- simple file copy program Program 8.1 */
#include <stdio.h>

void main(void)
{
    FILE *infile, *outfile; /* two stream pointers */
    int ch = 0, bytes = 0;  /* count the bytes copied */

/* try to open HELLO.C for read--only, binary file */

    if ((infile = fopen("hello.c","rb")) == NULL) {
       perror("Sorry about HELLO.C");
       exit (1);
    }

/* try to create/open HELLO.CBK for write--only, binary file.
   If file exists, delete old one first */

    if ((outfile = fopen("hello.cbk","wb")) == NULL) {
       perror("Sorry about HELLO.CBK");
       exit (1);
    }

/* both files open, so copy infile to outfile until EOF *,
    while ((ch = getc(infile)) != EOF) {
       putc(ch, outfile);
       ++bytes;
    }
/* close both to flush stream */

    fclose(infile);
    fclose(outfile);

/* report completion and stats */

    printf("\nTotal of %d bytes KOPY'd",bytes);

}
```

► *Program 8.1:* KOPY.C

Both files are opened as binary to solve the potential problem of copying the end-of-file (Ctrl-Z) code. Try changing the modes to "r" and "w" (or whatever) to check this out.

The actual copying is done with

```
while ((ch = getc(infile)) != EOF) {
   putc(ch, outfile);
   ++bytes;
}
```

There are more concise ways of doing this without using the **ch**, but my version is legible. Try **putc(getc(infile), outfile)** for fun—but you must watch the parentheses.

I did not use the file name HELLO.BAK since this extension is used by DOS—it would be impolite to erase a possibly useful file. Nor did I call the program COPY.C for obvious reasons!

When you have KOPY.EXE working, rename your HELLO.C and test the error message. You can try opening HELLO.CBK in mode "**ab**". If the file already exists, you will copy (append) HELLO.C to the end of HELLO.CBK.

Next I'll show you how to make KOPY.C a tad more flexible. The new version is VKOPY.C (Program 8.2). The **argc** and **argv** indentifiers are explained in the following section.

Do not run VKOPY from the QC menus. Compile and link to VKOPY.EXE and exit to DOS. Read the next section before running VKOPY from the DOS prompt.

```
/* vkopy.c -- improved file copy program Prog8.2 */
#include <stdio.h>

void main(int argc, char *argv[]) /* new! args for main() */
{
    FILE *infile, *outfile;
    int ch = 0, bytes = 0;

    if (argc != 3) {
        puts("\nUsage is VKOPY filename1 filename2\n");
        exit (1);
    }

    if ((infile = fopen(argv[1],"rb")) == NULL) {
        printf("\nSorry %s",argv[1]);
        perror("");
        exit (1);
    }

    if ((outfile = fopen(argv[2],"wb")) == NULL) {
        printf("\nSorry %s",argv[2]);
        perror("");
        exit (1);
    }

    while ((ch = getc(infile)) != EOF) {
        putc(ch, outfile);
        ++bytes;
    }

    fclose(infile);
    fclose(outfile);

    printf("\nTotal of %d bytes VKOPY'd",bytes);
}
```

► *Program 8.2: VKOPY.C*

► *Using main( ) with Command-Line Arguments* ►

C has an indispensible mechanism through which **main( )** can obtain parameters entered at the DOS command level. If I type VKOPY *file1 file2* at the DOS prompt, it would be nice to pass the two file names to VKOPY.EXE, making it more flexible and more like the official DOS command COPY. Any data entered after the command or program name can be considered as a command-line argument, but some conventions must be agreed on in order to cope with the variety of formats encountered. DOS and C consider each string, including the command name itself, to be a distinct argument. Obviously, strings are separated by spaces or tabs.

Two special identifiers, **argc** and **argv**, are used to pass to **main( )** the number of command-line arguments and pointers to each argument. You have to set up **main( )** as follows:

```
main(int argc, char *argv[ ])
{ ... }
```

argc will then provide the number of command-line arguments, including the command itself—so **argc** is never less than 1. The **argv[ ]** is our old friend from Chapter 5, an array of pointers to **char**, or, equivalently, an array of strings. Each of **argv[0]**, **argv[1]**,... up to **argv[argc – 1]** is a pointer to a command-line argument, namely a NUL-terminated string. The pointer **argv[argc]** is set to NULL to mark the end of the array.

You may now execute VCOPY by typing VKOPY HELLO.C HELLO.CBK on the command line (or you can choose two files of your own). **main( )** will access the following values:

argc = 3 (command plus 2 arguments).

argv[0] points to empty string "" (DOS 2.x or earlier).
argv[0] points to "C:\VKOPY\0" (DOS 3.0 or later. Note that drive and directory have been added. Your path may differ, of course.).

argv[1] points to "HELLO.C\0".
argv[2] points to "HELLO.CBK\0".
argv[3] is NULL.

VKOPY will also work with full-file path specifications, but, unlike the DOS COPY command, it will not default the output file name and path or handle wild cards.

Using an array of strings (or an array of pointers to **char**) solves the problem of variable-length arguments. You will sometimes see **argv** declared as **char **argv**, which is also an array of strings (see Chapter 5).

It is important to know that all the **argv[ ]** arguments are passed as strings, so a command line such as C>SEND 12 350.45 will not get you an integer and a floating-point number. You would have to convert 12 and 350.45 from ASCII to numeric using **atoi( )** (ASCII to integer) and **atof( )** (ASCII to FP double).

The white space between arguments is essential: the familiar commas used in C functions will not delimit command-line arguments. Quotation marks can be used to produce a single argument from entries containing white space. The following line has three arguments including SEND:

C>SEND "nice day" fish,chips

► *The env Argument* ►

main( ) will not accept any old arguments. Apart from **argc** and **argv**, the only other legal argument allowed is **env**, from which you can find out the DOS environment parameters (established with the DOS SET command). You can define **main( )** as follows:

```
main(int argc, char *argv[ ], char *env[ ])
{ ... }
```

Each **env[i]** returns a string of the form

```
"environment_var = environment_val"
```

until you reach a NULL pointer, which means that no more environment values have been SET.

You can also use **getenv( )** and **putenv( )** from STDLIB.H to access, change, or delete an environment value. They are declared like this:

```
     char *getenv(char *environment_var);
/* if arg is "PATH" for example, getenv returns the string found
   in the environment, e.g., "C:\;C:\BIN" or 0 if PATH not SET */
        int putenv(char *environment_string);
/* the arg string e.g., "PATH = B:\" will be added to the environment,
   or will overwrite an existing PATH setting. "PATH =" will
   clear any existing setting */
```

When you spawn *child processes* using the **exec...( )** family of functions to load and run other programs, you can also pass new environment values.

► *Your Environment Revealed* ►

Here is SHOALL.C (Program 8.3), which displays all the arguments mentioned. This can be run from within QC, but run it from the DOS prompt with some dummy arguments to test the command-line display. MS-DOS 3.0 and later versions will produce different displays than previous versions.

Figure 8.1 shows the screen display I get from SHOALL. The PROMPT shown has become very popular—it displays the date, time, and directory in reverse video at the top of the screen.

I now return to the standard I/O library routines.

► *The get...( ) AND put...( ) FAMILIES* ►

There are several variants on **getc( )** and **putc( )**, some of which you have already encountered. I list them all here with their revealing prototypes or macros and brief notes. (For simplicity I have omitted the **_CDECL** elements found in the STDIO.H and CONIO.H prototypes.)

► *fgetc( ) in STDIO.H*

int fgetc(FILE *fp); is a real function version of the **getc( )** macro.

```
/* shoall.c -- display command line & environment Prog8.3 */
#include <stdio.h>

void main(int argc, char *argv[], char *env[])
{
    int i;

    if (argc == 1)
        puts("\nSHOALL has no arguments");
    else {
        puts("\nSHOALL has following arguments:");
        for ( i=0; i<argc; i++)
            printf("%d:\t%s\n",i,argv[i]);
    }

    puts("\nDOS Environment Values:");
        for ( i=0; env[i] != NULL; i++)
            printf("%d:\t%s\n",i,env[i]);
}
```

► *Program 8.3: SHOALL.C*

```
 Sun  2-26-1989 / 13:42:36.43 : E:\BIN
E>shoall jim joe stan

SHOALL has following arguments:
Ø:        E:\BIN\SHOALL.EXE
1:        jim
2:        joe
3:        stan

DOS Environment Values:
Ø:        COMSPEC=C:\COMMAND.COM
1:        PROMPT=$e[s$e[1;1H$e[Øm$e[K$e[7m $d / $t : $p $e[Øm$e[u$n$g
2:        PATH=C:\;E:\BIN;E:\TUTORIAL;C:\BIN;
3:        LIB=E:\LIB;
4:        INCLUDE=E:\INCLUDE;

E>
```

► **Figure 8.1:** *SHOALL screen output*

► *fgetchar( ) in STDIO.H*

int fgetchar(void); is not in ANSI C and is the same as **fgetc(stdin)**. It grabs a byte from the standard input, which is usually the keyboard unless redirection is in force.

► *getchar( ) in STDIO.H*

getchar( ) is a simple macro defined as

#define getchar( ) getc(stdin)

so it takes no argument but simply returns a character as an **int** (or EOF on a failure) from **stdin**. This is an excellent illustration of the use of the special predefined file pointer **stdin**—this stream and its pointer are already **fopen**ed for you and do not have to be **fclosed**! getchar( ) is a holdover from the old line-buffered UNIX terminal days. **getch( )** and **getche( )** are more convenient for the PC console input.

► *getch( ) in CONIO.H*

int getch(void); also returns a single integer-character (or EOF) from the keyboard, regardless of where **stdin** is pointing. The character does not echo to the screen.

► *getche( ) in CONIO.H*

int getche(void); works exactly like **getch( )** except that the keyed character echoes to the screen.

► *ungetc( ) in STDIO.H*

int ungetc(char ch, FILE *fp); "undoes" a **getc( )** by pushing the **char ch** back on the argument stream, **fp**. **ungetc( )** is useful in many "look ahead" situations—you can grab a byte, test it, and reject it or push it back for the next **getc( )**. Without **ungetc( )** many scanning loops prove quite tricky to implement. **ungetc( )** always returns the integer-character you have pushed. Ungetting an EOF (but who would want to?) does not affect the stream and returns an EOF. If you **ungetc( )** twice without a **getc( )** in between, you effectively remove the first ***unget***ted character from the stream. Several operations, like **fseek( )** and **rewind( )**, also remove the effect of an **ungetc( )**.

► *ungetch( ) in CONIO.H*

int ungetch(int ch); is the console-only version of **ungetc( )**. Redirection is ignored.

► *getw( ) in STDIO.H*

int getw(FILE *fp); is not in ANSI C and works like **getc( )** but reads a 2-byte integer from the stream. You must be careful with **getw( )** for two reasons. First, the function will not worry about byte boundaries—you get the 2 bytes as found whether they represent a genuine **int** or not. Second, although **getw( )** returns EOF at the end of a stream, just testing for EOF is insufficient since − 1 is a legitimate **int** value. You must use **feof( )** or **ferror( )** as discussed in the **getc( )** section.

► *gets( ) in STDIO.H*

char *gets(char *str); reads a string into **str** from **stdin** until a newline character is received. The newline is replaced by a NUL in the returned string. A NULL pointer is returned on errors.

► *cgets( ) in CONIO.H*

You must place the maximum string length needed in **str[0]** before calling **cgets( )**, which is defined as

```
char *cgets(char *str);
```

cgets( ) always reads from the console (keyboard) and plays some tricks by returning the length of the input string into **str[1]**. The string type goes into **str[2], str[3],**.... If the maximum is reached before a newline character, input stops. A newline is converted to a NUL. The final string is always at least **str[0]** + 2 bytes long. The function returns **&str[2]**—there is no error signal.

Use of this function is not recommended because a user can type a string longer than **str**, causing unpredictable results. Use **cgets( )** or **fgets( )** instead.

► *fgets( ) in STDIO.H*

char *fgets(char *str, int n, FILE *fp); is a stream version of **cgets( )** that will read at most **n − 1** bytes from the stream into **str**. An earlier newline character will terminate but goes into the string. A NUL is always added at the end of **str**. A NULL pointer is returned on errors.

Before leaving all these **get...( )**s, take a quick look at the definition of **getc( )**, the one I started out with.

► *The Macro getc( )* ►

```
#define getc(f) (—(f)->_cnt >= 0 ? 0xff & *(f)->_ptr + + : _filbuf(f))
```

The **_cnt** component of **FILE** is an int marking the buffer-refill level. Each call on **getc( )** predecrements the level; while it is nonnegative, the first part of the **?...:** clause is invoked. This advances **_ptr**, the stream active position pointer, after grabbing the current byte. The upper byte (if any) is stripped by masking with 0xff. If the level goes negative, the function **_filbuf( )** is invoked to fill the buffer.

See if you can decipher the **putc( )** macro:

```
#define putc(c,f) (—(f)->_cnt >= 0 ? 0xff & (*(f)->_ptr + + = (char)(c)) \

           : _flsbuf((c),(f)))
```

I now give you all the **put...( )** variants with few comments since they follow, mutatis mutandis, the **get...( )** routines.

► *putchar( ) in STDIO.H*

This macro is defined in STDIO.H as

```
#define putchar(c) putc((c), stdout)
```

meaning that **putchar( )** will place a byte argument on the standard output. Note the essential parentheses in **(c)**. EOF is returned on errors.

► *fputc( ) in STDIO.H*

int fputc(int ch, FILE *fp); is the function version of the macro **putc( )**. EOF is returned on errors.

► *fputchar( ) in STDIO.H*

int fputchar(int ch); (not in ANSI C) is the same as **fputc(int ch,stdout)**. EOF is returned on errors.

► *putch( ) in CONIO.H*

int putch(int ch) is the console version of **putc( )**. No errors are signaled.

► *putw( ) in STDIO.H*

int putw(int w, FILE *fp); is not in ANSI C and writes **w** as 2 bytes into the stream, ignoring any alignment problems. EOF is returned on errors, but **ferror( )** should be used since EOF is a valid **int**.

► *puts( ) in STDIO.H*

int puts(char *str); is an old friend from Chapter 1. It displays the string plus a new line on the active **stdout**. On success, it returns the last character displayed; on failure you get an EOF.

▶ *cputs( ) in CONIO.H*

void cputs(char *str); works only on the console (screen) and with NUL-terminated strings. No newline character is appended and no value is returned whether it's successful or not.

▶ *fputs( ) in STDIO.H*

Like cputs( ), fputs( ) writes the NUL-terminated string with no newline character, but it writes to the designated stream. It's defined as

    int fputs(char *str, FILE *fp);

Like puts( ) it signals success by returning the last character, with EOF being returned on failures.

▶ *I/O HELP* ▶

The plethora of similarly named I/O routines certainly taxes the beginner's memory. So this seems an appropriate time to explore one of QuickC's most appealing features: the almost HyperCard-like set of linked help screens.

Press Alt-H to bring up the Help menu, then select C for Contents. Move the cursor to the Run-time Library legend and press F1 (or you can simply mouse-click on the adjacent button). You will see the screen shown in Figure 8.2. You can scroll around this multiscreen help section using PgUp and PgDn, then Esc when you feel glutted and wish to retire.

Note the three sections devoted to I/O: Streams, Low-level, and Console/Port. You select these, or any other topic of interest, in the usual way (position cursor, then press F1). Each selection reveals a list of relevant functions and a small menu offering Summary, Description, and Example. Browse around to your heart's content!

Apart from giving you instant on-line access to function formats and usage while you are programming, the QuickC Help system offers a useful cut and paste facility. Any portion of any help screen can be selected and copied into your source text without missing a beat. This is especially helpful in the case of unfamiliar or complex functions; you can cut and paste prototypes found in the help screen and use them as *templates* in your source code.

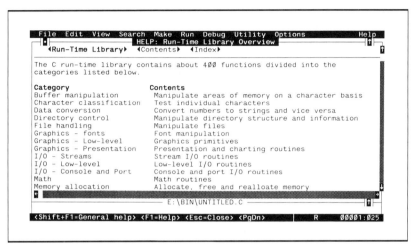

► **Figure 8.2:** *Run-time library help screen*

► *Help's Cut and Paste*

There are three steps in copying from help text to source code:

1. Select the help text segment by positioning your cursor at the first character to be copied. Then, hold the Shift key while you move the cursor to the last character to be copied. This will highlight the selected text.

2. Press the hot key Ctrl-Ins to copy the selected text to the internal "clipboard" buffer. (The long-winded equivalent is Alt-E for Edit, followed by C for Copy.)

3. Press F6 to return to your source window, and position the cursor at the point where you wish to insert the help text. Press the hot key Shift-Ins to paste from the clipboard to the source text (or use the longer method: Alt-E followed by P for Paste).

Mousers can achieve step 1 by click/dragging the cursor across the text to be selected.

► *MORE ON BUFFERING* ►

In the **FILE** structure you will see the magic number

#define BUFSIZ 512

BUFSIZ is an example of what is called a *manifest constant*.
Note also the **FILE** structure member called **base**:

```
        char *base
/* data transfer buffer */
/* base points to first byte of buffer! */
```

Each open (active) stream has a pointer, **file_var.base**, to access its private buffer of 512 bytes, where **file_var** is of type **FILE**. Since **file_var** is usually referenced via a file pointer (for example, **fp** of type **FILE** *) you would be more likely to see expressions such as **fp –> base**.

As you've seen, the standard I/O functions set up and control the members of *****fp** for you, so you rarely need direct access to the buffers. The STDIO.H functions therefore offer what is known as *buffered I/O*. You should, however, be aware of the fact that there are many *low-level* I/O routines available in QuickC that offer only the basic read/write tools for file access, leaving you to set up your own buffering strategy and attend to most of the housekeeping chores.

Some confusion arises when these latter routines are called *unbuffered* since, at some level or other, all I/O is buffered with either software or hardware—even a single-byte buffer is a buffer! Low-level I/O functions, as opposed to standard I/O functions, are declared in IO.H.

For advanced work, **setbuf( )** and **setvbuf( )** allow you to set up your own buffers and buffering strategy.

► *NON-ANSI C ROUTINES* ►

The following are non-ANSI C routines provided by Microsoft to maintain continuity in areas where many I/O versions prevail or because they are useful on the PC:

```
int       fcloseall         (void);
FILE      *fdopen           (int handle, char *type);
```

int	fgetchar	(void);
int	flushall	(void);
int	fputchar	(int c);
int	getw	(FILE *fp);
int	putw	(int w, FILE *fp);
int	remove	(const char *filename); /*erases a file*/
int	unlink	(const char *filename); /*erases a file*/
#define	fileno (f p)	((int)(unsigned char)(fp) –>_file
		/*returns the file handle of fp*/

► BLOCK I/O ►

There are two important stream routines still to cover. They allow you to read and write whole blocks of data with one deft function call. They are declared in STDIO.H as follows:

```
size_t fread (void *ptr, size_t size, size_t n, FILE *fp);
size_t fwrite (const void *ptr, size_t size, size_t n, FILE *fp);
```

The data type **size_t** is an ANSI C addition to improve portability. It is prede-fined as an integer type large enough to hold **sizeof( )** results. QuickC defines **size_t** as **unsigned int**.

The **fread( )** is given the usual stream argument, assumed to be open for reading or updating. In addition you tell it to read **n** items of data each of **size** bytes. The destination for all **n*size** bytes is the area pointed at by the generic **ptr**. You may recall that **void *ptr** allows **ptr** to be type cast as a pointer to any data type.

So, there are four arguments:

1. The source of the transfer is a stream opened for input equals **fp**.

2. The number of chunks equals **n**.

3. The size of each chunk equals **size**.

4. The receiving area (a pointer to memory) equals **ptr**.

Items 3 and 4 are closely related. If you are sending **int**s, then **ptr** must be of type pointer to **int**, so **size** must be **sizeof (*ptr)**, namely 2 bytes for QuickC. It is your responsibility to ensure that the destination can hold the total num-ber of bytes being sent, namely **(n * sizeof(*ptr))**.

The returned value of **fread( )** is the number of items sent, not the number of bytes.

fwrite( ) works similarly but in the opposite direction— *from* **ptr** as the source *to* the stream opened for output. The number and size of the elements being written are defined in exactly the same way.

A small difference you may have spotted in the declaration is that **ptr** is declared as **const**. The idea is that the source pointer is not changeable. This is not the same as saying that the objects being pointed at are invariant!

Block I/O gets exciting when you consider that the **n** items to be transferred from, say, memory to disk or disk to screen, can be records defined as arrays, structures, or unions of any complexity. A lot can be done with a single **fread** and **fwrite**. Indeed, I will conclude this chapter with SPLAYER.C (Program 8.4), a partial version of PLAYER.C that saves the player database to disk. The functions not reprinted here are exactly as found in PLAYER.C. The function **save_play( )** has been added, and **init_play** has been modified to call **save_play** after each record is entered.

```c
/* SPLAYER.C - a simple, disk version of PLAYER.C database */
/* Program 8.4 -- requires functions and main() from Program 6.1 */
/* overall strategy due to N. Gehani, AT&T Bell Labs */

#include <stdio.h>
#include <malloc.h>
#include <ctype.h>
#include <string.h>

#define FOUND 1
#define MISSING 0

#define PL_MAX 2        /* max number of player - vary for tests */
#define NAME_MAX 25     /* max name + 1 null */
#define HDG "Pl# Name                        Posn  RBI ERA     DATE Active

        typedef struct {
                unsigned char month, day;
                unsigned int year;
        } DATE;

        typedef unsigned char BOOL;

        typedef enum {
            X, P, C, I, S, O, D
        } POSITION;

        typedef struct player {

                char name[NAME_MAX];
                unsigned char player_number;
                POSITION player_position;
                unsigned int rbi;
                double era;
                DATE date_joined;
```

► *Program 8.4: SPLAYER.C*

```
                BOOL active;
             ) PLAYER_REC;


         static PLAYER_REC *pptr[PL_MAX];
/* global to all functions in this file,
   but not accessible elsewhere.
   Declares an array of 'pointers to PLAYER_REC structure' */

         static int pind;
/* player index used with pptr[] */

         static int db_size;
/* number of players in database */

/*----------------------------------------------*/
/* SAVE_PLAY - write n player records to PLAYER.DAT */
/*----------------------------------------------*/

int save_play(PLAYER_REC *play_ptr, int n)


{
    FILE *play_fp;
    int saved;

    play_fp = fopen("PLAYER.DAT","ab");
/* open binary file for append - each player is added at end */
    if (play_fp == NULL) {
        perror("PLAYER.DAT");
        exit(1);
    }
    saved = fwrite(play_ptr, sizeof(PLAYER_REC), n, play_fp);
/* number of player recs actually saved - n were requested */
/* return 0 if error */
    fclose(play_fp);
    if (saved == n)
        return saved;
    else
        return 0;
}

/*-------------------------------------*/
/* INIT_PLAY - set up player database    */
/* data in memory only - until Chapter 8! */
/*-------------------------------------*/
void init_play(void)
{
    int dbind;     /* local var - scans the database */
    char pos;      /* ASCII player position */

 for (dbind = 0; dbind < PL_MAX; dbind++) {
    if ((pptr[dbind]=(PLAYER_REC *)malloc(sizeof(PLAYER_REC)))
                              ==NULL) {
        puts("Memory Allocation Failure");
        exit(1);
    }

/* here pptr[dbind] points to an allocated record awaiting input */

    printf("\n#%3d Enter Player Number <99=exit>: ",dbind);
    scanf( "%d",&(pptr[dbind]->player_number) );

    if (pptr[dbind]->player_number == 99) break;

    printf("\n    Enter Player Name: ");
    scanf( "%s",pptr[dbind]->name );
```

► **Program 8.4:** SPLAYER.C (continued)

```
    /* Next item could be entered with getch() but I want to */
    /* show scanf() with %s                                  */
        printf("\n       Enter Player Position: ");
        scanf("%s",&pos);
        pos = toupper(pos);
        switch (pos) {
            case 'P': pptr[dbind]->player_position = P; break;
            case 'C': pptr[dbind]->player_position = C; break;
            case 'I': pptr[dbind]->player_position = I; break;

            case 'S': pptr[dbind]->player_position = S; break;
            case 'O': pptr[dbind]->player_position = O; break;
            case 'D': pptr[dbind]->player_position = D; break;
            default:  pptr[dbind]->player_position = X;
        }
        if (pptr[dbind]->player_position != P) {
            pptr[dbind]->era = 0.0;
            printf("\n       Enter Runs Batted In: ");
            scanf( "%d",&(pptr[dbind]->rbi) );
        }
        else {
            pptr[dbind]->rbi = 0;
            printf("\n       Enter Earned Run Average: ");
            scanf( "%lf",&(pptr[dbind]->era) );
        }
        printf("\n       Enter Date Joined (mm/dd/yyyy): ");
        scanf( "%2d/%2d/%4d", &((pptr[dbind]->date_joined).month),
                          &((pptr[dbind]->date_joined).year) );

        printf("\n       Active=Y or N? :");
        scanf( "%s",&pos);
        pptr[dbind]->active = ('Y' == toupper(pos));
    /* save one player rec in PLAYER.DAT */
    /* save_play allows future enhancement - save several records */
        if (save_play(pptr[dbind],1))
            puts("\nSaved in PLAYER.DAT");
        else
            puts("\nRecord not saved??");

    } /* end for loop */
    db_size = dbind;         /* set current size of database */

}
/*-------------end init_player--------------------*/
```

► *Program 8.4: SPLAYER.C (continued)*

► *SUMMARY OF CHAPTER 8* ►

◄► Files and devices come in all shapes and sizes, but C and DOS allow you to control them via a uniform logical concept called the stream.

◄► Input and output between different elements require buffering—most of which is done behind the scenes using high-level I/O functions and macros in STDIO.H.

◄► Streams can be redirected and piped by attaching them to files and devices. Most I/O functions can operate on streams with no prior knowledge of the physical devices or applications.

◄► C offers a rich array of I/O routines, both buffered (STDIO.H) and unbuffered (IO.H), formatted and unformatted.

◄► Text and binary streams require different treatment for EOF detection and CR/LF to new-line translation.

◄► **getc( )** and **putc( )** are single-byte I/O routines, but from these over 30 variations can be derived.

◄► Random access is obtained by setting a pointer to scan the stream. **fseek( )** and simple calculations can direct the pointer to any given record.

◄► Block I/O is accomplished via **fread( )** and **fwrite( )**.

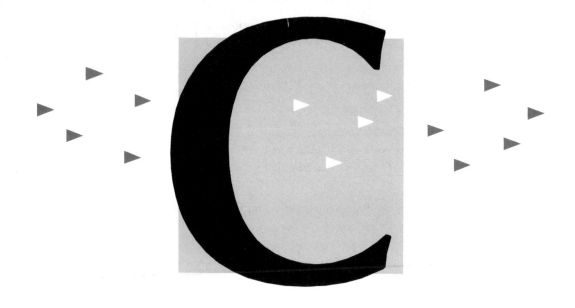

PRETTY PICTURES:
THE GRAPHICS TOOLBOX

► CHAPTER 9 ►

The screen displays you have produced so far, using **printf( )** and **puts( )**, for instance, have been restricted to monochrome ASCII text. To enter the more dazzling world of graphics and color requires three added ingredients: hardware (the appropriate graphics adapter card and monitor), graphics software tools (functions for drawing and color control), and a fair amount of programming savvy to cajole the hardware and software into sullen cooperation! This chapter aims to help you in this latter pursuit.

The hardware aspects largely depend on your personal tastes and pocketbook, although attractive graphics cards and high-definition monitors are no longer the preserve of the rich. Indeed, many PC's and clones now come equipped with high-definition monochrome adapters, such as the Hercules or work-alikes, which are supported by QuickC and which provide excellent graphics facilities. I am not alone in preferring high-resolution monochrome over fuzzy and garish colors for many applications. If, however, you can afford a crisp, high-density, amiable palette, QuickC will not object.

The good news for your budget is that your QuickC package already contains two comprehensive graphics libraries: GRAPHICS.LIB for all the basic video control, windowing, and drawing functions; and PGCHART.LIB for the more advanced presentation graphics charting functions such as bar charts, pie charts, and fancy graphs. There are two corresponding include files—GRAPH.H and PGCHART.H—containing many useful manifest constants, essential structure type definitions, and hundreds of function prototypes.

► ACCESSING THE GRAPHICS LIBRARIES ►

Before you tackle the examples in this chapter, you must ensure that these two libraries and their header files are accessible if needed by the QuickC compiler/linker. The #include <graph.h> and #include <pgchart.h> directives, of course, take care of the header files. More precisely, all your graphics programs will need GRAPH.H, but only those programs invoking presentation graphics functions or manifest constants will need to include PGCHART.H.

The simplest way of making the graphics libraries available, if you have enough spare hard-disk space, is to incorporate them into your combined libraries during the SETUP.EXE run. If you have already used SETUP without combining the graphics libraries, you can always run it a second time. When the prompt

Include in combined libraries: GRAPHICS.LIB [N]: PGCHART.LIB [N]

appears during SETUP, you should answer Y for both libraries. If you are squeezed for hard-disk space, you may want to forgo the luxury of incorporating the less-used PGCHART.LIB. You can even survive without putting GRAPHICS.LIB into the combined library, since there are ways of linking additional, noncombined libraries to your object code.

If one or both graphics libraries are *not* in the combined library, QC will lose no time in telling you: many "unresolved external references" messages will appear!

You can use QCL as a linker (or use LINK directly) to link the missing libraries with the *.OBJ file obtained via QC. Without embarking on a full discourse on the QCL and LINK syntax, the following examples should indicate the methods available. Assuming you have written MYGRAF.C, which uses functions from GRAPHICS.LIB and PGCHART.LIB, you can use Compile from the QC Make menu to obtain MYGRAF.OBJ. Then exit to DOS (by typing X) and type either

    C>QCL MYGRAF[.OBJ] \LIB\GRAPHICS.LIB \LIB\PGCHART.LIB

or

    C>LINK MYGRAF[.OBJ],,,NUL,\LIB\GRAPHICS[.LIB]
    +\LIB\PGCHART[.LIB]

The entries within [ ] are optional, since QCL and LINK default to .OBJ and .LIB extensions as indicated. Either command will produce MYGRAF.EXE, provided there are no errors. The path shown as \LIB\, of course, must correspond to the directory in which you have placed the graphics libraries.

You can also link *.LIB files (and other *.OBJ files in the case of multi-module programs) with MYGRAF.OBJ without leaving the QC environment.

Briefly, you create a program list or *.MAK file using the QC Make menu. These direct the QC linker to link all the elements listed (and can also trigger the recompilation of any modules that may have changed since the last compile/link operation). More on the QC Make facilities in Chapter 10.

In addition to the more common QuickC graphics functions covered in this chapter, an alphabetical listing of functions with complete specifications and notes can be found in Appendix F.

I'll give you enough geometrical and PC video-hardware knowledge to master the QuickC graphics routines, but don't expect any more here than the basics. The jungle starts when you try listing all the different adapters and monitors. This is an area, the cynics say, in which there are so many standards you are bound to find one you like. If you find references to objects irrelevant to your own installation, please be patient.

► THE DISPLAY ADAPTER ►

Every PC has a special *display adapter* circuit board containing some *display memory* (or *video memory*) that is physically distinct from your main RAM but nevertheless part of the address space of the CPU. The starting and ending absolute addresses of the display memory vary with the PC model and are usually of no direct interest to the user—the system knows where to find the video memory, and with some boards the programmer is actively discouraged from peeking and poking.

The size of the display memory, though, and its logical division into *pages* (or *planes*) is of importance since these dictate the sort of graphics tricks you can accomplish. The simplest adapters provide 4KB, with more expensive models offering 16KB, 64KB, 1MB, and ever upward.

The cathode ray tube (CRT) display unit (or *monitor*) is fed from the display memory via a programmable black box called the CRT controller chip. You can imagine one of the pages of the display memory being transformed in various ways to generate signals for your particular CRT screen. This page is called the *visual page*.

When you have more than one page of display memory available, you can independently load data into another page, the *active* page, which is ready to display almost instantly as required. Note that "active" refers to the invisible page, which is being replenished by the program, not the visual page, which is generating the display. The visual page must not be written to during the display cycle. Animation effects depend on flipping between active and visual pages.

▸ *RASTER SCAN* ▸

The transfer from memory to screen, in the form of a raster scan, is repeated 60 times per second (or 50 in some countries), giving the illusion of a steady display. Video memory is specially wired with multiple I/O ports to the CPU and the CRT controller. Simultaneous access by the CPU and CRT controller leads to a display aberration known as *snow*.

Between each refresh cycle an important event takes place: the electron beam painting the screen has to switch off and get from the bottom right corner back to the starting point at the top left corner (see Figure 9.1). This *vertical retrace* provides an important opportunity for the display memory to be updated by your program without causing snow. This is especially important if you have only one page of display memory. The key design elements

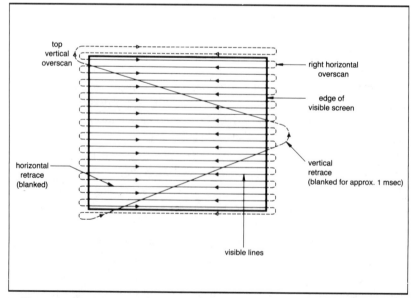

▸ **Figure 9.1:** *Raster scan and vertical retrace*

relevant to all graphics applications are the vertical retrace period (typically a millisecond or so), the memory-to-memory transfer rate, and the number of pages.

► DISPLAY MEMORY MAPS ►

Groups of bits or groups of bytes in memory are *mapped* to positions and attributes on the screen. The mapping varies according to which *video mode* is operative. Display adapters and monitors vary in the number and types of modes they can support.

There are many different modes, but they can be classified into two distinct groups—*text* and *graphics*.

► Text Mapping ►

With text mapping, two adjacent bytes in display memory map to a region of the screen large enough to display a single character. One byte specifies the character (you have 256 combinations with IBM extended ASCII), and the other byte controls the character's attributes (intensity, underlining, reverse video, suppression, blinking, and, possibly, color). Each character is generated by hardware and takes up a fixed area of the screen. The usual maxima are 80 characters per line and 25 lines per screen, as shown in Figure 9.2. A simple calculation shows that for an 80 by 25 text display you need $2 \times 80 \times 25 = 4000$ bytes per page.

► Text Coordinate Systems

Figure 9.2 also shows the *Cartesian* coordinate system used for text in QuickC: X, the column position, runs from 1 through 80 from left to right on each line, and Y, the line or row position, runs from 1 to 25 from top to bottom. QC's text functions refer to a text screen position as (row, column)—i.e., as (Y,X), the opposite order from that used in traditional (X,Y) or (column, row) Cartesian coordinates. The top left corner of the text screen is (1,1) and the bottom right corner is (25,80). Note this second quirk: the row or Y values increase from top to bottom, the reverse of conventional graphs

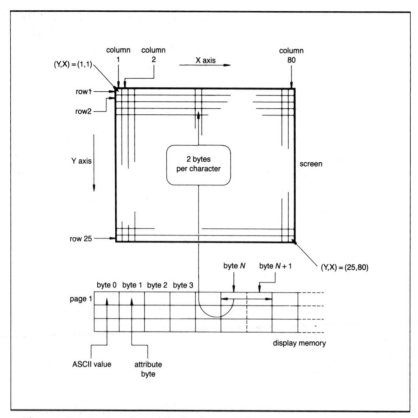

► **Figure 9.2:** *Memory-mapped display for normal text*

in which the Y axis points upward! To add to your confusion, you will encounter ways of inverting the Y axis in some graphics functions so that the second quirk is removed. Forewarned is forearmed!

The relation between row, column, and character position in a page of display memory is

character_offset = ((row − 1) × 80 × 2) + ((column − 1) × 2)

attribute_offset = character_offset + 1

You will also encounter text formats with 40 characters per line. The mapping principle is the same with these.

Pages usually start on even-kilobyte boundaries, so there are often unused bytes between pages. Finding the address of a character in the second and subsequent pages must allow for these gaps.

Now that you know something of text mapping, I'll show you how QuickC handles text windows.

► Text Windows

A text window is a mapping of display memory to a rectangular area of the screen. The minimum window is one row by one column, and the maximum is the whole screen, which is the default when your program starts. The **_settextwindow( )** function specifies four coordinates—two for the top left corner and two for the bottom right corner—using (row,column) coordinates. Thus

```
#include <graph.h>
...
_settextwindow(10, 20, 15, 30);
/* active text window has corners at (10,20), (10,30), (15,30), and (15, 30)
   going in a clockwise direction */
```

will create an active text window as shown in Figure 9.3. A call to **_settextwindow( )** with illegal coordinates will be ignored, and no error message will

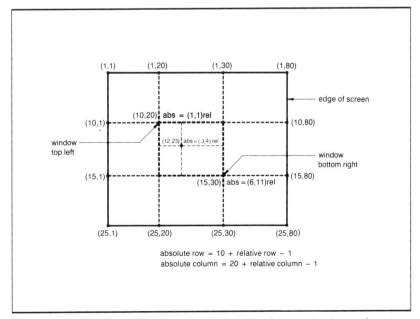

► **Figure 9.3:** *Absolute and relative text window coordinates using (row,column)*

be generated [**_settextwindow( )** returns **void**]. **_settextwindow( )** does not create borders, so you have to draw your own (Program 9.1 shows you how). **_settextwindow( )** simply alters the effect of certain display functions such as **_outtext( )** by sending output to the active window. The vital point to remember is that a window, once created, establishes a new set of local coordinates.

```c
/* TTEXT.C Program 9.1 Test bed for Text-modes */

#include <graph.h>
#include <stdio.h>

#define FALSE 0

#define T_BLACK          0
#define T_BLUE           1
#define T_GREEN          2
#define T_CYAN           3
#define T_RED            4
#define T_MAGENTA        5
#define T_BROWN          6
#define T_WHITE          7
#define T_DARKGRAY       8
#define T_LIGHTBLUE      9
#define T_LIGHTGREEN     10
#define T_LIGHTCYAN      11
#define T_LIGHTRED       12
#define T_LIGHTMAGENTA   13
#define T_LIGHTBROWN     14
#define T_LIGHTWHITE     15
#define T_BLINK          16
/* text colors */

void showvc(void);

struct videoconfig vc;

void main(void)
    {
    short start_row, start_column, start_f_color, start_cursor;
    short start_wrap;          /* initial state of wrapon option */
    long start_bk_color;       /* initial background color */
    struct rccoord rccoord, rc1; /* holds row, col cursor positions */
    char buff[255];            /* temp for sprintf() */
    int r, c;                  /* temp row,col */
    showvc();
/* displays current video mode facts, with pause */

    if (vc.adapter == _HGC)
        puts("You have a Hercules Mono adapter!\n");
    else
    {
        puts("Sorry, no HGC board!\n");
        exit (0);
    }

    if (_setvideomode(_HERCMONO) == FALSE)
    {
        puts("Sorry, but we cannot set HERCMONO mode!\n");
        exit (0);
    }
```

► *Program 9.1:* TTEXT.C

```
/* vary above for CGA, EGA, etc */

/* we are now in e.g. HERCMONO mode */
     showvc();
/* let's look at new values in videoconfig */
     rccoord =_gettextposition();  /* save current cursor row,col */
     start_row = rccoord.row;  start_column = rccoord.col;
     start_cursor = _gettextcursor();
/* save current cursor attribute */
     start_f_color = _gettextcolor();
     start_bk_color = _getbkcolor();
 /* save current text foreground and background colors */
     for (r=1; r <= vc.numtextrows; r++)
        for (c=1; c <= vc.numtextcols; c++)
           {
            _settextposition(r, c);
            _outtext("*");
           }
/* fill screen with asterisks, so we can test clearing a·
 * text window */

     _settextwindow(10, 20, 15, 40);
/* resets text window from initial full screen to a rectangle
 * with row/col coordinates (10,20),(10,40),(15,40),(15,20) in a
 * clockwise direction */

     _clearscreen(_GWINDOW);
/* clears only the text window */

     _settextposition(1,1);
/* sets cursor at 1,1, relative to window = (10,20) absolute */

     start_wrap = _wrapon(_GWRAPON);
/* turn word-wrap on and save previous wrapon status */

     _settextcolor(T_BLUE+T_BLINK);
     _setbkcolor((long) T_BLACK);
/* try different combinations here */

     _outtext("Watch for the wrap around...Hit any key...\n");
     getch();

/*      _settextcolor(_BLUE); _setbkcolor(_BLACK); */
/* see how text attributes interpret colors */

/* restore things...*/
     _settextwindow(1, 1, vc.numtextrows, vc.numtextcols);
     _wrapon(start_wrap);
/* restore prevous wrapon status */
     _settextcolor(start_f_color);
     _setbkcolor(start_bk_color);
/* restor previous foreground and background colors */
     _settextcursor(start_cursor);
     _settextposition(start_row, start_column);
/* restore previous cursor type and position */
     _setvideomode(_DEFAULTMODE);
     }

void showvc()
{
   _getvideoconfig(&vc);
   _clearscreen(_GCLEARSCREEN);
   _settextposition(1,1);
   puts("Your CURRENT Video Mode data:");
   printf("numxpixels  =%4d          numypixels=%4d\n",
                   vc.numxpixels, vc.numypixels);
```

► **Program 9.1:** *TTEXT.C (continued)*

```
    printf("numtextcols  =%4d           numtextrows=%4d\n",
                        vc.numtextcols, vc.numtextrows);
    printf("numcolors    =%4d          bitsperpixel=%4d\n",
                        vc.numcolors, vc.bitsperpixel);
    printf("numvideopages=%4d                  mode=%4d\n",
                        vc.numvideopages, vc.mode);
    printf("adapter      =%4d               monitor=%4d\n",
                        vc.adapter, vc.monitor);
    printf("video memory =%4dK bytes\n", vc.memory);

    printf("Your MONITOR is ");
    switch (vc.monitor) {
       case _MONO:
           puts("Monochrome");
           break;
       case _COLOR:
           puts("Color or Enhanced emulating color");
           break;
       case _ENHCOLOR:
           puts("Enhanced Color");
           break;
       case _ANALOGMONO:
           puts("Analog Mono");
           break;
       case _ANALOGCOLOR:
           puts("Analog Color");
           break;
       case _ANALOG:
           puts("Analog");
           break;
       default:
           puts("Unknown Monitor type");
           break;              /* reminder if future additions */
       }

    puts("Hit a key to proceed...");
    getch();
    _clearscreen(_GCLEARSCREEN);
    return;
}
```

▶ **Program 9.1:** *TTEXT.C (continued)*

As with all coordinate systems in mathematics, there are *absolute* and *relative* addressing methods. **_settextwindow( )** itself uses the absolute coordinates for the window corners, but many of QuickC's window functions use coordinates relative to the top left corner of the window, taking this position as (1,1). You get from relative to absolute coordinates by adding a displacement to each coordinate. This translation is illustrated in Figure 9.3. You'll meet several functions that perform these translation calculations for you.

QuickC allows you to find out where you are, save your cursor position, and move about with **_gettextposition( )** and **_settextposition( )**. The **_wrapon( )** function lets you control whether word wrap will occur when a text window edge is reached. With **_wrapon(_GWRAPOFF)** text sent beyond the left edge of a window simply disappears into the twilight zone. You use **_wrapon(_GWRAPON)** to ensure that text will wrap over to the next line. **_wrapon( )** returns the previous wrap status—a common C trick to help you keep track of what's going on, as well as helping you to restore the status quo.

► *Graphics Mapping* ►

The graphics memory map is fundamentally different from the text map. As shown in Figure 9.4, the screen in graphics mode is conceptually divided into a fine mesh of individual dots or *pixels* (picture elements). The dots are not, of course, Euclidean points, although it is often convenient to treat them as such. Note especially that pixels are referenced as (X,Y) or (column,row),

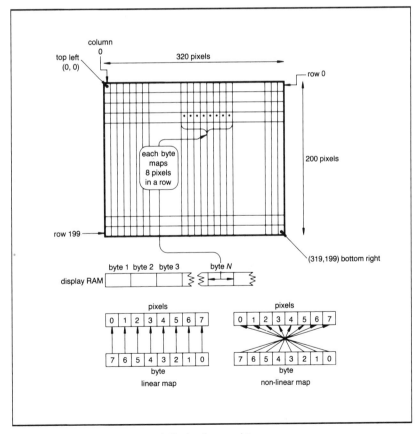

► **Figure 9.4:** *Memory-mapped display for graphics*

the exact reverse of the (row,column) text coordinates. This is a real pain in the plot when you write programs that mix the two coordinate systems. Write to your congressperson!

Any particular pixel can be suppressed or illuminated, which is the whole foundation for creating graphical images. The *resolution* of the display is described in terms of the number of pixels per line and the number of pixels per column. A 640 × 200-pixel display, for example, is considered *hi-res* (high-resolution) and will allow more detailed images than a 160 × 200-pixel *lo-res* (low-resolution) display. Some raster-scanning systems use interlacing, whereby odd- and even-numbered lines are displayed on successive scans. The viewer is not aware of this trickery and the programmer is only involved if interlacing affects the memory mapping. Even then, the graphics functions often hide you from the underlying complexity.

► The Impact of Resolution

Resolution is important when you want smooth curves and diagonal lines. Also, since monitor screens are wider than their height (or vice versa) and/or have pixels that are not perfect squares, there exists the *aspect-ratio* problem. The pixels I am looking at now as I type have an aspect ratio of 4:3 (4 units high and 3 units wide). This is especially noticeable when I try to draw exact squares and pleasant circles. To reduce distortion, certain *scaling* corrections have to be made in one direction or another. Most drawing functions include some aspect-ratio scaling, but you can provide your own corrections as well.

All the popular graphics adapter/monitor combinations offer a choice of resolutions. QuickC provides functions such as **_getvideoconfig( )** and **_setvideomode( )** to test which modes are available and to set, change, or restore a mode. Typically, for a given adapter, the trade-off is between resolution and the number of colors available. When we talk of selecting a video mode, we simply mean choosing a particular combination of palette and resolution (see Table 9.1).

► Pixel Encoding

To represent a pixel state as "on" or "off" requires only 1 bit of display memory, but a pixel may take from 1 to 16 bits when you take into account the possible coding of the pixel attributes. The actual number of bits depends

► **Table 9.1:** *Standard IBM PC video modes and QuickC mnemonics*

Mode	Type	Resolution	Colors/Attributes	Adapters	QC Mnemonic
-1	Original	Original	Original	All	_DEFAULTMODE
0	Text	40 × 25	16 g	CGA, EGA+	_TEXTBW40
1	Text	40 × 25	16 f		
			8 b	CGA, EGA+	_TEXTC40
2	Text	80 × 25	16 g	CGA, EGA+	_TEXTBW80
3	Text	80 × 25	16 f		
			8 b	CGA, EGA+	_TEXTC80
4	Graphics	320 × 200	4	CGA, EGA+	_MRES4COLOR
5	Graphics	320 × 200	4 g	CGA, EGA+	_MRESNOCOLOR
6	Graphics	640 × 200	2	CGA, EGA+	_HRESBW
7	Text	80 × 25	mono	EGA+, MDA	_TEXTMONO
8*	Graphics	720 × 348	mono	Hercules	_HERCMONO
13	Graphics	320 × 200	16	EGA+	_MRES16COLOR
14	Graphics	640 × 200	16	EGA+	_HRES16COLOR
15	Graphics	640 × 350	2	EGA+	_ERESNOCOLOR
16	Graphics	640 × 350	4/16**	EGA+	_ERESCOLOR
17*	Graphics	640 × 480	2	VGA	_VRES2COLOR
18*	Graphics	640 × 480	16	VGA	_VRES16COLOR
19*	Graphics	320 × 200	256	VGA	_MRES256COLOR
64*	Graphics	640 × 400	1/16	Olivetti	_ORESCOLOR

► * *does not correspond to standard IBM video mode number*
► ** *depends on video memory available*
► + *also available on most VGA adapters*
► f = *foreground color*
► b = *background color*
► g = *shades of gray in the color-suppressed modes on composite output. However, the RGB output carries full-color signals.*

on the *palette*, that is to say, the range of colors available. The words *attribute* and *color* are often used loosely and interchangeably to include such factors as intensity or shades of gray or even whether the characters are set to "blink" or not. Do not worry if you see color-coding schemes used with "monochrome" adapters and displays.

The display-memory requirements for a 320 × 200 resolution, 4-color system, taking 2 bits per pixel, would be 2 × 320 × 200 = 128,000 bits = 16KB per page. The same resolution on a 16-color display with 4 bits per pixel would need 32KB per page. If you want more colors and more pages, the memory requirements build up quite nicely, which explains the growth of EMS—the Extended Memory Specification system devised by Intel, Lotus, and others to beat the PC's 1MB addressing-space limit. There are also special ways of addressing display memory that conserve the PC's own address space.

The different ways in which the bits for each pixel can be stored in memory provide more complications. For some modes the mapping is linear; for others you find noncontiguous groups of bits representing banks of odd- and even-numbered lines. Tracking all these and masking off queer bits is a programmer's nightmare. Luckily, the QuickC graphics functions do most of the hard work. You'll see that once you have passed a mode argument to the initialization function **_setvideomode( )**, you work with the same set of high-level tools, however complex the pixel mapping happens to be.

► *Device Drivers*

The secret to interfacing software with so many different adapters and monitors is an intercessory program called the *graphics device driver*, written specially for each group of adapters. You are probably familiar with other device drivers such as disk and mouse drivers. Drivers perform all the nasty little signal translations between logical and physical objects.

All you really need to know about these esoteric driver programs is that you must have one (or more)! QuickC's libraries have built-in drivers for nine of the most popular graphics boards. With one exception, QC loads the appropriate driver for you automatically. If you want to run graphics with the Hercules family of adapters, you must load the special Hercules MSHERC.COM driver yourself before you start the day. Just type MSHERC at the prompt, or put this command in your AUTOEXEC.BAT file. Warning: Do not try to load MSHERC from within QC using the DOS shell!

► *Graphics Coordinates*

As with text mappings, we refer to positions on the graphics screen in terms of coordinates. With text modes, there is a definite, hardware-generated cursor that reminds us of the current position. With graphics modes there is no preordained cursor, but we still refer to the next writing position on the screen as the CP, though in this case it stands for *current position* rather than *cursor position*. If you want a visible cursor on a nontext graphics display, you have to generate one.

There are three other differences between graphics coordinates and text coordinates: in graphics (X,Y) refers to a pixel "point" rather than to a character position, the top left pixel is (0,0) not (1,1), and the coordinates are (column,row) *not* (row,column). Take another look at Figures 9.3 and 9.4 and make sure you understand these differences.

The resolution of the mode you are in dictates the legal range of values for X and Y. For a 640 × 200 resolution, X ranges from 0–639 (left to right) and Y ranges from 0–199 (top to bottom). The function **_getvideoconfig( )** allows you to determine the maximum values of X and Y for the currently reigning mode. You'll meet many such **get...( )** routines that, like **sizeof( )**, simplify the writing of portable code.

Later on, you'll find that QuickC allows you to transform the coordinate system in many ways. For example, you can reset the (0,0) origin to a more convenient point, and you can even invert the Y-axis direction to run from bottom to top (as with conventional mathematical graphs).

► *Pixel Geometry*

All the drawing primitives rely ultimately on selecting pixels according to some relation derived from analytical geometry. $Y = aX + b$ $(a, b <> 0)$, for instance, represents all the pixels on the unique straight line through the points $(0,b)$ and $(-b/a,0)$. $Y = b$ represents a horizontal line through $(0,b)$, and $X = b$ is the vertical line through $(b, 0)$. Similarly, the equation $(X-a)^2 + (Y-b)^2 = R^2$ represents a circle of radius R centered at (a,b), and so on. Euclidean planes and points, of course, cannot be represented on a finite screen with discrete pixels, so you constantly have to decide whether images are to be scaled, clipped, wrapped around, scrolled, or made to reappear on the opposite edge.

Enormous effort has been expended by graphics programmers to devise plotting algorithms that work in fast integer arithmetic, avoiding slow floating-point sums.

► *Three Types of Pixel Coordinates* ►

To master the QuickC graphics toolbox, you need to distinguish the three ways in which pixels can be addressed. Choosing the correct graphics function and passing it the proper values depends on whether you are dealing with *physical*, *viewport*, or *window* coordinates.

As far as a physical pixel "point" is concerned, the hardware needs two integers—the *physical* (also known as the *absolute*) coordinates—in order to locate the pixel on the real, physical screen with respect to the top left origin (0,0).

QuickC lets you establish a *virtual screen* or *viewport*, a rectangular area that may be all or part of the physical screen. The viewport's origin is its top left corner, so that viewport coordinates (also known as *logical* or *relative* coordinates) use integer coordinates relative to this new origin. You will also find viewport coordinates referred to simply as *view* coordinates. As you saw with text windows, the translation from logical to physical coordinates (and vice versa) is a simple $(X + X', Y + Y')$ mapping performed behind the scenes.

The default viewport in the absence of contrary commands is the whole screen, in which case the physical and view coordinate systems coincide. In the next section you'll see how viewports and origins can be set up and changed. The important point to digest now is that both physical and viewport coordinates are integer values. The following data structure, defined in GRAPH.H, indicates how such coordinates are usually stored:

```
struct xycoord {              /* (x,y) for pixels */
        short xcoord;         /* origin is (0,0) */
        short ycoord;
        };
```

For text modes the cursor coordinates are also integers, defined in a similar structure:

```
struct rccoord {              /* row/column for text */
        short row;            /* origin is (1,1)    */
        short col;
        };
```

Note the use of **short int** for improved portability.

Many QC functions return, or use as arguments, the **xycoord** structure for physical and view coordinates. As a simple example, the function **_getphys-coord( )** can be used to convert from view to physical coordinates. The prototype looks like this:

```
struct xycoord far _getphyscoord(short x, short y);
```

The physical coordinates corresponding to (X,Y) are returned in the **xycoord** structure. For example:

```
#include <graph.h>
...
short x, y, px, py;
struct xycoord xycoord;
...
/* set up a viewport here */
...
xycoord = _getphyscoord(x, y);
px = xycoord.xcoord;
py = xycoord.ycoord;
```

You can convert in the opposite direction, from physical to view coordinates, using **_getviewcoord( )**:

```
#include <graph.h>
...
short x, y, px, py;
struct xycoord xycoord;
...
/* set up a viewport here */
...
xycoord = _getviewcoord(px, py);
x = xycoord.xcoord;
y = xycoord.ycoord;
```

You may encounter an obsolete version of **_getviewcoord( )** called **_setlog-coord( )** meaning "set logical coordinates." It works in the same way as **_get-viewcoord( )**.

We now come to the third coordinate system, the window coordinates. First, some motivation. When plotting mathematical functions, the coordinates seldom appear naturally as integers between 0 and max X or max Y.

Life is much easier, therefore, if the (X,Y) in our equations and function calls can refer to floating-point numbers (positive or negative) measured from any convenient origin, with the Y axis oriented in the most convenient direction. Obviously you can always write private routines to massage your real (X,Y) values into suitable physical or view coordinates. You would usually have to round them off to whole numbers, then possibly add displacements to allow for the difference in the physical and logical origins. You may have to reverse the sign of Y to match the "nonstandard" orientation of the hardware, and, somewhere along the way, you will usually have to scale your coordinates to fit your particular graph size. All this is tedious stuff, especially if you want your graphs to appear sensibly on systems with different screen resolutions.

QuickC offers several remedies, howbeit at the expense of learning sets of *window* variants to some of the basic function calls. These variants accept special window coordinates as a pair of **double** arguments, defined via the **_wxycoord** structure, also in GRAPH.H:

```
struct _wxycoord {            /* window coordinates are FP */
        double wx;            /* origin is (0.0,0.0)      */
        double wy;
        };
```

You set up a window by first creating a viewport (unless you need the whole screen), then using **_setwindow( )**, as you'll see in detail soon. Consider a window as a special kind of "scaled" viewport within which you can use floating-point coordinates. You can also invert the sense of the Y axis.

The window function variants have the suffix **_w** tagged on the end of the function name: **_moveto( )** becomes **_moveto_w( )**, and so on. Both **_moveto( )** variants set the CP (current position) without actually displaying a pixel there. In the absence of a "cursor," of course, you get no immediate visual sign that **_moveto( )** has done anything. You normally follow **_moveto( )** with **_setpixel( )** and **_moveto_w( )** with **_setpixel_w( )** (or some other drawing command), which will soon reveal the position of the CP.

A few window functions take the **_wxycoord** structure as argument, rather than two separate **double**s. You can spot these through the special **_wxy** suffix. The **_getviewcoord( )** function you met earlier (converting physical to view coordinates) has two window variants to illustrate this fact. Consider the following prototypes from GRAPH.H:

```
struct xycoord far _getviewcoord_w(double wx, double wy);
/* converts from window to view coordinates */
```

```
struct xycoord far _getviewcoord_wxy(struct _wxycoord far pwxy);
/* also converts from window to view coordinates */
```

► *Viewports and Clip Regions* ►

We first consider three related functions used with viewports: **_setview-port( )**, **_setvieworg( )**, and **setcliprgn( )**. Establishing a viewport, as with a text window, requires the specification of the two physical points: the top left and bottom right limits of the viewport rectangle:

```
short tlx = 30, tly = 40, brx = 200, bry = 150;
  _setviewport(tlx, tly, brx, bry);
/* viewport is bounded by rectangle of 171 x 111 pixels, with
 * the top left corner at absolute (30,40) and the bottom right
 * corner at absolute (200,150) */

/* _setviewport( ) returns void */

/* Note that NO borders are created by this call */
```

This call achieves two purposes: first, the (0,0) origin for view coordinates will now be the physical point (column,row) = (30,40). The coordinate arguments in any subsequent drawing or positioning function calls will be interpreted relative to this new origin. Setting a pixel at (3,5), for instance, will give you a dot at absolute (33,45).

Second, the viewport rectangle serves as a *clip region*, meaning that no displays can occur outside the defined area. Lines and circles that attempt to stray out of bounds will be silently clipped. Remember that in the absence of a **_setviewport( )** call, the whole screen is the default viewport, and also, without any doubt, the whole screen acts as the maximum clip region!

_setvieworg( ) allows you to independently change the viewport origin without affecting the clip region:

```
struct xycoord xycoord;
...
xycoord = _setvieworg(40,60);
/* set absolute (40,60) to new origin
 * and return absolute coords of previous origin */
```

It is vital to note that the arguments for **_setvieworg( )** must always be given in physical, absolute coordinates. **_setvieworg( )** also returns the physical coordinates of the previous origin via an **xycoord** structure. This can be useful for temporary changes of origin. Notice that one important side effect of **_setvieworg( )** is that you may need negative coordinates to access regions north or west of the new origin.

You can also independently create a clip region within a viewport (or the whole screen) without changing the origin:

```
short ctlx = 50, ctly = 60, cbrx = 100, cbry = 90;
_setcliprgn(ctlx, ctly, cbrx, cbry);
/* clip region is a rectangle of 51 x 31 pixels, with
 * the top left corner at absolute (50,60) and the bottom right
 * corner at absolute (100,90) */
/* _setcliprgn( ) returns void */
/* Note that NO borders are created by this call */
```

_setcliprgn( ) must also take absolute, physical coordinates. Attempts at setting impossible viewports and clip regions will be ignored. The **_setviewport( )** call is effectively the same as first calling **_setvieworg( )** at the viewport's top left corner, then calling **_setcliprgn( )** with the viewport's dimensions.

Viewports do not come with visible surrounding rectangles, but you can easily create pretty frames by selecting a *line style* with **_setlinestyle( )** and then calling **_rectangle( )**. Unlike the text mode user-supplied rectangle, which is limited to using the IBM extended ASCII line and corner symbols, the graphics frames can be Louvres or Guggenheim to taste. Consider the following snippet:

```
_setlinestyle(mask);
_rectangle(fill_control, tlx, tly, brx, bry);
```

where **mask** is an unsigned short integer value representing the pixel pattern needed for line drawing. For example, a **mask** of 0x8888 would give a dotted line by repeating the pixel pattern 1000100010001000.

The **fill_control** argument can be either **_GBORDER** or **_GFILLINTERIOR** (constants defined in GRAPH.H), giving a simple border or solid, filled rectangle, respectively.

The fill pattern is set with **_setfillmask(fillmask)**, where **fillmask** is an 8 × 8 array of bits, with 1's set in the places where you want the pixel to show with the current color and 0's where the pixel is to be unchanged. As with the line-style **mask**, the **fillmask** pattern is repeated to fill the area. A **fillmask** set to xAAxAAxAAxAAxAAxAAxAAxAA, for example, would show a repeated 1010 pixel shading. If **fillmask** is set to NULL (the default), the rectangle is filled uniformly with the current color. The same filling mask, by the way, is used for flood filling other closed shapes, but care must be exercised to avoid "leaky" borders.

_getlinestyle( ) and **_getfillmask( )** allow you to save the current line and fill masks for subsequent restoration, as shown by the following prototypes:

```
unsigned short far _getlinestyle(void);
/* returns a 2-byte value representing the currently set
 * linestyle */
unsigned char far * far _getfillmask(unsigned char far *fillmask);
/* Note that the argument and return value are both far pointers
 * to unsigned char. In the smaller memory models, you should
 * type cast your arguments with (unsigned char far *)fillmask.
 * More on far functions and pointers at A LA MODE below.
 * Returns NULL if no fillmask has been set. */
```

The significance of the **far** keyword will emerge later.

Another advantage of viewports is that you can move arbitrary rectangles of graphics data (often referred to as graphics or bit images) between screen and memory, using the functions **_getimage( )**, **_imagesize( )**, and **putimage( )**. You'll see these in action soon.

► *QC Does Windows* ►

It is rather strange that the simple, homely concept of windows has generated such conflicting terminology in the computer industry. The viewport described above fits some people's idea of a window. However, QuickC uses the word *window* in a special sense to refer to a viewport with scaling and floating-point coordinates. Once you have established a viewport (including the whole-screen default case), you can create an associated window using **_setwindow( )**. Consider the following prototype:

```
void _setwindow(short invert, double wx1, double wy1,
                double wx2, double wy2);
```

The **invert** argument is set to true if you want the Y axis to increase from bottom to top—i.e., the origin will be (0,0) at the bottom left of the viewport with

(0,maxY) at the top left corner. Set **invert** to false to get the normal screen coordinates with (0,0) at top left and Y increasing from top to bottom. The two "points" (wx1,wy1) and (wx2,wy2) given in FP window coordinates represent the minimum and maximum values envisaged in your plotted graph. The basic idea is that subsequent calls to, say, **_setpixel_w( )** or **_lineto_w( )**, the special window variants of the drawing functions, will have their arguments scaled automatically to fit the stated window range within the given viewport. We'll return to this feature later.

► *TEXT-TEXT AND GRAPHICS-TEXT* ►

Having seen a little of the theory behind text and graphics memory maps, let's return to the different adapter/monitor combinations available. They fall into two main groups—those capable of text mode only, such as the IBM MDA, and those that can handle both text and graphics modes, such as the Hercules Graphics Card and the IBM CGA and EGA boards. The dual-purpose models can be switched between several different modes, some of which use text mappings and others of which use graphics mappings with different resolutions.

The standard IBM PC range provides internal hardware and ROM BIOS support for five distinct text modes and seven graphics modes (I exclude three graphics modes assigned exclusively to the PCjr). Which of these you can access depends initially on the adapter fitted and the drivers available. If you have the proper adapter and drivers, exploitation of the features provided in each mode then rests with your monitor.

I have to choose my words carefully. All multimode systems are capable of displaying text in text mode (normal ASCII plus attribute mapping) as well as text in graphics mode (using pixels to create characters in various ways). I'll call the former text-text and the latter graphics-text to avoid confusion.

There are two types of graphics-text: *bit-mapped fonts* and *stroked fonts* (also known as *vector-mapped fonts*). A bit-mapped font defines a fixed pixel pattern for each text symbol within a small rectangle. You can intermix graphics-text with normal graphics elements in display memory to provide legends for your graphs, pie slices, and bar charts.

You can use software to do creative (not to mention hideously unattractive) things with a graphics-text that you can't do with text mode text. Some examples are justification, rotation, inversion, magnification, Hebrew vowel pointing, and accenting. The bit-mapped approach has severe limitations, however, such as the well-known invasion of the "jaggies" when characters are enlarged beyond a certain size. Scaling up a bit-mapped character quickly reveals the rough edges.

The *stroked-font* approach can reduce some of these problems. Each character in a stroked font is coded as a drawing, using line and curve segments, rather than as a small set of pixels. Deep down, of course, everything displayed is really a set of pixels, and ultimately the resolution of the monitor sets the limit. With advanced splining techniques, however, the typographic disasters of magnification can be reduced. On the other hand, at smaller sizes, the bit-mapped characters are often crisper than the vector-mapped ones.

QuickC provides three bit-mapped fonts: Courier, Helv (Helvetica), and Tms Rmn (Times Roman); and three stroked fonts: Modern, Script, and Roman. The data tables defining these fonts are stored in *.FON files, compatible with the *.FON files used in Microsoft Windows.

Specialist vendors provide more exotic fonts that include foreign-language character sets. (See Appendix H.) In addition, the technique of scanning and digitizing from artwork has simplified the problem of creating fonts (especially when compared with the old, manual bit-picking methods).

To summarize, with text-text you are relying on a hardware character generator that takes an ASCII byte plus an attribute byte and forms its own character image for the monitor. Most computer printers are set up to handle text-text with just minor tweaks for attribute changes (bold, italics, underlining, and so on).

The graphics mapped fonts do it all with software. They take extra memory and CPU cycles but offer much in return—scaling, sloping, style changing, proportional spacing, and WYSIWYG (what you see is what you get) displays for desktop publishing. Printing graphics fonts is more difficult since the mappings and resolutions of screen and printer seldom match.

► SOME POPULAR DISPLAY ADAPTERS ►

Adapters such as IBM's Monochrome Display Adapter (MDA) work only with a single color in text mode. With the IBM extended ASCII code, you do get several line-segment symbols from which you can build up simple rectangular shapes and bar charts that a lay onlooker might consider to be "graphical." Although the MDA can only handle ASCII text, it excels at this task with crisp, high-resolution characters ideal for the mainstream of office word processing. The MDA has been widely cloned and imitated.

The IBM Color Graphics Adapter (CGA) can operate in seven modes, four for text (two mono and two color) and three for graphics (two mono and one color). The IBM Enhanced Graphics Adapter (EGA) provides all the CGA modes plus four additional modes (one mono text and three color graphics). The IBM Video Graphics Array (VGA) supports all the CGA and EGA modes, then adds three more (all high-resolution color graphics).

The Hercules Graphics Card (HGC) offers an excellent compromise, providing a high-resolution 720 × 348 in monochrome. It is quite feasible to have more than one adapter board fitted as long as each knows its place.

Table 9.1 lists the properties of each of the modes assigned in the *video byte* at address 0x40:0x49 of all true blue PC's. The mode numbers in Table 9.1 follow QuickC's conventions, although the numbers do coincide with IBM's internal video byte values for the text modes.

Since several adapters can share the same mode value, there is another byte at address 0x40:0x87, the *equipment byte*, which is used to encode, inter alia, the type of adapter. In theory, software can poll these bytes to discover what video boards are fitted. In practice, there are many near-clones and almost-compatibles out there to muddy the waters.

► A LA MODE ►

Summing up so far, your graphics adapter board can work in two distinct sets of modes: text-only modes and graphics modes. Text can be displayed in both modes, but for drawing fancy pictures such as circles and sine waves, you must be in a graphics mode and your monitor must be capable of displaying bit-mapped pixels. Some functions will output text in either mode, while other functions are limited to just one of the mode types. QuickC, however, offers the one function **_setvideomode( )** to select either a text or a graphics mode. The prototype tells the simple story:

```
short _FAR _setvideomode(short mode);
/* try to select the given mode; return zero if unsuccessful */
```

Before I discuss the action of this function, a brief detour might be useful to explain the use of **far** functions and pointers in graphics applications. The key fact behind the **_FAR** trick is that QuickC supplies one GRAPHICS.LIB and one PGCHART.LIB to work with all the memory models.

► *Far Away Functions* ►

The strange-looking **_FAR** in the previous prototype gets replaced either with nothing at all or with the more familiar modifier **far**, depending on various compiler options and memory model settings.

Note that all graphics library functions actually need the **far** keyword (either explicitly in the smaller models or implicitly in the large models), so that regardless of the memory model in force, pointers to these functions are 32 bits; such functions need not reside in the current code segment. Similarly, many of the internal data arguments accessed by the graphics library must be declared **far** since they may exist outside your program's data segment (more on this in Appendix E in the discussion of pointers and memory models).

The big snag is that **far** is a non-ANSI, or *extended*, keyword, so it cannot be used explicitly in prototypes without hindering portability. Hence, you will find the following conditional definitions in GRAPH.H (and elsewhere, in fact):

```
/* edited extract from GRAPH.H */
    #ifndef NO_EXT_KEYS  /* ANSI extensions have been enabled */
    #define _FAR  far  /* so 'far' is admitted */
    #else
        #ifdef M_I86LM  /* large model */
                #define _FAR  /* 'far' is not needed */
        #else
                #error /Za requires /AL when using graph.h
        /* don't disable ANSI extensions in small models! */
        #endif  /* ends if M_I86LM */
    #endif  /* ends if NO_EXT_KEYS)
```

(You'll find similar tricks applied to the other extended keywords such as **cdecl** and **pascal**.) If you follow this snippet through, you'll see that when you compile with non-ANSI extensions enabled (i.e., **NO_EXT_KEYS** *not* defined), **_FAR** becomes **far** in all the following prototypes of GRAPH.H, otherwise **_FAR** becomes empty for the large memory model. Trying to compile with GRAPH.H functions under a small model with ANSI extensions disabled (i.e., **NO_EXT_KEYS** defined) will result in an error message. In the QC environment, the Language Extension option (in the Options menu) defaults to On (**NO_EXT_KEYS** *not* defined), so leave it like that for graphics work in the smaller memory models. For QCL, the /Ze and /Za switches are used to enable and disable the ANSI C extensions—so avoid /Za unless you are also using the large memory model switch, /AL.

To simplify the following exposition, I will often omit the **_FAR** and **far** modifiers when showing you function prototypes. You should be aware of the role they are playing but not be overly concerned with the details.

► *Setting and Getting Video Modes* ►

Returning to the prototype

```
short _setvideomode(short mode);
/* try to select the given mode; return zero if unsuccessful */
```

the value of **mode** is set to a **short** integer representing the graphics mode you want to select. **mode** can be any of the mnemonics shown in Table 9.1—e.g., **_TEXTC80**, **_HERCMONO**, and so on. The **short** value returned by **_setvideomode( )** is true (nonzero) if the request is granted, otherwise false (zero). A false returned value indicates that the mode you requested was not available. The most common reason for **_setvideomode( )** to fail is that the video board(s) fitted do not support the target mode. More likely, now that composite boards come with endless rows of DIP switches, the chances are that the board *would* support the target mode *if* the switches were correctly set.

When writing programs for a wide range of systems and video boards, you must apply tests before and after each use of **_setvideomode( )** to avoid obvious calamities. Good programs try to inform the user why they cannot continue. The catch-22 is that bugs in graphics programs (or adapter boards) often prevent the display of diagnostic messages! It is useful to remember that messages can always be redirected to the printer.

Even when writing for a single "known" configuration, it is wise to test the result of **_setvideomode( )**:

```
if (_setvideomode(_ORESCOLOR) = = FALSE)
{
  puts("You need an Olivetti Graphics Board!\n");
  exit (0);
}
/* reach here if _ORESCOLOR mode selected */
```

Note the typical C "economy" of invoking a function as part of the conditional test.

Another popular method of selecting available modes depends on the probing function **_getvideoconfig( )**. You met this earlier as a means of exploring the features of your video hardware, such as the number of pixels available. **_getvideoconfig( )** is passed the address of a structure of type **videoconfig**, defined in GRAPH.H as follows:

```
struct videoconfig {
        short numxpixels;           /* number of pixels on X axis */
        short numypixels;           /* number of pixels on Y axis */
        short numtextcols;          /* number of text columns available */
        short numtextrows;          /* number of text rows available */
        short numcolors;            /* number of actual colors */
        short bitsperpixel;         /* number of bits per pixel */
        short numvideopages;        /* number of available video pages */
        short mode;                 /* current video mode */
        short adapter;              /* active display adapter */
        short monitor;              /* active display monitor */
        short memory;               /* adapter video memory in KB */
};
```

Calling **_getvideoconfig( )** fills the above structure with the relevant data for your current active video board, monitor, and mode. You can then test various fields and take the appropriate action. The **adapter** and **monitor** fields are usually the first to be checked out. Consider the following code extract:

```
struct videoconfig vc;  /* declare vc as a structure */
...
_getvideoconfig(&vc);   /* fill vc with active mode data */
if (vc.adapter = = _EGA)
{
  if (vc.monitor = = _ENHCOLOR)
  {
  /* an EGA board with enhanced color monitor has been
   * detected. Set an appropriate mode here */
  }
  else if (vc.monitor = = _COLOR)
  { ...
  }
  else ...
```

```
    }
    else if (vc.adapter = = _VGA)
    {
        /* set a mode available on a VGA board */
    }
    ...
    else
        puts("Sorry, you do not have the proper adapter board!\n");
```

The mnemonics and hex values for the various adapters and monitor types are shown in Table 9.2. The bit patterns assigned offer the scope for

► **Table 9.2:** *Video adapter and monitor mnemonics*

Mnemomic	Hex Value	Adapter
_MDPA	0x0001	Monochrome Display Adapter
_CGA	0x0002	Color Graphics Adapter
_EGA	0x0004	Enhanced Graphics Adapter
_VGA	0x0008	Video Graphics Array
_MCGA	0x0010	MultiColor Graphics Array
_HGC	0x0020	Hercules Graphics Card
_OCGA	0x0042	Olivetti Color Graphics Adapter
_OEGA	0x0044	Olivetti Enhanced Graphics Adapter
_OVGA	0x0048	Olivetti Video Graphics Array
Mnemonic	**Hex Value**	**Monitor Type**
_MONO	0x0001	Monochrome
_COLOR	0x0002	Color (or enhanced emulating color)
_ENHCOLOR	0x0004	Enhanced color
_ANALOGMONO	0x0008	Analog monochrome only
_ANALOGCOLOR	0x0010	Analog color only
_ANALOG	0x0018	Analog monochrome and color modes

bitwise operations when checking for matches. For example:

```
if (vc.adapter & 0x0040)
    puts("You have an Olivetti board\n");
```

The **switch/case** construct and other variants are possible, as you'll soon see, but for now the important point is to see how **_getvideoconfig( )** and the **videoconfig** structure work together.

The general graphics programming sequence goes like this:

1. Use **_getvideoconfig( )** to determine the monitor type and available modes. Warn if the hardware detected is inadequate for the purposes of the program.

2. If several modes are available, use some criterion such as best resolution or largest palette, or offer a menu choice.

3. Use **_setvideomode( )** to set the chosen mode, then test for success.

4. Use **_getvideoconfig( )** again to set all the video parameters of the selected mode into the **videoconfig** structure.

5. After completing the graphics routines, remember to restore the adapter to its default condition:

```
_setvideomode(_DEFAULTMODE);
```

► *TEXT MODES* ►

Now that you can set your adapter to any available mode, let's look at some of the text-only-mode functions, applicable to such modes as **_TEXT-MONO**, **_TEXTBW40**, **_TEXTC40**, **_TEXTBW80**, and **_TEXTC80**. Recall that the normal display functions in STDIO.H and CONIO.H are no longer adequate for several reasons. First, the standard and console output functions may not give you complete control over cursor position. Second, you cannot directly use the **printf( )** or **cprintf( )** formatting methods. Finally, the standard nongraphics display functions do not recognize the text windows and their associated coordinates that you can establish in the graphics text-only modes. The following bizarre snippet will reveal some of the important functions that overcome these limitations.

```
        short start_row, start_column, start_f_color, start_cursor;
        short start_wrap;           /* initial state of wrapon option */
        short start_toggle;         /* initial state of cursor on/off toggle */
        long start_bk_color;        /* initial background color */
        struct videoconfig vc;      /* vc holds current video data */
        struct rccoord rccoord, rc1;  /* hold row,col cursor positions */
        char buff[255];
        ...
        _getvideoconfig(&vc);       /* what's out there? */
        if ((vc.adapter = = _CGA) || (vc.adapter = = _EGA))
            puts("You have a CGA or EGA board!\n");
        else
        {
            puts("Sorry, no CGA/EGA board!\n");
            exit (0);
        }
        if (_setvideomode(_TEXTC80))
        {
            start_cursor = _gettextcursor( );
/* save current cursor attribute */
            start_toggle = displaycursor(_GCURSOROFF);
/* set cursor off and remember previous state */
            start_f_color = _gettextcolor( );
            start_bk_color = _getbkcolor( );
/* save current text foreground and background colors */
        }
        else
        {
            puts("Sorry, cannot set TEXTC80 mode!\n");
            exit (0);
        }
/* we are now in 80 col text, 16/8 CGA color mode */
        _getvideoconfig(&vc);   /* set all video data in vc */
        _settextwindow(10, 20, 15, 60);
/* resets text window from initial full screen to a rectangle
 * with row/col coordinates (10,20),(10,60),(15,60),(15,20) in a
 * clockwise direction */

        _clearscreen(_GWINDOW);
/* clear the text window */

        start_wrap = _wrapon(_GWRAPOFF);
/* turn word-wrap off and save previous wrapon status */
```

```
        rccoord = gettextposition( );  /* save current cursor row,col */
        start_row = rccoord.row;  start_column = rccoord.col;

        _settextposition(1,1);
        _outtext("Start at 1,1 relative to text window\n");
        rec1 = _settextposition(3, 4);
/* move text cursor to row 12 col 23; save previous position */

        _settextcolor(max(start_f_color + 1,15));
/* change foreground color unless max */
        sprintf(buff, "Prev. row = %d  Prev. column = %d
                NumColors = %d\n", rc1.row, rc1.col, vc.numcolors);
        _outtext(buff);

        sprintf(buff, "Available text rows = %d  text columns = %d\n",
                vc.numtextrows, vc.numtexcols);
        _outtext(buff);
/* last two lines replace a normal printf( ) */
        rccoord = _gettextposition( );     /* where are we now? */
/* answer is (rccoord.row, rccoord.col) */
        ...
        _wrapon(start_wrap);     /* restore previous wrapon status */
        sprintf(buff, "New row = %d  New column = %d\n",
                rccoord.row, rccoord.col);
        _outtext(buff);
        ...
        _settextcolor(start_f_color);
        _setbkcolor(start_bk_color);
/* restore previous foreground and background colors */

        _displaycursor(start_toggle);
        _settextcursor(start_cursor);
        _settextposition(start_row, start_column);
/* restore previous cursor on/off, type and position */
        ...
        _setvideomode(_DEFAULTMODE);
/* restore default video mode */
```

Note first that the **struct rccoord** defined in GRAPH.H as

```
struct rccoord {
     short row;
     short col;
};
```

is used as the return value in both **_gettextposition( )** and **_settextposition( )**. The simplified prototypes are:

```
struct rccoord _gettextposition(void);
/* returns the current absolute text cursor coordinates as
 * (rccoord.row,rccoord.col). There are no error indications */
struct rccoord _settextposition(short new_row, short new_col);
/* saves previous text cursor coordinates as (rccoord.row,
 * rccoord.col), and moves the cursor to new_row, new_col. There
 * are no error indications */
```

Setting a text window with **_settextwindow( )** affects the action of **_outtext( )** only when displayed text reaches the left vertical edge and the bottom horizontal base of the defined window. If **_wrapon(option)** is called with **option** set to **_GWRAPON**, the text will "wrap" over to the next line rather than "escape" from the text window. This is a coarse "word break" wrap—in other words, words can be split when wrapping occurs.

If you use **option** set to **_GWRAPOFF**, any characters trying to display beyond the left edge are simply clipped and discarded. Regardless of the **option** setting, though, when text reaches the bottom line of a text window, the text is always scrolled—i.e., the new bottom line pushes earlier lines upward, until the previous top line leaves the window forever.

The **_settextwindow( )** function has a simple prototype that tells the whole story:

```
void _settextwindow(short tlr, short tlc, short brr, short brc);
/* (tlr,tlc) are the top left row,column, (brr,brc) are the
 * bottom right row,column absolute coordinates of the text
 * window. Illegal parameters are ignored; there are no error
 * indications */
```

In the absence of any **_settextwindow ( )** calls, the whole screen is considered as the default text window. The **videoconfig** structure lets you determine the number of text rows and columns available: **vc.numtextrows** and **vc.numtextcols**.

Note that text windows are defined by the absolute coordinates of their corners, even if a previous text window has been established. Each text window removes the effects of any previous text window, and subsequent text positioning is done via (row,column) coordinates relative to the new top left corner, which is now considered to be (1,1).

The function **_clearscreen( )** takes a single mnemonic argument:

_GCLEARSCREEN	= 0 will clear the whole screen
_GVIEWPORT	= 1 will clear (and fill with the current background color) the current viewport (nontext modes)
_GWINDOW	= 2 will clear the current text window (all modes)

The prototype is

```
    void _clearscreen(short option);
/* clear or fill all or part of the screen according to current
 * mode, current window or viewport, and value of option. No
 * error indications */
```

There are three functions to control the cursor. In most graphics contexts, the normal "blinking" cursor of the Monochrome Display Adapter is a blinking nuisance, but in text modes a cursor can be useful. In fact, the CGA and EGA boards can display various cursor shapes in text mode. When you enter any graphics routine, however, the cursor is automatically hidden, but using **_displaycursor( )** you can control whether it remains hidden when the routine is exited. Consider the following prototype:

```
short _displaycursor(short toggle);
```

If **toggle** is set to **_GCURSORON** (or 1), the cursor will be restored upon exit from a graphics routine. If **toggle** is set to **_GCURSOROFF** (or 0), the cursor remains off. There are also two functions—**_gettextcursor( )** and **_settextcursor( )**—for determining and setting the text cursor attributes (blinking, solid block, underline, and so on). These seem to be hardware and BIOS dependent, so you should experiment to see how they work on your system. In the snippet I simply use them to save and restore the initial cursor. Incidentally, I find that many packages I use, including QuickC, have the bad habit of changing my cursor shape—e.g., from underline to hyphen—when I exit back to, say, WordStar. The small difference can be quite disconcerting during text editing.

The snippet also illustrates the important use of **sprintf( )** and **_outtext( )** when you want to format output in text modes. Note that **_outtext( )** can also display standard text in graphics modes. Later, you'll see how the

_outgtext( ) variant can be used to display graphics-text (fonts). **_outtext( )**
takes only a single string argument, hence the prior use of **sprintf( )** to format
the array of **char** called **buff**. I made it **buff[255]** to err on the side of safety.
Here's the **_outtext( )** prototype:

```
    void _outtext(char *text);
/ * display text from the current position. No error indications. */
```

The subject of color now rears its ugly head. Each time I feel that all is clear
and stable, some new XXXGA board arrives with larger palettes, higher resolution, and more complex calling schemes. In the next section I discuss the
simpler, almost obsolete CGA text color modes (also available, remember,
with EGA and VGA boards).

▶ *Text Color* ▶

The CGA text modes that offer color work as follows (provided you have a
color monitor, of course). You will recall that a text character and its attribute
are encoded in adjacent bytes. The screen cell displaying the character can
have a selected *background* color upon which the character appears in a
foreground color. The attribute byte encodes both these colors and a *blink-
enable flag* as follows:

Bits	Meaning
0–3	4 bits = 16 foreground colors possible
4–6	3 bits = 8 background colors possible
7	1 bit = blink-enable flag (0 = off, 1 = on)

It is instructive to look a little deeper at the seven color-encoding bits:

Bit	Meaning
0	Blue foreground
1	Green foreground
2	Red foreground
3	Intensity bit (0 = off, 1 = on)

4	Blue background
5	Green background
6	Red background

Sir Isaac Newton showed that mixing the three primary colors, red, green, and blue, in different proportions could produce all the colors of the visible spectrum. With the aid of the single intensity bit, the 8 simple mixes of the foreground primaries provide 16 different colors, 8 of which (low intensity) are also available as background colors. Clearly the same combination of low-intensity background and foreground colors is unacceptable—the character would merge with its background! Even with a high-intensity foreground, some of the background colors do not work very well (brown behind yellow, for example). The default attribute-byte setting, by the way, is 0x7, which gives white on black.

The 16 colors derived from these combinations are defined numerically as 0–15 as shown in Table 9.3. The numbers 16–31 represent the same colors but with "blinking" text. These numbers are used in the four color-manipulating functions **_settextcolor( )** and **_gettextcolor( )** for foreground and **_setbkcolor( )** and **_getbkcolor( )** for background colors.

The **_set...( )** functions do not alter the colors of previously displayed text—they simply set the color attributes for all *subsequently* displayed characters and their backgrounds until the attribute is changed again (or you exit the mode). Generally speaking, changing attributes and modes seldom affects the current display—you are setting things up to change the text that you output subsequently. Plan ahead! One rare exception is when you change a palette index on the EGA. The colors are immediately changed on the existing display, providing an opportunity for psychedelic effects that some programmers, alas, find hard to resist.

Here are the prototypes of the text color functions:

```
short _settextcolor(short color_value);
/* Set foreground color with color_value 0-31; 0-15 for steady
 * colors, 16-31 for blinking colors. Returns previous
 * foreground color_value. No error indications */

short _gettextcolor( );
/* Returns color_value of current foreground text /
long _setbkcolor(long color_value);
```

▶ **Table 9.3:** *Text colors*

Value	Color	Foreground/Background?
0	Black	Both
1	Blue	Both
2	Green	Both
3	Cyan	Both
4	Red	Both
5	Magenta	Both
6	Brown	Both
7	White	Both (light gray on some monitors)
8	Dark gray	Foreground only (or black)
9	Light blue	Foreground only
10	Light green	Foreground only
11	Light cyan	Foreground only
12	Light red	Foreground only
13	Light magenta	Foreground only
14	Light brown	Foreground only (or yellow)
15	Light white	Foreground only
+ 16		Adds blink to corresponding foreground color

```
/* Set background color with color_value 0-7.
 * Returns previous background color_value. No error indications.
 * Used also in nontext modes */

long _getbkcolor( );
/* Returns color_value of current background text. Used
 * also in some nontext modes */
```

The reason for the **long int** in the background color values is to allow their use in EGA, VGA, and other color modes. These need a 4-byte value to allow the encoding of additional mixes of red, green, and blue. For example, the

VGA allows 64 intensities for each of the RGB components, so that each color needs 6 bits. The EGA allows a 64-color palette using 2 bits (4 intensities) for each of the RGB primaries.

► *The Monochrome Attribute* ►

If you use these color-change calls on a monochrome adapter/monitor, the attribute bit pattern will be interpreted somewhat differently. The intensity and blinking bits work identically, but color bits allow only four distinct combinations:

► Normal "white on black" corresponds to attribute value 0x07, which is equivalent to **_settextcolor(15);** and **_setbkcolor(0);**.

► Underline, obtained with attribute value 0x01, corresponds to **_settextcolor(1);** and **_setbkcolor(0);**.

► Reverse video, obtained with attribute value 0x70, corresponds to **_settextcolor(0);** and **_setbkcolor(15);**.

► Hidden relates to attribute value 0x00, the same as **_settextcolor(0);** and **_setbkcolor(0);**. This can be useful for certain animated titling tricks.

On each of these you can superimpose high intensity and blinking, although it's hardly useful with hidden characters! You should experiment on your system to see the effect of combinations such as flashing reverse video, highlighted underlines, ad nauseam.

► *Text Mode Test Bed* ►

To give you a test bed for exploring the text-only modes, try out TTEXT.C, shown in Program 9.1. With the program comments to guide you, you should experiment to find the best combinations of foreground and background color for you own particular adapter/monitor. If you have not incorporated GRAPHICS.LIB in your combined library, proceed as follows:

1. Enter TTEXT.C using the QC editor.

2. Press Alt-M to get the Make menu.

3. Type S to set a program list.

4. Enter TTEXT.MAK as the file name.

5. Enter \LIB\GRAPHICS.LIB, then TTEXT.C. You will see these names appear in the program list window. (The actual order of the file names in a program list is not important.)

6. Press Alt-S to save your TTEXT.MAK file.

7. If you want to change or correct a *.MAK file, type E to use Edit from the Make menu. Boxes in the Edit menu let you Add/Delete, Clear all, or Save.

Whenever you invoke Run, Compile, Build, or Rebuild from QC, the compiler/linker looks at TTEXT.MAK for guidance. Depending on what has changed (and when) since TTEXT.EXE was last created, Run and Build will compile and/or link as needed. Rebuild will force a complete compile/link regardless.

▶ GRAPHICS MODES ▶

Getting into a graphics mode is no more difficult than getting into a text mode: You use the same **_getvideoconfig( )** and **_setvideomode( )** functions as outlined earlier. However, you do have the problem of working with more complex coordinate systems, and you have many more functions to worry about. From now on, I will be discussing the tools available in both GRAPHICS.LIB and PGCHART.LIB. Remember to include both GRAPH.H and PGCHART.H in your programs as needed and ensure that both libraries are accessible, either in the combined libraries or via your *.MAK files.

▶ *Graphics Mode Applications* ▶

Once you have successfully called **_setvideomode( )**, you have at your command all the spectacular display effects provided in the QuickC toolbox: lines, arcs, ellipses, bar charts, pie charts, graphs, scatter diagrams, and all the creative combinations imaginable. You can set colors (if you have them), line styles, and fill patterns from a given repertory or design your own. You can write text in the standard font or in any of the available fonts, with various magnifications.

► *Using Fonts* ►

As a starter, TFONT.C (Program 9.2) determines a few facts about the adapter you have, then explores the various fonts available. I have already mentioned the various *.FON files supplied with QuickC. Table 9.4 lists the six standard fonts with their characteristics. A growing number of vendors can supply other fonts in this format. You simply load such *.FON files to your hard disk and use them as in TFONT.C.

Figure 9.5 shows the output from TFONT.C.

► **Table 9.4:** *Standard *.FON typefaces and sizes*

Typeface	Mapping	Pixel Sizes	M/P	File Name
Courier	Bit	13×8, 16×9, 20×12	Mono	COURIER
Helv	Bit	13×5, 16×7, 20×8	Mono	HELV
		13×15, 16×6, 19×8		
Tms Rmn	Bit	10×5, 12×6, 15×8	Mono	TMSRMN
		16×9, 20×12, 26×16		
Modern	Stroked	Scaled	Prop	MODERN
Script	Stroked	Scaled	Prop	SCRIPT
Roman	Stroked	Scaled	Prop	ROMAN

```
/* Program 9-2 */
/* TFONT.C - play with *.FON files */

#include <stdio.h>
#include <conio.h>
#include <graph.h>

#define NFONTS 6

void init_graphics(void);
void exit_graphics(void);
/* function declarations */

struct videoconfig vc;
/* defined in graph.h */

int maxx, maxy;
/* X axis runs from 0-maxx; Y axis runs from 0-maxy */
/* Set in init_graphics() via struct vc */
```

► **Program 9.2:** *TFONT.C*

```
void main(void)
{

/* see what graphics cards you have in there -- set highest rez
 * mode and fill the struct vc with video mode parameters. */

        init_graphics();

/* need to register a font before using it */
        if (_registerfonts("SCRIPT.FON") < 0)
        {
            _outtext("Sorry! SCRIPT Font not available");
            exit (0);
        }
        _setfont("t'script'h20w15b");
/* specify typeface, h20,w15=character height,width in pixels
 * b=pick best fit. 'script' is now the 'current' font */

/* here you can use _getfontinfo(&fi) to find out more about the
 * selected font, e.g. fi.ascent, fi.pixwidth. See text */

        _rectangle(_GBORDER,0,0,maxx/2,maxy/2);
        _moveto(10,10);
/* sets cp for graphics text at absolute x=10, y=10 */
        _outgtext("This is a sample of SCRIPT");
/* _outgtext() is a variant of _outtext() for graphics text */

/* repeat for another font */
        if (_registerfonts("COURB.FON") < 0)
        {
            _outtext("Sorry! COURIER Font not available");
            exit (0);
        }
        _moveto(10,30);
        _setfont("t'courier'h16w9b");
        _outgtext("This is a sample of COURIER");

        exit_graphics();
/* Any-key exit, then restore to default graphics mode */
        _unregisterfonts();
/* frees memory when no more font-work needed */
}

/***** FUNCTION DEFINITIONS *****/

void exit_graphics(void)
{
        _rectangle(_GBORDER,0,maxy-80,maxx-30,maxy-10);
        _moveto(10,maxy-45);
        _outgtext("Returning to Default Mode -- Hit any key...");
        getch();
        _setvideomode(_DEFAULTMODE);
}

void init_graphics(void)
{
    _getvideoconfig(&vc);
    switch (vc.adapter)
    {
        case _CGA:
            _setvideomode(_HRESBW);    /* 640 x 200 BW */
            break;
        case _OCGA:
            _setvideomode(_ORESCOLOR);  /* 640 x 400 1 of 16 cols */
            break;
        case _EGA:
        case _OEGA:
```

► *Program 9.2:* TFONT.C (continued)

```
            if (vc.monitor == _MONO)
                _setvideomode(_ERESNOCOLOR);   /* 640 x 350 BW */
            else
                _setvideomode(_ERESCOLOR);     /* 640 x 350 4/16 cols
    */
            break;
        case _VGA:
        case _OVGA:
        case _MCGA:
            _setvideomode(_VRES2COLOR); /* 640 x 480 BW */
            break;
        case _HGC:
            _setvideomode(_HERCMONO);   /* 720 x 348 BW */
            break;
        default:
            printf("This program requires a CGA, EGA, VGA, or
    Hercules card\n" );
            exit (0);
    }
    _getvideoconfig(&vc);

    maxx = vc.numxpixels - 1;
    maxy = vc.numypixels - 1;
}
```

▶ **Program 9.2:** *TFONT.C (continued)*

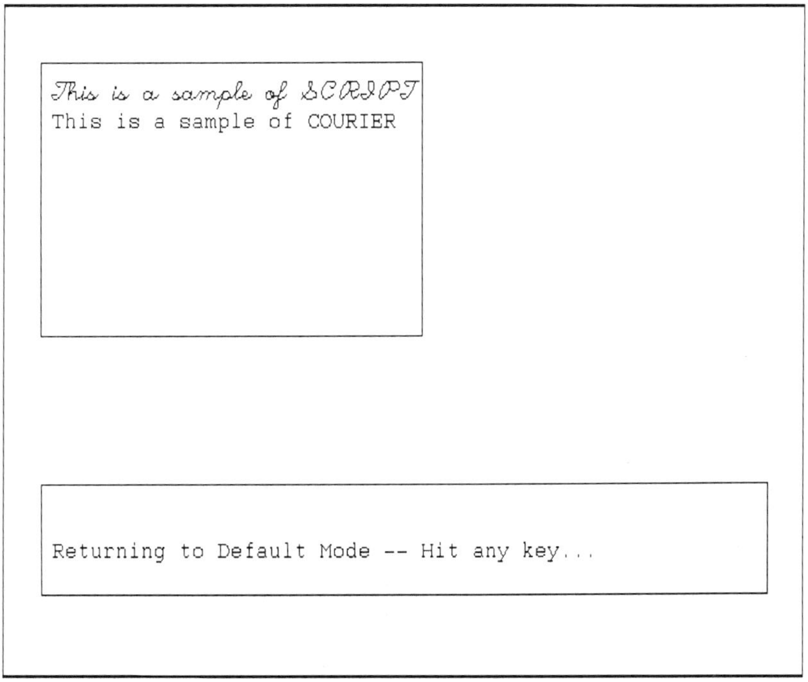

▶ **Figure 9.5:** *Output from TFONT.C*

► *Analysis of TFONT.C*

You must first ensure that the *.FON files you want to use are available on disk. Next, you use **_registerfonts( )** to load some basic font specification data (known as header information) into RAM. The prototype reveals all:

```
short _registerfonts(unsigned char *filespec);
/* filespec is the FON file name, including paths and wildcards,
 * allowing you to register several fonts. Returns the total
 * number of fonts registered or returns a negative number if
 * unsuccessful */
```

TFONT.C registers just one font at a time, taking 140 bytes of RAM. If you want to go wild and use all the fonts in a single program (a temptation that artists should resist), and provided you have enough RAM, you can replace SCRIPT.FON with *.FON. Note the standard test < **0** to detect a failure during font registration.

Before using a particular registered font, you must make it the *current font*. A call to **_setfont( )** does this and also allows you to specify the typeface and size required:

```
short _setfont(unsigned char *options);
/* The options string contains various option codes -- see below.
 * Returns true for success */
```

Invoking **_setfont( )** results in a disk access to load the font mapping data, so you should plan accordingly: try to display all you can in one font before switching to another font.

Table 9.5 shows the available option codes for the **options** string. The option letters are not case sensitive, you can list them in any sequence, and you can intersperse white space between groups of option codes for added legibility. Observe the use of single quotes in the **t'script'** entry. Yes, **t'tms rmn'** does need a space as shown.

If **_setfont( )** is successful, a structure called **_fontinfo** is set with data for the new current font:

```
struct _fontinfo
{
        int type          /* 1 = stroked font; 0 = bit-mapped font */
        int ascent        /* distance in pixels from top to bottom of
                           * tallest character; useful for creating
```

► **Table 9.5:** *Font option codes*

OpCode	Function
t	t'*fontname*' indicates the typeface, where *fontname* must be surrounded with single quotes, e.g., 'helv' or 'tms rmn' (note the space).
h*y*	*y* is the character height in pixels, e.g., **h13**.
w*x*	*x* is the character width in pixels, e.g., **w8**.
f	Select only a fixed (monospacing) font.
p	Select only a proportionally spaced font.
v	Select only a vector (stroked) font.
r	Select only a raster- (bit-) mapped font.
b	Select the best fit if a font of the exact size requested is not registered. If omitted, a failure will occur unless an exact size matched font is registered.
n*f*	Select font number *f*, e.g., **n2** will select the second registered font if two or more fonts are registered.

```
                             * proper line spacing */
        int pixwidth         /* width in pixels of character */
        int pixheight        /* height in pixels of character */
        int avgwidth         /* average width in pixels */
        char filename[68]    /* filename and path */
        char faceName[32]    /* font name */
};
```

As you can guess, knowing some of these facts is essential when you want to lay out your graphics text neatly. Also, if you have several fonts registered and you use the **b** option for best fit, the above structure must be examined to determine which font and size was selected.

You can probe the **_fontinfo** structure using **_getfontinfo( )** as follows:

```
struct _fontinfo fi;
...
_getfontinfo(&fi);
/* now you can access fi.ascent, fi.avgwidth, and so on */
```

Note the use of **_outgtext ( )** rather than **_outtext ( )** for all graphics text output.

The display starts at the CP, but where does it end? With different character widths and proportionally spaced fonts flying around, this is seldom a trivial question. To help you, there is a function called **_getgtextextent( )** that takes a single string argument and returns a **short int** giving you the total width of the string in pixels based on the current font:

```
short _getgtextextent(unsigned char *string);
/* returns total pixel width of string in the current font */
```

It is not the easiest function to spell consistently and correctly, but it's worth the effort to do so when your pretty legends keep falling outside their proper regions. Similarly, you may need to use fi.**ascent** to construct your **_move-to(x + fi.ascent + 5,y);** in lieu of conventional line feeds.

► *Drawing Lines and Filling Polygons* ►

In addition to creating pretty fonts, one of the most pleasurable aspects of computer graphics is seeing pages of boring code spring to life on the screen. There's no way I can do justice to this vast subject, on which whole libraries and industries have been built. Once you see how the functions for each pictorial element are invoked, it is really up to your artistic imagination to take over. Let's start with a simple example, TGRAF.C (Program 9.3), which fills the screen with randomly shaded circles. It introduces many of the basic functions.

```
/* Program 9-3 */
/* TGRAF.C - test-bed: draw/fill concentric circles */

#include <conio.h>
#include <graph.h>
#include <stdlib.h>

#define random(x) (rand() % (x))
/* returns a random number between 0 and (x-1)
 * rand() is declared in stdlib.h.  It returns a pseudorandom
 * integer in the range (0-32,767), so we use the modulus operator
 * to 'scale' down.  Note the generous use of ()'s.
 */

short circle(short fill, float asp, short x, short y, short r);
/* ANSI-C style prototype declaration */
```

► *Program 9.3:* TGRAF.C

```
struct videoconfig vc;

void main(void)
{
        int i;
        short cx, cy, cr, dr;
/* parameters for the circles - center coordinates & radii */

        short maxx, maxy;

        float aspect;
/* aspect ratio = maxy/maxx */

        int max_try;
/* number of iterations */

        _setvideomode(_HERCMONO);
        _getvideoconfig(&vc);
/* vary this according to you adapter */

        maxx = vc.numxpixels-1;   maxy = vc.numypixels-1;
/* set max values of x and y coordinates */

/*      aspect = (float) maxx/ maxy; */
        aspect = 1.66;
/* experiment to find a good correction factor for your
 * particular pixel shape.  On the Hercules Mono, I find
 * that aspect=1.66 gives a 'rounder' circle than the 'official'
 * value of 1.333... Aspect is used as a factor on the x-pixels
 * -- see circle() function definition
 */

        srand(17);
/* seed the random-number generator; random start */

        max_try = 37;
/* set number of circles to be drawn and filled */

        for (i=0; i<=max_try; i++) {

        cx = 40 + random(660);
        cy = 40 + random(280);
        cr = 20 + random(20);
        dr =  5 + random(20);
/* play with above numbers for different effects */

        circle(_GBORDER, aspect, cx, cy, cr+dr);
/* outer circle radius cr+dr */
        circle(_GFILLINTERIOR, aspect, cx, cy, cr);
/* inner circle radius cr */
/* You could experiment with different fill patterns */
/* Note how the filling area can be affected by nearby arcs */
/* BUT is it ART? */

    }

        _moveto(1,1);
        _outtext("Can you see this? Hit any key..");
        getche();

        _setvideomode(_DEFAULTMODE);
}

/********** FUNCTION DEFINITION ***********/
short circle(short fill, float asp, short x, short y, short r)
{
        return _ellipse(fill,(short)(x-r*asp),y-r,
                             (short)(x+r*asp),y+r);
```

► **Program 9.3:** TGRAF.C (continued)

```
        }
        /* normally the corners of the containing 'square' would be
         * (x-r,y-r) and (x+r,y+r) for a circle center (x,y) radius r;
         * We stretch out the 'square' along the x-axis to compensate
         * for the fact that y-pixels are larger than x-pixels.
         * Since _ellipse() returns TRUE for success, FALSE for failure,
         * you can test the return value of circle() if you wish.
         * Note that x-r*asp is 'promoted' to double, so we need to
         * typecast it to short
         */
```

► **Program 9.3:** *TGRAF.C (continued)*

To understand the drawing functions, you must know how to set the CP and the style and drawing color of the line elements. I have already examined some of these topics, but I will cover them again as a form of revision.

► *Setting the CP*

The graphics equivalent to setting the text cursor position with **_settext-position( )** is **_moveto( )** and its windows variant **_moveto_w( )**. You will recall that in graphics modes, CP stands for current position—the invisible pixel where the next drawing command will take effect. The prototypes are quite obvious:

```
struct xycoord _moveto(short x, short y);
/* Move CP to viewport coordinates (x,y), i.e., (x,y) is relative
 * to any viewport or _setvieworg( ) in force. The previous CP is
 * returned in an xycoord structure, e.g.,
 * (xycoord.xcoord,xycoord.ycoord). */

struct _wxycoord _moveto_w(double wx, double xy);
/* As above but using window coordinates */
```

► *What's My Line?*

Before calling certain drawing functions, such as **_lineto( )** or **_rectangle( )**, you have the option to set the line style, using the appositely named function **_setlinestyle( )**. This lets you choose between a solid line (the default) or one of your own line textures constructed from a 2-byte bit pattern. Ellipses and arcs must use the default solid line corresponding to a pattern of 0xFFFF.

_setlinestyle( ) is called like this:

```
short line_style = 0x9249; /* bit pattern 1001001001001001 */
_setlinestyle(line_style);
/* subsequent drawings will be with dotted line as shown */
```

Setting line styles does not affect the color attributes in any way. Remember that changing a line style does not affect the screen immediately—the impact is on lines still to be drawn.

The _**get...**( ) function corresponding to _**setlinestyle**( ) is called _**getline-settings**( ). It returns a **short int** representing the current **line_style** pattern:

```
short line_style;
line_style = _getlinesettings( );
/* line_style now gives you the current line settings. Useful for
 * restoring values later. If no line style has been set, you get
 * the default value 0xFFFF, a solid line */
```

► *Drawing the Line*

All the coordinates used in the drawing functions are specified relative to the current viewport, the top left corner of which is taken as (0,0). The functions for drawing linear segments are:

```
short _lineto(short end_x, short end_y);
/* draw a line in current style/color from CP to endpoint
 * specified in window-relative coordinates. If call is
 * successful true is returned, and the CP moves to the target
 * endpoint. Returns true if successful, else false. */

short _lineto_w(double end_wx, double end_wy);
/* as for _lineto( ) except for the window coordinates */
```

► *Triangles and Other Polygons*

You can easily concoct your own triangles, trapezia, and any known variety of polygon, open or closed, using the above line segment primitive. The key fact is that after using _**lineto**( ) to connect points A and B, the CP ends up at B, ready for the next line segment:

```
short Ax = 200, Ay = 0, Bx = 100, By = 100, Cx = 300, Cy = 100;
/* triangle needed is (A, B, C) */
```

```
short color = 4;          /* color-index: result will depend on palette */
_setcolor(color);         /* set drawing color */
_moveto(Ax, Ay);          /* CP at point A */
_lineto(Bx, By);          /* join A to B. CP now at B */
_lineto(Cx, Cy);          /* join B to C. CP now at C */
_lineto(Ax, Ay);          /* complete triangle. CP now back at A */
```

If you are deeply into drawing triangles, you can always create a **triangle( )** function with seven arguments: six coordinates and one fill control.

► *Ellipses, Circles, and Arcs*

You met the **_ellipse( )** function in TGRAF.C. There are three variants—one for viewport coordinates and two for window coordinates. They all return true for success and have the same basic structure:

```
short _ellipse(short fill, short x1, short y1,
                        short x2, short y2);
/* fill flag controls flood filling; (x1,y1) and (x2,y2) define
 * the bounding rectangle in relative viewport coordinates */

short _ellipse_w(short fill, double x1, double y1,
                        double x2, double y2);
/* fill flag controls flood filling; (x1,y1) and (x2,y2) define
 * the bounding rectangle in relative window coordinates */

short _ellipse_wxy(short fill, struct _wxycoord pwxy1,
                        struct _wxycoord pwxy2);
/* fill flag controls flood filling; pwxy1 and pwxy2 define
 * the bounding rectangle in structured window coordinates */

/* The _w and _wxy variants are actually defined as macros, but
 * the above equivalent formats are more helpful */
```

The significance of the bounding rectangle will be clear from Figure 9.6.

The **flood** flag can be **_GFILLINTERIOR** or **_GBORDER**, exactly as with the **_rectangle( )** function. Because ellipses are always drawn in the solid line style, the flood fill cannot "leak."

If you recall your first-grade geometry lessons, circles can be considered as ellipses with equal major and minor axes. To draw a circle, then, you simply ensure that the bounding rectangle is a square! (See the comments in Program 9.3.)

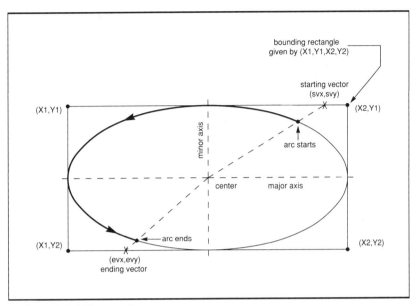

► **Figure 9.6:** *Ellipses and arcs*

The _**arc**( ) function draws elliptical arcs, including the special case of circular arcs. If you choose the parameters in a certain way, you can also achieve a closed curve, but _**ellipse**( ) does that for you already! Again, there are three variations of _**arc**( ) corresponding to the three coordinate systems:

```
short _arc(short x1, short y1, short x2, short y2,
           short svx, short svy, short evx, short evy);
/* (x1,y1) and (x2,y2) define the bounding rectangle;
 * (svx,svy) is the starting vector; (evx,evy) is the ending
 * vector for the arc -- see Figure 9.6 */


short _arc_w(double x1, double y1, double x2, double y2,
             double svx, double svy, double evx, double evy);
/* (x1,y1) and (x2,y2) define the bounding rectangle;
 * (svx,svy) is the starting vector; (evx,evy) is the ending
 * vector for the arc -- see Figure 9.6 */


short _arc_wxy(struct _wxycoord pwxy1, struct _wxycoord pwxy2,
               struct _wxycoord svxy,  struct _wxycoord evxy);
/* pwxy1 and pwxy2 define the bounding rectangle;
 * svxy is the starting vector; evxy is the ending
 * vector for the arc -- see Figure 9.6 */
```

```
/* The _w and _wxy variants are actually defined as macros, but
 * the above equivalent formats are more helpful */
```

► *Pies and Wedges*

Closely related to the _arc( ) function is _pie( ). The latter draws an elliptical arc using the same set of eight coordinates but then draws the bounding
radii (from the center of the ellipse to its starting and ending points) to give a
wedge-shaped object, not unlike an abstract slice of idealized pie. An extra
argument in _pie( ) is the fill flag you met with _ellipse( ) and _rectangle( ).
This allows the optional flood filling of your pie wedge. Very tasty.

```
short _pie(short x1, short y1, short x2, short y2,
           short svx, short svy, short evx, short evy);
/* (x1,y1) and (x2,y2) define the bounding rectangle;
 * (svx,svy) is the starting vector; (evx,evy) is the ending
 * vector for the pie -- see Figure 9.6 */

short _pie_w(double x1, double y1, double x2, double y2,
             double svx, double svy, double evx, double evy);
/* (x1,y1) and (x2,y2) define the bounding rectangle;
 * (svx,svy) is the starting vector; (evx,evy) is the ending
 * vector for the pie -- see Figure 9.6 */

short _pie_wxy(struct _wxycoord pwxy1, struct _wxycoord pwxy2,
               struct _wxycoord svxy,  struct _wxycoord evxy);
/* pwxy1 and pwxy2 define the bounding rectangle;
 * svxy is the starting vector; evxy is the ending
 * vector for the pie -- see Figure 9.6 */

/* The _w and _wxy variants are actually defined as macros, but
 * the above equivalent formats are more helpful */
```

Do not confuse _pie( ) in GRAPHICS.LIB with the more elaborate
_pg_chartpie( ) in PGCHART.LIB. Although you could hack out a series of
_pie( ) calls to give the traditional-style pie chart, the PGCHART.LIB version
does it for you automatically from any set of data, such as monthly sales or
market shares.

► *Filling In*

You have seen how rectangles, ellipses, and pie wedges can be flood-filled
using the fill flag. With _floodfill( ) you can flood fill the inside or outside of

any closed, "watertight" curve. The prototype is:

```
short _floodfill(short x, short y, short boundary_color);
/* flood from (x,y) with current fill pattern and color
 * until a region with boundary_color is reached */
```

There is an obvious window variant called **_floodfill_w( )** that takes **double** coordinate arguments.

The principle is that when you move the CP to any point within a closed figure (known as the flood *seed*) and call **_floodfill( )**, the interior of the figure is flooded with the prevailing pattern and color. These parameters are determined by calls to **_setfillmask( )**, which you saw earlier. If your CP is outside the closed figure, you get the possibly disconcerting phenomenon known as *exterior fill*, in which all or part of the surrounding screen is flooded. This also happens if the figure is not strictly closed—the flood fill leaks in or out and invades more of the screen than you bargained for!

A strict topological definition of "closed" is beyond the scope of this book, but you can imagine that with complex figures made up of arc sequences, overlapping circles and rectangles, and so on, the flood radiates out in all directions until it meets pixels of the color specified by **boundary_color** or the edge of the current viewport or clip region, whichever is nearer. The limits usually coincide with lines and arcs you have previously drawn, but the extent of the flood fill is actually controlled by the enclosing color, not by shapes per se.

An "empty" fill mask can be used to "unfill" by flooding with the current background color.

In TGRAF.C I used **WHITE** as the flood-fill border color for my monographics Hercules adapter since this is the "color" used to draw the circles. Similarly, I used **WHITE** as the fill color. The background color for mono displays is treated as **BLACK**, hence the confusing use of the term *two-color* for monochrome systems.

To keep track of the current fill pattern and color, you use the function **_getfillmask( )**, described earlier. The border color does not have to be stated explicitly since this is implied by the current drawing color (which is set via **_setcolor( )** as you'll see shortly).

▶ *PRESENTATION GRAPHICS* ▶

To add some graphical pizzazz to your statistical reports, QuickC offers several powerful, high-level functions in its presentation graphics library,

PGCHART.LIB. They make use of the automatic scaling concepts that underpin QC's window coordinate structure. Essentially, you have little more to do than set up a *data series*, usually an array of **double**s representing the *dependent variable*—that is to say, the basic observations or values to be "graphed." Then you have to establish a set of classes or categories representing the *independent variable*, against which your data series is to be plotted. The latter can be Old Father Time or simply a list of sales offices. You do not necessarily have to decide in advance whether you want to display the relationships as pie charts, bar charts, or conventional line graphs. By selecting various parameters in PGCHART functions, the same data can be quickly displayed in any or all of the popular formats. Equally important, the scaling of the axes and the display of appropriate legends are achieved with the minimum of tedious coding.

You should compile/link the CHRTDEMO program supplied with QuickC Version 2 at this point to give you an impressive preview of what is possible. You should create a CHRTDEMO.MAK file containing CHRTDEMO.C, CHRTSUPT.C, GRAPHICS.LIB, and PGCHART.LIB, then use Build in the Make menu. The source code for CHRTDEMO.C may prove a tad overwhelming if you are a beginner, but it will repay careful study when you have finished this chapter. In addition to showing all the PGCHART tricks, there is much code devoted to basic strategies such as selecting video modes and chart styles from menus.

To ease you more gently into PGCHART, I will go through some of the basic functions. All PG programs follow the same broad sequence:

1. Include both GRAPH.H and PGCHART.H function prototypes and manifest constants.

2. Use **_getvideoconfig( )** and **_setvideomode( )** to check the graphics equipment and set an appropriate video mode, as with any graphics program.

3. Use **_pg_initchart( )** to establish default data in various PGCHART data structures. In most cases these defaults provide the ideal bases for your charts.

4. Use **_pg_defaultchart( )** with arguments that establish the type of chart you need.

5. Set some parameters in a **chartenv** structure, such as strings representing titles and legends, numbers for color choices, border styles, and title justification.

6. Call the appropriate viewing function, such as **_pg_chartpie( )**, with arguments representing the data to be plotted.

7. Set a pause to study the chart and receive general acclamation.

8. Exit gracefully by restoring the status quo with a line such as **_set-videomode(_DEFAULTMODE)**.

By changing just a few lines (often just two lines!), the same program can produce bar charts (horizontal), column charts (vertical), or line charts.

► *Charts, Bars, and Pies* ►

To see this in action, consider STATS.C, listed as Program 9.4, which gives an optimistic bar chart for Marin county rainfall.

```
/* STATS.C:  Program 9.4 Rainfall Chart. */
#include <conio.h>
#include <string.h>
#include <graph.h>
#include <pgchart.h>

#define MONTHS 12

typedef enum {FALSE, TRUE} boolean;

float far value[MONTHS] =
{
   10.0, 14.0, 28.5, 19.0, 18.8, 16.0,
   12.0, 17.0, 25.5, 22.0, 15.0,  9.5
};
/* In the REAL world, above data would probably come from
 * a data file */

char far *category[MONTHS] =
{
  "JAN", "FEB", "MAR", "APR",
  "MAY", "JUN", "JLY", "AUG",
  "SEP", "OCT", "NOV", "DEC"
};

/* short far explode[MONTHS] = {0}; */
/* PIE variant: uncomment above */

main()
{
  chartenv env;
  int mode = _VRES16COLOR;
  /* Set highest rez mode available */
  while(!_setvideomode( mode ))
     mode--;
```

► *Program 9.4: STATS.C*

```
    if(mode == _TEXTMONO)
    {
/* keep decrementing mode 'til _setvideo() returns TRUE */

        puts("Sorry, we needs a GRAPHICS adapter!");
        return(0);
    }

    /* Initialize chart library */
    _pg_initchart();

    /* Set up defaults for horizontal bars */
    _pg_defaultchart(&env, _PG_BARCHART, _PG_PLAINBARS);

    /* _pg_defaultchart(&env, _PG_PIECHART, _PG_PERCENT); */
    /* Pie Variant: replace bar chart with % pie chart */


    /* Add titles and chart options */


    strcpy( env.maintitle.title, "Marin County Weather Inc." );
    env.maintitle.titlecolor = 6;
    env.maintitle.justify = _PG_CENTER;
    /* try _PG_LEFT or _PG_RIGHT to position main title */

    strcpy( env.subtitle.title, "RAINFALL, 1989" );
    env.subtitle.titlecolor = 6;
    env.subtitle.justify = _PG_CENTER;
    /* or _PG_LEFT or _PG_RIGHT for subtitle */

    strcpy(env.yaxis.axistitle.title, "Months");
    strcpy(env.xaxis.axistitle.title, "Inches");
    /* PIE variant: comment out above 2 lines */

    env.chartwindow.border = FALSE;

    /* Arguments for _pg_chart() are:
     *      env       - Environment variable in struct chartenv
     *      category  - Months are Category labels
     *      value     - Array of Rainfall Data
     *      MONTHS    - Number of data values */

    if(_pg_chart(&env, category, value, MONTHS))
    /* PIE variant: add explode arg between value and MONTHS */
    {
        _setvideomode(_DEFAULTMODE);
        _outtext("Error:  can't draw chart");
    }
    else
    {
        getch();
    /* Pause to admire! */

        _setvideomode(_DEFAULTMODE);
    }
    return(0);
}
```

► **Program 9.4:** *STATS.C (continued)*

Figure 9.7 shows the output of STATS.C.

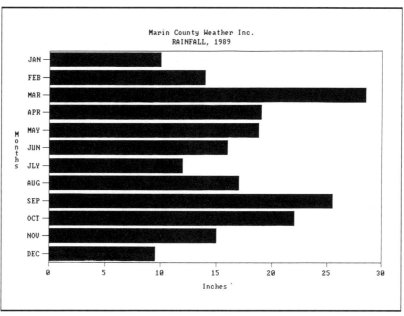

► **Figure 9.7:** *Output from STATS.C*

► *Analysis of STATS.C*

Basic to the PGCHART functions is the environment structure, defined as follows:

```
typedef
struct       {
short        charttype;      /* _PG_BARCHART, _PG_COLUMNCHART,
                              *  _PG_LINECHART,
                              *  _PG_SCATTERCHART, _PG_PIECHART */
short        chartstyle;     /* Style for selected chart type
                              *  _PG_PERCENT, _PG_PLAINBARS, etc.
windowtype chartwindow;      /* Window definition for overall
                              *  chart */
windowtype datawindow;       /* Window definition for data
                              *  part of chart */
```

```
titletype    maintitle;      /* Main chart title */
titletype    subtitle;       /* Chart subtitle */
axistype     xaxis;          /* Definition for X axis */
axistype     yaxis;          /* Definition for Y axis */
legendtype   legend;         /* Definition for legend */
} chartenv;
```

As you can see, **chartenv** contains further structures, such as **maintitle**, embedded in it, which explains such variables as **env.maintitle.title.** The functions in PGCHART access and update the **chartenv** structure in many ways. Here are some of the relevant prototypes to give you a flavor of what can be done.

```
short _pg_initchart(void);

short _pg_defaultchart(chartenv *env, short charttype,
                       short chartstyle);

short _pg_chartpie(chartenv *env, char **cat, float *val,
                   short *explode, short numcat);
```

Notice that **cat** is a pointer to the array of categories—in our example, the names of the months.

_pg_defaultchart( ) takes three arguments:

1. **&env**, a pointer to **env**, where **env** is of type **struct chartenv.** As with **_pg_initchart( )**, the default function fills up the **env** structure with appropriate data to control all the default actions of subsequent PG function calls.

2. The chart type, a **short** represented by one of the five mnemonics **_PG_BARCHART, _PG_COLUMNCHART, _PG_LINECHART, _PG_SCATTERCHART,** and **_PG_PIECHART** defined in the file PGCHART.H.

3. The chart style, another **short**, controls the appearance of the chart depending on the chart type. **_PG_PLAINBARS** and **_PG_STACKEDBARS** can be used with either the bar or column type. **_PG_PERCENT** and **_PG_NOPERCENT** work only with the pie chart. **_PG_POINTANDLINE** and **_PG_POINTONLY** control the appearance of the line and scatter charts.

The types of chart may need a little explanation. **_PG_COLUMNCHART** gives vertical bars rather than the horizontal bars used in STATS.C with **_PG_BARCHART**. **_PG_LINECHART** gives the conventional graph style with lines joining the plotted points. **_PG_SCATTERCHART** lets you study the relationships between two separate data series, **D1** and **D2**. Rather than plot each against **MONTHS**, say, you plot points with coordinates (d1i,d2i), where d1i is the ith value in **D1** and d2i is the ith value in **D2**.

Depending on the chart type you choose, you will need to set appropriate strings to give you main and subtitles. These and other parameters, such as colors and left or right justification or centering controls, are all transferred to parts of the **env** structure—for example:

```
strcpy(env.subtitle.title, "Your Subtitle String");
...
env.maintitle.titlecolor = Your_choice_of_color      /* short int */
```

You should study the various structures in PGCHART.H for advanced PG work, but simply by varying the lines in STATS.C as indicated in the comments, you can do quite a lot of fancy work without knowing **titletype**, **axistype**, **windowtype**, **legendtype**, or **paletteentry** in great detail.

Having set **env**, you use one of the three main display functions:

1. **_pg_chart( )** for bar, column, and line charts for a single data series. The **_pg_chartms( )** variant, where **ms** stands for multiple series, superimposes two or more separate plots against the same time or category axis. You need to set up higher dimensional arrays for the extra data series. The only limit here is the amount of RAM, although you should also avoid cluttering charts with too much information. Two or three data series is a reasonable upper limit!

2. **_pg_chartpie( )** for pie charts. There is, thankfully, no multiple series version of the pie chart. There is an additional argument called **explode**, which is an array of explode flags. Each flag controls a particular slice of the pie: 0 means no explosion; 1 means explode. Once again, this feature can lead to obscurity if overused. STATS.C suggests the line:

```
short far explode[MONTHS] = {0};
```

which confines all 12 monthly slices to nonexplosive behavior.

3.   _pg_chartscatter( ) takes two arrays of **float** data, **D1** and **D2**, and plots a scatter diagram from them:

```
short _pg_chartscatter(chartenv *env, float *D1, float *D2,
                       short n);
```

The X axis takes values from **D1**, and the Y axis takes values from **D2**. Each point plotted is a (d1i,d2i), where i ranges from 0 to n − 1. The multiple series variant is **_pg_chartscatterms( )**.

► *Multiple Data Series*

To improve legibility when plotting multiple data series, PG uses a special array of structures called PG palettes. Unlike the standard EGA and VGA palettes, which control only displayed colors, the PG palettes control colors, line and fill styles, and plot characters. The plot character, usually * or **x**, is the character used in line charts and scatter diagrams. A plot character is placed at each plotted point and joined up with lines to form the familiar ups and downs of a sales department, say.

Pools of line and fill styles and a pool of plot characters are provided so that each chart in a multiple series gets a unique combination of line and plot characters. Although pie charts are by definition single data series objects, they do make use of the PG palette array. Each pie slice uses a different PG palette to help distinguish the slices.

Similarly, a color pool of distinct colors is used to provide a different color for each data series, at least as far as this is possible. If you plot seven data series using a four-color mode, such as **_MRES4COLOR**, the color of the fifth series will duplicate that of the first series. The following **typedef**s from PGCHART.H will clarify the situation:

```
typedef unsigned char fillmap[8]   /* 8 x 8 bits */

typedef struct
{
  unsigned short color;
  unsigned short style;
  fillmap         fill;
  char            plotchar;
} paletteentry;
```

```
typedef paletteentry palettetype[_PG_PALETTELEN];
/* _PG_PALETTELEN is defined as 16, so palettetype is an array of
 *  16 PG palettes */
```

The **color** field should not be confused with the color or pixel values or color indexes used elsewhere. This **color** value is a PG-specific index to the color pool that will, depending on the adapter and mode, determine the colors used for each data series.

The **style** field works in a similar fashion by indexing to the line-style pool—a set of solid, dashed, or combination lines—and determines which line style is used for each data series. If the number of colors is less than the number of data series, choosing different line styles can help avoid duplication of display methods.

The **fill** field specifies an 8 × 8-bit fill pattern, just as you saw with _**floodfill**( ) and _**rectangle**( ). Again, you can envisage a pool of fill patterns, so that each data series can have its private variety for filling bars and pies.

Finally, the **plotchar** field in the **paletteentry** structure determines the plot character for line charts and scatter diagrams.

Although _**pg_initchart**( ) initializes the array of palette structures with convenient default values, you are free to poke your own data into them if you wish. Two function calls, _**get**...( ) and _**set**...( ), work as follows:

```
palettetype pal_s;
/* pal_s is a pointer, in fact an array of type struct paletteentry! */
...
_pg_initchart( );   /* init chartenv and palette array */
_pg_getpalette(pal_s);   /* get current settings */
...
pal_s[1].plotchar = 'X';
/* change plot character for 1st data series */
/* make any other changes here... */
_pg_setpalette(pal_s);
/* update palette */
```

Further customizing is done by changing the **chartenv** structure, as you saw in STATS.C. In fact, STATS.C only scratched the surface. Try adding lines to alter the defaults in the **axistype** structure:

```
typedef
struct    {
short     grid;        /* True = grid lines drawn; False = no lines */
```

```
short      gridstyle;      /* Style number from style pool
                            * for grid lines */
titletype  axistitle;      /* Title definition for axis */
short      axiscolor;      /* Color for axis */
short      labeled;        /* True = tic marks and titles drawn */
short      rangetype;      /* _PG_LINEARAXIS, _PG_LOGAXIS */
float      logbase;        /* Base used if log axis */
short      autoscale;      /* True = next 7 values calculated by system */
float      scalemin;       /* Minimum value of scale */
float      scalemax;       /* Maximum value of scale */
float      scalefactor;    /* Scale factor for data on this axis */
titletype  scaletitle;     /* Title definition for scaling factor */
float      ticinterval;    /* Distance between tic marks (world coord.) */
short      ticformat;      /* _PG_EXPFORMAT or _PG_DECFORMAT
                            * for tic labels */
short      ticdecimals;    /* Number of decimals for tic labels (max = 9)*/
}
axistype;
```

Recall that within **chartenv** you have two structures of type **axistype**—namely, **xaxis** and **yaxis**—so you have considerable scope for creating havoc! Try converting STATS.C from bar to line chart. Then change the **grid** field to true on both axes:

```
    env.xaxis.grid = TRUE;  /* gives vertical grid lines */
    env.yaxis.grid = TRUE;  /* gives horizontal grid lines */
 /* Note: grid lines are perpendicular to the chosen axis. Set
  * either or both to false, the default, to remove grid(s) */
```

Now you can play with **env.xaxis.gridstyle** to change the line style of the vertical grid lines. The *tic* marks referred to are the small marks along the axes that are labeled with data or category values (not to be confused with the axis titles). The **labeled** Boolean field determines if these will appear, the default being true. You can even ask for logarithmic scales to any base (the default is 10) on either axis and leave PG to do the math for you. Log scales are widely used when plotting values with large ranges or when one or both variables is known to vary exponentially. The **autoscale** field defaults to true, meaning that PG automatically calculates all the scaling factors for you. Unless this is set to false, you need not worry about the final seven fields in the structure.

Finally, you can alter the parameters held in the two **windowtype** structures in **chartenv**—namely, **chartwindow** (the overall chart window) and

datawindow (the smaller area holding your graphical data). These allow changes to the origins, border types, and the foreground or background colors of these windows. The defaults make best use of the whole screen, but for fancy zooming and clipping, you are free to change any or all of these defaults:

```
    env.datawindow.border = FALSE;
/* no border needed on data window */
    env.chartwindow.borderstyle = _PG_POINTANDLINE;
/* change border line style */
```

As you can see, the PG toolbox offers wonderful scope for your creative talents. Furthermore, study of the PG structures and functions will greatly enhance your C skills: they embody all the power and elegance of the C language.

► GRAPHICS IMAGES ►

I move now to the interesting topic of graphics images and how QC lets you save and move them between windows and screens. This operation plays a role in many aspects of graphics programming, including the glamorous application known as animation. If you understand the basic ideas behind pixel mapping, you will appreciate that moving parts of a graphics screen to memory and back again is not as simple as handling a predictable number of bytes with, say, **malloc( )**.

The basic functions are **_getimage( )** to store a graphics image to RAM and **_putimage( )** to reverse the process by displaying an image in RAM to the screen. The first question that arises is how to define the portion of the screen to be manipulated. The answer is that we define such regions as rectangular areas of the screen, and we can use either viewport or window coordinates to define our target image. So, you will find the usual **_w** and **_wxy** variants to most of the image transfer functions. The second question is how to create a buffer of the correct size to store the pixels that represent the image. The answer is **_imagesize(rectangle_args)**, which is smart enough to know what mode you are in and how to count the relevant bytes in video memory. Let's look at the three versions of **_imagesize( )**:

```
long _imagesize(short x1, short y1, short x2, short y2);
/* return number of bytes in the rectanglar area defined by the
 * view coordinates top left corner (x1,y1), bottom right corner
 * (x2,y2) */
```

```
long _imagesize_w(double x1, double y1, double x2, double y2);
/* return number of bytes in the rectanglar area defined by the
 * window coordinates top left corner (x1,y1), bottom right corner
 * (x2,y2) */

long _imagesize_wxy(struct _wxycoord pwxy1, struct _wxycoord pwxy2);
/* return number of bytes in the rectanglar area defined by the
 * window coordinates top left corner pwxy1, bottom right corner
 * pwxy2 */
 * Note: all coords are relative to current view origin */
```

Calling _imagesize( ) or one of its variants is always the first step since you will need the number of bytes in the image in order to **malloc** the correct buffer to hold the image. Now we can look at _getimage( ):

```
void far _getimage(short x1, short y1, short x2, short y2,
                        char far *buffer);
/* store the image found in the rectanglar area defined by the
 * view coordinates top left corner (x1,y1), bottom right corner
 * (x2,y2). Saved in buffer */
```

There are also obvious _w and _wxy versions of _getimage corresponding to the versions of _imagesize( ).

Now that your image is safely stored, you can either manipulate it in memory prior to redisplaying it, or you can use a trick built into _putimage( ):

```
void far _putimage(short x, short y, char far *buffer,
                        short action);
/* display image stored in buffer. Start display at relative
 * view coordinate (x,y). The action value determines the
 * interaction between the incoming and preexisting image.
 * There is a _putimage_w( ) version but no _wxy version */
```

Since the size and disposition of the image is known, you need only specify the top left corner of the target rectangle.

As you can see, when you move a bit image from memory to screen, you have a choice as to how the newly arriving pixels combine with the corresponding pixels already on the screen. **action** is a short integer parameter that controls this interaction. GRAPH.H defines the possibilities with the mnemonic constants _GPSET, _GPRESET, _GAND, _GPOR, and _GXOR.

These define the Boolean operations to be performed between each pixel value in the buffer and the corresponding value on the target screen. The visual result of all these bit confrontations is hardware dependent and is especially so with complex color graphics adapters and monitors. (There is more on this in Appendix F.) The following snippet will help you experiment on your own machine:

```
#include <graph.h>
/* lest you forget -- also remember graphics.lib in your .MAK file */
    /* set your video mode here */
    ...
    char far *buffer;
    /* for malloc( ) */

    int image_size;
    ...
    /* create some screen images here */

    image_size = _imagesize(10, 20, 300, 240);
    /* get number of bytes in the image (relative to view org) */
    buffer = (char far *) malloc(image_size);
    if (buffer = = NULL
    {
        outtext("Insufficient memory\n");
        exit(1);
    }
    _getimage(10, 20, 300, 240, buffer);
    /* buffer gets image_size bytes */
    ...
    /* do some more creative screen play */

    putimage(10, 20, buffer, _GXOR);
/* send original bit image to screen and XOR with current image.
 * Coinciding bits will cancel out (0 xor 0) = (1 xor 1) = 0, other
 * positions will be set (0 xor 1) = (1 xor 0) = 1 */

    /* try the other action values */
    ...
    free(buffer);
    /* deallocate */
    _setvideomode(_DEFAULTMODE);
    /* restore graphics */
```

► *The Active and Visual Pages* ►

If you are lucky enough to have more than one page of video RAM, you can play some clever tricks by flipping images quickly without using **_set-image( )** and **_putimage( )**. The number of pages potentially available depends on the total video RAM assigned and on the mode selected. The general formula is

bytes per screen = (number of bits per pixel) × (number of pixels
per screen)/8

number of pages = (total bytes video RAM) / (bytes per screen)

with suitable rounding to the lowest integer.

Alternatively, you can use **_getvideoconfig(&vc)**, then look at **vc.num-videopages**.

The mode dictates both the number of bits per pixel (palette size) and the number of pixels per screen (resolution). For example, a simple 4-color palette uses only 2 bits per pixel, allowing more pages than a 16-color palette. Similarly, a 640 × 200 resolution allows more pages than a 640 × 480 resolution. Some adapters use the video-RAM allocation by offering increased resolution modes rather than extra pages.

The standard CGA board has only one 16KB page for all its modes. Depending on the amount of video RAM and the selected mode, the standard EGA board can have from one to four pages and the VGA board can have one or two pages. The Hercules adapter provides two 32KB pages. There are now hundreds of special graphics boards available with every conceivable combination.

If your adapter supports pages, there are two important functions in the QuickC toolbox to examine. Look at the following prototypes:

```
short _setactivepage(int pagenum);
/* make pagenum the active page = send all graphics output,
 * including text, to this section of video RAM. Pages are numbered
 * from 0 to  maxpage – 1. Returns previous active page for
 * success; return a – ve value on failure. */


void far _setvisualpage(int pagenum);
/* make pagenum the visual page — screen displays come from the
 * this section of video RAM. Returns previous visual page for
 * success; returns a – ve value on failure. */
```

I explained the basic principles of video pages earlier in this chapter. To recap, all graphics output is directed to the active page, and all screen displays come from the visual page. When you first fire up in graphics mode, the default active and visual pages are both the same, usually 0. Unless you change this state of affairs, the various drawing routines will display their images immediately.

When you call _**setactivepage(N)**;, the active page is switched to page **N** if you have one and the value of the previous active page is returned; otherwise the call is ignored and a negative value is returned. Subsequent calls to any graphics output functions will not affect the screen, but the images build up in page **N**, literally behind the scenes. If you now call _**setvisual-page(N)**;, the contents of page **N** immediately appear, replacing the original display. If you time these calls properly, you can create many special effects, including primitive animation. As a simple test bed, look at PAGE.C, listed as Program 9.5. The _**setlinestyle( )** calls are there to remind you about "leaks" in flood fills. Ellipses always use solid lines regardless of line style.

```
/* Program 9-5 */
/* page - switching active & visual pages  */

#include <conio.h>
#include <graph.h>
#include <stdlib.h>

void main(void)
{
      _setvideomode(_HERCMONO);
/* set your favorite video mode & check vc.numvideopages */
/*      _setvisualpage(0); */
/*      _setactivepage(0); */
/* defaults - so not strictly needed */

      _setlinestyle(0xf0f0);
      _rectangle(_GBORDER,55,20, 340,200);
      _setlinestyle(0xffff);
      _ellipse(_GFILLINTERIOR,75,40, 320,180);
/* drawn in page 0 -- displayed */
      _setactivepage(1);
      _setlinestyle(0xf0f0);
      _ellipse(_GBORDER,55,20, 340,200);
      _setlinestyle(0xffff);
      _rectangle(_GFILLINTERIOR,75,40, 320,180);
/* drawn in page 1 -- not displayed */
      _setactivepage(0);
      _moveto(50,300);
      _outtext("Hit any key..");
      getch();
      _setvisualpage(1);
/* flip a la Spielberg! */
```

► **Program 9.5:** PAGE.C

```
        _setactivepage(1);
        _moveto(50,300);
        _outtext("Hit any key..");
        getch();
        _clearscreen(_GCLEARSCREEN);
/* clear graphics screen */

        _setvideomode(_DEFAULTMODE);

    }
```

► **Program 9.5:** *PAGE.C (continued)*

► GRAPHICS COLOR ►

I'll wind up this chapter with a survey of the various ways of selecting color in the popular CGA and EGA graphics modes. You have already seen some of the principles involved, but it's time for more detail.

Even if your hardware is strictly monochromatic, it is well worth reading the following sections to get a general grasp of the subject—it may tempt you to acquire the necessary equipment and put some color in your life. Although controlling color in graphics mode is more complex than in text mode, the QuickC tools do most of the hard work.

The first point to remember is that in a graphics mode each individual pixel has a color attribute. Rather than having a character cell with a foreground and background color (as with the color text modes), you now think in terms of a background color for the whole screen plus a color set for the pixel, which I'll call the drawing color. Two rarely used functions can handle individual pixel colors and are useful for plotting math functions:

```
short _getpixel(short x, short y);
/* returns the color or pixel value of the pixel at (x,y).
 * There is a _getpixel_w( ) version with double window
 * coordinates. Returns – 1 if unsuccessful. */

short _setpixel(short x, short y);
/* Set the pixel at (x,y) to the current color. Returns the
 * previous value of the target pixel if successful, else returns
 * – 1. Calling this with y to set successive values of F(x)
 * will plot the graph y = F(x). */
```

However, you are usually more interested in setting up background and drawing colors.

The values associated with a pixel's color are not usually absolute values—they often index into a table of colors representing the current palette available (the CGA has some exceptions, as you'll see). Most color adapters and monitors permit a wide range of color possibilities, but at any given time only a subset of these is available—namely, the current or active palette.

▶ *CGA Color Schemes* ▶

The palettes for the CGA are as listed in Table 9.6. These are the low-resolution CGA modes that allow 320 × 200 resolution and any one of the sets of four-color palettes listed for the drawing color. (The hi-res 640 × 200 CGA mode is two color only. I'll cover this later.)

You can see from this list that if you set a color value of 1, say, with **_set-color(1);**, the actual pixel color you get depends on which palette is active. It could be green, cyan, light green, or light cyan. To switch from light green to

▶ **Table 9.6:** *CGA palettes*

_MRES4COLOR Mode

Palette Number	Color Index Values		
	1	2	3
0	Green	Red	
1	Cyan	Magenta	
2	Light green	Light red	Yellow
3	Light cyan	Light magenta	White

_MRESNOCOLOR Mode

Palette Number	Color Index Values		
	1	2	3
0	Blue	Red	Light gray
1	Light blue	Light red	White

cyan, for example, you would have to change palettes from 2 to 1 with
_selectpalette(1);. The color values 1–3 are the drawing colors. What about
the background color? The background color has the color index value 0 for
all palettes, and this can represent any of the 16 different colors listed in
Table 9.7.

To set a CGA background color you use **_setbkcolor(color)**, where **color**
is any value listed in Table 9.7. So, in CGA mode, the following lines would
give you light cyan on a red background:

```
_selectpalette(3);
_setcolor(1);
_setbkcolor(4);
```

Other adapters that work like this are the Olivetti/AT&T and the MCGA
in lo-res.

The two-color, hi-res **_HRESBW** mode simply has a black, unchangeable
background and a colored foreground. To confuse everyone, a peculiarity of
this arrangement is that you must use **setbkcolor( )** with any of the 16 values
in Table 9.7 to set the *foreground* color. No, I don't make these rules, I just
pass them on! It's the PC hardware, I'm told.

► **Table 9.7:** *CGA background colors*

Color	Numeric Value	Color	Numeric Value
Black	0	Dark gray	8
Blue	1	Light blue	9
Green	2	Light green	10
Cyan	3	Light cyan	11
Red	4	Light red	12
Magenta	5	Light magenta	13
Brown	6	Light brown	14
White	7	Light white	15

To check the current drawing and background colors, you use **_getcolor( )** and **_getbkcolor( )**, which are declared as follows:

```
long _getbkcolor(void);
/* returns current background color value -- default is 0 */

short _getcolor(void);
/* returns pixel value of current drawing color -- default is the
 * highest legal value of the current palette */
```

► *EGA/VGA Color Schemes* ►

Both the EGA and VGA adapters have a true, user-changeable palette, offering 16 color values from a total range of 64 colors. The functions covered in this section apply equally to both boards, so I will not refer specifically to the VGA. The default palette gives you the 16 CGA colors listed in Table 9.7, so if you don't do anything to change things, **setcolor(0)** gives black, **setcolor(1)** gives blue, and so on. The EGA palettes are manipulated with **_remappalette( )** or **_remapallpalette( )**—the function **_selectpalette( )** is for CGA boards only and must *not* be used with EGA/VGA's.

To understand the tricks of EGA palette control, you need to distinguish color indices and actual (or hardware) color values. Table 9.8 lists the actual EGA color values and their mnemonics as defined in GRAPH.H.

► **Table 9.8:** *EGA actual color codes and mnemonics*

Mnemonic	Value	Mnemonic	Value
_BLACK	0x000000L	_GRAY	0x151515L
_BLUE	0x2a0000L	_LIGHTBLUE	0x3F1515L
_GREEN	0x002a00L	_LIGHTGREEN	0x153f15L
_CYAN	0x2a2a00L	_LIGHTCYAN	0x3f3f15L
_RED	0x00002aL	_LIGHTRED	0x15153fL
_MAGENTA	0x2a002aL	_LIGHTMAGENTA	0x3f153fL
_BROWN	0x00152aL	_LIGHTYELLOW	0x153f3fL
_WHITE	0x2a2a2aL	_BRIGHTWHITE	0x3f3f3fL

As you can guess, it's easier and safer to use the defined names than play around with the numbers. Leaving aside for the moment the significance of the actual color values, imagine that you were free to assign any real color to any particular color index. For example, the default EGA palette assigns the color index 1 to the real color blue. In the absence of any palette changes, **_setcolor(1)** would set the current drawing color to blue. If you now remap the palette with **_remappalette(1, _RED)**, a dramatic change occurs—not only do future calls to **_setcolor(1)** now set the drawing color to real red, but also all displayed pixels that were previously set to index 1 will switch from blue to red. You can be even more dramatic with **_remapallpalette-(color_array)**. This can reassign any or all of the color-index-to-real-color assignments, with immediate effect on all displayed pixels whose indices may have changed.

The index values of the pixels (also known as their pixel values) have not altered, but their interpretation by the hardware undergoes a sudden, possibly psychedelic mutation. Look at the following prototypes:

```
long _remappalette(short index, long actual_color);
/* Changes palette color at index to machine color actual_color.
 * Returns the previous machine color of the index arg if
 * successful, otherwise returns − 1 on failure. */

short _remapallpalette(long far *colors_array);
/* Assigns new actual colors to all color values. Replaces the current
 * palette with the machine colors found in the array
 * colors_array.
 * Returns 0 if successful, − 1 if failure. */
```

► SUMMARY OF CHAPTER 9 ►

◄ ► The two libraries GRAPHICS.LIB and PGCHART.LIB provide many powerful functions for PC graphics. They can be combined in your xLIBxx library or you can link them with your object code using *.MAK files or the external linker.

◄ ► The basics of video-display technology were covered. Key concepts are raster scanning, mapping video RAM to the screen, display adapters, color and monochrome monitors, and text and graphics modes.

◄ ► QuickC provides drivers for all the popular graphics boards and has functions that can detect the hardware fitted and initialize the graphics system [_**getvideoconfig( )** and **_setvideomode( )**].

◄ ► Text mode and graphics mode have different video mapping schemes, but separate sets of functions handle most of the bit- and byte-counting operations for you.

◄ ► Graphics text relies on a set of *.FON files and special functions to load fonts for use with **_outgtext( )**.

◄ ► QuickC offers several different screen coordinate systems:

text = (row,col) absolute or relative to text windows.

graphics = (short x,short y) for viewports, absolute or relative.

graphics = (double x,double y) for windows, absolute or relative.

◄ ► PGCHART.LIB provides high-level calls for bar, column, and pie charts and scatter diagrams.

◄ ► Appendix F has a handy alphabetical listing of all the graphics, font, and PG functions with prototypes and brief descriptions.

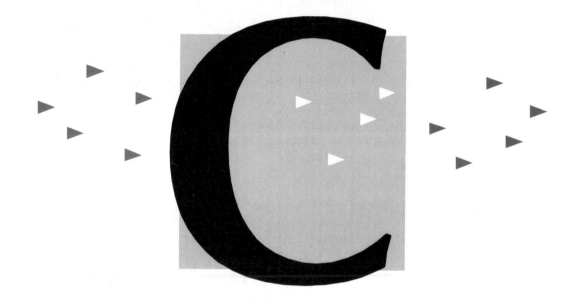

ODDS && SODS

► *CHAPTER 10* ►

This chapter covers several topics that for various reasons did not quite fit in the mainstream of my exposition so far. There were many moments when I had to resist the temptation of making "just another little detour!" Also, there are some aspects of C that only assume importance when your programs blossom into full-scale, real-world projects.

Among the latter is the topic I discussed briefly in Chapter 7: the division of large programs into separately compilable files or *modules*. (I'll define this term more precisely shortly.) This involves a study of LIB, the Microsoft Library Manager; LINK, the stand-alone overlay linker; the Make facility built into QC; and a simple overview of the QCL command-line compiler.

To conclude this chapter I'll present some more advanced topics, including the use of recursion and pointers to functions.

► *THE LIB LIBRARY MANAGER* ►

Although you have encountered libraries at various stages of your work with QuickC, they have been more or less lurking in the background and taken for granted. This, of course, is one of the merits of QuickC: The journey from writing C source code to running a .EXE file can be completed within the QC integrated environment without worrying too much about the various intermediate .OBJ files needed during the linking process. Each time you call **printf( )** or any of the hundreds of C library functions, the machine code for that function must eventually be linked with your code before the final .EXE file can be created. The linker built into QC does this for you, guided where necessary by your program lists or *.MAK files.

In the bad, old, prelibrary days, you might have had hundreds of separate files of machine code: PRINTF.OBJ, PUTS.OBJ, and so on. The linker would have had to search around, accessing mass storage (a deck of cards, perhaps) until all function references had been resolved and the appropriate machine code incorporated into the .EXE file.

The library concept simplifies this process by combining sets of .OBJ files (including code and/or data) into one or more library files (with the usual extension .LIB). The linker now has an easier time locating the object code for all referenced functions. In addition to access speed, an important side benefit is that disk space is conserved. There is also a conceptual advantage: a whole set of diverse functions is safely encapsulated in one higher-level object, namely, a library. To recap an earlier theme: C is a *small core* language based on a few keywords; its power stems from libraries of standard functions, complemented by user- or vendor-supplied functions.

The price you pay is that you need to maintain your libraries: creating libraries, adding new modules from .OBJ files, removing dead wood, updating modules, combining libraries, listing their contents, checking them for consistency, and so on. The Microsoft LIB utility does all this for you once you have mastered its command-line syntax. LIB is a tool known as a *librarian* or *library manager*. It will help you in many ways as your programs become more complex and need to be broken down into separately compiled files of functions. Your frequently used functions (and any associated data tables) can be put into your own personal libraries using LIB. LIB will also help when you want to revise the modules sitting in your libraries.

In a real sense, you are extending C with your own functions. You may even be able to sell your LIB files to other users—this is a growing market for the smaller developer who does not want to compete in the hectic end-user applications market. The small ads in computer magazines reveal a wide variety of specialist toolkits for use with QuickC. LIB allows you to incorporate other vendors' selected modules or whole libraries into your own libraries. To exploit these possibilities you need to know a little more about program modules, libraries, and linkers.

► *What Is a Library?* ►

A library is a file with the extension .LIB that contains a set of .OBJ modules (compiled code and data) together with lists of identifiers to aid the linker. (QuickC can handle library files with extensions other than .LIB, but .LIB is the usual default extension so it's safer to follow this convention.)

► *What Is a Module?*

Think of a module as an .OBJ file sitting inside a .LIB file without the .OBJ extension. Although we are dealing with QuickC, remember that these

.OBJ modules need not necessarily have originated from QuickC or indeed any brand of C! The Microsoft assembler (MASM) and most of the Microsoft languages can produce .OBJ modules for LIB (if certain rules are followed).

If STAN.OBJ is added to a library, for example, a module STAN (no extension) will be set up with an indexing mechanism to allow fast retrieval. The module may possibly contain several functions and diverse data elements; it all depends on what STAN.C (or STAN.PAS, or whatever) contained at the time it was compiled!

► *Standard Combined Libraries*

When you installed QuickC you will recall that SETUP.EXE asked you which combined library or libraries were needed depending on which memory model or models you would be using. SETUP then proceeded to accumulate the correct .OBJ files as modules in one or more *combined* libraries. For our simple needs, we opted for the SLIBCE library (small memory model with floating-point math by software emulation) or SLIBC7 (if you have a math coprocessor). The first letter—S, M, C, or L—indicates the memory model: small, medium, compact, or large (also used for the huge memory model). The middle letters—LIBC—mean "combined library," and the final character can be E for "emulation" or 7 for hardware FP math using the 8087/80827.

When you compile/link MYPROG.C in a particular memory model, QuickC passes the name of the *default library* to the linker, which then automatically links SLIBCE.LIB or SLIBC7.LIB with MAIN.OBJ, together with any other .OBJ files or libraries specifically requested. This is true for both QC (the integrated compiler/linker) and for QCL (the external command-line compiler/linker), although the invocation mechanisms are different. Note that if a library is specified, only those modules referenced by other programs or modules are passed to the final MYPROG.EXE. You can prove this by observing that SLIBCE.LIB occupies 206,343 bytes, whereas HELLO.EXE is merely 7447 bytes!

You may recall from Chapter 9 that you can add GRAPHICS.LIB and PGCHART.LIB to your combined SLIBCE.LIB when you run SETUP or, failing that, you need to explicitly link them when building graphics programs. Since these two graphics libraries are used for all memory models, you will remember that some tricks were needed in GRAPH.H and PGCHART.H to accommodate the different pointer sizes. When you create your own libraries, you must also watch for similar situations and adopt a suitable strategy: Either establish separate libraries for the five memory models, or resort to **#ifdef** dodges to produce correct function prototypes.

► *Why Use Libraries?* ►

To stress the importance of libraries, let's look at a concrete example.

Suppose you write a program called MYMAIN.C that calls functions you have coded in files MYFUNC1.C and MYFUNC2.C. Presumably, these functions are considered to be of general use; otherwise they might as well reside in MYMAIN.C. One way of proceeding is to precompile the two function files, giving MYFUNC1.OBJ and MYFUNC2.OBJ. When you compile/link MYMAIN.C, you tell the system to link these .OBJ files. The most convenient way to do this with QC is to specify a program list using the Make menu. This creates an ASCII file called MYMAIN.MAK. You can look on MYMAIN.MAK as a kind of advanced DOS .BAT file that QC uses to perform a sequence of compiles and conditional links. (The external NMAKE facility, which is beyond the scope of this book, lets you execute .MAK files outside the QC IDE but with more complex options.)

To keep things simple, MYMAIN.MAK contains the three file names

MYMAIN.C

MYFUNC1.OBJ

MYFUNC2.OBJ

of your program list, together with various control commands that specify the following *dependencies*:

MYMAIN.EXE depends on linking MYMAIN.OBJ, MYFUNC1.OBJ, and MYFUNC2.OBJ (plus the default combined library).

MYMAIN.OBJ depends on compiling MYMAIN.C.

This means that the QC Build command will automatically recompile/relink depending on what has changed since the last recompile/relink. QC always checks the date/time stamps on relevant files before deciding what needs to be done to produce a good, up-to-date MYMAIN.EXE.

If any supporting file has changed, certain recompilations or relinks are triggered on the dependent files; otherwise time is saved by avoiding redundant processing. Note carefully that the above .MAK file does not contain any reference to MYFUNC1.C or MYFUNC2.C, so don't expect it to recompile these. It simply checks the date/times of the two function .OBJ files in relation to MYMAIN.C, MYMAIN.OBJ (if it exists), and MYMAIN.EXE (if it exists) to see which is the most current.

The above program list is a sensible one if MYFUNC1.C and MYFUNC2.C are stable, tried, and tested (or maybe you don't have the two .C files!). If they are still subject to change, the answer is to replace MYFUNC1.OBJ with MYFUNC1.C and replace MYFUNC2.OBJ with MYFUNC2.C in the MYMAIN.MAK file. This adds two more dependencies:

MYFUNC1.OBJ depends on compiling MYFUNC1.C.

MYFUNC2.OBJ depends on compiling MYFUNC2.C.

A Build command now may trigger a recompilation of, say, MYFUNC1.C if a change is detected, followed by a relinking. Note that MYFUNC2 will not be recompiled if MYFUNC2.C has not been changed since the last build. Remember, too, that the command Rebuild All ignores the previous build history and recompiles/relinks everything in sight!

QC also checks the relative date/time of MYMAIN.MAK! You will get a warning, **Build environment has changed**, before the build occurs if you have changed the .MAK file since the last build. The QC Make facility should suffice for most multiprogram work, but NMAKE is available for more complex dependencies.

► *Your Personal Include Files*

Before we leave the subject of dependencies, consider the very common situation in which you examine your MYFUNC1.C file and find that it starts with a whole bunch of #includes and #defines, many of which occur also in MYFUNC2. It is meet and proper to consider creating a MYOWN.H header file:

```
/* myown.h – includes & defines for myfunc1, myfunc2 */
#include <stdio.h>
#include <stdlib.h>
#include <conio.h>
#ifndef BUFSIZ
#define BUFSIZ 512
```

```
#endif
/* more of the same */

extern double anyfunc(char *chptr, struct mine *sptr);
/* and so on */
```

Your function source files can now start with

```
/* myfunc1.c – set of widget-splining functions */
#include <myown.h>
/* or use #include "myown.h" if it's in current directory */

/* more includes, defines, declarations unique to this module */

/* all your functions come here */
/* end of myfunc1.c */


/* myfunc2.c – set of widget-extrusion functions */
#include <myown.h>

/* or use #include "myown.h" if it's in current directory */

/* more includes, defines, declarations unique to this module */

/* all your functions come here */
/* end of myfunc2.c */
```

but now you need to watch the impact of include file changes on the final .EXE. The QC Make facility will ignore changes to include files and may tell you that MYMAIN.EXE is up to date. So using Rebuild All is advisable in such cases. NMAKE, however, allows you to include #**include** file dependencies explicitly.

► *On the Make*

Whenever you invoke Build, whether you do so directly from the Make menu or indirectly with Run, the .MAK file ensures that MYFUNC1.OBJ and MYFUNC2.OBJ are included in the list of files to be linked. The appropriate xLIBCy.LIB is linked for you automatically. You now have MYFUNC.EXE.

► *Simple QCL Applications*

You can also compile MYMAIN.C and link in your two function files with a QCL command line, as follows:

```
C>QCL MYMAIN MYFUNC1.OBJ MYFUNC2.OBJ
```

This produces MYMAIN.EXE because the base name is the first one given on the QCL line. Alternatively

```
C>QCL MYMAIN MYFUNC1.C MYFUNC2.C
```

will achieve the same ends by first compiling all three functions before linking. You can also compile each file separately and then use LINK with the three .OBJ files as follows:

```
C>QCL /c MYMAIN
C>QCL /c MYFUNC1
C>QCL /c MYFUNC2
C>LINK MYMAIN.OBJ MYFUNC1.OBJ MYFUNC2.OBJ
```

Note the /c flag, which means, "Just compile, don't link."

The end result of all these methods is MYMAIN.EXE, all ready to run and amaze your family.

The above set of QCL and LINK options will cover most of your simple needs. In fact, there are hundreds of options beyond the scope of this book. They allow you to control such things as optimization, warning levels, and memory model.

► *Exploiting Your Function Files* ►

So far, so good. But suppose you now write NEWMAIN.C and compile it to NEWMAIN.OBJ. It may or may not call functions in MYFUNC1.OBJ and/or MYFUNC2.OBJ. How should you link NEWMAIN.OBJ? As projects get larger and more complex, you can spend much time poring over your listings trying to remember which functions are in which files so you can decide which .OBJ files need to be linked. Taking the safe and easy way out by always linking all possible .OBJ files has the disadvantage of inflating NEWMAIN.EXE.

LIB comes to the rescue. If you use LIB to create a MYFUNC.LIB file from MYFUNC1.OBJ and MYFUNC2.OBJ (and possibly others), you can link NEWMAIN.OBJ with MYFUNC.LIB without worrying about which .OBJ file contains which functions. The linker will pull in only those .OBJ modules needed by NEWMAIN.OBJ. A .LIB file is so organized that LINK (or any compatible linker) can determine the module in which any referenced function or external variable is located. An added bonus is that the size of the collected .OBJ modules is nearly always smaller than the sum of the individual .OBJ files. (You'll see shortly that there is no need to keep an .OBJ file separately on disk after it's safely incorporated in a library.)

Once they are embedded in MYFUNC.LIB, the .OBJ sets of code are more correctly referred to as *modules* rather than as *files*. As modules within a library they are still referenced by their original .OBJ names (MYFUNC1 and MYFUNC2), but you don't name the drive, path, or extension.

► *What Is a Librarian?* ►

LIB can create new .LIB files, add modules to existing libraries, and delete modules from existing libraries. It can extract a module from a library and recover the original .OBJ file, and it can also add all the modules of one library to another. Finally, but not least, LIB lets you examine the contents of a library by creating a list file. These tasks are known as *library maintenance*. The software that performs them is called a librarian or library manager.

► *Creating and Adding to a Library* ►

To create the MYFUNC.LIB file, you use LIB at the DOS command level as follows:

```
C>LIB MYFUNC[.LIB] +MYFUNC1[.OBJ] +MYFUNC2[.OBJ];
```

LIB assumes the obvious extensions shown as defaults. Wildcards are not allowed. The plus signs immediately before the .OBJ file names indicate additions to the library. If MYFUNC.LIB already exists, the above line adds both .OBJ files to it; otherwise LIB creates a new file called MYFUNC.LIB and then adds the .OBJ files. This example assumes that all three files are in the current directory. If they are elsewhere, you must specify their drives and paths—but remember that LIB stores only the module names after stripping off any extraneous rubbish.

You could later add a module called MYFUNC3 to \QC, remove the original MYFUNC2, and add in all the modules from another library called OEM.LIB with one command line:

    C>LIB MYFUNC +\QC\MYFUNC3 −MYFUNC2 +OEM.LIB;

Notice the minus sign used for module deletion. No path or extension is needed with a − (delete) action since module names are just module names! If you unnecessarily add paths or extensions, LIB will quietly remove them. The \QC\ *is* needed for adding MYFUNC3 because LIB needs to locate the .OBJ file (.OBJ is the default). Inside the library, though, the module retains no clue to its original directory.

You can present these + and − actions in any sequence because LIB sorts them before processing your requests. The removals are always performed before the additions. The following line appears pointless yet is very common and sensible:

    C>LIB MYFUNC −MYFUNC1 +MYFUNC1;

Yes, you are replacing MYFUNC1 with a new version. The following line would have the same effect:

    C>LIB MYFUNC +MYFUNC1 −MYFUNC1;

This operation is so common that LIB allows you to use the following short-hand equivalent:

    C>LIB MYFUNC − +MYFUNC1;

If you try to remove a module that isn't there, LIB will inform you of the irresolvable quandary it faces. Similarly, LIB balks at adding a module that already exists, forcing you to do the − + trick.

Ah! But what if you remove MYFUNC2 from MYFUNC.LIB but do not have MYFUNC2.OBJ somewhere as a separate file? Alas, unless MYFUNC2 exists within another library, it has now disappeared. If you kept

MYFUNC2.C, of course, no lasting harm is done—you can always recompile. LIB offers *module extraction* as an alternative to recompilation. What LIB putteth together, LIB can also pulleth asunder! In

    C>LIB MYFUNC *MYFUNC2;

the * (extract) operator recovers the MYFUNC2 module and writes it out to MYFUNC2.OBJ, either creating this file or overwriting any existing file of that name. This recovers the .OBJ file in the exact format it had during the original addition operation. If the requested module is not found, you get a suitable message and no new file is created.

   As you may guess, a safe way to remove a module without losing it is to combine − and * as follows:

    C>LIB MYFUNC − *MYFUNC2;

This creates MYFUNC2.OBJ and then removes the module MYFUNC2 from MYFUNC.LIB. In this case, indicating the drive and path makes sense if you want to extract the module and save it in another directory. The drive and path would be used by the * but ignored by the − .

   The following lines are all equivalent to the previous example:

    C>LIB MYFUNC − *MYFUNC2;

    C>LIB MYFUNC *MYFUNC2 − MYFUNC2;

    C>LIB MYFUNC − MYFUNC2 *MYFUNC2;

► *LIB Syntax* ►

The LIB librarian can be invoked in two distinct ways:

1. If you type C>LIB and then press Enter, LIB will prompt you for four arguments:

    Library name: Enter the main library to be operated on.

    Operations: Enter the operation commands.

    List file: Enter the list file name.

    Output library: Enter the new library name.

As you may guess, some or all of these fields can be omitted. The minimum entry is just the library name. Entering a ; terminates the dialogue. To understand the various options and defaults, consider the second LIB usage since the two are closely related.

2. In the second method, you supply the arguments in a command line as follows:

   C>LIB *libname* [*options*] [*commands*] [,[*listfile*][,[*newlib*]]][;]

As you can see, the only mandatory argument is the library name. A few examples will clarify the situation:

► Entering LIB MYLIB; or LIB MYLIB.LIB; will perform a consistency check on MYLIB.LIB. This checks that all the modules indexed are present, and vice versa.

► Entering LIB MYLIB ,STAN.LST; will perform the consistency check and then create (or overwrite) a cross-reference list file called STAN.LST. This lists all the public symbols in MYLIB.LIB, followed by a list of all the modules in MYLIB.LIB.

► Entering LIB MYLIB +MYOBJ; will add MYOBJ.OBJ to the library MYLIB.

► Entering LIB MYLIB − *MYOBJ, , NEWLIB copies the module MYOBJ to a file MYOBJ.OBJ and makes a new library called NEWLIB.LIB, which is the same as MYLIB except that MYOBJ is missing. MYLIB is unchanged.

► *LIB Commands List*

The optional *commands* list is any sequence of file names (with or without drive and paths) preceded by combinations of the action symbols + (add a module), − (delete a module), and * (extract a module), as described earlier. The legal combinations are − * (extract and then remove) and − + (remove and then add). Suitable error messages are given if you try to remove or extract a nonexistent module or add an existing module. You should be careful with * since it could overwrite a later .OBJ version with an earlier version without warning.

Only the + action is possible with a library file name. You can add all the modules in one library to another, but you can only remove and extract single modules. To rename a module, you have to extract it, rename the .OBJ file, and then add the renamed file.

► *Listing the LIB Contents*

The optional file name (*listfile*) appearing after a comma at the end of the command line receives a listing of the library modules in alphabetical order with their offsets and size in bytes. After each module a list of the public symbols defined in that module appears, also in alphabetical sequence.

These public symbols represent all the external identifiers you studied in Chapter 7: function names, global variables, and **extern**ed variables defined in the original source files. The compiler passes these to the .OBJ files (for direct linking purposes) and LIB passes them to the .LIB files (for selective linkage).

LIB listings are only produced if you enter a comma followed by a file name or the device-file names CON (screen display) or PRN (direct printer output).

Similarly

C>LIB MYFUNC, MYLIB.PRT;

will create a file called MYLIB.PRT that contains the module names and public symbols. You can study this file at your leisure. You will find it instructive to list the modules in SLIBCE.LIB, the small memory model support library, and you will see many familiar names in the symbol list.

In normal, default QuickC operation, these identifiers retain their uppercase and lowercase source code spellings but have an underscore (_) prepended. When mixing C and case-insensitive Pascal code, as discussed in Chapter 5, some care is needed to avoid inadvertent clashes since the **pascal** modifier converts symbols to uppercase. These conversions are important in understanding the /I (short for /IGNORECASE) and /NOI (short for /NOIGNORECASE) *options* in LIB.

► *The LIB/LINK Case-Sensitivity Problem*

The /I and /NOI options provide compatibility with both case-insensitive languages and case-insensitive linkers.

As I mentioned, LIB maintains a table of all the public symbols (such as function names and global variables) defined in its member modules. This table is consulted by LINK or some alien linker to determine which modules to pull in. We clearly cannot allow duplicates in any set of tables, so whenever we add a module to a library, LIB has to check that the new symbols being added are unique. If they are not, an error is signaled and the new module is rejected.

The question arises, Is case relevant? Are the entries **_sum** and **_SUM**, for instance, different? As far as the C language and QuickC's LINK linker are concerned, they are indubitably distinct; however, many old-fashioned linkers and languages are case insensitive and cannot differentiate! Remember that a linker is not really concerned about the origin of the .OBJ files (they can come from almost any high- or low-level language) as long as they follow an agreed format.

If you use the /I flag, you force LIB to be case insensitive as a sop to the older regimes. LIB would therefore reject a new module defining **_sum** if the symbol **_SUM** already existed in that library's symbol table. In Pascal mode, in fact, this would be a genuine error.

The /NOI option, which is the default, tells LIB *not* to ignore case—in other words, to behave case sensitively like C does. This feature may not concern you, but it is important for software developers who may have no control over the linkers used by their customers.

Summing up, if you include the /NOI flag or exclude the /I flag, LIB becomes case sensitive and your library is less portable because many linkers match the early single-case computer languages.

If you intend to use only LINK and case-sensitive languages, you can safely omit the /I option; otherwise it is wiser to include it.

Incidentally, if you ever get a long list of **identifier unknown** linker-error messages showing names with underscores, it probably indicates that you failed to include a .LIB file. The likely candidates are GRAPHICS.LIB or PGCHART.LIB (since they are outside the normal combined libraries unless you specifically asked for their inclusion when running SETUP).

► *LIB Response Files* ►

The final LIB feature to be covered is the *response file*—an ASCII text file you can create to help you automate repetitive maintenance operations on your libraries. The idea is that if you have a response file called UPDATE.RSP, say, containing the line

    MYLIB − +NEW.OBJ − +REV.OBJ;

its contents can be pulled into the command line by typing

    LIB @UPDATE.RSP

at the prompt. The leading @ causes the following file name to be read into the command line, exactly as if you had typed

    LIB MYLIB − +NEW.OBJ − +REV.OBJ;

at the prompt. I gave the response file an extension .RSP as a recognition aid—in fact, any extension or none is OK. Apart from saving keystrokes, the response file solves the problem of DOS command lines being limited to 127 characters. A response file can be as long as you like provided that you use an & to indicate a continuation line:

    MYLIB + − REVISED1.OBJ + − REVISED2.OBJ + − REVISED3.OBJ &

    + NEWONE.OBJ − OLDONE *REVIEW.OBJ;

The response file need not contain the entire command entry—you can enter some fields by hand and have the rest pulled in from the response file. You can even use several response files in the same command. If REV.RSP was the file holding the previous lines, and you set up files MYPATH and LIBLST to contain

    \QC\NEWLIB\

and

    , LIBLST.LST;

respectively, you could type

    /LIB @REV.RSP − *@MYPATH SPECIAL @LIBLIST;

at the prompt. The response file shortcut is also available with LINK, and the syntax is identical.

► *FUNCTIONS AT WORK* ►

In this final section I want to touch on two important aspects of functions: functions as arguments to other functions and recursive functions. These are big subjects that fill many esoteric volumes, so, like the Winchester read-head, I can only scratch the surface.

► *Pointers to Functions* ►

When the compiler meets the declaration of an array such as **char name[30];**, you know that the identifier **name** is translated as a pointer (the constant pointer to the **char** at address **&name[0]**). So **name** plays a dual role as array name and pointer.

In the same way, the names of declared functions also play a second role as pointers. The syntax distinguishes between **func(arg);** as a call to **func** and the isolated identifier **func** as a pointer. If you encounter the following declaration:

```
int (*func_ptr)(void);
```

you can deduce that **(*func_ptr)** is playing the role of a function taking no arguments and returning an **int**. C's declaration syntax is based on the "template for action" principle. What the declaration has achieved is similar to the other pointer declarations you have encountered—e.g., **int *ptr;** does not create an **int** but creates an uninitialized variable of type pointer to integer. Similarly, the **func_ptr** declaration creates not a function but an uninitialized variable of type pointer to function of type F, where F is "takes no arguments and returns an integer." Before being used this pointer must be initialized with an appropriate value. If you define

```
int myfunc(void)
{ /* body here */
}
```

then **myfunc** is a respectable candidate for **func_ptr**:

```
func_ptr = myfunc;
i = *func_ptr( );
/* same as i = myfunc( ); */
```

In the first assignment it is tempting but wrong to use **&myfunc** on the right side. This is as wrong as using **&name** rather than the true pointer, **name**. Since **func_ptr** now has a valid, non-NULL value, the indirection is valid and ***func_ptr( )** is a legal invocation of a function.

Function pointers can be used just like other pointers. You can store them in arrays, structures, and unions. For example, you can have

```
struct action_table {
int (*func1)( );
float (*func2)( );
action_table *node;
} my_table;
```

Here you can store function pointers representing actions to be taken under different circumstances. Saving formulas in spreadsheet cells can be achieved with this approach.

Function pointers can be arguments to functions, and they can be returned as values by functions. Functions cannot return arrays or functions per se, but they can return pointers for these objects. When all the dust from the pointer controversy settles, you can say that the dangers are offset by the power and elegance of being able to pass and effectively return arrays and functions to and from functions.

A simple but instructive example is **qsort( )**, which is prototyped in STDLIB.H as follows:

```
void qsort(void *base, size_t nelem, size_t width,
           int (*fcmp)( ) );
```

The arguments are as follows:

base is the pointer to the first (0th) element of the table to be sorted.
nelem is the number of entries in the table.
width is the size in bytes of each element to be sorted.

Ah ha—what is the final parameter? Yes, it's a pointer to a user-supplied function called the *comparison function*. You tell **qsort( )** how to sort by indicating what you mean by "greater," "equal," and "less than." Your **fcmp( )** must be defined so that **fcmp(ptr1, ptr2)** returns − 1 if ***ptr1** is less than ***ptr2**, 0 if ***ptr1** equals ***ptr2**, and + 1 if ***ptr1** is greater than ***ptr2**. **ptr1** and **ptr2** are declared as pointers to elements of the table to be sorted.

The sort, based on C. A. R. Hoare's quicker-sort, is therefore applicable to any numerical or symbolic ordering sequence you can possibly dream up. For simple lexicographic string sorts, you can use any of the **strcmp( )** variants in STRING.H because these return the prescribed **int** values. For more complex sorts, you write **my_comp( )** and pass **my_comp** as the pointer argument.

► *Recursion* ►

(*Recursive* adj. See *Recursive* [Kelly-Bootle, Stan. *The Devil's DP Dictionary*. New York: McGraw-Hill, 1981.])

C shares a valuable property with most modern structured languages in its support of *recursion* both for functions and data structures.

You saw recursive data structures in Chapter 5, where a structure member could be a pointer to its own structure.

I mentioned in Chapter 7 that a function can call any function within its scope and that this allows **func( )** to call **func( )** recursively. To avoid an infinite regress, you need to ensure that each call to **func( )** somehow converges to some measurable, terminating goal. Recursion also occurs when A calls B, B calls C, and C calls A. This is equally allowed in C, provided the scoping rules are followed. Recursion offers an elegant solution to many problems where each stage of computation is defined in terms of the same function, although in theory any recursive solution has an equivalent nonrecursive formulation. The classic illustration is factorial(N), which is defined a ($N \times$ factorial($N - 1$)) unless N equals 0 [factorial(0) is defined as 1]. Another example is the exponentiate or power function, since $X^N = X \times (X^N - 1)$. Consider the function **exp(X, N)** for non-negative **N**, defined as follows:

```
double exp(double X, int N)
{
if (N < 0) return (− 1);
/* error */
```

```
if (N == 0) return (1);
else return (X*exp(X, N – 1));
}
```

Each time **exp( )** calls itself, the exponent argument is reduced by 1, guaranteeing an end to the sequence. You should try this with different values, noting that for very large values of **N** you may get stack overflow. Program 10.1, MYEXP.C, gives you a bare-bones platform to experiment with.

```
/* Prog 10.1 myexp.c - tests recursion */
#include <stdio.h>

double myexp(double X, int N)
{
        if (N < 0) return (-1);
        if (N == 0) return (1);
        else return (myexp(X,N-1)*X);
}

void main()
{
        double x = 0; int n = 0; char ch = '\0';

        do {
          puts("Enter N and X:");
          scanf("%d %lf",&n, &x);
          printf("N=%d, X=%f\n",n,x);
          printf("X^N=%f\n",myexp(x,n));}
        while ((ch = getch()) != 'X');
}
```

► *Program 10.1:* MYEXP.C

MATH.H contains the standard power function

```
double pow(double x, double y);
/* toil and trouble? */
```

for more exotic calculations of x^y. You might want to compare its accuracy with **myexp( )** when **y** is a whole number.

► *SUMMARY OF CHAPTER 10* ►

◄► LIB is a simple but effective object code library manager. You can create and maintain .LIB files using command-line option switches and/or response files. You can + (add), − (remove), or * (extract) .OBJ files to or from any .LIB file. LIB also lets you display, print, or write to disk the members of a .LIB file. The /I and /NOI switches give you compatibility with case-insensitive languages and linkers. The QuickC-supplied LINK linker syntax was explained.

◄► You saw how and why libraries are used in C—both for efficiency and control of large projects. The QC Make facility was also explained in the context of maintaining multifile programs. .MAK files allow you to express the interdependencies of .C and .OBJ files.

◄► Pointers to functions allow you to write "generic" functions such as **qsort( )** that take a function pointer as an argument. The syntactical key is that **func** as an identifier is taken as the pointer to the function, whereas **func(args)** is used to declare, define, or invoke the function.

◄► Recursion—I gave you a brief, tantalizing peek at a topic of great importance. Recursive data structures are widely used in C, allowing a **struct** member to point to itself (in a manner of speaking). Recursive functions call themselves directly or indirectly. To avoid infinite loops and exhausted stacks, some tested criterion in the recursion must ensure an exit. The function X^Y (exponentiate) was coded recursively as a simple example.

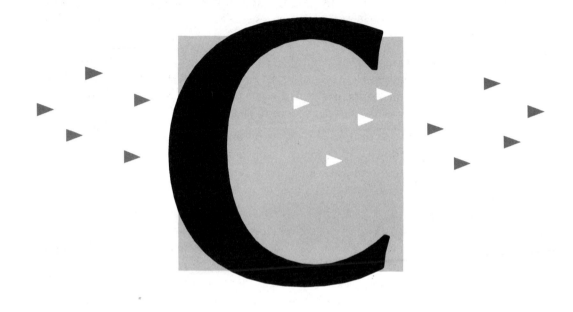

NAILING YOUR BUGS

► *CHAPTER 11* ►

► *FOR ALL YOU DO, THIS BUG'S FOR YOU!* ►

First, let's step back and consider the nature of the beast. What exactly are bugs, and how can they be squashed? If you have tried any of the examples in this book, you have almost certainly encountered unexpected results from time to time, just as I did when devising the programs! Bugs are the critters that take the blame for a program misbehaving in some way.

The entomological taxonomy of bugs, though, is quite complicated and still the subject of intense computer scientific debate. To say that a program misbehaves implies that you have a firm and formal picture of what constitutes "correct" behavior. A program intended to compute factorial N, for instance, may give erroneous results (or loop forever with no results) if you input too big an N or a negative or fractional value of N. It is even possible to envisage a bizarre factorial N program that works fine for all values of $N < 50$ except for $N = 7$ and $N = 39$.

Is the problem with the program for failing to trap such input, or with the definition of factorial N, or with the limited capacity of your registers, or with the user of the program? Furthermore, the "defect" may not be discovered for many years because it was never subjected to "dubious" input, reminding us that bugs can and do "lurk" undetected simply because it may be impossible to test a large program with all possible input combinations. Testing each module as it is developed is mandatory, of course, but there is no automatic guarantee that your modules will cooperate as planned.

You may have also heard the ironic in-joke that bugs are simply "undocumented features." The truth is that as your program grows in complexity, it becomes increasingly difficult to define exactly how it should behave under all circumstances. Certain nonfatal quirks may surface, and it is often cheaper to change the program specifications than modify the code. There are limits to this, of course. If your factorial program tells you that 4! (pronounced "factorial 4") is 23 rather than 24, no amount of redefinition and redocumentation will save you from the scorn of your potential user base.

Studies of large software projects reveal two frightening facts:

1. As the number of bugs is reduced, it becomes exponentially harder to remove the residual bugs—whence the old saw "Let sleeping bugs lie."

2. The code used to remove bugs, often called a *patch*, has a higher propensity for error than the original code owing to the possibility of subtle side effects.

Remember too that a program can run correctly with a given compiler/OS/hardware mix and yet fail when ported to some other system. More often than you may imagine, a version change of the OS or compiler, or a change in the parameters and defaults used during compilation/linking, can dramatically affect the behavior of your code. In these cases, where exactly is the "bug"?

► Errors—Ancient and Modern ►

The mere act of typing, whether you are copying from a list or transferring your inward thoughts, is remarkably error-prone. And so is the task of proofreading when you compare two documents. The study of this problem goes back many centuries before the advent of computer programs. Even the most conscientious scribes copying revered manuscripts slipped up occasionally, as any biblical commentary will confirm. Two classes of error are common enough to attract special nomenclature by textual scholars: *dittography* and *haplography*.

With dittography, the scribe, possibly because of some interruption, copies a piece of text for the second time. A modern version of this occurs with word processors when a block of text is wrongly duplicated. Haplography is the opposite problem: When copying text that contains repeated groups of characters, the eye moves ahead and a section is inadvertently omitted. It is surprisingly difficult sometimes to spot such aberations (such as the missing *r*!) in your own work but not when you are reading someone else's efforts. The actual perception, that is to say, the message sent from eye to brain, of what you have written is so easily colored by what you *intended* to write. It may seem a trite observation, but you may not be the best person to debug your own code. If, however, you are working alone, then you must develop the concentration needed to achieve clinical objectivity.

I have already mentioned the differences between syntactical (compile time) and semantic (run time) errors in a program (Chapter 1). In real life, these two classes of errors can overlap in disconcerting ways. You can sometimes make "syntax" errors that generate legal code with unintended "semantic" side effects. The C language is especially prone to such problems.

Gross syntax errors are trapped by the compiler but may generate a rash of "misleading" error messages. This is because the impact of a syntax error may extend beyond its immediate neighborhood. It may take several statements, for example, before a misspelling, such as typing **far** or **fur** in place of **for**, can be diagnosed by the compiler!

There are far more ways of getting a program wrong than there are ways of getting it right, so it is difficult to formulate precise rules for debugging. If the final, erroneous output (or lack of any output) from the program run is your only guide, you need a lot of luck to locate the bug immediately. It can be useful to embed various display statements in a program under development so that intermediate results can be observed. The aim is to work back from the known faulty result to the prime cause or causes. In Chapter 5, I explained how **#define DEBUG 1** and **#if DEBUG** can be used to provide optional displays that are easily switched on or off as your debugging proceeds without extensive source code modifications: Simply replace **#define DEBUG 1** with **#define DEBUG 0** and the **#if DEBUG** sections are omitted.

If the computed value **(a * b / c)** is wrong, for example, you make sure that you did not enter **(a / b * c)**, then trace back to see whether **a**, **b**, and **c** were computed correctly. In many cases, these three variables are set from other calculations, and you enter a confusing maze of possibilities. The only advice here is the obvious need for patient, logical detective work with large sheets of plain paper to note the effect of *single* changes to the program. Changing too many parameters at once is a common temptation. In the above example, you might try setting **a = 1** and bypassing the function that computes **a**. This approach involves lots of time editing and recompiling. Source-level debugging offers several time-saving tricks, as you'll shortly see.

Before I show you some real examples, let me explain the principles of the source code debugger and establish some of the jargon you will need.

► *SOURCE-LEVEL DEBUGGING* ►

It is worth stressing, first of all, that debuggers do not actually debug your code! Sorry about that. You alone must determine why the program is misbehaving and make the corrections. Apart from locating syntax errors, the compiler, linker, and run-time support system have no innate ability to guess your intentions. It can even be proved that no general metaprogram exists that can detect endless loops. What debuggers can do is allow you to "freeze," inspect, and interact with a program while it is executing, thereby giving you useful clues pointing to the problems.

Before the advent of the source-level debugger, debugging high-level-language run-time errors was a major problem. The most you could expect was a *core dump* showing you the contents of memory and registers at selected moments of execution. The rather gloomy sounding *postmortem* dump was often triggered automatically when the program *abended* (i.e., ended through abortion). Relating pages of obscure octal or hex listings back to your legible source code was a real pain.

The popularity of *interpreters* over compilers can be traced to their obvious advantages in debugging: Each line of code is interpreted and executed immediately, pinpointing most errors for an instant fix. Reduced execution speed, however, is the price to be paid. A compromise that is emerging offers a C interpreter for program development, after which you switch to a compiler to get your final *.EXE.

The source-level debugger still remains the most popular approach to debugging, offering major advantages over the old core-dump approach. First, symbol table data is made available in various ways so that, during execution, variables can be referenced by their original source code names rather than via memory locations.

Second, *breakpoints* can be set at the source code level, allowing you to run a program up to a selected line or statement. When the program stops, you can peek at variables, expressions, and registers and optionally change their values. From this point you can step through the program, statement by statement, optionally performing function calls as one step (using Step Over) or stepping through each statement defining the function (using Trace Into). You can then go full-speed ahead to the next breakpoint.

You can also arrange for the debugger to display continuously (dynamically) the values of selected variables or expressions, known as *watch values*, as the program runs. A variant of this feature allows the values of all local variables to be displayed. As the program passes through its functions, the set of local variables will be dynamically updated.

You can also set *watchpoints*. A watchpoint acts like a breakpoint by halting execution; however, the criterion for stopping the run is not confined to a particular statement. A typical watchpoint might be the Boolean expression **sum = = 0**. The debugger monitors the value of (**sum = = 0**) and stops execution whenever this evaluates to true (nonzero). The watchpoint expression can be any combination of C language operators and valid identifiers that evaluate to true or false (0), so you have a powerful tool that can temporarily halt a program when any critical condition is reached.

Another useful feature is suggestively named *animation*. With animation activated, the program runs in slow motion with each successive statement highlighted on the screen. You can press any key to pause. Breakpoints, watch values, and watchpoints can all be used in conjunction with animation, and you can set the speed of execution. Animation proves useful in getting an overall picture of control flow and function call sequences.

While on the subject of function calls, the Calls... feature is worth noting. This allows you to inspect all the function calls (and their arguments) made by your program up to the time you started your debugging session.

A final feature to be noted is the *History* command. Briefly, this lets you record your actions during a debugging session so that you can "replay" the session at a later date. You'll soon see how complex a debugging session can be, so the History facility can prove invaluable, especially when you are faced with "intermittent" bugs. In order to isolate hardware and software problems, it is essential to be able to repeat debugging sequences exactly.

To sum up, the modern source code debugger is a miracle of systems software. It gives you intimate control over how your ∗.EXE files will run and provides a fly-on-the-chip picture of what's going on. The major hurdle is that the debugger has to share the same CPU, memory, run-time support, and OS as the .EXE file with no nasty side effects.

Let's see how you can exploit these features with the QuickC menus and hot keys.

► *USING THE QUICKC INTEGRATED DEBUGGER* ►

The Run, Debug, View, and Options menus each control various aspects of the QC integrated debugger. As you can guess, the View/Windows menu plays an important role since the debugger has lots to tell you, and the QuickC window system is exploited to the full, with windows available to display watch values, local variables, and registers in addition to the familiar source, output, and Error windows.

► *Setting Debug Mode* ►

The first selection needed before you can use the debugger is made with the Options menu. Fire it up with Alt-O, then select the Make... submenu. Figure 11.1 shows you the dialog box displayed, which allows you to set the Build flag to debug mode.

If there is a dot alongside the Debug legend, the Build flag is already set to Debug and you can press Esc to return to the source window. If the dot shows alongside the Release legend, you should press the left arrow (or mouse-click on the Debug button) to get the dot showing in the Debug button. Then click on <OK> or press Enter to save this option. Later, when you want to turn off debugging, you simply move the dot back to the Release button and press Enter. Changes in this flag are noted as environment changes by QC, so expect rebuild prompts when you try to run a program after such changes.

The key point here is that the *.OBJ and *.EXE programs you build with the Build flag set to Debug carry special debugging data. When the Build flag is set to Debug, the debugger also generates additional files with extensions .ILK (incremental linking), .SYM (symbol), and .MDT (module description tables) for use with the debugger. These files all carry the same base name as your program.

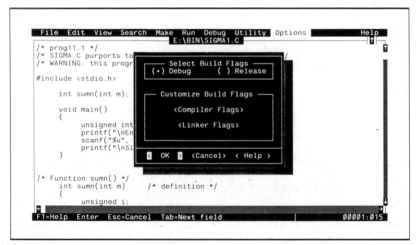

► *Figure 11.1:* Options/Make dialog box

The additional debugging data do not affect the normal execution of the .EXE file, but once you have debugged a program, you should reset the Build flag to Release and rebuild your program. The reduction in file size can be considerable: my HELLO.OBJ, for example, drops from 1815 bytes to 407 bytes when I shed the debugging data; HELLO.EXE reduces from 16,868 bytes to 7447 bytes. (Your figures may differ, but the percentage reductions will be comparable.) You can also erase the *.ILK, *.SYM, and *.MDT files once you are happily debugged.

To simplify our discourse I will refer to *.EXE programs that have been compiled/linked with the Debug option active as debuggable programs. For future reference, if and when you graduate to the Microsoft Optimizing C Compiler (currently Version 5.1), note that QuickC debuggable programs are compatible with the more complex CodeView debugger but usually not the other way round.

You will find that QC is, as usual, quite friendly in prompting you when necessary. For example, if you try to debug a nondebuggable program, regardless of the state of the Build flag, QC will warn you and ask if you want to rebuild it in debug mode.

► *Debugging SIGMA.C* ►

Enter SIGMA1.C, the version of SIGMA.C as listed in Program 11.1, and set the program list to SIGMA1.C. This step is not essential with single-file programs, but it is a good habit to develop since SIGMA1.C might become part of a multifile project. After checking that the Options/Make Build flag is set to Debug, compile and link SIGMA1.C using the Make/Build menu.

SIGMA.C is supposed to calculate the sum of the first N natural numbers: 1 + 2 + ... + N, where N is entered by the user. However, this version of SIGMA.C contains some deliberately instructive errors, ranging from the obvious to the less obvious.

Now select Go from the Run menu (or the hot key equivalent, F5) to run SIGMA from within the QC environment. Since you have not yet set any breakpoints or watchpoints (and animation is off), the program will run normally, stopping only for **scanf( )** keyboard input. The user screen will display **Enter a number:**. Type 3 and press Enter. Make a note of the answer given for Sigma 3, then press any key to return to the source screen.

You do have some control over screen swapping during a debugging session. The Options/Run / Debug... menu lets you choose between three

```
/* prog11.1 = SIGMA.C version 1 */
/* SIGMA1.C purports to sum first n integers: 1+2+...+n */
/* WARNING: this program has deliberate bugs */

#include <stdio.h>

    int sumn(int m);     /* declaration */

    void main()
    {
        unsigned int n;
        printf("\nEnter a number: ");
        scanf("%u", &n);
        printf("\nSigma %u = %lu", n, sumn(n) );
    }


/* Function sumn() */
    int sumn(int m)       /* definition */
    {
        unsigned i;
        unsigned long sum;

        for (i=0; i < m; i++)
            sum =+ i;
        return sum;
    }
```

▶ *Program 11.1:* SIGMA1.C

screen-swapping strategies:

1. Auto: The screen swaps from source to output for both screen display and keyboard input. This is the best option for beginners.

2. On: The screen swaps to output after each executable statement. Use this only with programs calling for mouse and BIOS video routines.

3. Off: The screen swaps only for output.

Regardless of which option you select, remember the useful hot key F4, which lets you flip between the source screen and output screen at any time. During forthcoming debugging sessions, you'll find it useful to return to the scene of the crime! For small programs such as SIGMA with modest output requirements, you may wish to experiment with the View/Windows menu; you can have both the output and source screens as windows sharing the screen—simply select Output window in the Windows menu. Then you can use View/Maximize (or Ctrl-F10) to zoom into either window or Ctrl-F4 to close the output screen (the source window is always open, by the way). F6 toggles the *active* window—that is to say, the window holding the active cursor. But before you get carried away with these tricks, let's not forget the job in hand: debugging SIGMA.C.

The correct answer for Sigma 3 should be 3 + 2 + 1 = 6, but SIGMA is not behaving as it should. Run the program again with different values of **n** and see if you can discern any pattern in the erroneous output.

The answers given by my SIGMA1.C are

Sigma 1 = 65536   not so good—should be 1

Sigma 2 = 131073   terrible—should be 3

Sigma 3 = 196610   worse—should be 6

You should always keep a note of the results with simple inputs—such as 1, 2, or 3—then look through the source code for any obvious errors. The wrong answers here immediately suggest that we have somehow mixed up signed and unsigned numbers. Because this is an artificial debugging exercise, I will assume that you do not immediately spot the bugs responsible.

To give you some practice with the debugging features, I'll show you first how to *single-step* through the program.

► Single-Stepping ►

There are two single-stepping commands, both in the Run menu and both with convenient hot keys: Step Over (F10) and Trace Into (F8). The differences will emerge presently.

Try selecting Step Over from the Run menu, or use the handy hot key F10. The first thing that happens is that QuickC checks the Build flag; if this is not set to Debug, or if SIGMA.EXE is not debuggable, you get a warning and an offer to rebuild. If you confirm, QC will rebuild in debug mode before obeying your Step Over command.

Even if SIGMA.EXE is debuggable, QC still checks the program's dependencies from the program list and, if necessary, rebuilds to obtain the latest .EXE file. In this latter respect, Step Over (F10) initially behaves just like Go (F5). With Step Over, however, the program will be executed one step (statement) at a time.

A highlighted band, which I'll call the *execution band*, now appears to indicate the execution point. As you single-step, this band advances past each executable line of code, indicating the statement line *about to be executed*. Notice that nonexecutable lines, such as comments and **#includes** are skipped, so initially the debugger will stop at the first executable line, the opening block marker { of the function **main( )**. You are still free to move the source edit cursor around and this still indicates the point where edit changes occur. But notice that the execution band is quite independent.

F10 is just one of several ways of initiating a debugging session. You can restore single-stepping at any moment using Run/Restart or its hot key, Shift-F5. This reloads SIGMA.EXE into memory and puts the execution point back to the start; however, Restart does *not* trigger execution and it doesn't alter any of the debugging conditions.

You should now try the other single-stepper, Run/Trace Into or, more conveniently, the equivalent hot key, F8. Notice how the execution band steps through successive lines for each F8 Trace Into operation, following the actual run sequence. This does not always match the physical sequence of the source code statements, so show no surprise when the highlighted band jumps around during **while, for,** and other control loops.

Just like F10, F8 can be used to initiate a debugging session. QuickC will check debuggability and program list dependencies in exactly the same way. So, how do F8 and F10 differ?

► Tracing and Stepping

F8 (Trace Into) and F10 (Step Over) both single-step in the same way until you reach a statement calling a user-supplied function. As the names imply, F8 single-steps (traces) into the function's statements, whereas F10 steps over the function, executing it as a single step. Note that F8 can only trace into a debuggable function—that is, a function whose source code is available to the debugger. Also, of course, the function must have been compiled/linked originally with the Debug option on, and the auxiliary symbol files mentioned earlier must be available.

For example, a QuickC-supplied library function such as **printf( )** cannot usually be traced into because it was not compiled in debug mode. As you have seen, this would bloat the library without due cause. Both F8 and F10, then, will simply execute **printf( )** as a single step. Normally, of course, there would be no practical point in stepping through the individual statements of **printf( )** or any other supplied library function. You are really interested in debugging *your* code not Microsoft's!

If you have purchased any vendors' library source, you may wish to create debuggable versions of their functions as an educational exercise, but for now I will assume that you will always step over vendor-supplied functions rather than trace into them.

The usual approach is to use F8 while debugging called functions, but once these have been corrected, you can save time by switching to F10.

Note again the vital difference between the *cursor* position and the execution band position. These two are quite independent. The cursor indicates your current position in the QC editor, whereas the execution band indicates the next statement to be executed by the debugger. The difference is exploited by the Continue To Cursor command in the Run menu (hot key F7), which allows you to execute all statements between the execution band and the line holding your current cursor (provided, of course, that such statements exist). Rather than setting breakpoints, which "stick" until cleared, you can move your cursor ahead of the execution band, then use Continue To Cursor (F7).

Also, the independent cursor lets you edit any part of your code in the usual manner during a debugging session. Some care is needed with cut and paste, since the block marker highlight can be confused with the execution band. Remember to use File/Save and Make/Build before resuming the debugging session. More on this later.

For now, just keep pressing F8 to step line by line, noticing how the execution band follows the source code. When you pass the **printf( )** statement, the user screen will momentarily display the prompt and then return to the source screen with the **scanf( )** line highlighted. When you press F8 to execute the **scanf( )** statement, you return automatically to the user screen and the system waits for you to enter a number, just as if you were running normally.

After entering **n**, you are returned to the source screen with the execution band on the next line:

```
printf("\nSigma %u = %lu", n, sumn(n) );
```

If you press F8 now, execution of **printf( )** calls the function **sumn( )**. It is important to note that although the execution band tracks line by line, a typical C line may contain several statements, possibly including calls to functions. The debugger will execute these in the correct sequence as specified by the C syntax.

Because **sumn( )** is a debuggable function and in the same module as **main( )**, you will see the execution band move down into the **sumn( )** source code. Had you used F10, all the steps of the function **sumn( )** would have been invoked in one fell swoop.

As you press F8 to step through **sumn( )**, notice that the single statement within the **for** loop will be invoked as many times as the parameters dictate. In our simple example, the execution band seems to remain on the same statement, **sum = + i;**, but be not alarmed! The statement *is* being executed each time you press F8—indeed, this sequence gives you a useful clue as to whether the **for** loop is correctly coded (in fact, you've probably spotted some gross errors in the **for** loop already).

Keep pressing F8 until the **for** loop terminates; then on through the **return** statement; then back to **main( )**, where the **printf( )** is completed. Once again, the action returns to the output screen where the answer **Sigma n =** appears. Jot down the results, then press Shift-F5 to restart. Notice that if you keep single-stepping past the end of **main( )**, you will start again at the beginning of **main( )**. Using the Restart command is just a safety-first habit to clear any possible detritus.

This is a useful point at which to try out another useful feature of QuickC. It's the Function command in the Search menu, and it only works during execution and with debuggable programs. You can enter a function name, such as **sumn**, and Search/Function will lead you to the function's entry point in the source. No big deal here, I agree, but it's handy when your programs get bigger.

The foregoing drill was intended to give you a feel for the single-stepping hot keys. However, we have not yet tackled the bugs—we have simply been running a buggy program one bug at a time! In the next session, you will learn how to peek and poke or, more politely, how to evaluate and modify the values of variables and expressions at selected points in the run sequence.

► WATCH YOUR EXPRESSIONS! ►

Repeat the previous debugging session and enter n = 2, then stop at the **for** loop in **sumn( )**:

```
for (i = 0; i < m; i + +)
sum = + i;
return sum;
```

Now select Debug/Watch Value. The Watch Value dialog box shown in Figure 11.2 lets you enter a variable name or expression in the Expression field. You then select <Add/Delete>, and the variable name or expression is added to the List box. You delete watch expressions by selecting them from the list and choosing <Add/Delete>.

For now, type **sum** in the Expression field and select <Add/Delete>. The idea is that whenever **sum** changes in value, its value will appear in the Debug window, just above the source window, as shown in Figure 11.3.

► *A Quick Detour Round the Windows* ►

We'll now have a quick diversion, including some recaps, on windows before we proceed. The Debug window is one of eight window types supported by QuickC: source, Debug, Help, Locals, Registers, Notepad, output, and Error. A maximum of five of these types can be displayed at any one time, so certain pairs of windows share the same display areas:

Debug/Help: the Debug window shares with Help.

Locals/Registers: the Locals window shares with Registers.

Notepad/Output: the Notepad window shares with Output.

The source and Error windows have their own reserved areas and do not share.

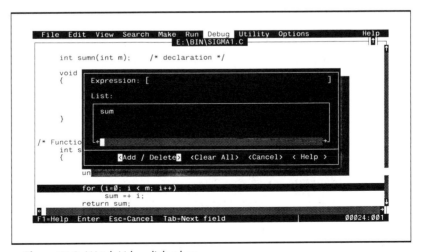

► *Figure 11.2:* Watch Value dialog box

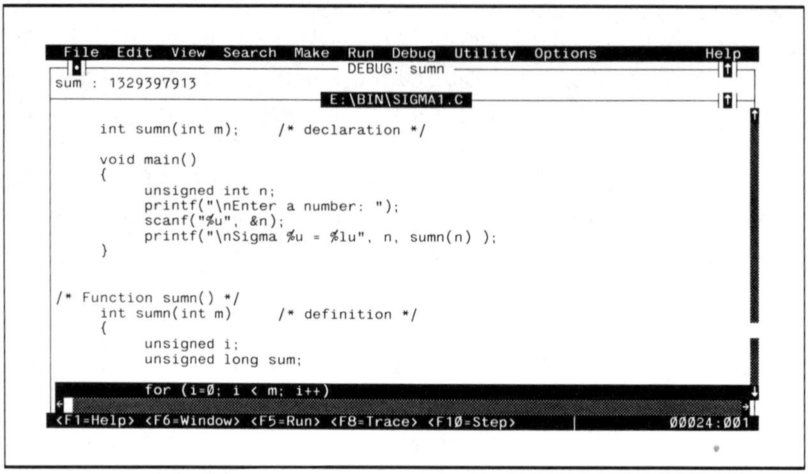

```
 File  Edit  View  Search  Make  Run  Debug  Utility  Options        Help
─────────────────────────── DEBUG: sumn ──────────────────────────────
sum  : 1329397913
─────────────────────── E:\BIN\SIGMA1.C ──────────────────────────────
    int sumn(int m);     /* declaration */

    void main()
    {
         unsigned int n;
         printf("\nEnter a number: ");
         scanf("%u", &n);
         printf("\nSigma %u = %lu", n, sumn(n) );
    }


/* Function sumn() */
    int sumn(int m)        /* definition */
    {
         unsigned i;
         unsigned long sum;

         for (i=0; i < m; i++)

<F1=Help> <F6=Window> <F5=Run> <F8=Trace> <F10=Step>          00024:001
```

► **Figure 11.3:** *Debug window*

Windows are *opened* either with the View/Windows menu or as a result of some action. For example, setting a watch value automatically opens the Debug window. The source window is special: it is opened whenever you enter QC and it cannot be closed. At any time, just one window has the honor of being the *current* or *active* window, signaled by the presence of the cursor. F6 moves the current window around from one open window to the next. The shared pairs, such as Debug and Help, if both are open, can be "flipped" using Ctrl-F6 as a toggle switch—they cannot both be displayed simultaneously. Ctrl-F4 closes the current window, unless that happens to be the source window.

Displayed windows survive when you use the File menu to load another program, although the data displayed obviously changes. More often than not, the visible part of a window will not be large enough to display all the data available. You can always scroll up and down in the active window, or you can resize it (zoom) with Ctrl-F8 or via View/Maximize (Ctrl-F10).

You can set "bookmarks" in windows to help you find your place after making forays into other windows. Ctrl-K-n (where n ranges from 0 to 3) lets you set up to four bookmarks per window. You then use Ctrl-Q-n to find a bookmark. This approach will be familiar to WordStar users.

The neat thing is that you can edit the Debug window directly: make it current with F6, then edit away to change the watch expressions, just as if you were editing source code. Then use F6 to return to the source window.

► *The Watch Values at Work* ►

You can format the watch value using a simplified form of the **printf( )** conversion type. For example, entering **sum,d** tells QC to display **sum** as a signed decimal integer. The other modifiers are shown in Table 11.1.

You should now have a value for **sum** in the Debug window. In my case, I get the value 1329397913 for **sum**; your value may be different but equally bizarre. Can you explain the weird value revealed? Yes, the local variable **sum** has not been initialized. Since the aim is to accumulate 1 + 2 + ... in **sum**, clearly we should set **sum** to 0 before the **for** loop.

► *Bug Number 1*

We have uncovered our first bug—an instructive one to be sure. Most bugs are bugs of omission rather than bugs of commission. Here, we failed to initialize a local variable. The probability that the rubbish found in **sum**

► **Table 11.1:** *Watch value format codes*

Letter Code	Format	Value val	Display val,code
d,i	Signed decimal integer	100	100
u	Unsigned decimal integer	200	200
o	Unsigned octal integer	300	0454
x	Hexadecimal integer	500	1f4
f	Floating point (six decimal places)	1./2.	0.500000
e	Floating point (scientific notation)	1./2.	0.5000000e + 000
g	Floating point (shorter of f, e)	1./2.	0.5000000
c	Single character	66	B
s	String	"Bill"	"Bill"
z	Structure field names	{2, 'X'}	mystruct.a : 2 mystruct.b : 'Z'

will be 0 is too low to form the basis of a sound program! (Review Chapter 7 if you are not clear about initializing local variables.) There are four ways to correct this bug:

1. Define **sum** as a static variable so that it is set to 0 automatically.

2. Initialize **sum** in the definition as follows:

   unsigned long sum = 0;

3. Initialize **sum** in the **for** loop as follows:

   for(i = 0,sum = 0; i < m; i + +)

4. As a temporary patch, without changing the source code, you can change the value of **sum** using the Modify Value... command in the Debug menu. This brings up a dialog box rather like the Watch Value box (see Figure 11.4). The difference is the presence of a Value field.

Let's concentrate on this fourth method for the moment. Type **sum** in the Expression field, move down to the Value field, and enter 0 (or you can enter any other constant or legal expression that evaluates to a constant). Then

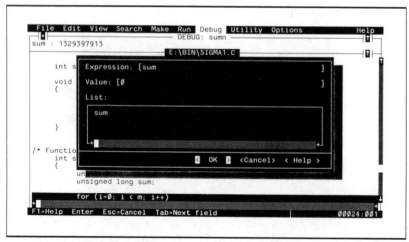

▸ *Figure 11.4:* Modify Value dialog box

press Enter to signify OK. You can sometimes save typing by selecting a variable name for the Expression field from the List box.

You can enter any expression, such as **sum + 1** or **sum/(i∗3)**, in the Value field, provided that the variables used are currently defined and within the scope of the current function. Such expressions are evaluated according to the normal rules of C, then assigned to **sum**. Note that you cannot modify the value of a whole array or structure with a single entry: you have to make individual entries for each member.

When you resume execution, the new value of **sum** will be in force. If you type a new value and then change your mind, you can edit or cancel, but once you select OK, the new value will be assigned. The Value field, like the Expression field, can be scrolled left or right to accommodate long expressions using the left and right arrows and the Home and End keys. Setting new values during a run allows you to probe and test a program in many ways without changing the source code. It is often the only way to deliberately pass invalid-parameter data to a function in order to test your error-trapping routines.

If you enter a variable that is out of scope, QC will warn you with an "invalid expression" message. Check your spelling, and if you are correct, just ignore the warning. Once the program reaches the point at which your local expression comes into scope, its proper value will be shown.

For the moment, we have set **sum** to 0 without correcting the source code. Before we correct the source, I want to reveal another common, diabolical situation in debugging—how one bug can mask the presence of another.

► *Bug Number 2*

Press F8 once through the **sum = + i;** statement, and watch the value of **sum** in the Debug window. The plot gets thicker: **sum** is now 0! Had we not bothered to set a watch on **sum** before entering the loop, this result—**sum** equals 0—might have led to complacency.

Look carefully at the following statement in the **for** loop:

```
sum = + i;
```

Of course—this should read **sum + = i;**, as explained in the discussion of compound assignments in Chapter 2. In the early days of C, the compound assignments were actually written **= +** , **= /**, and so on. This led to some syntactic ambiguities: Does **sum = + i;** mean **sum = (+ i);** or **sum (= +) i;**? So the compound assignments were revamped from **= op** to **op =** .

Correct this line to show **sum + = i;**, and while you are at it, add **sum = 0** in the **for** loop initialization, as discussed in the previous section. Now do a File/Save As SIGMA1.C to be safe, then use F8 (Trace Into) again. QuickC will cleverly recompile/relink before resuming the single-stepping. (I have kept each successive correction of SIGMA as a separate file to avoid confusion. In the real world, only major changes would justify keeping previous copies.)

Program 11.2 shows SIGMA2.C, the result of this correction to SIGMA1.C.

Alas, you will still find that **n = 1** gives Sigma 1 as 65536, yet if you evaluate **sum** just before the **return** statement, you find that **sum** is 0.

This directs our attention to the line

```
printf("\nSigma %u = %lu", n, sumn(n) );
```

in **main( )**. Yes, **sumn( )** has been defined as returning an **int**, yet **sum** is an **unsigned long** and the format string uses **%lu** for an **unsigned long** variable. We must either change **sum** to **int** and change the **%lu** to **%d** or, preferably, redefine **sumn( )** to return an **unsigned long**. SIGMA would benefit

```
/* prog11.2 = SIGMA.C version 2 */
/* SIGMA2.C purports to sum first n integers: 1+2+...+n */
/* WARNING: this program still has bugs */

#include <stdio.h>

    int sumn(int m);     /* declaration */

    void main()
    {
        unsigned int n;
        printf("\nEnter a number: ");
        scanf("%u", &n);
        printf("\nSigma %u = %lu", n, sumn(n) );
    }


/* Function sumn() */
    int sumn(int m)      /* definition */
    {
        unsigned i;
        unsigned long sum;

        for (i=0,sum=0; i < m; i++)   /* initialize sum */
            sum += i;                 /* was =+ */
        return sum;
    }
```

► *Program 11.2: SIGMA2.C*

from the larger range, and we know the answer is always nonnegative. You need to alter both the declaration and definition of **sumn( )** to show

unsigned long sumn(int m);

...

unsigned long sumn(int m)

{

...

Program 11.3 shows SIGMA3.C, the version of SIGMA.C after these corrections have been made to SIGMA2.C.

Now use File/Save As SIGMA3.C to save your changes, use Shift-F5 to restart the program, and then rerun it using Run/Go (or F5). Are we any closer to our elusive target?

Well, now we get the *less* wild results

Sigma 1 = 0   should be 1

Sigma 2 = 1   should be 3

Sigma 3 = 3   should be 6

```
/* prog11.3 = SIGMA.C version 3 */
/* SIGMA3.C purports to sum first n integers: 1+2+...+n */
/* WARNING: this program still has a bug */

#include <stdio.h>

    unsigned long sumn(int m);    /* declaration */

    void main()
    {
        unsigned int n;
        printf("\nEnter a number: ");
        scanf("%u", &n);
        printf("\nSigma %u = %lu", n, sumn(n) );
    }


/* Function sumn() */
    unsigned long sumn(int m)      /* definition */
        {                          /* return type now matches sum */
        unsigned i;
        unsigned long sum;

        for (i=0,sum=0; i < m; i++)   /* initialize sum */
            sum += i;                  /* was =+ */
        return sum;
        }
```

► *Program 11.3:* SIGMA3.C

The answers are still wrong, but because Sigma 2 is showing the correct value for Sigma 1, and Sigma 3 gives us the proper value for Sigma 2, we can hazard a guess that the **for** loop is terminating too soon. Of course, you might spot the reason for this right away by examining the source, but to reveal more debugging tricks, I will show you how to set up breakpoints and watchpoints.

▶ *SETTING AND USING BREAKPOINTS* ▶

Load and build the latest version of SIGMA.C (SIGMA3.C), if you haven't already done so, press F10 [setting the execution band at the start of the body of **main( )**], then position the cursor on the **for** loop line. Now press F9 to set a breakpoint. The breakpoint line will appear highlighted; but try not to confuse this with the execution band sitting at **main( )**. Try pressing F9 again with the cursor on the existing breakpoint line. The breakpoint will clear and the highlight will disappear. Note that you cannot place a breakpoint on a non-executable line such as **int sum;**—the system will bleep at you if you try.

The Debug/Breakpoint menu offers an alternative method of checking, setting, and clearing breakpoints. The Breakpoint dialog box, shown in Figure 11.5, lets you set and clear breakpoints by line number. If this sounds crude and à la BASIC, notice that the bottom right-hand information box on the QC screen tells you the line number as well as the column position of the current cursor, which is quite helpful.

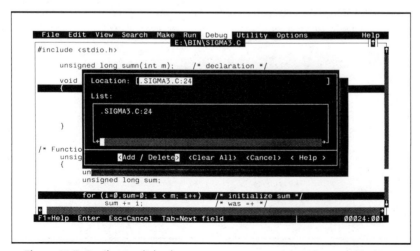

▶ *Figure 11.5:* Breakpoint dialog box

In the Location field you can enter **filename.c:nnn** to set a breakpoint at line nnn of program FILENAME.C. The default file name is the base name of the file being debugged.

The Breakpoint dialog box has the familiar List box giving you a useful view of all breakpoints set. You can set as many breakpoints as you wish, and you can clear them all from the dialog box using <Clear All>. Using Restart (Shift-F5) does *not* alter the breakpoint settings.

If you pay attention, you really should never confuse a breakpoint highlight with an execution band. In any case, as you'll shortly see, they do coincide whenever the breakpoint does its job by stopping execution!

If you now select Run/Go (F5), the program will run at normal speed, stopping for **scanf( )** input and then coming to rest at the breakpoint line, with the execution band and breakpoint line coinciding. You can now note the value of **sum** in the Watch window as you press F8 (Trace Into), F10 (Step Over), or F7 (Continue To Cursor). QuickC will always monitor your dependencies, so if you have changed any constituent module, a recompile/relink occurs.

If you edit a file with breakpoints and then try to continue the debugging session, you get the prompt **Source modified, <OK> to Rebuild?**. As you might guess, it can be tricky for QuickC to maintain breakpoints during certain edits—for example, when you delete a breakpoint line. Note, though, that if you use File/Save to save a file, load another file, then reload the original file, it will retain any previously set breakpoints.

This is a great help when you are debugging across several different modules. But if you leave QC, the breakpoints disappear. You can also clear breakpoints individually by positioning the cursor and using the F9 toggle. Or you can clear all your breakpoints using the Debug/Breakpoint... menu.

► *Setting Watchpoints* ►

Select the Debug/Watchpoint... menu (note the key letter is p not W) to display the Watchpoint dialog box, as shown in Figure 11.6. You can enter any Boolean expression in the Expression field using basic integer, real, or pointer variables (arrays, structures, and unions are not allowed but their members are, provided they are basic types) together with the arithmetic operators (**+ - * / %**), relational operators (**= = != > >= < <=**), or bitwise and logical operators (**& ¦ && ‖ << >>**). You use parentheses as needed for the usual C associativity and precedence rules (or for improved legibility).

Type **i = = 2** in the Expression field to gain some vital experience. Since you have entered an expression containing an out-of-scope identifier, namely **i**, you will get an "invalid expression" warning box with the question **Use anyway? <Yes> <No> <Cancel> <Help>**, as shown in Figure 11.7.

Show no alarm! Just say Yes! Any variables that are not local to the current execution point will remain undefined until you trace into their scope. For instance, **i** is undefined (out of scope) in **main( )**, but once you reach **sumn( )**, **i** becomes local and defined. You will not, of course, incur this warning with watchpoint expressions using global or local, in-scope variables.

Once you press Enter (or click in the <OK> button), the Boolean expression **i = = 2** appears in the List box. The program will pause whenever the condition **(i = = 2)** evaluates to true, just as if you had programmed **if (i = = 2) pause( );** after every statement affecting the value of **i**. To delete a watchpoint, you select it from the List box and select <Add/Delete>. You can clear all watchpoints by selecting <Clear All>.

After a watchpoint pause, you are free to continue execution with any of the familiar run variants: F5 (Go, full-speed ahead), F8 (Trace Into, single-step), F10 (Step Over, single-step), or F7 (Continue To Cursor at full speed). You can also interrupt further execution with Ctrl-C or Ctrl-Break.

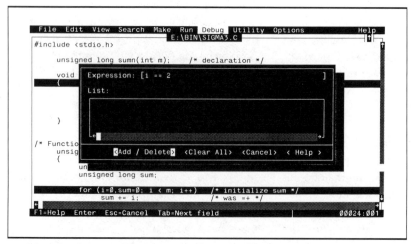

► *Figure 11.6: Watchpoint dialog box*

► **Figure 11.7:** *Watchpoint expression warning*

► *Now Back to the Bugs* ►

At this stage in the debugging odyssey, you should have:

1. A watch value set for **sum**

2. A breakpoint on the **for** loop statement

3. A watchpoint set for i = = **2**

Because we have narrowed down the remaining bug (or bugs) in SIGMA3.C to the **for** loop, one way to proceed would be to set up additional watch values for the other variables in the loop—namely, **m** and i. Well, there is an alternative, using a feature known as the Locals window. Let's see how it works.

► *The Locals Window* ►

The Locals window allows you to peek at all the local variables as your program is running. It works rather as if you had selected all such variables in the Expression field of the Watch Value dialog box. However, as you trace in and out of functions, the Locals window automatically changes the watch list for you to match the new set of local variables as they move into scope.

To invoke the Locals window, select View/Windows... then select Locals. The window will appear at the top of your screen (see Figure 11.8), below the Debug window.

To see how the Locals and Registers windows share this area, try opening the Registers window using View/Windows.... Then use Ctrl-F6 to switch between the two. The register values you see are interesting but irrelevant to our present intents. Do not (ever) attempt to change these values without careful forethought. Bring back the Locals window with Ctrl-F6 (or you can close the Registers window by using F6 to make it current, then using Ctrl-F4).

Now press F8 (Trace Into), enter n = 3 at the **scanf( )** statement, then continue with F8 to trace into the **for** loop. You will observe the three variables' values in the Locals window. The variable **m**, of course, will remain equal to 3, the value passed from **main( )**. Now for some serious debugging! Note the values of **i** and **sum** as you use F8 to step through the **for** loop. The bug will be readily exposed:

loop 1:   m = 3, i = 0, sum = 0

loop 2:   m = 3, i = 1, sum = 1

loop 3:   m = 3, i = 2, sum = 3

Notice (you cannot help but notice!) the Watchpoint window shown in Figure 11.9 advising you that the condition i = = 2 has been encountered.

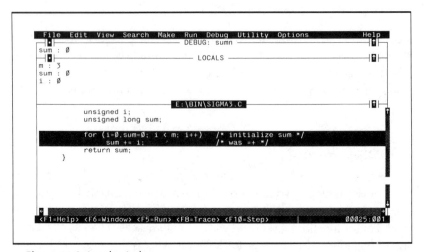

► *Figure 11.8: Locals window*

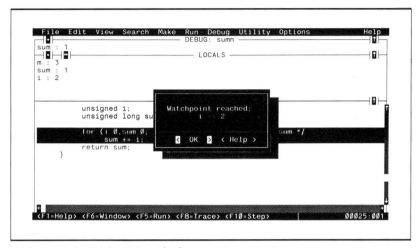

► **Figure 11.9:** *Watchpoint reached*

You press Enter (meaning OK) to return to the execution point. At this point you can amend the watchpoints, breakpoints, or watch values, depending on the situation, or you can resume execution in any of the modes we have discussed. For practice, why not delete the watchpoint before proceeding?

Now continue with F8 (Trace Into). The loop will exit with **sum = 3** and i = 3 because the i + + has made the loop condition (i < m) false.

► *Bug Number 3*

It should be clear (at long last!) that the loop is ending too soon: The condition (i < m) terminates the loop after **Sigma (m – 1)** has been accumulated. The easiest fix is to change the loop condition to (i < = m). (Check out Chapter 4 if you are rusty on the **for** loop.) Alternatively, you could change the initializer to i = 1, but if so, you must watch out for the special case n = 0 (see later).

Change SIGMA3.C to SIGMA4.C as shown in Program 11.4. If you still have a breakpoint on the **for** statement, you can use F5 (Go), which will trigger a rebuild, then run SIGMA at full speed until the **scanf( )** statement. Enter n = 3, then use F5 again to reach the breakpoint. Now use F8 to step through the loop. You should see the following more promising sequence in the Locals window:

loop 1:   m = 3, i = 0, sum = 0

```
/* prog11.4 = SIGMA.C final version 4 */
/* SIGMA4.C computes sum of first n natural numbers */
/*          with sigma 0 = 0 */

#include <stdio.h>

        unsigned long sumn(int m);    /* declaration */

        void main()
        {
        unsigned int n;
        printf("\nEnter a number: ");
        scanf("%u", &n);
        printf("\nSigma %u = %lu", n, sumn(n) );
        }

        unsigned long sumn(int m)    /* definition */
        {
        unsigned i;
        unsigned long sum;

        for (i=0,sum=0; i <= m; ++i)
                sum += i;
        return sum;
        }
```

▸ *Program 11.4: SIGMA4.C*

loop 2:   m = 3, i = 1, sum = 1

loop 3:   m = 3, i = 2, sum = 3

loop 4:   m = 3, i = 3, sum = 6

The loop now exits with **sum = 6** and i = 4 because (**i < = m**) is now false. Try a few other values of **n** to convince yourself that this version of SIGMA is now correct.

There still remains a "philosophical" problem with SIGMA. How do we define **Sigma n** for n < = 0? **Sigma 0** could reasonably be defined as 0 (the sum of the first 0 integers); if so, then SIGMA.C works for n = 0. For n < 0, it would be wiser to say that **Sigma n** is *undefined*. Because **n** has been declared as **unsigned int**, SIGMA.C as it stands would generate misleading rubbish for n < 0. I will leave you to revamp SIGMA.C to trap negative input. Hint: Change **n** to **signed int** to allow the test **if** (n < 0).

SIGMA.C was a short, artificially doctored program to illustrate debugging some common errors and give you some practice in navigating the comprehensive QuickC menus. Remember the ever-present, context-sensitive Help facilities, which provide concise reminders when needed. (Appendix H offers some hints on exploiting the Help system.)

► *THE DEBUG HISTORY RECORD* ►

QuickC offers an advanced facility called History, whereby you can record a whole debugging session for "playback" later. The general idea is that with Debug/History On activated, QC can save all your debug commands in a .HIS file and/or all your data inputs in a .INP file. Each file is optional and is named according to your base program or .MAK file name.

Bring up the Options/Run / Debug menu and select one of the options Record ALL, Record Debug Commands, or Record User Input. A dot appears in the adjacent button. Record ALL means that you'll get both the .HIS and .INP files when recording with History On selected.

If either of these files exist when you request History On, you are asked whether you want to use them or clear them and create fresh history files. A dot appears alongside the History On legend to signal its active status. Further, a D appears on the status lines to remind you that you are saving (or replaying) debugging history; an I signifies that a .INP file is being saved (or replayed).

The .HIS file remembers all your watchpoints and breakpoints and exactly how you single-stepped, provided only that you use the QC editor and not your own! Each location in the program at which execution paused or single-stepped is recorded as a *history point*. These points allow you to skip forward or backward through a history file, as you'll see later.

While History On is active, you can use Debug/Undo to cancel your previous debugger command, almost as though you were correcting a tape recording of your actions. Likewise, you can use Debug/Replay to reconstruct the recorded session (less, of course, any undone actions). History must also be on during a replay. The .INP file, if one has been saved, will automatically supply the keyboard entries made during the recorded session. If you decided not to save a .INP file, the playback session simply prompts you for input in the usual way.

Before running a replay, you are asked to load a .HIS and a .INP file (defaulting to the base names previously saved). This allows you to keep different debugging sessions available for replaying on the same program.

Some obvious restrictions apply if you have edited your program since the previous debug session was saved. Naturally, you must have History On selected during all edits. Even so, some edits may invalidate your history files, and any edits that alter the control flow will certainly upset your replay, so it is wiser to repeat and rerecord your debug session after an edit to remove any doubts.

During a replay you "use up" entries from your .INP file (if you have one), but at any point you can elect to discard any residual entries still left in .INP, provided History On is selected, and supply such entries manually through the keyboard. You do this with the Debug/Truncate User Input menu command. You can also bypass or repeat parts of your .HIS file by using Shift-F10 to browse forward to the next history point or Shift-F8 to browse backward to the previous history point. Subsequently selecting Debug/Replay then executes the history file from the current history point, offering much scope for getting completely out of synchronization! At least QC will warn you if any input is incompatible with the particular C statement encountered in the program. I leave you to play around with the History facility by repeating the last SIGMA debug session with History On selected.

► SUMMARY OF DEBUGGING COMMANDS ►

Table 11.2 provides a brief summary of the debugging and related commands provided with QuickC Version 2.

► WHAT NEXT? ►

As you have seen, the QuickC package provides an inexhaustible treasure of features to help you develop your own programs quickly and effectively. An area I have barely touched on is the integration of C and assembly-language tools in QuickC. This answers the common criticism that C is inefficient for certain space-critical and time-critical tasks. QuickC lets you embed your own optimized in-line, low-level code wherever this is needed without the need for an independent assembler such as the Microsoft macro assembler (MASM).

As your projects become more ambitious, possibly edging toward Microsoft's OS/2, the "software platform of the future," you will sooner or later graduate to the more comprehensive Microsoft Optimizing C Compiler, currently at Version 5.1, with Version 6.0 imminent, and the famed CodeView window-based source-level debugger. The Microsoft Windows programming environment is emerging as a successful bridge between DOS and the Presentation Manager of OS/2, harnessing the power of the 80286. The Windows Development Kit from Microsoft, of course, is written in and is used almost entirely with C. Also, with the growth of the 80386-based XENIX and

▶ *Table 11.2:* Debugging and related commands

Menu Sequence	Hot Key	Function
Search/**F**unction...	n/a	Display a function declaration
Run/**G**o	F5	Run program until breakpoint or watchpoint
Run/**R**estart	Shift-F5	Reload program and reset execution point
Run/**C**ontinue To Cursor	F7	Run program from execution band to current cursor
Run/**T**race Into	F8	Single-step, including function statements
Run/**S**tep Over	F8	Single-step over functions
Run/**A**nimate	n/a	Slow-motion single-step; set speed with Option/Run / Debug .
View/**O**utput Screen	F4	Toggle between source and user screens
View/Maximi**z**e	Ctrl-F10	Zoom current window
View/**W**indows...	n/a	Open/close windows
Debug/**C**alls...	n/a	List function calls and arguments
Debug/**B**reakpoint...	F9	Toggle breakpoint on/off by cursor position or line number
Debug/Watch**p**oint...	n/a	Set/clear watchpoint expressions
Debug/**W**atch Value...	n/a	Set/clear watch expressions; open Debug window
Debug/**M**odify Value	n/a	Set value of watch expressions
Debug/**H**istory	n/a	Turn on History feature; record session in .HIS and/or .INP files
Debug/**U**ndo	n/a	Delete last operation from history file(s)
Debug/**R**eplay	n/a	Replay a recorded debugging session from history file(s)

► **Table 11.2:** *Debugging and related commands (continued)*

Menu Sequence	Hot Key	Function
Debug/**T**runcate User Input	n/a	Clear all/part of .INP history file
Options/**M**ake...	n/a	Set Build flag to Debug or Release; set to Debug to create debuggable programs
Options/**R**un / Debug...	n/a	Specify a command line that will be written to .MAK file; set animate speed; set screen swap option: Auto, On, Off
Help/**T**opic	F1	Context-sensitive help (also mouse right button, provided Options/Display set)
None	F6	Switch next open window to current window
None	Ctrl-F6	Switch between a pair of shared opened windows—e.g., Debug/help, Locals/Registers, Notepad/output
None	Ctrl-F8	Resize current window
None	Ctrl-F4	Close current window (source window excepted)
None	Shift-F10	Browse forward to next history point in a .HIS file
None	Shift-F6	Browse backward to previous history point in a .HIS file

UNIX market (not to mention the rival Motorola platforms), a knowledge of C is well-nigh indispensible. Looking beyond that, there is the promise of 80486-based PC's capable of running OS/2 and UNIX, so the need for C competence is bound to keep growing.

In spite of all the layers of complexity and potential frustration, programming in general (and coding in C in particular) has no rival as an activity in which your skill and patience can bring rich rewards—not only financially in a rapidly growing, programmer-hungry marketplace but also at a personal-achievement level.

If you have stayed the course this far, I dare to hope that your appetite has been whetted for a deeper study of C. Appendix H lists some useful resources for consolidation and more advanced work. From the hundreds of books on C available, I recommend the three listed in Appendix H as a minimum start-up library.

Although there is much to learn, I have tried to ensure that you will not have too much to unlearn. When a language passes a certain threshold of usage, there is very little that can dislodge it—as shown by BASIC, COBOL, and FORTRAN. C has certainly achieved this degree of immortality, so good C programmers will never be short of job opportunities.

To some programmers, the ANSI C standard, like all standards, threatens a rather moribund immortality without the fun of diversity and innovation. Yet C has already been postincremented with the arrival of Bjarne Stroustrup's object-oriented C++, which comes from the same AT&T Bell Labs that gave us the original K&R C. The C you have been learning forms a subset of C++, so mastery of QuickC will prepare you for this bright future.

Do write to me care of SYBEX. Your comments and criticisms are always welcome and will help me to improve future editions of this book.

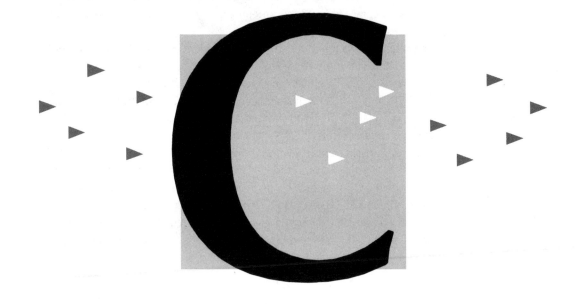

ASCII CODE CHART

► *APPENDIX A* ►

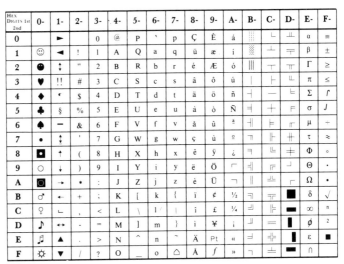

Hex Digits 1st / 2nd	0-	1-	2-	3-	4-	5-	6-	7-	8-	9-	A-	B-	C-	D-	E-	F-
0		►		0	@	P	`	p	Ç	É	á	░	└	╨	α	≡
1	☺	◄	!	1	A	Q	a	q	ü	æ	í	▒	┴	╤	β	±
2	☻	↕	"	2	B	R	b	r	é	Æ	ó	▓	┬	╥	Γ	≥
3	♥	‼	#	3	C	S	c	s	â	ô	ú	│	├	╙	π	≤
4	♦	¶	$	4	D	T	d	t	ä	ö	ñ	┤	─	╘	Σ	⌠
5	♣	§	%	5	E	U	e	u	à	ò	Ñ	╡	┼	╒	σ	⌡
6	♠	▬	&	6	F	V	f	v	å	û	ª	╢	╞	╓	µ	÷
7	•	↨	'	7	G	W	g	w	ç	ù	º	╖	╟	╫	τ	≈
8	◘	↑	(	8	H	X	h	x	ê	ÿ	¿	╕	╚	╪	Φ	°
9	○	↓	)	9	I	Y	i	y	ë	Ö	⌐	╣	╔	┘	Θ	∙
A	◙	→	*	:	J	Z	j	z	è	Ü	¬	║	╩	┌	Ω	·
B	♂	←	+	;	K	[	k	{	ï	¢	½	╗	╦	█	δ	√
C	♀	∟	,	<	L	\	l	|	î	£	¼	╝	╠	▄	∞	ⁿ
D	♪	↔	-	=	M	]	m	}	ì	¥	¡	╜	═	▌	φ	²
E	♫	▲	.	>	N	^	n	~	Ä	₧	«	╛	╬	▐	ε	■
F	☼	▼	/	?	O	_	o	⌂	Å	ƒ	»	┐	╧	▀	∩	

► **Table A.1:** *U.S. ASCII table*

Hex Digits 1st / 2nd	0-	1-	2-	3-	4-	5-	6-	7-	8-	9-	A-	B-	C-	D-	E-	F-
0		►		0	@	P	`	p	Ç	É	á	░	└	ð	Ó	-
1	☺	◄	!	1	A	Q	a	q	ü	æ	í	▒	┴	Ð	β	±
2	☻	↕	"	2	B	R	b	r	é	Æ	ó	▓	┬	Ê	Ô	=
3	♥	‼	#	3	C	S	c	s	â	ô	ú	│	├	Ë	Ò	¾
4	♦	¶	$	4	D	T	d	t	ä	ö	ñ	┤	─	È	õ	¶
5	♣	§	%	5	E	U	e	u	à	ò	Ñ	Á	┼	ı	Õ	§
6	♠	▬	&	6	F	V	f	v	å	û	ª	Â	ã	Í	µ	÷
7	•	↨	'	7	G	W	g	w	ç	ù	º	À	Ã	Î	þ	¸
8	◘	↑	(	8	H	X	h	x	ê	ÿ	¿	©	╚	Ï	Þ	°
9	○	↓	)	9	I	Y	i	y	ë	Ö	®	╣	╔	┘	Ú	¨
A	◙	→	*	:	J	Z	j	z	è	Ü	¬	║	╩	┌	Û	·
B	♂	←	+	;	K	[	k	{	ï	ø	½	╗	╦	█	Ù	¹
C	♀	∟	,	<	L	\	l	|	î	£	¼	╝	╠	▄	ý	³
D	♪	↔	-	=	M	]	m	}	ì	Ø	¡	¢	═	¦	Ý	²
E	♫	▲	.	>	N	^	n	~	Ä	×	«	¥	╬	Ì	¯	■
F	☼	▼	/	?	O	_	o	⌂	Å	ƒ	»	┐	¤	▀	´	

► **Table A.2:** *Multilingual ASCII table*

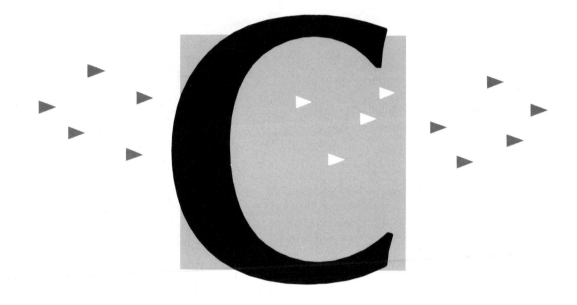

INSTALLATION AND CUSTOMIZING SUMMARY

► *APPENDIX B* ►

This appendix gives a brief, "get you started," QuickC Version 2 installation guide, followed by a discussion of the important facilities for customizing your development environment.

► *GETTING STARTED* ►

Have you already made backup copies of your ten QuickC floppies? If not, do so now. Also, sign and return your QuickC registration card. Print the contents of README.DOC to pick up any recent changes or corrections.

► *Hardware Needs* ►

You need an IBM PC, PC/XT, PC/AT, or PS/2 or genuine compatible with MS-DOS (or PC-DOS) Version 2.1 or later and at least 448KB of available RAM. As in most walks of life, the more memory you have the better.

Although you can run QuickC with two floppy drives, a hard-disk drive with one or two floppies makes life so much sweeter. You get a bargain with QuickC, so if you lack mass storage, treat yourself to a 20MB hard disk—they are cheaper now than many C compilers and are certainly cheaper than floppy drives were five years ago.

► *Rapid Installation* ►

There are three basic steps to installing QuickC:

1. Building one or more *combined* libraries from the component libraries provided on the three library floppies.

2. Copying some optional extra files to your hard disk.

3. Setting up directories, CONFIG.SYS, and environment variables.

These are all handled by the SETUP.EXE program on the SETUP floppy (although you'll see shortly that you can perform step 3 on your own).

► *SETUP Screen 1*

Insert the SETUP floppy in drive A. Run the SETUP.EXE program by typing SETUP, then pressing Enter, at the A> prompt.

Answer the questions posed by SETUP. Use Enter at each prompt to give you the default entry shown in square brackets, where N means No and Y means Yes. When in doubt, use the default answer. As you become more familiar with the ramifications, you may wish to alter these options. It is reassuring to know that you can rerun SETUP at any time without causing irreversible havoc.

Here are the questions asked by SETUP:

Source of compiler files [A:] :

This tells SETUP which floppy drive you will be using to load the QuickC floppies. The usual place is drive A:, but if you have a drive B: that you want to use, enter B: here.

Installing on a hard-disk drive [Y] :

If you don't have a hard disk, answer N here. Later you will be prompted to load a scratch floppy in B: (or A:). Some of the later screen prompts are not applicable and will not appear. I'll return to the twin-floppy installation procedure in a moment.

Math Options: Emulator [Y]: 8087 [N] :

This question determines which set of math libraries will be added to your combined library. If you do *not* have a math coprocessor (either the 8087 or 80287), you *must* answer Y for the emulator and N for the 8087. If you have a math coprocessor, you are free to answer N for emulator and Y for 8087. If you do, it means that your programs will run *only* on systems with a math coprocessor, but your combined library is not lumbered with unused floating-point emulation routines. Since the emulator can detect the presence of a math coprocessor and switch to exploiting it, saying Y to the emulator quiz offers the most flexibility (at the cost of increasing the size of your combined libraries). It is legal but unfruitful to say Y to both questions.

Memory Models: Small [Y]: Medium [N]: Compact [N]: Large/Huge [N]:

Each Y you give here will result in the creation of a distinct combined library for the selected memory model. All four libraries require a total of about 6MB of disk space. For QuickC work within the QC environment, only the small library is needed. If and when you are ready to use the QCL command-line compiler with larger projects (total code or total data exceeding 64KB) you can rerun SETUP with the /L switch and add one or more of the larger memory model libraries. All the programs in this book are well within the small model, so use the defaults indicated.

Do you want to change any of the above options [Y]:

This final question lets you retract any earlier choices. On a second, change cycle, your earlier answers become the new defaults, so pay attention! If you are happy, answer N (you don't want to change). You are next asked:

Include in combined libraries: GRAPHICS.LIB [N]: PGCHART.LIB [N]:

If you plan frequent use of any of the graphics or presentation graphics functions, answering Y to both questions simplifies your future programming chores at the cost of increasing hard-disk usage. Answering N to either or both, however, does not preclude the use of the library functions in your programs, but you will have to explicitly link the appropriate libraries, as explained in Chapter 9.

► *SETUP Screen 2*

The next screen determines which of the optional extra files will be transferred to your hard disk. The questions you are asked are:

Install Microsoft Mouse [Y]:

Answer Y if you have a Microsoft or compatible mouse or if you plan to use one in the future. The presence of the mouse driver, MOUSE.COM, will do no harm if you are mouse-free.

Copy documentation files [Y]:

Answering Y will copy all the *.DOC files, such as README.DOC, to your hard disk. If you have disk space, this is a good idea: even if you print out these files, it is convenient to have them available on line.

Copy the DOS patch file [N]:

Certain PC compatibles have BIOS and other quirks that need this patch.

Copy sample C programs [N]:

Beginners should, if possible, copy the sample C programs for inspection and compilation. The more C source you study, the better. The PGCHART demos are particularly enlightening (see Chapter 9).

Copy the QuickC tutorial files [N]:

Since you can run through this IDE tutorial directly from the floppy, the default, N, seems a good choice.

► SETUP Screen 3

You must now decide where all the QuickC files are to be stored on your disk. Much depends on how your disk is currently organized. Beginners should follow the suggested defaults, assuming, of course, that the target hard-disk partition is C:. Whatever letter your chosen drive happens to be, you should use the suggested directories. Your choices here must match the following PATH, LIB, and INCLUDE variables set up in the environment:

```
Directory for Executable files [C:\QC2\BIN]
Directory for Libraries [C:\QC2\LIB]
Directory for Include files [C:\QC2\INCLUDE]
Directory for Sample files [C:\QC2\SAMPLES]
Directory for Tutorial files [C:\QC2\TUTORIAL]
```

If the selected directories do not exist, you will be asked to confirm before SETUP creates them for you.

At this point, SETUP checks your available disk space and warns you if your requests cannot be accommodated. For the default options, you'll need about 3MB. The bulk of this is the small memory model combined library, SLIBCE.LIB (or SLIBC7.LIB if you selected the math coprocessor library). Selecting all four libraries calls for 6MB. If your disk is overoccupied, you must either make some room (try ERASE *.BAK, for example) or reconsider your options and rerun SETUP.

► *The Feeding of the Floppies*

SETUP now orders you to insert the QuickC floppies in its preferred sequence, during which time it is busy copying files and building combined libraries.

► *Configuration and Environment*

Finally, you must adjust your CONFIG.SYS, if necessary, and check that your AUTOEXEC.BAT will set your PATH, LIB, and INCLUDE environment variables. To help you, SETUP creates two files for you: NEW-CONF.SYS and NEW-VARS.BAT.

Your CONFIG.SYS must have a files = N line (this sets the maximum number of files that DOS can open at any one time to N), where N can be at least 20. If you have such a line with N > = 20, do nothing—all is well. Otherwise add or edit the line to show files = 20. Similarly, CONFIG.SYS must have a line showing buffers = B, where B is at least 10. Do not disturb any other lines you may find in your CONFIG.SYS.

NEW-VARS.BAT will reflect the directory choices you made during the third SETUP screen. If you picked the default directories, this file will contain

PATH = C:\QC2\BIN [; followed by any previous paths you may have set]

set LIB = C:\QC2\LIB

set INCLUDE = C:\QC2\INCLUDE

PATH tells DOS where, and in which sequence, to look when you type a command that is not in your current directory. Since the QuickC executables, such as QC.EXE, LINK.EXE, LIB.EXE, and so on, are to be in the directory C:\QC2\BIN, the latter should be included somewhere in your path. This allows you to run QC even when you are logged in some other drive or directory. The INCLUDE and LIB variables tell QuickC where to find the *.H and *.LIB files when preprocessing and linking.

If you want to set this environment while booting, you must alter your AUTOEXEC.BAT to include the above three lines; otherwise you can just type NEW-VARS.BAT after your normal boot. Incidentally, QuickC does not take kindly to some TSR (terminate and stay resident) programs. The POP-DOS2 utility, for example, which I have used safely for five years with every type of package, prevents QC from operating. If POPDOS2 is loading from your AUTOEXEC.BAT, you should remove it.

Remember that your changes to CONFIG.SYS and AUTOEXEC.BAT do not become effective until you have rebooted. One point regarding PATH may lead to puzzling effects. If you have a non-QuickC program around called LINK (it's a common name), you must ensure that it is not inadvertently invoked when you try to use the QuickC LINK.EXE, and vice versa. The position of directories in PATH should be watched.

► *Twin Floppies* ►

Returning to the SETUP procedure if you don't have a hard disk, when you answer N to the earlier question:

Installing on a hard-disk drive [Y] :

you will eventually be asked:

Drive to use to build combined libraries [B:]
Do you want to change any of the above options [Y]:

If the drive for feeding the QuickC floppies was A:, then take the default answer B: for building the libraries. Otherwise, you will be feeding in the QuickC floppies to B: and building up on A:. You will need to have a blank, formatted disk ready for each combined library you have requested plus one extra, "scratch" floppy (also blank and formatted) for intermediate files during the buildup. After SETUP is complete, this scratch disk can be cleared and used for other jobs.

Your PATH must include both A: and B: drives, so make sure that your AUTOEXEC.BAT includes the line

set PATH = A:\;B:\

Running QuickC with two floppy drives requires a certain amount of disk swapping, so you will soon develop an urge to move up to hard-disk status.

► CUSTOMIZING ►

QuickC lets you vary several features to suit your personal lifestyle.

► Session Options ►

You have already met what might be called "session options," various choices you can make on the fly with the Options menu. These are saved in QC.INI from one session to another but are readily altered for the job in hand. The Full Menus option, described in Chapter 1, is a good example. You have also seen the Options/Make menu, in Chapter 11, whereby you can build debuggable or nondebuggable programs. The Options/Display menu gives you a dialog box for choosing sets of colors for window background, menus, and highlighting. You can also select the LCD option for monochrome or liquid crystal display. Be aware that if you wrongly select one of the color options on a monochrome system, you may not be aware of the fact until you come to cut and paste or set breakpoints: everything works fine but the highlighted bands will be missing.

Here are some of the other customizing features in the Options/Display menu:

► **Scroll Bars**   If you don't have a mouse, you can turn off the scroll bars to gain some extra window space.

► **Tab Stops**   You can enter a number to set the number of spaces between successive tabs; the default is eight spaces.

► **Right Mouse Button**   The right mouse button defaults to F1, the context-sensitive help invoker, while Shift with the right mouse button normally compiles a program and runs it to the cursor position (the same as F7). You can reverse these two assignments by clicking in the appropriate section of the Right Mouse Button box. For example, if you find you are running to the cursor position more often that you are seeking help, you can assign the simpler action (press right mouse button) to F7.

► **Prompt Before Saving Files**   With this option toggled off (no dot in the box), QC will save changed files without the boring inquisition.

► **Search Multiple Help Topics**   You can search through QuickC's comprehensive help database using the Search/Find menu. Normally such searches are made only in the currently displayed help topic. The Search Multiple toggle lets you extend the search throughout the current help file.

► *Customizing the Editor* ►

If you have ever used more than one word processor or text editor, you will know the angst that results in trying to remember if Ctrl-T will delete a word or scroll up a page—and finding that you made the wrong choice. The QuickC editor is closely based on MicroPro's popular WordStar editing sequences. This is a sensible choice (followed also by Borland's Turbo C), but it may not suit you if you've been brought up with VolksWriter or WordPerfect or vi. QuickC therefore offers two ways of customizing the QC editor: a complete switch to any of four preset editing regimes or a personalized editing scheme where you set your own mapping between key-group and edit-action.

Taking the precanned approach first, QC has four binary *key files*: QC.KEY, ME.KEY, BRIEF.KEY, and EPSILON.KEY. You invoke your choice as follows:

C>QC /k:keyfilename

The default is QC.KEY, representing the WordStar-like mapping discussed earlier. ME.KEY gives you the Microsoft Editor (as supplied with C 5.1 and other Microsoft language products); BRIEF.KEY and EPSILON.KEY correspond to the Brief and Epsilon editors. Your choice is stored in QC.INI, so you don't have to use the /k: switch again until you want to change the editing strategy.

To set up your own personalized editing sequences, you use MKKEY, the Make Key utility. You first create an ASCII version of a binary .KEY file, then edit it to reflect your choices. Finally you convert your edited ASCII file back to, say, MYOWN.KEY. You then use this binary file with the \k: switch to bring up QC under your own editing scheme.

The binary-to-ASCII conversion uses the following syntax:

C>MKKEY -c ba -i input.key -o output.asc

where INPUT.KEY can be any available .KEY file (usually, you would start with QC.KEY or the one nearest your requirements). The OUTPUT.ASC file is a simple list of editing actions with their corresponding keystrokes—e.g., Del : CTRL-G—which you alter in the obvious way. You can convert this file back to a .KEY file as follows:

MKKEY -c ab -i output.asc -o myown.key

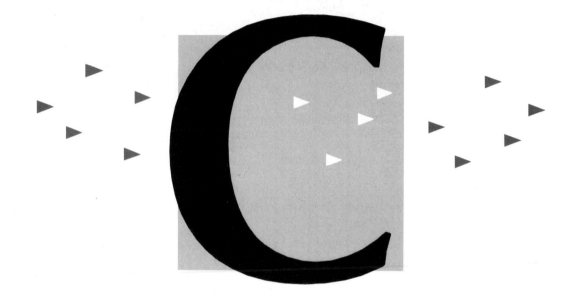

printf() AND
scanf() FORMATS

► *THE printf( ) FAMILY* ►

All the **printf( )** variants send formatted data to some device or destination: the screen, the standard output device (**stdout**), a specified stream, or a specified character array. Once you understand how **printf( )** works, the variants follow quite naturally.

Here is a brief summary of each variant with its prototype as defined in STDIO.H or CONIO.H. The notation , ... is the official ANSI C prototyping syntax to indicate a variable number of arguments of undetermined data type. (I have omitted the **_CDECL** modifier for clarity.) All these functions return the total number of bytes transferred, but this number is rarely used.

► *printf( )*

int printf (const char *format, ...); writes to **stdout**. A more helpful syntax is

printf("[text][%format][text][%format]...",[arg1,arg2,...]);

where each **%format** is matched with an **argN**. The arguments can be constants, variables, or expressions.

► *cprintf( )*

int cprintf (char *format, ...); writes to console. Line feeds are not translated as newline characters.

► *fprintf( )*

int fprintf (FILE *fp, const char *format, ...); writes to stream **fp**.

► *sprintf( )*

int sprintf (char *buffer, const char *format, ...); writes to character array (ending the string with a NUL character).

► *vprintf( )*

    int vprintf (const char *format, va_list arglist); writes to **stdout** with arguments from **va_arg** array.

► *vfprintf( )*

    int vfprintf (FILE *fp, const char *format, va_list arglist); writes to stream **fp** with arguments from **va_arg** array.

► *vsprintf( )*

    int vsprintf (char *buffer, const char *format, va_list arglist); writes to character array (ending the string with a NUL character) with arguments from **va_arg** array.

    The **v**... variants allow you to supply variable-argument functions that use the formatting features of **printf( )**. They are listed here for completeness but are beyond the scope of this book.

► *The printf( ) Family Format String* ►

    char *format indicates a special string that you supply to control formatting—i.e., how each argument is converted and displayed. For each argument to be formatted there must be a corresponding element in the format string.

    The format string can contain any number of the following groups of items:

1. Literal text (displayed unchanged)

2. Format specifications—a sequence of symbols preceded by %

A format specification (FS) looks like this:

% [flags] [width] [.precision] [F ¦ N ¦ h ¦ l ¦ L] type

where ¦ means select one only, and the square brackets indicate that the enclosed item is optional. The *[F ¦ N ¦ h ¦ l ¦ L]* is called the *size* field.

A minimal FS would be **%d** with type **d** indicating that a single integer argument would be converted to ASCII and displayed as follows:

```
printf("%d",my_int);              /* display my_int - no newline */

printf("%d\n",my_int);            /* display my_int plus newline */

printf("This = %d\n",my_int);     /* display This = my_int plus newline */
```

► *The Conversion-Type Field*

Although appearing last in the syntax list, the conversion type is the main element (and often the only one you need). It specifies the data type of the argument to be converted. In the absence of any overriders from the other fields (see below), you will get the following conversions:

Type	Input	Output
"d"	integer	Signed decimal integer
"i"	integer	Signed decimal integer
"o"	integer	Unsigned octal integer
"u"	integer	Unsigned decimal integer
"x"	integer	Unsigned hex with "a", "b", etc.
"X"	integer	Unsigned hex with "A", "B", etc.
"f"	FP	Signed decimal: *[–]dd...d.dddddd* (all FP arguments can be **float** or **double**)
"e"	FP	Signed scientific: *[–]d.dddd e [+ ¦ –]ddd*
"E"	FP	Signed scientific: *[–]d.dddd E [+ ¦ –]ddd*
"g"	FP	Signed: either "f" or "e" depending on size
"G"	FP	Signed: either "f" or "E" depending on size
"c"	char	Single character display
"s"	*char	Sequence of characters until NUL or precision limit reached. The pointer argument is taken as **near** or **far** depending on the memory model.

"%"		"%%" needed to display "%"
"n"	*int	Special argument to capture number of charac-ters displayed. The pointer argument is taken as **near** or **far** depending on the memory model.
"p"	**far** pointer	Displays **far** pointers as **SSSS:OOOO** (segment: offset) in hex.

► The Size Field

The next thing to look for is the optional size field, a single letter in front of the type field used to indicate a **short** or **long** integer argument or a **near** or **far** pointer argument. There are four possibilities:

Size	Action
"F"	Affects pointer arguments only: treats them as **far**. Used only with **%p**, **%n**, and **%s** (non-ANSI).
"N"	Affects pointer arguments only: treats them as **near**. Used only with **%p**, **%n**, and **%s** (non-ANSI).
"h"	For **d**, **i**, **o**, **u**, **x**, **X**: treats as a **short int**. Overrides the default size for numeric input.
"l"	For **d**, **i**, **o**, **u**, **x**, **X**: treats as a **long int**. Overrides the default size for numeric input. For **e**, **E**, **f**, **g**, **G**: treats as a **double** rather than as a **float**. Overrides the default size for FP numbers.
"L"	Prefix for **e**, **E**, **f**, **g**, **G**: specifies a **long double**.

► Size and Type Examples

Typical combinations encountered are

"%ld" for decimal **long int**
"%Lf" for decimal **long double**
"%lu" for decimal **unsigned long int**
"%hd" for decimal **short int**
"%ho" for octal **unsigned short int**

► *The Flags Field*

This is a sequence of characters controlling the following features:

"−"   Left justification: pad with spaces to right. If omitted, right justification: pad left with spaces or zeroes.

"+"   If a signed value is being formatted, always show a leading sign symbol ("+" or "−").

blank   Omit "+" if value is >= 0. Always show "−" if value is < 0.

"#"   Specifies an "alternative form" conversion (see below) usually involving whether 0's or decimal points will appear.

► *The Width Field*

This field contains either a number or a "*", as follows:

"N"   At least **N** characters will appear. If less are needed, pad right or left according to the flags field (see above).

"0N"   At least **N** characters will appear. If less are needed, pad left with zeroes.

"*"   The argument preceding the one to be formatted contains the width field to be used—i.e., you supply an extra argument **N** or **0N**.

► *The Precision Field*

The precision field, if present, always starts with a period. It governs the maximum number of characters to be displayed and the minimum number of digits to be displayed.

Precision Field	Action
none or "."	Default precision depending on the type. 1 for **d, i, o, u, x, X**; 6 for **e, E, f**. All significant figures for **g, G**. Until NUL for **s**. **c** types are unaffected.

".0"   Use default for **d**, **i**, **o**, **u**, **x**, **X**. Omit decimal point for **e**, **E**, **f**.

" .N"   For **d**, **i**, **o**, **u**, **x**, **X** at least **N** digits will display. Left pad with 0 if necessary. No truncation ever. For **e**, **E**, **f** you get **N** digits after the decimal point. The last digit is rounded. For **g**, **G** types you get at most **N** significant digits. For **c** types there is no effect. For **s** types no more than **N** characters will appear.

"*"   As for width, the field is to be found in the argument list preceding the value to be converted.

► *The "#" Alternative Forms*

As noted earlier, # appearing in the flags field modifies the conversion. Here's how:

Type Field	Effect of # Flag
c, s, d, i, u	No effect
o	0 prepended to a nonzero argument
x, X	0x or 0X prepended to argument
e, E, f	Always display a decimal point
g, G	As with **e** and **E**, but trailing zeroes will not be removed

► *Examples of printf( )* ►

I'll divide my examples into appropriate categories.

► *Characters and Strings*

Given **char ch** = 'A'; and **char name[5]** = "Stan";:

printf("ch = %c",ch); displays ch = A
printf("ch = %5c",ch); displays ch = *ssss*A (leading spaces)
printf("ch = %-5c",ch); displays ch = A*ssss* (trailing spaces)
printf("ch = %05c",ch); displays ch = 0000A

printf("Name = %s",name); displays Name = Stan
printf("Name = %6s",name); displays Name = *ss*Stan
printf("Name = %*s",6,name); displays Name = *ss*Stan (* means
                                     "take next int arg as width")
printf("Name = %06s",name); displays Name = 00Stan
printf("Name = % – 6s",name); displays Name = Stan*ss*
printf("Name = %.3s",name); displays Name = Sta (a small precision
                                     truncates)
printf("Name = %2s",name); displays Name = Stan (a small width
                                     never truncates)

► *Integers*

Given int i = 453;, int j = – 89;, and long int li = 78998:

printf("i = %d",i); displays i = 453
printf("i = %2d",i); displays i = 453
printf("i = %3d",i); displays i = 453
printf("i = %4d",i); displays i = *s*453
printf("i = % – 5d",i); displays i = 453*ss*
printf("i = % + d",i); displays i = + 453
printf("i = % + 05d",i); displays i = + 0453
printf("i = % + – 6d",i); displays i = + 453*ss*

printf("i = %5.1d",i); displays i = 453 (precision ignored)
printf("i = %.6d",i); displays i = 000453
printf("i = %o",i); displays i = 705 (octal)
printf("i = %#o",i); displays i = 0705 (leading 0 octal)
printf("i = %05o",i); displays i = 00705 (pad octal)
printf("i = %x",i); displays i = 1c5 (hex)
printf("i = %X",i); displays i = 1C5 (hex)
printf("i = %#x",i); displays i = 0x1c5 (hex)
printf("i = %06x",i); displays i = 0001c5 (hex)

printf("j = %d",j); displays j = – 89
printf("j = % + d",j); displays j = – 89
printf("j = %2d",j); displays j = – 89
printf("j = %4d",j); displays j = *s* – 89

printf("j = % – 5d",j); displays j = – 89ss
printf("j = %06d",j); displays j = – 00089
printf("j = %.8",j); displays j = – 000089

printf("li = %ld",li); displays li = 78998
printf("li = % + ld",li); displays li = + 78998
printf("li = %8ld",li); displays li = sss78998
printf("li = %08ld",li); displays li = 00078998
printf("li = %.8ld",li); displays li = 00078998
printf("li = % – 8ld",li); displays li = 78998sss

► Floating Point

The type "%f" works with **float** or **double** arguments since **float**s are converted to **double** before formatting is performed. Assuming that **float height** or **double height** contains 2500.3498537

printf("Height = %T",height);

will display as shown below given the listed width/precision/type combinations:

Combinations	Screen Display and Notes
"%f"	Height = 2500.349854 (default = "%.6f" rounded)
"%.0f"	Height = 2500 (no decimal point)
"% + .0f"	Height = + 2500 (sign always shown " + " or " – ")
"% .0f"	Height = 2500 (sign only if " – ")
"%.1f"	Height = 2500.3 (rounded)
"%.2f"	Height = 2500.35 (rounded)
"%.3f"	Height = 2500.350 (rounded)
"%6.2f"	Height = 2500.35 (width ignored—too small)
"%9.2f"	Height = ss2500.35 (pad blanks to 9 columns)
"%09.2f"	Height = 002500.35 (pad zeroes to 9 columns)
"%14f"	Height = sss2500.349854 (same as "%14.6f")
"%14.0f"	Height = ssssssssss2500 (no decimal point)

"%#14.0f"	Height = *sssssssss*2500. ("#" gives decimal point)
"% – 6.2f"	Height = 2500.35 (width ignored—too small)
"% – 9.2f"	Height = 2500.35*ss* (pad right spaces to 9 columns)
"% – 09.2f"	Height = 2500.35*ss* (zero is ignored)
"% – 14f"	Height = 2500.349854*sss* (default is "% – 14.6f")
"% – 14.0f"	Height = 2500*ssssssssss* (no decimal point)
"% – #14.0f"	Height = 2500.*ssssssssss* ("#" gives decimal point)
"%e"	Height = 2.5003499e + 003 (default = %.6e)
"%.3e"	Height = 2.500e + 003
"%.3g"	Height = 2.500e + 003
"%15.4E"	Height = *ssss*2.5003E + 003 (leading spaces)
"%015.4E"	Height = 00002.5003E + 003
"% + 015.4E"	Height = + 0002.5003E + 003
"% – 15.4e"	Height = 2.5003e + 003*ssss* (trailing spaces)
"% – +15.4E"	Height = + 2.5003E + 003*sss* (trailing spaces)

(Exponent always displays sign symbol and three digits. Mantissa is always d.dddd....)

If **height** were declared as **long double**, you would use "%Le" or "%LE". The displays would not be affected.

► THE scanf( ) FAMILY ►

The functions in the **scanf( )** family all perform formatting operations on input from the keyboard, standard input (**stdin**), a stream, or a string. The formatted data is placed in arguments given by **&arg1**, **&arg2**, and so on. Their prototypes from STDIO.H are listed below. (I have omitted the **_CDECL** modifier for clarity.)

► scanf( )

int scanf (const char *format, ...); accepts input from **stdin**. Returns number of input characters successfully converted.

► *cscanf( )*

  int cscanf (const char *format, ...); accepts input from keyboard.

► *fscanf( )*

  int fscanf (FILE *fp, const char *format, ...); accepts inputs from stream **fp**.

► *sscanf( )*

  int sscanf (const char *buffer, const char *format, ...); accepts data from
  NUL-terminated character array.

► *vscanf( )*

  int vscanf (const char *format, va_list arglist); accepts data from **stdin**—
  uses arguments from **va_arg** array.

► *vfscanf( )*

  int vfscanf (FILE *fp, const char *format, va_list arglist); accepts data
  from stream **fp**—uses arguments from **va_arg** array.

► *vsscanf( )*

  int vsscanf (const char *buffer, const char *format, va_list arglist);
  accepts data from buffer—uses arguments from **va_arg** array.

  The **v**... variants allow you to supply variable-argument functions that use
  the formatting features of **scanf( )**. They are listed here for completeness but
  are beyond the scope of this book.

► *The scanf( ) Format String* ►

  The format string is used to control how each input packet is converted,
  formatted, and saved in the matching argument. The rules generally follow a
  similar pattern for **printf( )** but in the opposite direction, as it were! For

example, "%d" converts a decimal integer to an **int**. The matching argument must be a pointer to **int**, say, **&int_arg**, whereupon **int_arg** will receive the converted value:

```
int int_arg;

scanf("%d",&int_arg);
/* if you key in 345, int_arg will receive 345 */
```

Staying with this simple case, two inputs would be handled as follows:

```
int int_arg1, int_arg2;

scanf("%d%d",&int_arg1, &int_arg2);
/* if you key in 345 whitespace 67,
   int_arg1 will receive 345 and int_arg2 will get 67 */
```

The idea is that **scanf( )** parses the input received under the control of the format string. The format string can hold groups of the following objects:

1.   Format specifications signaled by the "%" symbol.

2.   Literal text: any symbols, including white space, other than "%". The function of these is *not* to display [as with **printf( )**] but to *match* and discard identical characters being keyed. Any mismatch here causes **scanf( )** to terminate.

Any white space in a literal section serves to discard any amount of white space being keyed, but other literals must be matched on a one-by-one basis. As soon as you key a character other than white space, it enters the **scanf( )** parser. It either matches a literal in the format string and gets discarded or starts a conversion process depending on the next "%" sequence encountered. Subsequent keystrokes contribute to the input until one of several events occurs:

1.   If it's a stream input, EOF may be reached.

2.   A white space is encountered.

3.   An inappropriate character is keyed—for example, an alphabetic in a numeric field.

4.   The number of characters exceeds a specified width.

In the simple case above, I keyed 345 followed by a space. This told
scanf( ) to process the input, and since there was a "**%d**" in situ, the conversion was made to decimal. The same happened when I entered the second
number, 67, followed by a new line. Again the conversion was triggered, this
time with the second "**%d**". Each packet of input, therefore, must match
something in the format string. In the next example, I alter **scanf( )** to accept
two fixed field numbers separated by /

```
    int int_arg1, int_arg2;

    scanf("%3d/%2d",&int_arg1, &int_arg2);
/* if you key in 345/67 return
    int_arg1 will receive 345 and int_arg2 will get 67 */
```

The format string now converts three digits, discards the /, and then converts
two digits.
    Two important warnings: you must use pointer arguments, and you must
balance the format string with the number and type of entries. Excess arguments are evaluated but otherwise ignored. Having more "**%**" elements
than arguments, however, leads to unpredictable calamities.
    The syntax of the format string is

% [*] [width] [F ¦ N ¦ h ¦ l] type

Let's look at the type first—there are important differences from **printf( )**:

Type	Input	Output Argument
"d"	decimal integer	int *arg
"D"	decimal integer	long int *arg
"o"	octal integer	int *arg
"O"	octal integer	long int *arg
"i"	any integer	int *arg
"I"	any integer	long int *arg

"u"	unsigned decimal	**unsigned int *arg**
"U"	unsigned decimal	**unsigned long int *arg**
"x"	hex integer	**int *arg**
"X"	hex integer	**long int *arg** (non-ANSI)
"e"	FP	**float *arg**
"E"	FP	**float *arg**
"f"	FP	**float *arg**
"g"	FP	**float *arg**
"G"	FP	**float *arg**
"s"	string	**char array[ ]** (allow for final NUL)
"c"	character	**char *arg** (if width is given use **char arg[**width**]**). Converts next character input including white space. Use "%1c" to skip one white-space character.
"%"		No conversion with "%%". The second "%" is stored.
"n"	none	**int *arg** will store the number of successful characters up to the "%n".
"p"	far pointer	**void far **ptr_arg** (accepts **SSSS:0000** in hex format).

► Selective Conversion

You can use regular expressions as explained in Appendix G to allow ranges of input to be matched and converted. For example:

"%[A – Z]" will catch all uppercase input.
"[^a – c]" will catch all ASCII except "a", "b", and "c".

► *Assignment Suppression*

A "%*T" combination (where "*" is not the pointer sign!) causes the matching input field of type **T** to be scanned but discarded.

► *Width Specifier*

This sets the number of characters to be scanned and converted.

► *Size and Type Modifiers*

The **F¦N¦h¦I** field works like that for **printf( )**, allowing you to override the default or declared size of the argument.

Size	Action
"F"	Treat argument pointer as **far** (non-ANSI).
"N"	Treat argument pointer as **near** (non-ANSI).
"h"	For **d, i, o, u, x, X**: convert to **short int**. Ignored for **D, I, O, U, X**.
"I"	For **d, i, o, u, x, X**: convert to **long int**. Ignored for **D, I, O, U, X**. For **e, f**: convert to **double**.

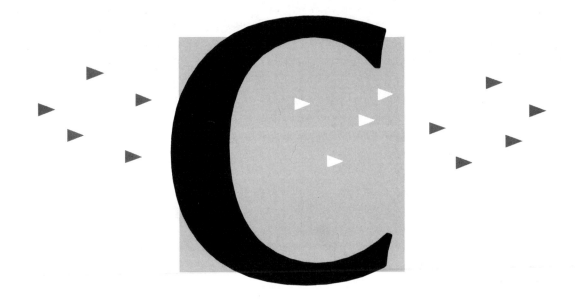

COMPUTER MATH BASICS

► NUMBER SYSTEMS ►

The decimal integer (whole number) 562 represents $5 \times 10^2 + 6 \times 10^1 + 2 \times 10^0$.

$X^n = X \times X \times \ldots$ (n factors)
$X^0 = 1$ for all X because $X^m/X^n = X^{m-n}$
$X^{-n} = 1/X^n$
$X^n \times X^m = X^{n+m}$

The *base* of decimal notation is 10. This means that the contribution of C_n, the nth numeral from the right, is $C_n \times 10^n$ (n starts from 0 not 1, so you often see the strange notation 0th position). C_n is a numeral in the range 0–9.

More generally, a number Z in base B notation is expressed as $Z = C_n \times B^n + C_{n-1} \times B^{n-1} + \ldots + C_1 \times B^1 + C_0 \times B^0$ where each C_i is in the range 0 to $(B-1)$.

If $B > 9$ you have to invent extra symbols to represent the decimal values 10, 11, and so on.

The most common bases used in computer math are 2 (binary notation), 8 (octal), and 16 (hexadecimal or hex).

► Binary ►

If the base is 2, the only permitted values for C_i are 0 and 1. The bit is the basic "binary digit" taking the values 0 (off, clear, or reset) and 1 (on or set).

Counting up in binary goes 0, 1, 10, 11, 100, 101, 110, 111, 1000, and so on. Decimal 13 = binary 1101 = $8 + 4 + 0 + 1 = 1 \times 2^3 + 1 \times 2^2 + 0 \times 2^1 + 1 \times 2^0$.

► Octal ►

When the base is 8, only the numerals 0–7 are used:

Decimal 12 = octal 014 = $1 \times 8^1 + 4 \times 8^0$

C distinguishes octal constants with a leading 0, which is why the octal equivalent of decimal 12 is 014. (This convention can easily trap the unwary.)

► Hexadecimal ►

If the base is 16, you need six more symbols than with decimal notation.

Hex	Decimal
A	= 10
B	= 11
C	= 12
D	= 13
E	= 14
F	= 15

Decimal $123 = 7 \times 16^1 + 11 \times 16^0 =$ hex 7B. C uses *0x* to distinguish hex constants from decimal and octal constants—for example, hex 0x56 = $5 \times 16^1 + 6 \times 16^0 = 86$ decimal.

► STORAGE CONVENTIONS ►

Most computers store numbers internally in binary form in fixed units of 4 (nibble), 8 (byte), 16 (word), or 32 (long word) bits. Numbers are usually stored without a specific + or − symbol to indicate whether they are positive or negative. (One exception is binary-coded decimal [BCD], in which 4 bits are used to encode each decimal digit or sign.)

► UNSIGNED AND SIGNED NUMBERS ►

Distinguishing postive and negative numbers relies on special modes and conventions. In *unsigned mode* all values are taken as positive, and you simply add up all bit values as powers of 2. In *signed mode* various conventions can apply to signal a negative value.

The most common conventions are *one's complement* and *two's complement*, where the most significant bit (MSB) in position 3, 7, 15, or 31 is a *sign bit*: 0 for positive, 1 for negative. These conventions evaluate binary numbers to decimal values as shown in Table D.1. The table just lists nibbles, but bytes, words, and long words follow the same pattern.

Two's complement is used on the IBM PC family and most other systems. One's complement is quite rare, but C does not specify any particular internal number representation. Note that one's complement has two ways of recording 0 (+0 and −0), whereas two's complement has a unique 0 but

► *Table D.1:* *Decimal values of nibbles*

Binary	Signed		Unsigned
	One's Complement	Two's Complement	
0111	7	7	7
0110	6	6	6
0101	5	5	5
0100	4	4	4
0011	3	3	3
0010	2	2	2
0001	1	1	1
0000	0	0	0
1111	−0	−1	15
1110	−1	−2	14
1101	−2	−3	13
1100	−3	−4	12
1011	−4	−5	11
1010	−5	−6	10
1001	−6	−7	9
1000	−7	−8	8

more negative numbers than positive numbers (+8 is outside and −8 is inside the legal range of a nibble). From here on, signed numbers will be assumed to be in two's complement format.

► *BYTE, WORD, AND LONG WORD RANGES* ►

It is vital to have a feel for the legal ranges of groups of bits in the various modes since they are directly related to C's integer data types.

char (1 byte)

unsigned range:	0 to +255 decimal
	0 to +0377 octal
	0 to +0xFF hex
signed range:	−128 to +127 decimal
	−0200 to +0177 octal
	−0x80 to +0x7F hex

(short) int (2 bytes)

unsigned range:	0 to +65535 decimal
	0 to +0177777 octal
	0 to 0xFFFF hex
signed range:	−32768 to +32767 decimal
	−0100000 to +077777 octal
	−0x8000 to +0x7FFF hex

long (4 bytes)

unsigned range:	0 to +4294967295 decimal
	0 to +037777777777 octal
	0 to +0xFFFFFFFF hex

signed range:	
	− 2147483648 to + 2147483647 decimal
	− 020000000000 to + 017777777777 octal
	− 0x80000000 to + 0x7FFFFFFF hex

► CARRY AND OVERFLOW ►

Unsigned addition follows the normal rules until you reach the upper limits. If you add 1 to 0xFFFF the answer flips to 0x0000, but the carry bit "emerging" from the top is stored by the CPU in a condition code register (CCR). The C language does not mandate any specific warning—it assumes all unsigned calculations are performed modulo 2^n where n is the number of bits in the data type. The modulo or remainder operator is explained in Chapter 3.

Signed arithmetic in two's complement format does not suffer from carry. It so happens that the sums turn out correctly if you ignore the carry:

Decimal		**Binary**
5		0101
+ − 3		+ 1101
2	ignore carried 1	0010 (decimal 2)

However, signed arithmetic can suffer from overflow, meaning that a number can be generated that exceeds the signed range for the data type:

Decimal	**Binary**
4	0100
+ 5	+ 0101
9	1001 (decimal − 7 in signed mode)

In this example + 9 is not expressible in 4 bits. C mandates that overflow create "an undefined result," leaving the implementor to decide on the appropriate action. The CPU's CCR has a flag to indicate overflow.

If you mix signed and unsigned arithmetic, several subtle errors can arise. For example, ch = − 128 is legal for a signed **char**, but if you negate it with − ch the result is not + 128 since that would exceed + 127, the maximum valid value for signed **char**s.

► *FLOATING-POINT FORMAT* ►

The basic FP notation expresses any number X, integral or fractional, as

$$X = M \times B^n$$

where M is called the *mantissa*, B is the *base*, and n is the *exponent*. In base 10, you could write $3.7 = 37 \times 10^{-1}$ or $3.7 = 0.37 \times 10^{1}$, so there is no unique FP expression for a given number.

In base 10, this notation is shortened to $X = MEn$ or *Men*—e.g., $3.7 = 37E-1 = 3.7E0 = 37e-1 = 0.37e1 = 0.037E2$ and so on. This is called *scientific* or *E* notation.

Internally, base 2 is used. In base 2 the "decimal" point is really a binary point, so 0.1 (binary) $= 1/2 = 1 \times 2^{-1}$. Bits to the right of a binary point represent $1/2$, $1/4$, $1/8$, and so on. Multiplying by 2 is equivalent to shifting the binary point to the left; dividing by 2 is the same as shifting the binary point to the right. This follows the familiar operation with decimal points and powers of 10.

C has two FP formats: single precision (**float**) and double precision (**double**). (A third format, **long double**, exists, but in QuickC this is the same as **double**, as allowed by the ANSI C standards.)

► *The float Format* ►

The data type **float** takes up 4 bytes (32 bits) as follows:

sign bit	1 bit (0 = positive, 1 = negative)
exponent	8 bits (range 0–255, but 127 is subtracted from this field to give actual exponents in the range −127 to +128. This is called "excess 127 format.")
mantissa	23 bits to the right of the binary point with an implied 1.0 to the left, so effectively 24 bits (see below)

To ensure a unique internal representation for each FP number, the exponent is adjusted so that the mantissa has a single 1 before its binary point. For example, 2 is stored as $(1.0) \times 2^{1}$ rather than as $(0.1) \times 2^{2}$. This *normalization* means that the 1 in front of the binary point need not be stored! (It is always there, so why waste a bit?). Nor do you waste space with leading 0's—just shift left until you hit the first 1. If you don't find a 1, then you have a zero FP.

Zero FP's are stored specially with 0's in all positions. (If the normal rules were applied to a **float** with 32 0's, they would give a value of $+1.0 \times 2^{-127}$, which is small but nonzero! A zero mantissa with a zero exponent therefore needs special decoding to give a true zero.)

For nonzero FP numbers the *implied bit* is added back before the mantissa is used in a calculation. So, although there are 23 bits in the mantissa, it really provides a precision of 24 significant bits.

The largest mantissa value is 1.11111... (23 1's after the binary point). This is approximately equal to 2, so the largest **float** is approximately 2×2^{128} or 3.4E38. The smallest positive **float** has a mantissa of 1.0000...01 and exponent -127, so its value is approximately $1 \times 2^{-127} = 1.0E-38$. The smallest negative **float** is $-3.4E38$.

The "excess 127" trick in the exponent gives a wider range for the absolute value of large numbers: 2^{128} compared with 2^{-127} for small numbers. A simple signed, or "excess 128," exponent would reverse this, giving 2^{127} for large and 2^{-128} for small numbers. The IBM BASIC FP format uses the latter, a fact that you might find invaluable one rainy night.

The 32 bits thus allocated for a **float** have fields that straddle byte boundaries. The resulting bit twiddling adds to the FP-management overhead and stresses the advantage of a dedicated math coprocessor such as the 8087. Although C has bit-field operators, emulating the 8087 by software is one area where the speed and tightness of assembly language is essential.

► *The double Format* ►

Double-precision values take 8 bytes (64 bits) allocated as follows:

sign bit	1 bit (0 = positive, 1 = negative)
exponent	11 bits (range 0–2048, but 1023 is subtracted from this field to give actual exponents in the range -1023 to $+1024$. This is called "excess 1023 format.")
mantissa	52 bits to the right of the binary point with an implied 1.0 to the left, so effectively 53 bits

Following the same logic as for **float**, you can see that the ranges for **double** are thus:

Maximum positive: 2×2^{1024} = 1.8E308 (approximately)

Minimum negative: = − 1.8E308

Minimum positive: 1×2^{-1023} = 1.0E − 309 (approximately)

► *FP Constants* ►

C treats the constant **2** as an **int** and **2.0** or **2.** as a **double** even though a **float** would be adequate. To force **2.0** into the smaller **float** format, use **2.0F**. This saves RAM but not CPU cycles since **float**s are internally promoted to **double**s before any expression is evaluated. You can also use scientic notation for FP constants.

► *FP Precision* ►

The enormous range of **double** variables disguises the true precision available. The width of the mantissa, effectively 53 bits, is the real guide. When you add FP numbers, their exponents must be adjusted so that their true binary points are aligned. This often leads to the loss of significant figures in the smaller number as it is shifted to the right. In an extreme case, adding *B* to *A* will not alter *A*! **float** gives you the equivalent precision of 7 decimal places, while **double** boosts this to about 17 places.

Programmers need to be constantly aware of the precision of the numbers used in expressions. It is quite easy to have a variable **x** holding, say, 1.999999 that is displayed as 2.00000 (**printf( )** rounds up for display purposes only), yet the conditional test **if (x == 2.0) {...}** fails. Testing for equality between FP numbers is nearly always hazardous, and even testing for **y > x** will sometimes deceive you. It is useful to define a constant, **EPSILON**, representing the smallest significant number for the precision being aimed at. If you are using numbers with only 3 reliable decimal places, you could set **EPSILON** to 0.0005. You would then test **if (fabs(x − y) < EPSILON) {...}**. Numbers differing by less than **EPSILON** are effectively equal.

► *ABSOLUTE VALUES* ►

fabs( ) returns the absolute value of an FP number or expression by setting the sign bit to zero. In other words, **fabs(− 2.0)** equals **fabs(2.0)** equals 2.0.

There are variants of the function **fabs( )** for other data types—for example, **int abs(int_arg)** is the variant for **ints**. **abs(_1)** returns + 1, but **abs(– 32768)** will not work! Why not? Because + 32768 is not a valid **int**, as I warned you earlier. **long labs(long_arg)** gives you the absolute value of a **long int**. The macro **cabs(Z)** returns the absolute value of the complex number Z. **struct complex** is declared as

```
struct complex {
    double X, Y;          / * real and imaginary parts */
};
```

The variable Z would be written as $Z = X + iY$ (where i is one of the square roots of -1) in traditional mathematics. X represents the *real* component and Y the *imaginary* component of the complex number Z. **cabs( )** returns mod Z, written $|Z|$, which is the distance from $(0,0)$ to (X,Y) in the complex plane, namely the positive square root of $(X^2 + Y^2)$. The function **hypot(X,Y)** achieves the same result.

► GENERAL MATHEMATICAL FUNCTIONS ►

QuickC offers all the standard mathematical functions specified by the ANSI C draft. Their declarations can be found in MATH.H, STDLIB.H, and FLOAT.H. Appendix F gives their prototypes.

In addition to logarithmic functions (both natural and base 10), and exponential and power routines, QuickC offers the usual trigonometric functions **cos( )**, **sin( )**, **tan( )**, their inverses **acos( )**, **asin( )**, **atan( )**, and their hyperbolic cousins **cosh( )**, **sinh( )**, and **tanh( )**. They all take and return **double** values. These routines are invaluable for many graphics and image-processing applications, which are unfortunately beyond the range of this book.

What is worth knowing, in general terms, is how QuickC handles FP errors. The function **matherr( )** is called internally whenever an FP error is detected:

```
int matherr (struct exception/*x);
```

You'll see the **exception** structure in a moment.

Typical errors include illegal arguments (*domain* errors) and illegal return values (*range* errors). Many of the standard math functions have singularities—

for example, **tan(x)** increases rapidly as **x** approaches 90 degrees, at which value it is officially infinite. MATH.H defines the following mnemonics for error type:

```
DOMAIN = 1          /* argument domain error : log ( – 1) */
SING  = 2           /* argument singularity : pow (0, – 2)) */
OVERFLOW = 3        /* overflow range error : exp (1000) */
UNDERFLOW = 4       /* underflow range error : exp ( – 1000) */
TLOSS = 5           /* total loss of significance : sin(10e70) */
PLOSS = 6           /* partial loss of signif. : not used */
```

matherr( ) fills an **exception** structure giving you the function name, the error type, and, if possible, the offending values:

```
struct exception
{
    int       type;            /*error type*/
    char      *name;           /*name of function causing
                                 error*/
    double    arg1, arg2, retval;   /*args causing error, and
                                 returned value*/
};
```

If these values are above **MAXDOUBLE** or below **MINDOUBLE**, matherr( ) substitutes **HUGE_VAL** (the FP equivalent to infinity) or 0, respectively.

► USEFUL LIMITS ►

I conclude this brief survey of computer math with the useful defines found in LIMITS.H. They are worth studying, especially the section handling limits for signed and unsigned **char**—the spirit of ANSI C's portability is enshrined in this kind of code. Note that the minimum signed values are set 1 above the legal minimum.

```
/* Copyright (c) 1985-1989, Microsoft Corporation.  All rights
 * reserved. */

#ifndef _CHAR_UNSIGNED
#define CHAR_MAX    127        /* maximum char value */
#define CHAR_MIN    – 127      /* minimum char value */
```

```
#else
#define CHAR_MAX      255
#define CHAR_MIN      0
#endif

#define SCHAR_MAX     127          /* maximum signed char value */
#define SCHAR_MIN     -127         /* minimum signed char value */
#define UCHAR_MAX     255          /* maximum unsigned char value */
#define CHAR_BIT      8            /* number of bits in a char */
#define USHRT_MAX     0xffff       /* maximum unsigned short value
                                      */
#define SHRT_MAX      32767        /* maximum (signed) short value */
#define SHRT_MIN      -32767       /* minimum (signed) short value */
#define UINT_MAX      0xffff       /* maximum unsigned int value */
#define ULONG_MAX     0xffffffff   /* maximum unsigned long value */
#define INT_MAX       32767        /* maximum (signed) int value */
#define INT_MIN       -32767       /* minimum (signed) int value */
#define LONG_MAX      2147483647   /* maximum (signed) long value */
#define LONG_MIN      -2147483647  /* minimum (signed) long value */
```

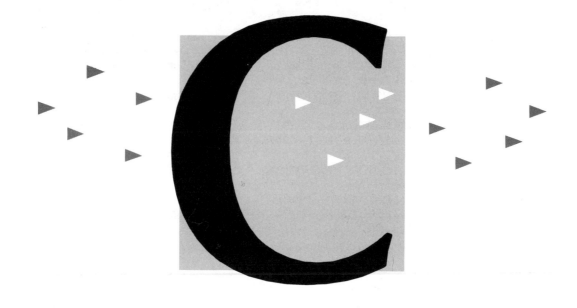

8088/8086 REGISTERS:
LOW-LEVEL STUFF

► *APPENDIX E* ►

► *PREAMBLE* ►

How much do you really need to know about the CPU in your PC? For writing reasonably sized programs entirely in QuickC, the answer is, "Very little, but it never hurts to have a general feel for what's going on inside!"

If your program size exceeds certain limits or if you want to do some macho low-level programming with QuickC's pseudo register variables or assembly language in order to improve control and speed, then you must become more (and more) familiar with your CPU's architecture and instruction set.

The term *systems programming* is often used to describe delving into the chip's registers or tapping directly into DOS, as opposed to *applications programming*, in which you usually rely on the standard functions to hide the inner details. QuickC blurs this distinction somewhat by providing intermediate tools. For instance, you can call DOS and BIOS services directly without needing a great deal of knowledge of how interrupts work.

This appendix gives you an introductory overview of the 808x registers and their role in QuickC. It may help you decide how much deeper you want to swim.

Creating large programs requires some knowledge of the QuickC memory models, which in turn calls for an understanding of the 808x addressing modes.

► *MEMORY ADDRESSING AND THE 808X* ►

QuickC, like other C compilers for the IBM PC family, has to accommodate the architectural quirks of the Intel 808x and 80x86 families of CPU's, in particular the segment:offset addressing scheme (see Figure E.1).

As shown, the effective address comes out 20 bits wide, giving a 1MB (2^{20}) address space of overlapping 64KB segments, but two 16-bit values, a segment and an offset, are needed to address each byte. Let's see how registers are used to store these.

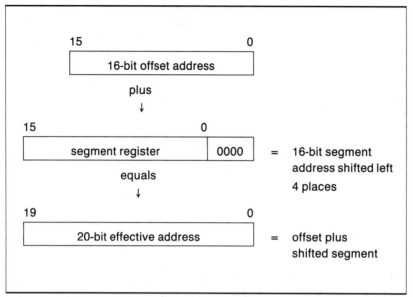

► *Figure E.1:* Segment:offset addressing

► *Segment Registers* ►

A register can be viewed as a small, superfast storage device built into the CPU. The 808x has 14 registers, each 16 bits wide. Most machine instructions use these registers in one way or another for arithmetic, control, and memory access.

Your PC keeps track of code, data, stack, and "extra" segments by storing their current segment addresses in four special-purpose registers:

CS	code segment register
DS	data segment register
SS	stack segment register
ES	extra segment register

► *Pointer and Index Registers* ►

The offset values from which the effective address is calculated can come from a variety of registers. Typical arrangements are:

CS + IP (instruction pointer) = instruction address, e.g., pointer to a function

DS + BX (base register)   = address of data in RAM, e.g., a static variable

SS + SP (stack pointer)   = address of data on stack, e.g., a local variable

ES + DI (destination index)   = address of a string in RAM

(DS is also often combined with an index register, either SI [source index] or DI [destination index]. SS can also be combined with BP [base pointer].)

The above is just a selection of the many ways the offset value is derived. For a fixed segment address, the offset register can index any byte of the 64 KB associated with that segment address, which is often called the *base address*.

► *Data Registers* ►

The 808x has four 16-bit data registers, each of which can also be treated as two 8-bit registers. AX, for example, is a 16-bit accumulator that can also be referenced as AH (high byte) and AL (low byte). The other registers have specialized duties: CX is for loop counting, BX is for indexing, and DX is for arithmetic and I/O, but these roles can vary depending on the instruction.

The complete register disposition is shown in Figure E.2.

► *Instruction Pointer* ►

The IP is the approximate equivalent of the PC (program counter) in other CPU's. When added to the CS, it gives the execution address of the next instruction. Because of the built-in instruction pipeline, this is not quite the "next - fetch - address" found in conventional program counters (since the instruction has already been fetched!).

► *Status Flags* ►

The status flags register uses 9 of the 16 bits to flag various processor or arithmetical states: carry, parity, auxiliary carry, zero, sign, trap (single-step mode), interrupt enable, direction (for string increment/decrement), and overflow. The other 7 bits are unused.

► *Pointers and the Memory Models* ►

Pointers to data can be simple 16-bit objects (called **near** pointers) provided that your data fits in one 64KB segment. This is because the segment

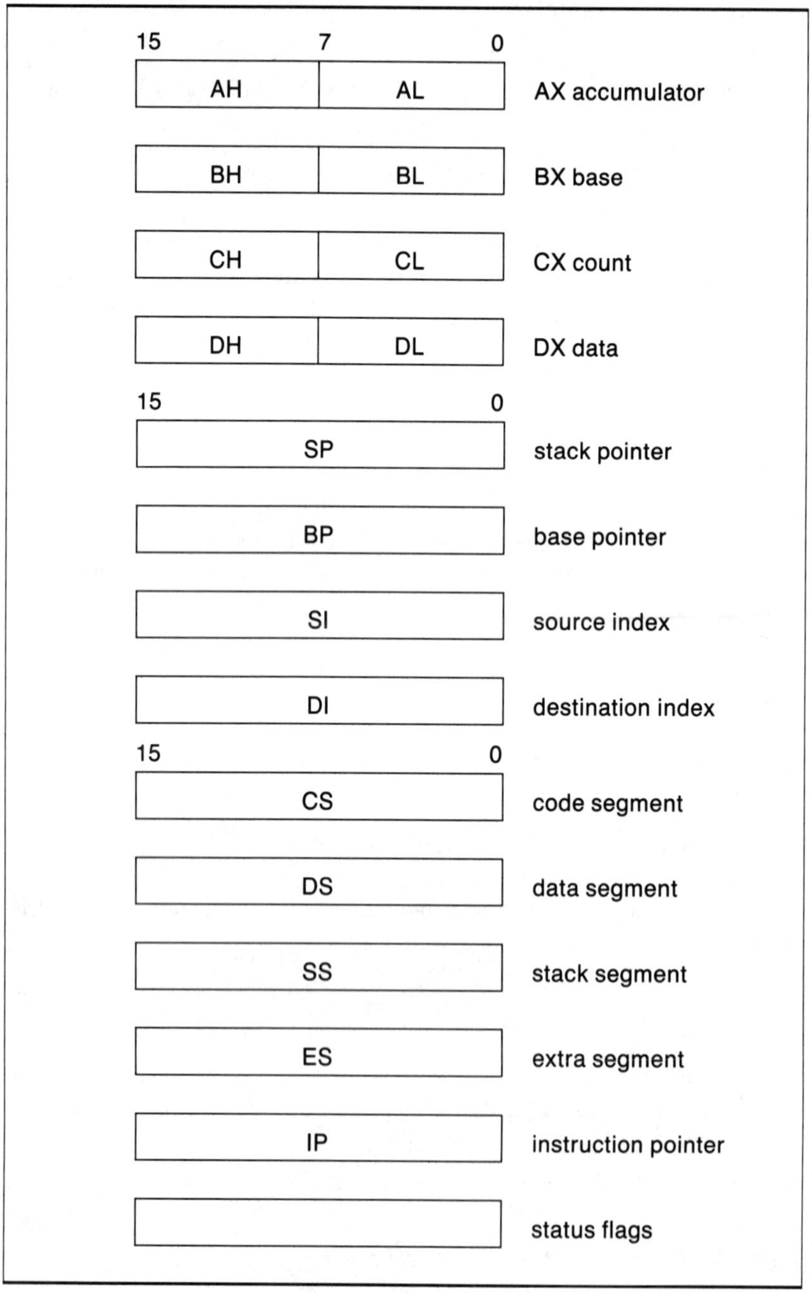

15	7	0	
AH	AL		AX accumulator
BH	BL		BX base
CH	CL		CX count
DH	DL		DX data

15	0	
SP		stack pointer
BP		base pointer
SI		source index
DI		destination index

15	0	
CS		code segment
DS		data segment
SS		stack segment
ES		extra segment
IP		instruction pointer
		status flags

► *Figure E.2: 808x registers*

part of the address is fixed and you need specify only the offset in order to get the effective address of an operand. Similarly, pointers to functions can be 16-bit **near** pointers if your code fits in a 64KB segment. In order to exceed these limits for either data, code, or both, two additional types of 32-bit pointers, known as **far** and **huge** pointers, are needed to specify both the segment and offset values.

QuickC offers five memory models: small, medium, compact, large, and huge. Each of these determines a default pointer type for data and code references.

The default model is small and uses **near** pointers for data and code, allowing you a 64KB maximum for data and a 64KB maximum for code. You need not fret about pointer size unless you exceed either limit.

Even when you have programs beyond the limits, you can let QuickC adjust the pointer types by selecting the appropriate memory model. You do this by adding − A*x* to the QCL command line, where *x* can be S, M, C, L, or H (the first letter of the memory model needed).

Each memory model gives you one of the four following combinations: (near-data, near-data), (near-data, far-code), (far-data, near-code), or (far-data, far-code).

The default pointer type, **near** or **far**, may not always be the most economical. If you understand how pointers relate to your code and data segments, you can safely use the type modifiers **near** and **far** to override the defaults. The **huge** modifier is always needed explicitly. **huge** pointers are normalized to allow simpler arithmetic. **far** pointers cannot readily be compared for size since the same effective address can have many segment:offset representations (see Chapter 5).

The basic principle here is that **near** pointers can only access data in the current segment, and **near** functions can only be called from within their own code segment.

The reason QuickC provides you with separate run-time libraries for each memory model is that functions and pointer arguments need to be declared as **near** or **far** for optimum performance.

You will find in Chapter 9 that the graphics library, GRAPHICS.LIB, is used for all models. Its functions are all declared as **far** for this reason. (Also, a graphics function may have to access video memory outside the **near** pointer range.)

► *ASSEMBLY LANGUAGE AND QUICKC* ►

You can combine assembly-language code with QuickC in two distinct ways. First, using MASM (the official Microsoft macro assembler), you write and assemble your code to an .OBJ module, then LINK it with QuickC .OBJ files.

Second, you can supply *in-line* assembly code, which turns out to be simpler but slightly less versatile than linking full-blown assembled modules. In-line assembly code, as the name implies, is written directly into the C source. You need to prefix each such line with the keyword **_asm** (non-ANSI C) to give the compiler fair warning. The code following an **_asm** is treated as a line of normal 808x assembly code until either a newline character or semi-colon is reached:

```
_asm mov ax,my_int_var        /* you can use C variables! */
_asm xor di,di                /* you must use C style comments.
                                 MASM style comments are illegal */
puts("\nThis is normal QuickC");
```

Alternatively, a whole block of assembly code can follow **_asm** if you surround the block with { and }. Since I am not teaching assembly language here, I cannot go into much detail. Suffice it to say that the **_asm** lines are embedded in the assembly code that QuickC is producing from the C code prior to giving the final .OBJ file. The advantages of being able to mix assembly-language symbols and normal C identifiers, including structures and functions, should be obvious. Less obvious are the savings compared with independent assembly modules, which need countless housekeeping details to set up for LINK and memory-model compatibility.

► *PRAGMAS* ►

ANSI C allows a special set of directives called **#pragma**s. The name is derived from "pragmatic," indicating that pragmas serve as practical, ad hoc solutions to many portability problems. The general idea is that any compiler designer can invent private pragmas for machine-specific compiler direction without fear of breaking the ANSI rules. Pragmas devised for compiler A may or not be recognized by compiler B, but at least they cause no bother if they are *not* recognized. Pragmas are entered in the source code just like **#define**s—that is, you can start a line of source code with **#pragma**

pragma_name [args, ...], where the **args**, if any, depend on the particular pragma_name.

QuickC currently supports five pragmas, defined briefly as follows:

```
#pragma check_stack ([on | off])
/* turns stack checking on and off in conjunction with the QCL
 * switch /Gs */

#pragma check_pointer (on | off)
/* turns on or off special NULL pointer checking in conjunction
 * with the QCL switch /Zr */

#pragma skip
/* starts a new page when listing source code */

#pragma title "title_string"
/* creates a title heading for each page of a source code listing */

#pragma pack ([1 | 2 | 4])
/* determines whether structures are to aligned on byte, word, or
 * long word boundaries in conjunction with the QCL /Zp switch */
```

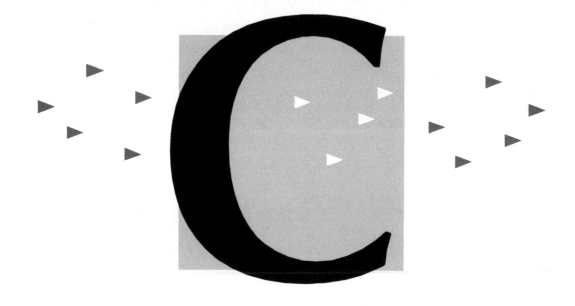

COMPLETE FUNCTION
REFERENCE

► *APPENDIX F* ►

► *PROTOTYPES OF STANDARD FUNCTIONS* ►

► *abort* ►

abort	abnormally terminates a process
Prototype	void abort(void);
Prototype in	stdlib.h and process.h

► *abs* ►

abs	absolute value
Prototype	int abs(int i);
Prototype in	stdlib.h

► *access* ►

access	determines accessibility of a file
Prototype	int access(char *filename, int amode);
Prototype in	io.h

► *acos* ►

acos	trigonometric function
Prototype	double acos(double x);
Prototype in	math.h

► _argc, _argv ►

_argc	count of command-line arguments
_argv	array of command-line arguments
Prototype	extern int_argc; extern char**_argv;
Prototype in	dos.h

► asctime ►

asctime	converts date and time to ASCII
Prototype	#include <time.h> char *asctime(struct tm *tm); .
Prototype in	time.h

► asin ►

asin	trignometric function
Prototype	double asin(double x);
Prototype in	math.h

► assert ►

assert	tests a condition and possibly aborts
Prototype	#include <assert.h> #include <stdio.h> void assert(expression);
Prototype in	assert.h

► atan ►

atan	trigonometric arctangent function
Prototype	double atan(double x);
Prototype in	math.h

► *atan2* ►

atan2	trigonometric arctangent function, calculates arctan (y/x)
Prototype	double atan2(double y, double x);
Prototype in	math.h

► *atexit* ►

atexit	registers termination function
Prototype	int atexit(atexit_t func)
Prototype in	stdlib.h

► *atof* ►

atof	converts a string to a floating-point number
Prototype	double atof(char *nptr);
Prototype in	math.h and stdlib.h

► *atoi* ►

atoi	converts a string to an integer
Prototype	int atoi(char *nptr);
Prototype in	stdlib.h

► *atol* ►

atol	converts a string to a **long**
Prototype	long atol(char *nptr);
Prototype in	stdlib.h

► *bdos* ►

bdos	MS-DOS system call
Prototype	int bdos(int dosfun, unsigned dosdx, unsigned dosal);
Prototype in	dos.h

► *_bios_disk* ►

_bios_disk	hard/floppy-disk I/O
Prototype	unsigned _bios_disk(unsigned service, struct diskinfo_t diskinfo);
Prototype in	bios.h

► *_bios_equiplist* ►

_bios_equiplist	checks equipment
Prototype	unsigned _bios_equiplist(void);
Prototype in	bios.h

► *_bios_keybrd* ►

_bios_keybrd	keyboard service via INT 0x16
Prototype	unsigned _bios_keybrd(unsigned service);
Prototype in	bios.h

► *_bios_memsize* ►

_bios_memsize	returns memory size
Prototype	unsigned _bios_memsize(void);
Prototype in	bios.h

► *_bios_printer* ►

_bios_printer	printer I/O services
Prototype	unsigned _bios_printer(unsigned service, unsigned printer, unsigned data);
Prototype in	bios.h

► *_bios_serialcom* ►

_bios_serialcom	serial communications services via INT 0x14
Prototype	unsigned _bios_serialcom(unsigned service, unsigned serial_port, unsigned data);
Prototype in	bios.h

► *_bios_timeofday* ►

_bios_timeofday	gets/sets system clock count via INT 0x1A
Prototype	unsigned _bios_timeofday(int service, long timeval);
Prototype in	bios.h

► *bsearch* ►

bsearch	binary search
Prototype	void *bsearch(const void *key, const void *base, size_t nelem, size_t width, int(*fcmp)(const void *, const void *));
Prototype in	stdlib.h

► *cabs* ►

cabs	absolute value of complex number
Prototype	double cabs(struct complex znum);
Prototype in	math.h

► *calloc* ►

calloc	allocates main memory
Prototype	void *calloc(size_t nelem, size_t elsize);
Prototype in	stdlib.h and malloc.h

► *ceil* ►

ceil	rounds up
Prototype	double ceil(double x);
Prototype in	math.h

► *cgets* ►

cgets	reads string from console
Prototype	char *cgets(char *string);
Prototype in	conio.h

► *_chain_intr* ►

_chain_intr	interrupts chaining service
Prototype	void _chain_intr(void(interrupt far *target));
Prototype in	dos.h

► *chdir* ►

chdir	changes working directory
Prototype	int chdir(char *path);
Prototype in	direct.h

► *chmod* ►

chmod	changes access mode of file
Prototype	#include <sys\stat.h> #include <sys\types.h> #include <io.h> int chmod(char *filename, int permiss);
Prototype in	io.h

► *chsize* ►

chsize	changes file size
Prototype	int chsize(int handle, long size);
Prototype in	io.h

► *_clear87* ►

_clear87	clears floating-point status word
Prototype	unsigned int_clear87 (void);
Prototype in	float.h

► *clearerr* ►

clearerr	resets error indication
Prototype	void clearerr(FILE *stream);
Prototype in	stdio.h

► *clock* ►

clock	reports elapsed processor time
Prototype	clock_t clock(void);
Prototype in	time.h

► *close* ►

close	closes a file handle
Prototype	int close(int handle);
Prototype in	io.h

► *_control87* ►

_control87	manipulates floating-point control word
Prototype	unsigned int _control87(unsigned int newvals, unsigned int mask);
Prototype in	float.h

► *cos* ►

cos	trigonometric function
Prototype	double cos(double x);
Prototype in	math.h

► *cosh* ►

cosh	hyperbolic functions
Prototype	double cosh(double x);
Prototype in	math.h

► *cprintf* ►

See Appendix C.

► *cputs* ►

cputs	sends a string to the screen

Prototype	int cputs(const char *string);
Prototype in	conio.h

► creat ►

creat	creates a new file or rewrites an existing one
Prototype	#include <sys\stat.h>
	#include <sys\types.h>
	#include<io.h>
	int creat(char *filename, int permiss);
Prototype in	io.h

► cscanf ►

See Appendix C.

► ctime ►

ctime	converts date and time to a string
Prototype	char *ctime(time_t *clock);
Prototype in	time.h

► dieeetomsbin ►

dieeetomsbin	converts IEEE doubles to MS binary format
Prototype	int dieeetomsbin(double *src8, double *dst8);
Prototype in	math.h

► difftime ►

difftime	computes difference between two times

Prototype	double difftime(time_t time2, time_t time1);
Prototype in	time.h

▶ _*disable* ▶

_*disable*	disables interrupts
Prototype	void _disable(void);
Prototype in	dos.h

▶ *div* ▶

div	divides two integers, returning quotient and remainder
Prototype	#include <stdlib.h> div_t div(int numer, int denom);
Prototype in	stdlib.h

▶ *dmsbintoieee* ▶

dmsbintoieee	converts MS binary **doubles** to IEEE format
Prototype	int dmsbintoieee(double *src8, double *dst8);
Prototype in	math.h

▶ *dosexterr* ▶

dosexterr	gets extended error (MS DOS 3 or later)
Prototype	int dosexterr(struct DOSERR *eblkp);
Prototype in	dos.h

► *_dos_allocmem* ►

_dos_allocmem	allocates paragraphs of memory
Prototype	unsigned _dos_allocmem(unsigned size, unsigned *segment);
Prototype in	dos.h

► *_dos_close* ►

_dos_close	closes a file via 0x3E system call
Prototype	unsigned _dos_close(int handle);
Prototype in	dos.h

► *_dos_creat* ►

_dos_creat	creates a new file via 0x3C system call
Prototype	unsigned _dos_creat(char *path, unsigned attribute, int *handle);
Prototype in	dos.h

► *_dos_creatnew* ►

_dos_creatnew	creates a new file via 0x5B system call
Prototype	unsigned _dos_creatnew(char *path, unsigned attribute, int *handle);
Prototype in	dos.h

► *_dos_findfirst* ►

_dos_findfirst	seeks file-name matches via 0x4E system call
Prototype	unsigned _dos_findfirst(char *path, unsigned attribute, struct find_t *buffer);
Prototype in	dos.h

► _dos_findnext ►

_dos_findnext	seeks next file-name match via 0x4F system call
Prototype	unsigned _dos_findnext(struct find_t *buffer);
Prototype in	dos.h

► _dos_freemem ►

_dos_freemem	releases memory block after **_dos_allocmem( )**
Prototype	unsigned _dos_freemem(unsigned segment);
Prototype in	dos.h

► _dos_getdate ►

_dos_getdate	gets current date via 0x2A system call
Prototype	void _dos_getdate(struct dosdate_t *date);
Prototype in	dos.h

► _dos_getdiskfree ►

_dos_getdiskfree	gets disk info via 0x36 system call
Prototype	unsigned _dos_getdiskfree(unsigned drive, struct disfree_t *diskptr);
Prototype in	dos.h

► _dos_getdrive ►

_dos_getdrive	gets current disk drive via 0x19 system call
Prototype	void _dos_getdrive(unsigned *drive);
Prototype in	dos.h

► *_dos_getfileattr* ►

_dos_getfileattr	gets file or directory attributes via 0x43 system call
Prototype	unsigned _dos_getfileattr(char *path, unsigned *attributes);
Prototype in	dos.h

► *_dos_getftime* ►

_dos_getftime	gets last date and time of file update via 0x57 system call
Prototype	unsigned _dos_getftime(int handle, unsigned *date, unsigned *time);
Prototype in	dos.h

► *_dos_gettime* ►

_dos_gettime	gets current system time via 0x2C system call
Prototype	void _dos_gettime(struct dostime_t *time);
Prototype in	dos.h

► *_dos_getvect* ►

_dos_getvect	gets current interrupt vector value via 0x35 system call
Prototype	void (interrupt far *_dos_getvect(unsigned intnum))( );
Prototype in	dos.h

► *_dos_keep* ►

_dos_keep	installs a TSR program via 0x31 system call
Prototype	void _dos_keep(unsigned return_code, unsigned memsize);
Prototype in	dos.h

► _dos_open ►

_dos_open	opens a file via 0x3D system call
Prototype	unsigned _dos_open(char *path, unsigned mode, int *handle);
Prototype in	dos.h

► _dos_read ►

_dos_read	reads count bytes from file via 0x3F system call
Prototype	int _dos_read(int handle, void far *buffer, unsigned count, unsigned *bytes);
Prototype in	dos.h

► _dos_setblock ►

_dos_setblock	changes segment size via 0x4A system call
Prototype	unsigned _dos_setblock(unsigned size, unsigned segment, unsigned *maxsize);
Prototype in	dos.h

► _dos_setdate ►

_dos_setdate	sets current system date via 0x2B system call
Prototype	unsigned _dos_setdate(struct dosdate_t date);
Prototype in	dos.h

► _dos_setdrive ►

_dos_setdrive	sets current default disk drive via 0x0E system call
Prototype	void _dos_setdrive(unsigned drivenum, unsigned *tot_drives);
Prototype in	dos.h

► _dos_setfileattr ►

_dos_setfileattr	sets file or directory attributes via 0x43 system call
Prototype	unsigned _dos_setfileattr(char *path, unsigned attributes);
Prototype in	dos.h

► _dos_setftime ►

_dos_setftime	sets date and time stamp on file via 0x57 system call
Prototype	unsigned _dos_setftime(int handle, unsigned date, unsigned time);
Prototype in	dos.h

► _dos_settime ►

_dos_settime	sets current system time via 0x2D system call
Prototype	unsigned _dos_settime(struct dostime_t *time);
Prototype in	dos.h

► _dos_setvect ►

_dos_setvect	sets current value of interrupt vector via 0x25 system call
Prototype	void _dos_setvect(unsigned intnum, void(interrupt far *handler)( ));
Prototype in	dos.h

► _dos_write ►

_dos_write	writes count bytes to a file via 0x40 system call

Prototype	unsigned _dos_write(int handle, void far *buffer, unsigned count, unsigned *bytes);
Prototype in	dos.h

▸ *dup* ▸

dup	duplicates a file handle
Prototype	int dup(int handle);
Prototype in	io.h

▸ *dup2* ▸

dup2	duplicates a file handle
Prototype	int dup2(int oldhandle, int newhandle);
Prototype in	io.h

▸ *ecvt* ▸

ecvt	converts a floating-point number to a string
Prototype	char *ecvt(double value, int ndigit, int *decpt, int *sign);
Prototype in	stdlib.h

▸ *_enable* ▸

_enable	enables interrupts via STI machine instruction
Prototype	void _enable(void);
Prototype in	dos.h

► *eof* ►

eof	detects end of file
Prototype	int eof(int handle);
Prototype in	io.h

► *exec...* ►

exec...	functions that load and run other programs
Prototype	int execl(char *pathname, char *arg0, arg1, ..., argn, NULL);
	int execle(char *pathname, char *arg0, arg1, ..., argn, NULL, char *envp[ ]);
	int execlp(char *pathname, char *arg0, arg1, ..., argn, NULL);
	int execlpe(char *pathname, char *arg0, arg1, ..., argn, NULL, char *envp[ ]);
	int execv(char *pathname, char *argv[ ]);
	int execve(char *pathname, char *argv[ ], char *envp[ ]);
	int execvp(char *pathname, char *argv[ ]);
	int execvpe(char *pathname, char *argv[ ], char *envp[ ]);
Prototype in	process.h

► *_exit* ►

_exit	terminates program after calling **atextit( )** and **onexit( )**
Prototype	void _exit(int status);
Prototype in	process.h and stdlib.h

► *exit* ►

exit	terminates program

Prototype	void exit(int status);
Prototype in	process.h and stdlib.h

► exp ►

exp	exponential function; returns e^x
Prototype	double exp(double x);
Prototype in	math.h

► _expand ►

_expand	changes size of allocated memory block
Prototype	void _expand(void *block, size_t size);
Prototype in	malloc.h

► fabs ►

fabs	absolute value
Prototype	double fabs(double x);
Prototype in	math.h

► fclose ►

fclose	closes a stream
Prototype	int fclose(FILE *stream);
Prototype in	stdio.h

► fcloseall ►

fcloseall	closes open streams

Prototype	int fcloseall(void);
Prototype in	stdio.h

► *fcvt* ►

fcvt	converts a floating-point number to a string
Prototype	char *fcvt(double value, int ndigit, int *decpt, int *sign);
Prototype in	stdlib.h

► *fdopen* ►

fdopen	associates a stream with a file handle
Prototype	FILE *fdopen(int handle, char *type);
Prototype in	stdio.h

► *feof* ►

feof	detects end of file on stream
Prototype	int fflush(FILE *stream);
Prototype in	stdio.h

► *ferror* ►

ferror	detects errors on stream
Prototype	int ferror(FILE *stream);
Prototype in	stdio.h

► *fflush* ►

fflush	flushes a stream

Prototype	int fflush(FILE *stream);
Prototype in	stdio.h

► *fgetc* ►

fgetc	gets character from stream
Prototype	int fgetc(FILE *stream);
Prototype in	stdio.h

► *fgetchar* ►

fgetchar	gets character from stream
Prototype	int fgetchar(void);
Prototype in	stdio.h

► *fgetpos* ►

fgetpos	gets the current file pointer
Prototype	int fgetpos(FILE*stream, fpos_t, *pos);
Prototype in	stdio.h

► *fgets* ►

fgets	gets a string from a stream
Prototype	#include <stdio.h>
	char *fgets(char *string, int n, FILE *stream);
Prototype in	stdio.h

► *_fheapchk* ►

_fheapchk	checks far heap for consistency

Prototype	int _fheapchk(void);
Prototype in	malloc.h

► _fheapset ►

_fheapset	checks far heap and fills unused area
Prototype	int _fheapset(unsigned fill);
Prototype in	malloc.h

► _fheapwalk ►

_fheapwalk	traverses far heap one node per call
Prototype	int _fheapwalk(struct _heapinfo *entry);
Prototype in	malloc.h

► fieeetomsbin ►

fieeetomsbin	converts IEEE **floats** to MS binary format
Prototype	int fieeetomsbin(float *src4, float *dst4);
Prototype in	math.h

► filelength ►

filelength	gets file size in bytes
Prototype	long filelength(int handle);
Prototype in	io.h

► fileno ►

fileno	gets file handle

Prototype	int fileno(FILE *stream);
Prototype in	stdio.h

► *floor* ►

floor	returns largest integer value less than or equal to **x**
Prototype	double floor(double **x**);
Prototype in	math.h

► *flushall* ►

flushall	clears all buffers
Prototype	int flushall(void);
Prototype in	stdio.h

► *fmod* ►

fmod	calculates **x** modulo **y**, the remainder of **x/y**
Prototype	double fmod(double **x**, double **y**);
Prototype in	math.h

► *fmsbintoieee* ►

fmsbintoieee	converts MS binary to IEEE **float** format
Prototype	int fmsbintoieee(float *src4, float *dst4);
Prototype in	math.h

► *_fmsize* ►

_fmsize	returns size of far heap memory block allocation
Prototype	size_t _fmsize(void far *buffer);
Prototype in	malloc.h

► *fopen* ►

fopen	opens a stream
Prototype	#include <stdio.h> FILE *fopen(char *filename, char *type);
Prototype in	stdio.h

► *FP_OFF* ►

FP_OFF	gets far address offset
Prototype	unsigned FP_OFF(char far *farptr);
Prototype in	dos.h

► *FP_SEG* ►

FP_SEG	gets far address segment
Prototype	unsigned FP_SEG(char far *farptr);
Prototype in	dos.h

► *_fpreset* ►

_fpreset	reinitializes floating-point math package
Prototype	void _fpreset( );
Prototype in	float.h

► *fprintf* ►

See Appendix C.

► *fputc* ►

fputc	puts a character on a stream

Prototype	int fputc(int ch, FILE *stream);
Prototype in	stdio.h

► *fputchar* ►

fputchar	puts a character on **stdout**
Prototype	int fputchar(char ch);
Prototype in	stdio.h

► *fputs* ►

fputs	puts a string on a stream
Prototype	int fputs(char *string, FILE *stream);
Prototype in	stdio.h

► *fread* ►

fread	reads data from a stream
Prototype	int fread(void *ptr, size_t size, nitems, FILE *stream);
Prototype in	stdio.h

► *free* ►

free	frees allocated block. Use **_ffree( )** and **_nfree** in large and small models, respectively.
Prototype	void free(void *ptr);
Prototype in	stdlib.h and malloc.h

► *_freect* ►

_freect	returns number of **malloc( )** calls possible with available memory

Prototype	unsigned _freect(size_t size);
Prototype in	malloc.h

► *freopen* ►

freopen	replaces a stream
Prototype	FILE *freopen(char *filename, char *type, FILE *stream);
Prototype in	stdio.h

► *frexp* ►

frexp	splits a **double** number into mantissa and exponent
Prototype	double frexp(double value, int *eptr);
Prototype in	math.h

► *fscanf* ►

See Appendix C.

► *fseek* ►

fseek	repositions a file pointer on a stream
Prototype	int fseek(FILE *stream, long offset, int fromwhere);
Prototype in	stdio.h

► *fsetpos* ►

fsetpos	positions the file pointer on a stream
Prototype	int fsetpos(FILE *stream, const fpos_t *pos);
Prototype in	stdio.h

► *fstat* ►

fstat	gets open file information
Prototype	int fstat(char *handle, struct stat *buff)
Prototype in	sys\stat.h and sys\types.h

► *ftell* ►

ftell	returns the current file pointer
Prototype	long ftell(FILE *stream);
Prototype in	stdio.h

► *ftime* ►

ftime	gets current time
Prototype	void ftime(struct timeb *time_ptr);
Prototype in	sys\types.h and sys\timeb.h

► *fwrite* ►

fwrite	writes to a stream
Prototype	int fwrite(void *ptr, size_t size, size_t nitems, FILE *stream);
Prototype in	stdio.h

► *gcvt* ►

gcvt	converts floating-point number to string
Prototype	char *gcvt(double value, int ndigit, char *buf);
Prototype in	stdlib.h

► *getc* ►

getc	gets character from stream
Prototype	int getc(FILE *stream);
Prototype in	stdio.h

► *getch* ►

getch	gets character from console, no echoing
Prototype	int getch(void);
Prototype in	conio.h

► *getchar* ►

getchar	gets character from stream
Prototype	int getchar(void);
Prototype in	stdio.h

► *getche* ►

getche	gets character from keyboard, echoes to screen
Prototype	int getche(void);
Prototype in	conio.h

► *getcwd* ►

getcwd	gets current working directory
Prototype	char *getcwd(char *buf, int n);
Prototype in	direct.h

► *getenv* ►

getenv	gets string from environment
Prototype	char *getenv(char *envvar);
Prototype in	stdlib.h

► *getpid* ►

getpid	gets the process ID of calling process
Prototype	int getpid(void);
Prototype in	process.h

► *getpsp* ►

getpsp	gets the program segment prefix
Prototype	unsigned getpsp(void);
Prototype in	dos.h

► *gets* ►

gets	gets a string from a stream
Prototype	char *gets(char *string);
Prototype in	stdio.h (**fgets, gets**) conio.h (**cgets**)

► *getw* ►

getw	gets integer from stream
Prototype	int getw(FILE *stream);
Prototype in	stdio.h

► *gmtime* ►

gmtime   converts date and time to Greenwich Mean Time

Prototype   struct tm *gmtime(long *clock);

Prototype in   time.h

► *halloc* ►

halloc   version of **malloc( )** for huge arrays

Prototype   void huge *halloc(long n, size_t size);

Prototype in   malloc.h

► *_harderr* ►

_harderr   sets user-supplied error handling for INT 0x24
                    hardware errors

Prototype   void _harderr(void (far *fptr( )));

Prototype in   dos.h

► *_hardresume* ►

_hardresume   allows _harderr( ) handler to return to DOS

Prototype   void _hardresume(int result);

Prototype in   dos.h

► *_hardretn* ►

_hardretn   allows _harderr( ) handler to return to application

Prototype   void _hardretn(int error);

Prototype in   dos.h

► _heapchk ►

_heapchk	checks heap for consistency
Prototype	int _heapchk(void);
Prototype in	malloc.h

► _heapset ►

_heapset	checks heap and fills unused area
Prototype	int _heapset(unsigned fill);
Prototype in	malloc.h

► _heapwalk ►

_heapwalk	traverses heap one node per call
Prototype	int _heapwalk(struct _heapinfo *entry);
Prototype in	malloc.h

► hfree ►

hfree	deallocates a block from earlier **halloc( )** call
Prototype	void hfree(void huge *buffer);
Prototype in	malloc.h

► hypot ►

hypot	calculates length of hypotenuse
Prototype	double hypot(double x, double y);
Prototype in	math.h

► *int86* ►

int86	general 8086 software interrupt interface
Prototype	int int86(int intr_num, union REGS *inregs, union REGS *outregs);
Prototype in	dos.h

► *int86x* ►

int86x	general 8086 software interrupt interface
Prototype	int int86x(int intr_num, union REGS *inregs, union REGS *outregs, struct SREGS *segregs);
Prototype in	dos.h

► *inp* ►

inp	reads a byte from specified port
Prototype	int inp(unsigned port);
Prototype in	conio.h

► *inpw* ►

inpw	reads a word from specified port
Prototype	unsigned inpw(unsigned port);
Prototype in	conio.h

► *intdos* ►

intdos	general MS-DOS interrupt interface
Prototype	int intdos(union REGS *inregs, union REGS *outregs);
Prototype in	dos.h

► *intdosx* ►

intdosx	general MS-DOS interrupt interface
Prototype	int intdosx(union REGS *inregs, union REGS *outregs, struct SREGS *segregs);
Prototype in	dos.h

► *is...* ►

is...	character classification macros
Prototype	int isalnum(int ch);
	int isalpha(int ch);
	int isascii(int ch);
	int iscntrl(int ch);
	int isdigit(int ch);
	int isgraph(int ch);
	int islower(int ch);
	int isprint(int ch);
	int ispunct(int ch);
	int isspace(int ch);
	int isupper(int ch);
	int isxdigit(int ch);
Prototype in	ctype.h

► *isatty* ►

isatty	checks for device type associated with handle
Prototype	int isatty(int handle);
Prototype in	io.h

► *itoa* ►

itoa	converts an integer to a string
Prototype	char *itoa(int value, char *string, int radix);
Prototype in	stdlib.h

► *kbhit* ►

kbhit	checks for recent keystrokes
Prototype	int kbhit(void);
Prototype in	conio.h

► *labs* ►

labs	gives **long** absolute value
Prototype	long labs(long n);
Prototype in	stdlib.h

► *ldexp* ►

ldexp	calculates $x \times 2^{exp}$
Prototype	double ldexp(double x, int exp);
Prototype in	math.h

► *ldiv* ►

ldiv	divides two **long**s, returns quotient and remainder
Prototype	#include <stdlib.h> ldiv_t ldiv(long lnumer,long ldenom):
Prototype in	stdlib.h

► *lfind* ►

lfind	performs a linear search
Prototype	char *lfind(char *key, char *base, unsigned *num, unsigned width, int(*compare)(const void *elem1, *elem2));
Prototype in	search.h

► *localtime* ►

localtime	loads date and time into a **tm** structure
Prototype	struct tm *localtime(long *clock);
Prototype in	time.h

► *locking* ►

locking	locks designated part of a file
Prototype	int locking(int handle, int modes, long nbyte);
Prototype in	sys\locking.h and io.h

► *log* ►

log	logarithm function in(**x**)
Prototype	double log(double x);
Prototype in	math.h

► *log10* ►

log10	logarithm function $\log_{10}(x)$
Prototype	double log10(double x);
Prototype in	math.h

► *longjump* ►

longjump	provides nonlocal **goto**; used with **setjmp( )**
Prototype	void longjump(jmp_buf env, int value);
Prototype in	setjmp.h

► _lrotl ►

_lrotl	rotates an **unsigned long** value to the left
Prototype	unsigned long _lrotl(unsigned long lvalue, int count);
Prototype in	stdlib.h

► _lrotr ►

_lrotr	rotates an **unsigned long** value to the right
Prototype	unsigned long _lrotr(unsigned long lvalue, int count);
Prototype in	stdlib.h

► lsearch ►

lsearch	performs a linear search; adds key at end if not found
Prototype	char *lsearch(char *key, char *base, unsigned *num, unsigned width, int(*compare)(const void *elem1, *elem2));
Prototype in	search.h

► lseek ►

lseek	moves read/write file pointer
Prototype	long lseek(int handle, long offset, int fromwhere);
Prototype in	io.h and stdio.h

► ltoa ►

ltoa	converts a **long** to a string
Prototype	char *ltoa(long value, char *string, int radix);
Prototype in	stdlib.h

► _makepath ►

_makepath	creates a single path name
Prototype	void _makepath(char *path, char *drive, char *dir, char *fname, char *ext;)
Prototype in	stdlib.h

► malloc ►

malloc	allocates main memory. Use **_fmalloc( )** and **_nmalloc( )** for large and small memory models, respectively.
Prototype	void*malloc(size_t size);
Prototype in	stdlib.h and malloc.h

► matherr ►

matherr	processes errors during math.h functions
Prototype	int matherr(struct exception *x);
Prototype in	math.h

► max ►

max	returns larger of two numbers (any type)
Prototype	type max(type a, type b);
Prototype in	stdlib.h

► _mem..., mem... ►

_mem...	sets of functions for memory array manipulation
mem...	

Includes	memccpy( ), memchr( ), memcmp( ), memcpy( ), memicmp( ), _memmax( ), memmove( ), memset( )
Prototypes in	memory.h and string.h

► _memavl ►

_memavl	returns number of bytes of available memory in default data segment
Prototype	size_t _memavl(void);
Prototype in	malloc.h

► min ►

min	returns smaller of two numbers (any type)
Prototype	type min(type a, type b);
Prototype in	stdlib.h

► mkdir ►

mkdir	creates a directory
Prototype	int mkdir(char *pathname);
Prototype in	direct.h

► mktemp ►

mktemp	makes a unique file name
Prototype	char *mktemp(char *template);
Prototype in	direct.h

► *mktime* ►

mktime   converts local time to calendar time

Prototype   time_t mktime(struct *time_ptr);

Prototype in   time.h

► *modf* ►

modf   splits into integer part and fraction

Prototype   double modf(double value, double *iptr);

Prototype in   math.h

► *movedata* ►

movedata   copies bytes

Prototype   void movedata(unsigned segsrc, unsigned offsrc,
                            unsigned segdest, unsigned offdest, unsigned
                            numbytes);

Prototype in   memory.h and string.h

► *_msize* ►

_msize   returns size of memory block allocation

Prototype   size_t _msize(void *buffer);

Prototype in   malloc.h

► *_nheapchk* ►

_nheapchk   checks near heap for consistency

Prototype   int _nheapchk(void);

Prototype in   malloc.h

► *_nheapset* ►

_nheapset	checks near heap and fills unused area
Prototype	int _nheapset(unsigned fill);
Prototype in	malloc.h

► *_nheapwalk* ►

_nheapwalk	traverses near heap one node per call
Prototype	int _nheapwalk(struct _heapinfo *entry);
Prototype in	malloc.h

► *_nmsize* ►

_nmsize	returns size of memory block allocation
Prototype	size_t _msize(void near *buffer);
Prototype in	malloc.h

► *onexit* ►

onexit	creates a register of functions to be performed on normal program exit; MS version of **atexit( )**
Prototype	onexit_t onexit(onexit_t func);
Prototype in	stdlib.h

► *open* ►

open	opens a file for reading or writing
Prototype	#include <fcntl.h> #include <sys\stat.h> #include <sys\types.h> int open(char *pathname, int access[,int permiss]);
Prototype in	io.h

► *outp* ►

outp	writes a byte to designated port
Prototype	int outp(unsigned port, int byte);
Prototype in	conio.h

► *outpw* ►

outpw	writes a word to designated port
Prototype	int outpw(unsigned port, unsigned word);
Prototype in	conio.h

► *perror* ►

perror	prints an error message to **stderr**
Prototype	void perror(const char *string);
Prototype in	stdio.h

► *pow* ►

pow	computes x^y
Prototype	double pow(double x, double y);
Prototype in	math.h

► *printf* ►

See Appendix C.

► *putc* ►

putc	outputs a character to a stream

Prototype	int putc(int ch, FILE *stream);
Prototype in	stdio.h

► *putch* ►

putch	puts a character on screen
Prototype	int putch(int ch);
Prototype in	conio.h

► *putchar* ►

putchar	writes a character to a stream
Prototype	int putchar(int ch);
Prototype in	stdio.h

► *putenv* ►

putenv	adds a string to current environment
Prototype	int putenv(char *envvar);
Prototype in	stdlib.h

► *puts* ►

puts	writes a string to a stream
Prototype	int puts(char *string);
Prototype in	stdio.h

► *putw* ►

putw	writes a word to a stream

Prototype	int putw(int w, FILE *stream);
Prototype in	stdio.h

► *qsort* ►

qsort	sorts using the quick sort routine
Prototype	void qsort(void *base, size_t nelem, size_t width, int(*fcmp)( ));
Prototype in	stdlib.h

► *raise* ►

raise	sends a signal to executing program
Prototype	int raise(int signal);
Prototype in	signal.h

► *rand* ►

rand	random number generator
Prototype	int rand(void);
Prototype in	stdlib.h

► *read* ►

read	reads from a file
Prototype	int read(int handle, void *buf, unsigned nbyte);
Prototype in	io.h

► *realloc* ►

realloc	changes the size of an allocated block of memory

Prototype	void *realloc(void *ptr, size_t newsize);
Prototype in	stdlib.h and malloc.h

► *rename* ►

rename	renames a file
Prototype	int rename(char *oldname, char *newname);
Prototype in	stdio.h

► *rewind* ►

rewind	repositions a stream's file pointer
Prototype	#include <stdio.h> int rewind(FILE *stream);
Prototype in	stdio.h

► *rmdir* ►

rmdir	removes target directory if empty
Prototype	int rmdir(char *pathname);
Prototype in	direct.h

► *rmtmp* ►

rmtmp	erases all temporary files created by **tmpfile( )**
Prototype	int rmtmp(void);
Prototype in	stdio.h

► *_rotl* ►

_rotl	rotates a value to the left

Prototype	unsigned _rotl(unsigned value, int count);
Prototype in	stdlib.h

► _rotr ►

_rotr	rotates a value to the right
Prototype	unsigned _rotr(unsigned value, int count);
Prototype in	stdlib.h

► sbrk ►

sbrk	resets the break value for the calling process by adding **incr** bytes to the break value
Prototype	void *sbrk(int incr);
Prototype in	malloc.h

► scanf ►

See Appendix C.

► _searchenv ►

_searchenv	searches for file in paths given by **env_vars**
Prototype	void _searchenv(char *filename, char *env_vars, char *path);
Prototype in	stdlib.h

► segread ►

segread	gets current segment-register values
Prototype	void segread(struct SREGS *segregs);
Prototype in	dos.h

► *setbuf* ►

setbuf	allows user-controlled buffering for streams
Prototype	void setbuf(FILE *stream, char *buffer);
Prototype in	stdio.h

► *setjmp* ►

setjmp	used with **longjump( )** to get nonlocal **goto**s
Prototype	int setjmp(jmp_buf env);
Prototype in	setjmp.h

► *setmode* ►

setmode	sets mode of open file
Prototype	int setmode(int handle, unsigned mode);
Prototype in	io.h and fnctl.h

► *setvbuf* ►

setvbuf	allows user-controlled stream buffering
Prototype	int setvbuf(FILE *stream, char *buffer, int type, size_t size);
Prototype in	stdio.h

► *signal* ►

signal	allows a process to define the interrupt handler signals from DOS
Prototype	void (*signal(int sig, void *func(int sig[,int subcode])))(int sig);
Prototype in	signal.h

► *sin* ►

sin	computes sine of **x** (radians)
Prototype	double sin(double x);
Prototype in	math.h

► *sinh* ►

sinh	computes the hyperbolic sine of **x**
Prototype	double sinh(double x);
Prototype in	math.h

► *sopen* ►

sopen	opens a file with various shared/exclusive permissions
Prototype	int sopen(char *path, int oflag, int shflag, int permission_mode);
Prototype in	fcntl.h, sys\types.h, sys\stat.h, share.h, and io.h

► *spawn...* ►

spawn...	functions that create and run other processes (children)

Prototype	int spawnl(int mode, char *pathname, char *arg0, arg1, ..., argn, NULL);
	int spawnle(int mode, char *pathname, char *arg0, arg1, ..., argn, NULL, char *envp[ ]);
	int spawnlp(int mode, char *pathname, char *arg0, arg1, ..., argn, NULL;
	int spawnlpe(int mode, char *pathname, char *arg0, arg1, ..., argn, NULL, char *envp[ ]);
	int spawnv(int mode, char *pathname, char *argv[ ]);
	int spawnve(int mode, char *pathname, char *argv[ ], char *envp[ ]);

	int spawnvp(int mode, char *pathname, char *argv[ ]);
	int spawnvpe(int mode, char *pathname, char *argv[ ], char *envp[ ]);
Prototype in	process.h and stdio.h

► _splitpath ►

_splitpath	splits a path name into its four basic components: drive, directory, file name, and extension
Prototype	void _splitpath(char *path, char *drive, char *dir, char *filename, char *extension);
Prototype in	stdlib.h

► sprintf ►

See Appendix C.

► sqrt ►

sqrt	calculates square root
Prototype	double sqrt(double x);
Prototype in	math.h

► srand ►

srand	initializes random number generator
Prototype	void srand(unsigned seed);
Prototype in	stdlib.h

► sscanf ►

See Appendix C.

► *stackavail* ►

stackavail	returns size of stack space available in bytes
Prototype	stack_t stackavail(void);
Prototype in	malloc.h

► *stat* ►

stat	gets information about open file
Prototype	int stat(char *pathname, struct stat *buff)
Prototype in	sys\stat.h and sys\types.h

► *_status87* ►

status87	gets FP status word for 8087/80287 math coprocessor
Prototype	unsigned _status87(void);
Prototype in	float.h

► *stime* ►

stime	sets time
Prototype	int stime(long *tp);
Prototype in	time.h

► *stpcpy* ►

stpcpy	copies one string into another
Prototype	char *stpcpy(char *destin, char *source);
Prototype in	string.h

► *str...* ►

str...   family of string manipulation functions

Prototype   char   *   strcat(char *destin, char *source);
                   char   *   strchr(char *str, char c);
                   int   strcmp(char *str1, char *str2);
                   char   *   strcpy(char *destin, char *source);
                   int   strcspn(char *str1, char *str2);
                   char   *   strdup(char *str);
                   int   stricmp(char *str1, char *str2);
                   int   strcmpi(char *str1, char *str2);
                   unsigned   strlen(char *str);
                   char   *   strlwr(char *str);
                   char   *   strncat(char *destin, char *source, int
                                 maxlen);
                   int   strncmp(char *str1, char *str2, int maxlen);
                   char   *   strncpy(char *destin, char *source, int
                                 maxlen);
                   int   strnicmp(char *str1, char *str2, unsigned
                                 maxlen);
                   int   strncmpi(char *str1, char *str2, unsigned
                                 maxlen);
                   char   *   strnset(char *str, char ch, unsigned n);
                   char   *   strpbrk(char *str1, char *str2);
                   char   *   strrchr(char *str, char c);
                   char   *   strrev(char *str);
                   char   *   strset(char *str, char ch);
                   int   strspn(char *str1, char *str2);
                   char   *   strstr(char *str1, char *str2);
                   double   strtod(char *str, char **endptr);
                   long   strtol(char *str, char **endptr, int base);
                   unsigned
                   long   strtoul(char *str, char *.*endptr, int base);
                   char   *   strtok(char *str1, char *str2);
                   char   *   strupr(char *str);

Prototype in   string.h or stdlib.h

► _strdate ►

_strdate	formats the current date in target buffer
Prototype	char *_strdate(char *date);
Prototype in	time.h

► _strerror ►

_strerror	returns pointer to error message string
Prototype	char *_strerror(const char *string);
Prototype in	string.h

► strerror ►

strerror	returns pointer to error message string
Prototype	char *strerror(int errnum);
Prototype in	string.h

► _strtime ►

_strtime	formats the current time in target buffer as hh:mm:ss
Prototype	char *_strtime(char *time);
Prototype in	time.h

► swab ►

swab	swaps bytes
Prototype	void swab(char *from, char *to, int nbytes);
Prototype in	stdlib.h

► *system* ►

system	issues an MS-DOS command
Prototype	int system(char *command);
Prototype in	stdlib.h

► *tan* ►

tan	trigonometric tangent function
Prototype	double tan(double x);
Prototype in	math.h

► *tanh* ►

tanh	computes the hyperbolic tangent of **x** (radians)
Prototype	double tanh(double x);
Prototype in	math.h

► *tell* ►

tell	gets current position of file pointer
Prototype	long tell(int handle);
Prototype in	io.h

► *tempnam* ►

tempnam	creates temporary file in another directory
Prototype	char *tempnam(char *dir, char *prefix);
Prototype in	stdio.h

► *time* ►

time	gets time of day
Prototype	time_t time(time_t *tloc);
Prototype in	time.h

► *tmpfile* ►

tmpfile	opens a binary "scratch" file
Prototype	FILE *tmpfile(void);
Prototype in	stdio.h

► *tmpnam* ►

tmpnam	creates a unique file name
Prototype	char *tmpnam(char *sptr);
Prototype in	stdio.h

► *toascii* ►

toascii	translates characters to ASCII format
Prototype	int toascii(int c);
Prototype in	ctype.h

► *_tolower* ►

_tolower	translates characters to lowercase
Prototype	int _tolower(int c);
Prototype in	ctype.h

► *tolower* ►

tolower   translates characters to lowercase

Prototype   int tolower(int c);

Prototype in   ctype.h

► *_toupper* ►

_toupper   translates characters to uppercase

Prototype   int _toupper(int c);

Prototype in   ctype.h

► *toupper* ►

toupper   translates characters to uppercase

Prototype   int toupper(int c);

Prototype in   ctype.h

► *tzset* ►

tzset   corrects times for different zones and daylight savings
                         rules by setting global variables depending on values
                         in the **TZ** environment variable

Prototype   void tzset(void);

Prototype in   time.h

► *ultoa* ►

ultoa   converts an **unsigned long** to a string

Prototype   char *ultoa(unsigned long value, char *string, int
                         radix);

Prototype in   stdlib.h

► *umask* ►

umask   sets file-permission mask of current process

Prototype   int umask(int permission_mode);

Prototype in   sys\types.h, sys\stat.h, and io.h

► *ungetc* ►

ungetc   pushes a character back onto input stream

Prototype   int ungetc(char c, FILE *stream);

Prototype in   stdio.h

► *ungetch* ►

ungetch   pushes a character back to the keyboard buffer

Prototype   int ungetch(int c);

Prototype in   conio.h

► *unlink* ►

unlink   deletes a file, if possible

Prototype   int unlink(char *filename);

Prototype in   dos.h

► *utime* ►

utime   sets modification time stamp on target file

Prototype   int utime(char *path, struct utimbuf *times);

Prototype in   sys\types.h and sys\utime.h

► *va_...* ►

va_alist	macros to allow access to functions with a variable number of arguments
Includes	va_arg, va_del, va_end, va_list, va_start
Defined in	stdarg.h and stdio.h

► *vfprintf, vprintf, vsprintf* ►

See Appendix C.

► *_write* ►

_write	writes to a file
Prototype	int _write(int handle, void *buf, unsigned nbyte);
Prototype in	io.h

► *write* ►

write	writes to a file
Prototype	int write(int handle, char *buf, unsigned nbyte);
Prototype in	io.h

► *QUICKC GRAPHICS FUNCTIONS—SUMMARY* ►

This section lists separately the graphics, presentation graphics, and graphics font functions.

► *Graphics* ►

Before listing and summarizing the graphics functions in alphabetical order, here are some of the graphics structures you will need to understand the function prototypes.

► *Graphics Structures*

► *struct rccoord* ►

```
struct rccoord {
     short row;                    /* text row coordinate = Y axis! */
     short col;                    /* text column coordinate = X axis! */
     };
```

```
/* as returned by _gettextposition( ) etc. */
```

► *struct xycoord* ►

```
struct xycoord {
     short xcoord;                 /* viewport X coordinate */
     short ycoord;                 /* viewport Y coordinate */
     };
```

```
/* as returned by _getviewcoord( ) etc. */
```

► *struct _wxycoord* ►

```
struct _wxycoord {
     double wx;                    /* window X coordinate */
     double wy;                    /* window Y coordinate */
     };
```

```
/* as used in _getwindowcoord( ) etc. */
```

► *struct videoconfig* ►

```
struct videoconfig {
     short numxpixels;             /* number of pixels on X axis */
     short numypixels;             /* number of pixels on Y axis */
```

```
        short numtextcols;          /* number of text columns available */
        short numtextrows;          /* number of text rows available */
        short numcolors;            /* number of actual colors */
        short bitsperpixel;         /* number of bits per pixel */
        short numvideopages;        /* number of available video pages */
        short mode;                 /* current video mode */
        short adapter;              /* active display adapter */
        short monitor;              /* active display monitor */
        short memory;               /* adapter video memory in KB */
};

/* as used with _getvideoconfig( ) etc. */
```

► Graphics Functions

All the following functions and macros are prototyped in GRAPH.H.

► _arc ►

```
short far _arc(short x1, short y1, short x2, short y2, short svx, short svy,
              short evx, short evy);
```

```
/* Draws an elliptical arc in a counterclockwise direction. The
ellipse is that one bounded by a rectangle with top left
corner at logical coordinates (x1,y1) and bottom right corner
at (x2,y2). The points (svx,svy) and (evx,evy) determine the
start and end vectors of the arc. Returns FALSE if
unsuccessful, else TRUE.
*/
```

► _arc_xy ►

```
short far _arc_xy(struct xycoord xy1, struct xycoord xy2, struct xycoord sv,
                  struct xycoord ev);
```

```
/* As for _arc( ), but the four point arguments are supplied in the
xycoord structure format.
*/
```

► _arc_wxy ►

```
#define _arc_wxy(pwxy1, pwxy2, pwxy3, pwxy4) \
        _arc_xy(_getviewcoord_wxy(pwxy1), _getviewcoord_wxy(pwxy2),
                _getviewcoord_wxy(pwxy3),
                _getviewcoord_wxy(pwxy4))
```

/* Macro defining _arc_wxy( ) in terms of _arc_xy( ). _arc_wxy( )
takes its arguments as window coordinate pointers but
otherwise works exactly like _arc( ) and _arc_xy( ).
_getviewcoord_wxy( ) converts window coordinates to viewport
coordinates.
*/

► _clearscreen ►

```
void far _clearscreen(short area);
```

/* area = _GCCLEARSCREEN, _GVIEWPORT, or _GWINDOW */
/* Erases target area and fills with current background color. */

► _displaycursor ►

```
short far _displaycursor(short toggle);
```

/* toggle = _GCURSORON or _GCURSOROFF*/
/* Determines if cursor will be turned back on again when you
exit a graphics routine. Returns previous state of toggle.
*/

► _ellipse ►

```
short far _ellipse(short control, short x1, short y1, short x2,
                   short y2);
```

/* control = _GFILLINTERIOR or _GBORDER */
/* Draws ellipse bounded by rectangle with top left corner at

(x1,y1) and bottom right corner at (x2,y2). Returns FALSE if
unsuccessful, else TRUE.
*/

► *_ellipse_xy* ►

short far _ellipse_xy(short, struct xycoord, struct xycoord);

/* A version of _ellipse( ) that uses the xycoord viewport-strucure
coordinates as point arguments.
*/

► *_ellipse_w* ►

#define _ellipse_w(control, wx1, wy1, wx2, wy2) _ellipse_xy(control, \
            _getviewcoord_w(wx1,wy1), _getviewcoord_w(wx2,wy2))

/* Macro giving the window coordinate version of _ellipse( ). */

► *_ellipse_wxy* ►

#define _ellipse_wxy(control, pwxy1, pwxy2) _ellipse_xy(control, \
            _getviewcoord_wxy(pwxy1), _getviewcoord_wxy(pwxy2))

/* Macro giving a window-structure coordinate version of
_ellipse( ).
*/

► *_floodfill* ►

short far _floodfill(short x, short y, short boundary_color);

/* Floods an area using current color and fill mask. Starts
filling at (x,y) and spreads until a border of color
boundary_color is reached. If (x,y) is inside a closed

figure, the interior will be filled; otherwise the outside
region is flooded. Filling a figure drawn with _lineto( ) or
its variants will 'leak' unless you use the solid line style
given by mask = 0xFFFF. Returns nonzero if successful,
otherwise 0.
*/

► _floodfill_xy ►

short far _floodfill_xy(struct xycoord xy, short boundary_color);

/* The viewport-structure coordinate version of _floodfill( )
using xycoord structure to supply the seed point position.
*/

► _floodfill_w ►

#define _floodfill_w(wx, wy, boundary) \
        _floodfill_xy(_getviewcoord_w(wx,wy), boundary)

/* Macro defining the window coordinate version of _floodfill( ).
You supply the seed point as a pair of doubles.
*/

► _getactivepage ►

short far _getactivepage(void);

/* Returns the current active page number, as set by a previous
_setactivepage( ). Default is 0. The active page is an area
of video memory to which your graphics output is directed for
possible display later. In multipage video systems, you can
designate a distinct visual page, representing the video memory
to be displayed. See also _getvisualpage( ), _setvisualpage( ).
*/

► _getbkcolor ►

long far _getbkcolor(void);

/* Returns the pixel (color) value of the current background
color. The default value is 0 in the absence of any specific
_setbkcolor( ) calls. There is no special error indication.
*/

► _getcolor ►

short far _getcolor(void);

/* Returns the pixel (color) value of the current drawing color.
The default value is the maximum legal value for the current
palette, in the absence of any specific _setcolor( ) call.
*/

► _getcurrentposition ►

struct xycoord far _getcurrentposition(void);

/* Returns the current logical coordinates of the CP (current
position) in an xycoord structure.
*/

► _getcurrentposition_w ►

struct _wxycoord far _getcurrentposition_w(void);

/* The window variant of _getcurrentposition( ). Returns the
window coordinates of the CP in a _wxycoord structure.
*/

► _getfillmask ►

unsigned char far * far _getfillmask(unsigned char far *mask);

/* Returns the current fill mask, an 8 x 8 array of bits used to
set the pattern used when filling closed figures. See
_setfillmask( ) and _floodfill( ) for details. If no fill mask
has been set, _getfillmask( ) returns NULL.
*/

► _getimage ►

void far _getimage(short x1, short y1, short x2, short y2,
                   char far *image_buffer);

/* Saves the bit pattern of the image displayed in the rectangle
bounded by top left (x1,y1), bottom right (x2,y2). The image
is stored in the area pointed at by the image_buffer pointer.
To ensure that this buffer is large enough, you first use
_imagesize( ) to determine the number of bytes needed for the
particular adapter and graphics mode in force. The stored
image can be redisplayed using _putimage( ).
*/

► _getimage_xy ►

void far _getimage_xy(struct xycoord, struct xycoord, char far *);

/* Version of _getimage( ) using viewport xycoord structure
coordinates. Use with corresponding version of _putimage_xy( ).
*/

► _getimage_w ►

#define _getimage_w(wx1, wy1, wx2, wy2, buffer) \
                 _getimage_xy(_getviewcoord_w(wx1,wy1), \
                 _getviewcoord_w(wx2,wy2), buffer)

/* Window coordinate version of _getimage( ). Same action except
it takes the rectangle definition from pairs of double
arguments. See corresponding version of _putimage_w( ).
*/

► *_getimage_wxy* ►

```
#define _getimage_wxy(pwxy1, pwxy2, buffer) \
                _getimage_xy(_getviewcoord_wxy(pwxy1), \
                _getviewcoord_wxy(pwxy2), buffer)
```

/* Version of _getimage( ) using window-structure coordinates.
*/

► *_getlinestyle* ►

```
unsigned short far  _getlinestyle(void);
```

/* Returns the current line style as previously set using
_setlinestyle( ). Line styles are 16-bit masks repesenting the
bit pattern used in various line-drawing routines. The bit
pattern is repeated as a line is drawn. The default line-
style mask is 0xFFFF, representing a solid line (all bits set).
*/

► *_getlogcoord* ►

```
struct xycoord far _getlogcoord(short x, short y);
```

/* Obsolescent version of _getviewcoord( ). Converts the physical
(absolute) coordinates (x,y) to the logical (viewport relative)
coordinates, returned in an xycoord structure. No errors are
returned.
*/

► *_getphyscoord* ►

```
struct xycoord far  _getphyscoord(short rel_x, short rel_y);
```

/* Converts the logical (viewport relative) coordinates
(rel_x,rel_y) to physical (absolute) coordinates, returned in
an xycoord structure. There is no error return.
*/

► _getpixel ►

short far _getpixel(short x, short y);

/* Returns the pixel (color) value of the pixel at the logical
point (x,y). Failure is signaled by a return of − 1.
*/

► _getpixel_xy ►

short far _getpixel_xy(struct xycoord wxy);

/* A version of _getpixel( ) that uses viewport-structure
coordinate for the argument point.
*/

► _getpixel_w ►

#define _getpixel_w(wx, wy) \
        _getpixel_xy(_getviewcoord_w(wx,wy))

/* Macro giving a window coordinate version of _getpixel( ).
(wx,wy) is given as two doubles; _getviewcoord( ) is used to
convert these to viewport-structure coordinates.
*/

► _gettextcolor ►

short far _gettextcolor(void);

/* Returns the current foreground text color as previously set by
_settextcolor( ). The default value is the highest legal value
for the particular adapter, mode, and palette in force.
*/

► *_gettextcursor* ►

short far _gettextcursor(void);

/* Returns the current text cursor value, as previously set by
_settextcursor( ).
*/

► *_gettextposition* ►

struct rccoord far _gettextposition(void);

/* Returns the current text 'cursor' position as (row,column) in
an rccoord structure. This position should not be confused
with the graphics current position.
*/

► *_getvideoconfig* ►

struct videoconfig far * far _getvideoconfig(struct videoconfig
                                                        far vc*);

/* Gets the data on your current video settings into a
videoconfig structure defined as follows:

```
struct videoconfig {
        short numxpixels;        /* number of pixels on X axis */
        short numypixels;        /* number of pixels on Y axis */
        short numtextcols;       /* number of text columns available */
        short numtextrows;       /* number of text rows available */
        short numcolors;         /* number of actual colors */
        short bitsperpixel;      /* number of bits per pixel */
        short numvideopages;     /* number of available video pages */
        short mode;              /* current video mode */
        short adapter;           /* active display adapter */
        short monitor;           /* active display monitor */
        short memory;            /* adapter video memory in KB */
};
```

Once you have called _setvideomode(mode); with a suitable value for
mode, you can call _getvideoconfig(&vc); and then examine each
parameter of interest: vc.memory, vc.numxpixels, and so on.
*/

► *_getviewcoord* ►

struct xycoord far _getviewcoord(short x, short x);

/* Converts from viewport (x,y) coordinates to viewport-structure
coordinates—e.g., xycoord.xcoord and xycoord.ycoord.
*/

► *_getviewcoord_w* ►

struct xycoord far _getviewcoord_w(double wx, double wy);

/* Converts from window to viewport-structure coordinates. */

► *_getviewcoord_wxy* ►

struct xycoord far _getviewcoord_wxy(struct _wxycoord far
*pwxy);

/* Converts from window-structure coordinates to viewport-
structure coordinates.
*/

► *_getvisualpage* ►

short far _getvisualpage(void);

/* Returns the current visual page number as set by a previous
_setvisualpage( ). The default is 0. See also
_getactivepage( ), _setactivepage( ). Useful only if your
adapter offers more than one page of video memory.
*/

► *_getwindowcoord* ►

struct _wxycoord far _getwindowcoord(short x, short x);

/* Converts from viewport (x,y) to window coordinates. */

► *_getwindowcoord_xy* ►

struct _wxycoord far _getwindowcoord_xy(struct xycoord xy);

/* Converts viewport-structure coordinates to window coordinates. */

► *_imagesize* ►

long far _imagesize(short x1, short y1, short x2, short y2);

/* Returns the number of bytes needed to store the image displayed
in the rectangle defined by the top left point (x1,y1) and the
bottom right point (x2,y2). Usually followed by a malloc( )
(or equivalent) call to create a buffer for storing the image
with _getimage( ).
*/

► *_imagesize_xy* ►

long far _imagesize_xy(struct xycoord tl, struct xycoord br);

/* This version of _imagesize( ) takes a pair of viewport-structure
arguments to define the top left and bottom right points of
the target rectangle. Returns the number of bytes in the
image exactly as with _imagesize( ), _imagesize_wxy( ), and
_imagesize_w( ).
*/

► *_imagesize_w* ►

#define _imagesize_w(wx1, wy1, wx2, wy2) _imagesize_xy(\
            _getviewcoord_w(wx1,wy1), _getviewcoord_w(wx2,wy2))

/* Macro giving the window coordinate version of _imagesize( ).
The rectangle arguments are given as four doubles, which are
converted to viewport-structure coordinates using
_getviewcoord_w( ).
*/

► _imagesize_wxy ►

```
#define _imagesize_wxy(pwxy1, pwxy2) _imagesize_xy( \
              _getviewcoord_wxy(pwxy1), _getviewcoord_wxy(pwxy2))
```

/* Macro giving the window-structure coordinate version of
_imagesize( ). The rectangle arguments are given as two window
structures, which are converted to viewport-structure coordinates
using _getviewcoord_wxy( ).
*/

► _lineto ►

```
short far  _lineto(short x, short y);
```

/* Draws a line in the current drawing color and line style from
the current position to the viewport coordinates (x,y). If
successful, TRUE is returned, and the current position becomes
the endpoint (x,y). If call is unsuccessful, a FALSE (0) is
returned.
*/

► _lineto_xy ►

```
short far  _lineto_xy(struct xycoord xy);
```

/* A version of _lineto( ) using a viewport structure to pass the
endpoint coordinates.
*/

► *_lineto_w* ►

```
#define _lineto_w(wx, wy) \
        _lineto_xy(_getviewcoord_w(wx,wy))
```

/* The window coordinate version of _lineto( ), in which you supply
the endpoint argument as a pair of doubles.
*/

► *_moveto* ►

```
struct xycoord far  _moveto(short x, short y);
```

/* Moves the CP (current graphics drawing position) to the
logical point (x,y). No drawing takes place. Returns the
logical (viewport) coordinates of the previous CP as an
xycoord structure. No error return.
*/

► *_moveto_xy* ►

```
struct xycoord far  _moveto_xy(struct xycoord xy);
```

/* This version of _moveto( ) takes the endpoint argument as a
viewport xycoord structure—e.g., (xy.xcoord,xy.ycoord) but
otherwise works just like _moveto( ).
*/

► *_moveto_w* ►

```
#define _moveto_w(wx, wy) \
        _getwindowcoord_xy(_moveto_xy(_getviewcoord_w(wx,wy)))
```

/* Macro defining the window coordinate version of _moveto( ).
The endpoint is given as a pair of doubles (wx,wy). Note how
_getviewcoord_w( ) converts these to an xycoord viewport

coordinate structure, which _moveto_xy( ) can handle.
_moveto_xy( ) returns an xycoord structure of the original
point, which _getwindow_w( ) then converts to a window-
structure _wxycoord. So, _moveto_w( ) moves the CP to (wx,wy) and
returns the starting point in window format.
*/

► _outtext ►

void far _outtext(unsigned char far *text_string);

/* Displays the text_string starting at the current text
position. Unlike printf( ), no formatting takes place, so you
often need to use sprintf( ) first. No error or return value.
Use outgtext( ) when displaying text with *.FON characters
-- see font functions section at the end of this appendix.
*/

► _pie ►

short far _pie(short control, short x1, short y1, short x2, short y2,
                short svx, short svy, short evx, short evy);

/* _pie( ) works like _arc( ) but goes on to draw two lines
from the center of the bounding rectangle to the arc's endpoints, thereby creating a wedge-shaped slice of pie. See
_arc( ) for an explanation of the arguments. As with
_ellipse( ) you can set control to _GFILLINTERIOR or _GBORDER to
control the interior flood-filling action. The pie is drawn
counterclockwise using the current drawing color. Any filling is
done with the current fill style and color. The line-style
setting is ignored: as with arcs and ellipses, pies are always
drawn with a solid line. Returns TRUE for success, FALSE
for failure.
*/

► _pie_xy ►

short far _pie_xy(short control, struct xycoord xy1, struct
                xycoord xy2, struct xycoord sv,
                struct xycoord ev);

/* This version of _pie( ) uses viewport xycoord structure
arguments for each of the four points. See _arc( ) and
_ellipse( ) xycoord structure variants.
*/

► _pie_wxy ►

```
#define _pie_wxy(control, pwxy1, pwxy2, pwxy3, pwxy4) _pie_xy(control, \
                _getviewcoord_wxy(pwxy1),
                _getviewcoord_wxy(pwxy2), \
                _getviewcoord_wxy(pwxy3),
                _getviewcoord_wxy(pwxy4))
```

/* The window-structure coordinate version of _pie( ). See the
explanations for _arc( ) and _ellipse( ) window variants.
*/

► _putimage ►

```
void far  _putimage(short x, short y, char far *image_buffer,
                short action);
```

/* Transfers the bit image stored at image_buffer to the screen
starting at logical (viewport) coordinates (x,y). The actual
display will depend on the existing image and the value set in
the argument action as follows:

Action Value	Display Logic
_GAND	Logically AND the two images; same colors will be unchanged, different colors will produce effects depending on the adapter and pixel mapping.
_GOR	Logically OR the two images; the incoming image will be superimposed without erasing original image.
_GPRESET	Logically invert each point of the incoming image; creates a 'negative' effect.
_GPSET	Display the new image exactly as it appeared when captured with _getimage( ).
_GXOR	Logically XOR (exlusive OR) the two images; inverts any point on screen where a point exists on incoming

image; allows an image to be moved about without
disturbing the background (since two successive XORs
restore original point).

_putimage( ) usually relies on an earlier _getimage( ).
There is no return value or error indication.
*/

► _putimage_xy ►

void far _putimage_xy(struct xycoord xy, char far *image_buffer,
                       short action);

/* Version of _putimage( ) using a viewport xycoord structure to get
the starting point for the image display. See similar variant
of _getimage( ).
*/

► _putimage_w ►

#define _putimage_w(wx, wy, image, action) \
        _putimage_xy(_getviewcoord_w(wx,wy), image, action)

/* Macro defining the window coordinate version of _putimage( ).
See the similar variant of _getimage( ) for an explanation.
*/

► _rectangle ►

short far _rectangle(short control, short x1, short y1,
                     short x2, short y2);

/* Draw a rectangle with top left at (x1,y1) viewport (relative)
coordinates and bottom right at (x2,y2). Use the current
line style and drawing color. The control argument controls
whether filling takes place using the current color and fill

mask. See _ellipse( ) and _floodfill( ). If control =
_GFILLINTERIOR, filling takes place. If control = _GBORDER, no
filling is done. Returns TRUE (nonzero) if successful,
otherwise FALSE (0).
*/

► _rectangle_xy ►

```
short far  _rectangle_xy(short control, struct xycoord xy1,
                        struct xycoord xy2);
```

/* Version of _rectangle( ) allowing use of viewport xycoord
structure arguments for the two rectangle endpoints. See
_ellipse( ) for similar variant.
*/

► _rectangle_w ►

```
#define _rectangle_w(control, wx1, wy1, wx2, wy2) _rectangle_xy(control,
                    _getviewcoord_w(wx1,wy1),
                    _getviewcoord_w(wx2,wy2))
```

/* Macro giving the window coordinate version of _rectangle( ).
See _ellipse( ) for similar variants.
*/

► _rectangle_wxy ►

```
#define _rectangle_wxy(control, pwxy1, pwxy2) _rectangle_xy(control,
                    _getviewcoord_wxy(pwxy1), _getviewcoord_wxy(pwxy2))
```

/* Macro giving the window-structure coordinate version of
_rectangle( ). See _ellipse( ) for similar variant.
*/

► _remapallpalette ►

short far _remapallpalette(long far *color_index_array);

/* Changes all the mappings from color number (index) to real
color on EGA, MCGA, VGA, and compatible adapters. The default
mapping is

0	Black
1	Blue
2	Green
3	Cyan
4	Red
5	Magenta
6	Brown
7	White
8	Dark gray
9	Light blue
10	Light green
11	Light cyan
12	Light red
13	Light magenta
14	Yellow
15	Bright white

Placing the long integers {a, b, c, d,...} in the
color_index_array argument, you would reassign pixels with value
a to Black, b to Blue, and so on. The effect of the call is
immediate: the new color scheme will be displayed instantly.
See also _selectpalette( ), _remappalette( ).
*/

► _remappalette ►

long far _remappalette(short color_index, long real_color);

/* Remaps the color_index to the real_color. Works immediately
to change all pixels being displayed with the value color_index
to the new real_color. Works only with CGA, MCGA, VGA, and
comparable adapters. Returns FALSE if successful, otherwise
−1. See also _selectpalette( ), _remapallpalette( ).
*/

► *_selectpalette* ►

short far _selectpalette(short palette_number);

/* Used only with _MRES4COLOR and _MRESNOCOLOR CGA/EGA
modes to select a palette. See Table 9.6 for the various color mappings for
each palette number. The palette you select determines which actual color
corresponds to each color index. Returns the value of the previous
palette_number. There is no error indication: illegal arguments are ignored.
See also _settextcolor( ), _setbkcolor( ), _gettextcolor( ), _getbkcolor( ).
*/

► *_setactivepage* ►

short far _setactivepage(short page_number);

/* If you have a multipage video adapter, you can designate one page as
active and another page as visual. Graphics output goes to the active page
of video memory, while the screen display reflects the contents of the visual
page. By switching page_number from active to visual, you can flip the
display instantly to display that page. See also _setvisualpage( ). If
successful, _setactivepage( ) returns the page number of the previous
active page; otherwise a − ve number is returned. By default, both active
and visual pages start life as page 0. The videoconfig structure has a field,
numvideopages, holding the number of pages available for the current
mode.
*/

► *_setbkcolor* ►

long far _setbkcolor(long color_number);

/* Used in text modes to set the background color. See Table 9.7 for the
colors available in CGA color text modes. See also _settextcolor( ), which is
used to set the foreground color, i.e., the color that text characters will
display against the current background color. Changing these colors does
not affect the immediate appearance of your text (as with _remappalette( )
in nontext graphics modes), rather it affects the colors of subsequent

displays. Returns the value of the previous background color. There are no error warnings: silly arguments are just ignored.
*/

▶ *_setcliprgn* ▶

void far _setcliprgn(short x1, short y1, short x2, short y2);

/* Defines a clipping rectangle, i.e., a region of the screen outside of which all graphical output is suppressed. By default, the whole screen is the initial clipping region. The coordinates of the clipping region are given by top left corner (x1,y1), bottom right corner (x2,y2). These points are always specified as absolute, physical coordinates, regardless of any viewports you may have previously set. There is no error warning should you supply illegal arguments. See also _setvieworg( ), _setviewport( ). When you issue drawing commands, any output destined for areas outside your clip region is simply lost without complaint. _setcliprgn( ) does not alter any relative coordinate system established with _setvieworg( ) or setviewport( ).
*/

▶ *_setcolor* ▶

short far _setcolor(short color_number);

/* Sets the current drawing color to the color indexed by color_number in the current graphics color palette. The actual color therefore depends on the adapter and its palette mappings. These are controlled with _remappalette( ) and _remapallpalette( ). Consult these entries for more details; also see Table 9.8 for the EGA palette descriptions. Do not confuse with _settextcolor( ) and _setbkcolor( ) used with text modes. Returns the previously set color number. The default, when you first start, is the highest number in the current palette.
*/

▶ *_setfillmask* ▶

void far _setfillmask(unsigned char far *fill_mask);

/* Sets the current fill mask to the 8 x 8 array of bits in fill_mask. Subsequent calls to functions that flood fill closed figures will use this mask

to determine the fill pattern. If no mask has been set, 'plain' fills are made using the current drawing color. When designing a fill mask, use squared graph paper; pencil in selected squares in an 8 x 8 grid until a pleasing effect is obtained, e.g., diagonal shading. Then write down eight binary numbers: 00100101, and so on, where 1's represent shaded squares. You can then construct the fill_mask array in hex: {x25, ...}. The small pattern you create is repeated throughout the flooded region, with 1's lighting up pixels in the current drawing color. See also _rectangle( ), _floodfill( ), _pie( ), _getfillmask( ). There is no return value or error signal.
*/

► *_setlinestyle* ►

void far _setlinestyle(unsigned short line_mask);

/* Line-drawing functions such as _lineto( ) and _rectangle( ) use a solid line style by default. To get dotted lines, you set up a 16-bit line_mask and call _setlinestyle( ). Each 1 in the mask produces a pixel lighted in the current drawing color, with gaps where the mask has 0. The default mask is therefore given by 0xFFFF. As with _setfillmask( ) you can use graph paper to design appropriate line-style masks, e.g., 1010101010101010 = 0xAAAA will give a fine dotted effect. There is no return value or error indication. See also _getlinestyle( ). Note that ellipses and arcs are not affected by the line-style setting.
*/

► *_setlogorg* ►

struct xycoord far _setlogorg(short, short);

/* This is an obsolete version of _setvieworg( ). */

► *_setpixel* ►

short far _setpixel(short x, short y);

/* Illuminates (sets) the pixel at viewport coordinates (x,y) with the current drawing color. Returns previous color value of that pixel if successful;

returns − 1 if unsuccessful. The actual color displayed at (x,y) depends on the mode and palette selected and on the color index in force. See _setcolor( ), remappalette( ), _remapallpalette( ).
*/

► _setpixel_xy ►

short far _setpixel_xy(struct xycoord xy);

/* A version of _setpixel( ) allowing you to specify the pixel position as an xycoord structure.
*/

► _setpixel_w ►

#define _setpixel_w(wx, wy) \
        _setpixel_xy(_getviewcoord_w(wx,wy))

/* Macro defining the window coordinate version of _setpixel( ). The pixel is referenced by two double values.
*/

► _settextcolor ►

short far _settextcolor(short color_number);

/* Used with CGA/EGA color text modes to set the foreground color of the actual text characters. These appear against a rectangle of pixels, the (background) color of which is independently set using _setbkcolor( ). Table 9.6 lists the various color numbers available. Color numbers in the range 0–15 represent normal, unblinking colors; adding 16 to these values causes the characters to blink. See also _gettextcolor( ), _setbkcolor( ), _getbkcolor( ).
*/

► *_settextcursor* ►

short far _settextcursor(short);

/* Used in text mode to set the shape and attributes of the cursor. Machine dependent. See _gettextcursor( ).
*/

► *_settextposition* ►

struct rccoord far _settextposition(short row, short col);

/* Sets the cursor position in text modes to (row,col), where row is in the range 1 – numtextrows and col is in the range 1 – numtextcols. The (row,col) is relative to the top left corner [taken as (1,1)] of any text window in force. The default text window is the whole screen. Returns the previous absolute cursor position in an rccoord structure: struct rccoord {short row; short col};. See also _gettextposition( ), _outtext( ), _settextwindow( ).
*/

► *_settextrows* ►

short far _settextrows(short rows);

/* For those systems allowing a choice of lines, e.g., 25 or 43, you can set the number of lines required. Returns 0 if error; else returns the number of rows set. See also _setvideomoderows( ).
*/

► *_settextwindow* ►

void far _settextwindow(short r1, short c1, short r2, short c2);

/* Establishes a text window with top left corner at (r1,c1) and bottom right corner at (r2,c2), where the coordinates are absolute (physical) taking (1,1) as the top left of the whole screen. Once set, a text window has four effects:

1. Coordinates in subsequent calls to _settextposition( ) are taken as relative to the top left corner of the text window.
2. The _wrapon( ) function can be used to control how text behaves when it reached the right edge of the window. See _wrapon( ) for an explanation.
3. Scrolling occurs when text reaches the bottom edge of the window.
4. The area cleared by _clearscreen( ) can be confined to the area of the text window, by using _GWINDOW as the area argument. See _clearscreen( ).

There is no return value or error indication. See also _outtext( ), _gettextposition( ), _settextposition( ).
*/

▸ _setvideomode ▸

short far _setvideomode(short mode);

/* Sets the video mode, if possible, to the argument mode. Returns FALSE (0) if the mode is unavailable; else returns TRUE. See also _getvideoconfig( ).
*/

▸ _setvideomoderows ▸

short far _setvideomoderows(short mode, short rows);

/* A variant of _setvideomode( ) allowing you to set the number of rows for those systems offering a choice, e.g., 25- or 43-line monitors. Returns the number of rows set if successful; otherwise returns 0.
*/

▸ _setvieworg ▸

struct xycoord far _setvieworg(short x, short y);

/* Allows you to change the viewport origin from (0,0), the top leftmost pixel, to the point (x,y) given in absolute viewport coordinates. Once set, all relative viewport coordinates will be measured as though the new origin

were (0,0). The current viewport rectangle or clip region (if any) is not affected. Returns the absolute coordinates of the previous origin via an xycoord structure. See _setviewport( ).
*/

► *_setviewport* ►

void far _setviewport(short x1, short y1, short x2, short y2);

/* Establishes a rectangular viewport with top left corner at (x1,y1) and bottom right corner at (x2,y2) given in absolute, physical coordinates. The effect is identical to the following: _setvieworg(x1,y1);, followed by _setcliprgn (x1,y1,x2,y2);. In other words: the new logical origin for subsequent view coordinates is (x1,y1), and all graphical output is clipped by the defined rectangle. The default viewport is the whole screen. See _setvieworg( ), setcliprgn( ), _getwindowcoord( ), _getviewcoord( ). There is no return value; daft arguments are ignored.
*/

► *_setvisualpage* ►

short far _setvisualpage(short page_number);

/* If you have a multipage video adapter, you can designate one page as active and another page as visual. Graphics output goes to the active page of video memory, while the screen display reflects the contents of the visual page. By switching page_number from active to visual, you can flip the display instantly to display that page. See also _setactivepage( ). If successful, _setvisualpage( ) returns the page number of the previous visual page; otherwise a − ve number is returned. By default, both active and visual pages start life as page 0. The videoconfig structure has a field, numvideopages, holding the number of pages available for the current mode.
*/

► *_setwindow* ►

short far _setwindow(short invert_Y, double wx1, double wy2,
                     double wx2, double wy2);

```
/* Establishes a window coordinate system with the origin at top left corner
(wx1,wy1) and bottom right at (wx2,wy2). All window coordinates are FP
double values. If the invert_Y flag is set to TRUE, the direction of the Y axis
is taken a increasing upward from a bottom left origin at (wx1,wy1);
otherwise the Y axis increases from top to bottom. See also
_getviewcoord_w( ) and many other _w and _wxy variants. Returns 0 if
unsuccessful.
*/
```

► _wrapon ►

```
short far _wrapon(short wrap_control);
```

```
/* With wrap_control set to _GWRAPON (the default), text being displayed
in a text window will wrap over the next line whenever it reaches the right
edge. To prevent wrapping, call  *_wrapon(_GWRAPOFF);. With wrapping
off, excess text will disappear. See _settextwindow( ), _outtext( ).
*/
```

► *Presentation Graphics* ►

Before I list the presentation graphics functions, here are some important error codes, data structures, and **typedef**s used throughout the PGCHART library.

► *PG Error Codes*

Mnemonic	Value	Description
_PG_NOTINITIALIZED	102	Library not initialized
_PG_BADSCREENMODE	103	Graphics mode not set before charting
_PG_BADCHARTSTYLE	04	Chart style invalid
_PG_BADCHARTTYPE	104	Chart type invalid
_PG_BADLEGENDWINDOW	105	Invalid legend window specified

_PG_BADCHARTWINDOW	07	x1 = x2 or y1 = y2 in chart window spec.
_PG_BADDATAWINDOW	107	Chart window too small
_PG_NOMEMORY	108	Not enough memory for data arrays
_PG_BADLOGBASE	05	Log base <= 0
_PG_BADSCALEFACTOR	06	Scale factor = 0
_PG_TOOSMALLN	109	Number of data points <= 0
_PG_TOOFEWSERIES	110	Number of series <= 0

Error values greater than 100 terminate the chart routine; others will cause the default values to be used in place of the invalid arguments encountered.

► PG Structures and typedefs

► *struct axistype* ►

```
typedef struct {
    short      grid;          /* TRUE = grid lines drawn; FALSE no lines
                                 */
    short      gridstyle;     /* Style number from style pool for grid lines
                                 */
    titletype  axistitle;     /* Title definition for axis */
    short      axiscolor;     /* Color for axis */
    short      labeled;       /* TRUE = tic marks and titles drawn */
    short      rangetype;     /* _PG_LINEARAXIS, _PG_LOGAXIS */
    float      logbase;       /* Base used if log axis */
    short      autoscale;     /* TRUE = next 7 values calculated by
                                 system */
    float      scalemin;      /* Minimum value of scale */
    float      scalemax;      /* Maximum value of scale */
    float      scalefactor;   /* Scale factor for data on this axis */
    titletype  scaletitle;    /* Title definition for scaling factor */
    float      ticinterval;   /* Distance between tic marks */
    short      ticformat;     /* _PG_EXPFORMAT or
                                 _PG_DECFORMAT for tic labels */
```

```
    short        ticdecimals;   /* Number of decimals for tic labels
                                    (max = 9) */
} axistype;
```

/* The main chart environment structure, chartenv, holds two fields of
type struct axistype, one for the X axis, one for the Y axis. Each field in
axistype determines the appropriate property for an axis.
_pg_defaultchart( ) sets up convenient defaults for you, but you can
override any of these by direct assignments to particular fields.
*/

► *type charmap* ►

```
typedef unsigned char charmap[8];
```

/* Used for character bit maps */

► *struct chartenv* ►

```
typedef struct {
    short        charttype;      /* _PG_BARCHART,
                                    _PG_COLUMNCHART,
                                    _PG_LINECHART,
                                    _PG_SCATTERCHART,
                                    _PG_PIECHART */
    short        chartstyle;     /* Style for selected chart type */
    windowtype   chartwindow;    /* Window definition for overall chart */
    windowtype   datawindow;     /* Window definition for data part of chart
                                    */
    titletype    maintitle;      /* Main chart title */
    titletype    subtitle;       /* Chart subtitle */
    axistype     xaxis;          /* Definition for X axis */
    axistype     yaxis;          /* Definition for Y axis */
    legendtype   legend;         /* Definition for legend */
} chartenv;
```

/* Main chart environment structure. Fields are set using _pg_default-
chart( ), although you are free to alter some or all of the default settings.
*/

► *type fillmap* ►

```
typedef unsigned char fillmap[8];
/* Used to define pattern bit maps in each PG palette. See typedef for
struct paletteentry.
*/
```

► *struct legendtype* ►

```
typedef struct {
    short          legend;          /* TRUE = draw legend; FALSE = no
                                       legend */
    short          place;           /* _PG_RIGHT, _PG_BOTTOM,
                                       _PG_OVERLAY */
    short          textcolor;       /* Internal palette color for text */
    short          autosize;        /* TRUE = system calculates size */
    windowtype     legendwindow;    /* Window definition for legend */
} legendtype;
```

```
/* Each field of struct legendtype controls some aspect of the chart legend.
The legend field in struct chartenv is of type struct legendtype, so
_pg_defaultchart( ) sets up default values for your legend style. You can
override these with direct assignments, e.g., env.legend.place =
_PG_BOTTOM;.
*/
```

► *struct paletteentry* ►

```
typedef struct {
        unsigned short    color;
        unsigned short    style;
        fillmap           fill;
        char              plotchar;
} paletteentry;
```

```
/* Basic PG palette structure, not to be confused with the graphics adapter
palettes on CGA, EGA, and the like. See typedef palettetype for more
details.
*/
```

► *type palettetype[]* ►

typedef paletteentry palettetype[_PG_PALETTELEN];

/* Establishes an array of structures of type paletteentry. The constant
_PG_PALETTELEN is currently set at 16 in PGCHART.H. Each plot in a
multiseries chart uses a different palettetype member, giving a distinct color,
style, fill, and plotchar. The style number is an index to the style pool, an
array defined in typedef styleset (see below).
*/

► *type styleset[]* ►

typedef unsigned short styleset[_PG_PALETTELEN];

/* A set of line-style masks similar to those used in the graphics library [see
_setlinestyle( ), _getlinestyle( )]. Mulitiseries plots can therefore use
different line styles as well as colors to help legibility.
*/

► *struct titletype* ►

```
typedef struct  {
    char     title[_PG_TITLELEN];    /* Title text */
    short    titlecolor;             /* Internal palette color for title text */
    short    justify;                /* _PG_LEFT, _PG_CENTER,
                                         _PG_RIGHT */
} titletype;
```

/* Determines the text, color, and positioning of various chart titles. See,
e.g., the axistitle field in struct axistype.
*/

► *struct windowtype* ►

```
typedef struct  {
    short    x1;             /* Left edge of window in pixels */
    short    y1;             /* Top edge of window in pixels */
```

```
    short    x2;           /* Right edge of window in pixels */
    short    y2;           /* Bottom edge of window in pixels */
    short    border;       /* TRUE for border, FALSE otherwise */
    short    background;   /* Internal palette color for window background
                             */
    short    borderstyle;  /* Style bytes for window border */
    short    bordercolor;  /* Internal palette color for window border */
} windowtype;
```

/* Used to establish the specifications for the three windows used in a PG chart: chart window, data window, and legend window. In struct chartenv you'll find fields called chartwindow and datawindow of type struct windowtype. The third window is 'hiding' in the field legend of type struct legendtype. Watch for the extra level of 'indirection,' e.g., env.chartwindow.bordercolor compared with env.legend.legendwindow.bordercolor.
*/

► PG Functions

► _pg_initchart ►

short far _pg_initchart(void);

/* PG primary function: Initializes your PG application by setting default values in various PG structures. Returns FALSE (0) if successful! All PG applications must call _pg_initchart( ) early on in their lives.
*/

► _pg_defaultchart ►

short far _pg_defaultchart(chartenv far *env, short charttype,
                              short chartstyle);

/* PG primary function: For a given choice of charttype and chartstyle, this function fills up the env structure (see typedef struct chartenv above) with useful default values. charttype and chartstyle can be selected from the following predefined mnemonics:

charttype	Possible chartstyles
_PG_BARCHART	_PG_PLAINBARS, _PG_STACKEDBARS
_PG_COLUMNCHART	
_PG_LINECHART	_PG_POINTANDLINE, _PG_POINTONLY
_PG_SCATTERCHART	
_PG_PIECHART	_PG_PERCENT, _PG_NOPERCENT

To vary any of the default settings, you need to assign your own choices, field by field, to the env structure. See the chartenv structure definition above.
*/

▸ _pg_chart ▸

```
short far _pg_chart(chartenv far *env, char * far *cat_array,
                    float far *val_array, short num_vals);
```

/* PG primary function for single data series: Having chosen a bar, column, or line chart with _pg_defaultchart( ) and added title text etc., you can call _pg_chart( ), the main drawing function for such charts. env, of course, must point to the same chartenv structure in both functions. The other arguments are as follows:

cat_array	An array of category names {"Mon", "Tue", ...};. The number of these will equal num_vals.
val_array	An array of the FP values to be plotted—e.g., { 0.354, 7.245, ...};. There will also be num_vals of these.
num_vals	The number of values to be plotted (also equals the number of categories).

Returns FALSE (0) if successful, otherwise TRUE! Remember to program a pause [e.g. getch( )] after _pg_chart( ).
*/

▸ _pg_chartms ▸

```
short far _pg_chartms(chartenv far *env,
                      char * far *cat_array,
                      float far *val_matrix,
```

```
short num_vals, short num_series,
short dim_array,
char * far *labels_array);
```

/* PG primary function for ms (multiple series) data: This is the ms version of _pg_chart( ). Having chosen a bar, column, or line chart with _pg_defaultchart( ) and added titles etc., you can call _pg_chartms( ), the main drawing function for ms charts. env, of course, must point to the same chartenv structure in both functions. The other arguments are as follows:

cat_array   An array of category names {"Mon", "Tue", ...};. The number of names will equal num_vals.

val_matrix   A two-dimensional array of the FP values to be plotted, one 'array' for each data series, e.g.,

```
{ { 0.354, 7.245, ...},
  { 9.897, 6.099, ...},
    ...
};
```

There will be num_vals values in each data series.

num_vals   The number of values to be plotted in each series (also equals the number of categories).

num_series   The number of data series to be plotted.

dim_array   Second dimension of val_matrix.

labels_array   An array of labels for the data series, e.g., {"NW Sales", "SE Sales", ...};.

Returns FALSE (0) if successful, otherwise TRUE! Remember to program a pause [e.g. getch( )] after _pg_chartms( ).
*/

► _pg_chartscatter ►

```
short far _pg_chartscatter(chartenv far *env,
                           float far *x_val_array,
                           float far *y_val_array,
                           short num_vals);
```

/* PG primary function for single data series: This is the scatter chart version of _pg_chart( ). Having chosen a _PGSCATTERCHART with _pg_defaultchart( ) and added title text etc., you can call _pg_chart-scatter( ), the main drawing function for such charts. env, of course, must point to the same chartenv structure in both functions. The other arguments are as follows:

x_val_array	An array of the FP values to be plotted on the X axis, e.g. { 0.354, 7.245, ...};. There will be num_vals of these.
y_val_array	An array of the FP values to be plotted on the Y axis, e.g. { 0.675, 7.123, ...};. There will also be num_vals of these.
num_vals	The number of values to be plotted.

Returns FALSE (0) if successful, otherwise TRUE! Remember to program a pause [e.g., getch( )] after _pg_scatterchart( ).
*/

► *_pg_chartscatterms* ►

```
short far _pg_chartscatterms(chartenv far *env,
                    float far *x_val_matrix,
                    float far *y_val_matrix,
                    short num_vals,
                    short num_series, short dim_array,
                    char farfar *labels_array);
```

/* PG primary function for ms (multiple series) data: This is the ms version of _pg_scatterchart( ); where

x_val_matrix	A two-dimensional array of the FP values to be plotted, one 'array' for each X data series, e.g., { { 0.354, 7.245, ...}, { 9.897, 6.099 ....}, ... };
y_val_matrix	A two-dimensional array of the FP values to be plotted, one 'array' for each Y data series, e.g., { { 9.321, 8.985, ...}, { 0.089, 3.165, ...}, ... };
num_series	The number of data series to be plotted.
dim_array	Second dimension of the value matrix.
labels_array	An array of labels for the scatter charts, e.g., {"NW Sales", "SE Sales", ...};.

Each scatter plot consists of plotchars at each (xi,yi), where xi and yi are corresponding values in one of the val_matrix arrays. Each data series will have a unique plotchar. Returns FALSE (0) if successful, otherwise TRUE! Remember to program a pause [e.g., getch( )] after _pg_chartscatterms( ).
*/

► *_pg_chartpie* ►

```
short far  _pg_chartpie(chartenv far *env,
                        char * far *cat_array,
                        float far *val_array,
                        short far *explode,
                        short num_vals);
```

/* PG primary function for pie charts: This is the pie chart version of _pg_chart( ). Having chosen a _PGPIECHART with _pg_defaultchart( ) and added title text etc., you can call _pg_chartpie( ), the main drawing function for such charts. env, of course, must point to the same chartenv structure in both functions. The other arguments are as follows:

cat_array	An array of category names, {"Unix", "DOS", ...};. The number of these will equal num_vals.
val_array	An array of the FP values for the pie slices, e.g., { 2000.00, 6000.00, ...};. There will also be num_vals of these.
explode	An array of explode flags, e.g., {0,0,1,1, ...};. A 1 in the nth position causes the nth pie slice to 'explode, i.e., be drawn as an isolated wedge. Slices corresponding to a 0 flag remain in the pie!
num_vals	The number of values to be plotted (also equals the number of categories equals the number of slices).

Returns FALSE (0) if successful, otherwise TRUE!
Remember to program a pause [e.g., getch( )] after _pg_chartpie( ).
*/

► *_pg_analyzechart* ►

```
short far  _pg_analyzechart(chartenv far *env,
                            char * far *cat_array,
                            float far *val_array,
                            short num_vals);
```

/* PG secondary function: Works exactly like _pg_chart( ) by calculating
and filling the PG structures, but does not display a chart. Useful for
customizing your charts.
*/

► _pg_analyzechartms ►

```
short far  _pg_analyzechartms(chartenv far *env,
                             char * far *cat_array,
                             float far *val_matrix,
                             short num_vals, short num_series,
                             short dim_array,
                             char farfar *labels_array);
```

/* PG secondary function: Works exactly like _pg_chartms( ) by calculating
and filling the PG structures, but does not display a chart. Useful for
customizing your charts.
*/

► _pg_analyzescatter ►

```
short far  _pg_analyzescatter(chartenv far *env,
                             float far *x_val_array,
                             float far *y_val_array,
                             short num_vals);
```

/* PG secondary function: Works exactly like _pg_chartscatter( ) by
calculating and filling the PG structures, but does not display a chart. Useful
for customizing your charts.
*/

► _pg_analyzescatterms ►

```
short far  _pg_analyzescatterms(chartenv far *env,
                             float far *x_val_matrix,
                             float far *y_val_matrix,
                             short num_vals,
```

```
                         short num_series, short dim_array,
                         char far *labels_array);
```

/* PG secondary function: Works exactly like _pg_chartscatterms( ) by
calculating and filling the PG structures, but does not display a chart. Useful
for customizing your charts.
*/

► *_pg_analyzepie* ►

```
short far  _pg_analyzepie(chartenv far *env,
                         char * far *cat_array,
                         float far *val_array,
                         short far *explode,
                         short num_vals);
```

/* PG secondary function: Works exactly like _pg_chartpie( ) by calculating
and filling the PG structures, but does not display a chart. Useful for
customizing your charts.
*/

► *_pg_getpalette* ►

```
short far  _pg_getpalette(paletteentry far *pe);
```

/* PG secondary function: Fills a paletteentry structure with details of the
current PG palette: color, style, fill, and plotchar. Not to be confused with the
graphics library palette functions. Returns 0 for success, nonzero for failure.
*/

► *_pg_setpalette* ►

```
short far  _pg_setpalette(paletteentry far *pe);
```

/* PG secondary function: Sets a new current palette according to the fields
set in *pe. See typedef struct paletteentry and _pg_getpalette( ). Returns 0
for success, nonzero for failure.
*/

► *_pg_resetpalette* ►

short far _pg_resetpalette(void);

/* PG secondary function: Resets all members of the palette pool to their
original default settings. See typedefs for paletteentry and palettetype.
Returns 0 for success, nonzero for failure.
*/

► *_pg_getstyleset* ►

void far _pg_getstyleset(unsigned short far *style_array);

/* PG secondary function: Fills a styleset array with details of the current
style pool. The style field in the paletteentry structure indexes an array of
line styles called styleset. Each entry determines the line style (mask) used
for line graphs. See also _pg_setstyleset( ). There are
_PGPALETTELEN = 16 styles in the style pool.
*/

► *_pg_setstyleset* ►

void far _pg_setstyleset(unsigned short far *style_array);

/* PG secondary function: Allows you to vary PG's default set of line styles
by changing the style pool. See also _pg_getstyleset( ).
*/

► *_pg_resetstyleset* ►

void far _pg_resetstyleset(void);

/* PG secondary function: Resets all members of the style pool to their
original default settings. See typedef styleset, _pg_setstyleset( ),
_pg_getstyleset( ).
*/

► _pg_getchardef ►

short far _pg_getchardef(short ch, unsigned char far *chmap);

/* PG secondary function: Obtains the charmap array for ch. See typedef
charmap. Returns 0 for success, nonzero for failure.
*/

► _pg_setchardef ►

short far _pg_setchardef(short ch, unsigned char far *chmap);

/* PG secondary function: Lets you set up a character bit map for ch. See
_pg_getchardef( ) and typedef charmap. Returns 0 for success, nonzero for
failure.
*/

► Graphics Fonts ►

This last section lists QuickC's graphics font structures and functions.

► Graphics Font Structures

► struct _fontinfo ►

```
struct _fontinfo {
    int    type;          /* b0 set = vector, clear = bit map */
    int    ascent;        /* Pixel height from top to baseline */
    int    pixwidth;      /* Character width in pixels */
                          /* 0 = proportional spacing */
    int    pixheight;     /* Character height in pixels */
    int    avgwidth;      /* Average character width in pixels */
    char filename[81];    /* File name including path */
    char facename[32];    /* Font name */
};
```

/* This is the basic structure telling you everything about the current font.
See _setfont( ) and _getfontinfo( ).
*/

► *Graphics Font Functions*

The following functions are all prototyped in GRAPH.H.

► *_getfontinfo* ►

short far _getfontinfo(struct _fontinfo far *fontinfo_ptr);

/* Fills a _fontinfo structure with details of the current font. You declare,
e.g., struct _fontinfo my_fontinfo, then call _getfontinfo(&my_fontinfo);.
See also struct _fontinfo, _setfont( ).
*/

► *_getgtextextent* ►

short far _getgtextextent(unsigned char far *text_string);

/* Returns the total length in pixels that the given text string would occupy if
displayed in the current font. Used to ensure that legends fit nicely in boxes.
*/

► *_outgtext* ►

void far _outgtext(unsigned char far *text_string);

/* This is the fonts version of _outtext( ). Use _moveto( ) to position the CP;
_outgtext( ) then displays the given text string starting at this CP. The CP
moves to the end of the fonts text display.
*/

► _registerfonts ►

short far _registerfonts(unsigned char far *font_filespec);

/* Initializes the font or fonts in the font_filespec string. Before you can use a font, three steps are needed: ensure that the .FON file is available; register the font with _registerfonts( ); set the font with _setfont( ). The registering function reads a header from a .FON file. By using wildcards in the font_filespec argument, you can register more than one font with this call. Returns the number of fonts successfully registered. Returns a – ve number on failure, so it is mandatory to test this before proceeding. See also _setfont( ).
*/

► _setfont ►

short far _setfont(unsigned char far *option_string);

/* Sets the registered font matched by the options in the option_string as the *current* font. All subsequent font displays will appear in this font until a further _setfont( ) call. The option string contains an option code followed possibly by a parameter, e.g.:

"t'<fontname>' [h<pixelheight>] [w<pixelwidth>] [v] [r] [b] [n<fontnumber]>"

The b option code lets the function pick the 'best' match among the registered fonts. The n option code lets you choose the font by number from the registered font list, e.g., n2 picks the second registered font. _setfont( ) causes a file access to retrieve font data, so avoid any unecessary font changes during a program: if possible, display all text in a given font before switching fonts. _setfont( ) returns 0 for success, nonzero for failure. You must test before trying to use _outgtext( ).
*/

► _unregisterfonts ►

void far _unregisterfonts(void);

```
/* Cancels the current registered list of fonts and frees up any memory
allocated for font data tables. Each registered font takes about 140 bytes of
RAM. No return value or error indications.
*/
```

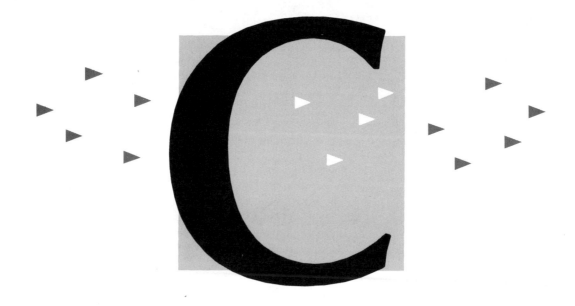

THE QUICKC HELP SYSTEM

► *APPENDIX G* ►

QuickC has set new standards in the quest for instant, on-line help for the user. By exploiting the concept of multilinked texts, often referred to as hypertext, Microsoft has gone beyond the traditional approach of simply displaying a fixed burst of advice whenever the user requests it.

In the very early days, you had to exit the current job in hand and type a phrase such as HELP SPOOL in order to receive a message saying, **HELP SPOOL? TRY HELP ABACUS, ASSEMBLY, BABBAGE, ...** In such systems you had to know the permissible keywords and spell them just so. Matters gradually improved in two directions: You could invoke help without leaving your application; and a single hot key would provide, when possible, context-sensitive help. The latter, however, was only coarsely related to what you were doing at the time, and to "correct" this deficiency, you were often bombarded with an excess of information. The ability to browse and thread through related help topics was limited, and apart from reading or printing the help screens, there was nothing else you could do with the glut of information.

The QuickC Help facility introduced with Version 2 has created an entirely new tool for beginners and advanced users alike. The help database not only provides a wealth of information on the QuickC menus and commands but also constitutes an on-line reference to the C language, available while you are programming. As well as reading the stuff, you can cut and paste it to other windows, such as the Notepad and source windows.

The Help facility is organized under the general headings Keywords/Topics and Index/Contents.

Before we explore these, there is a small chore to be done if you use a mouse. Select the Options/Display menu and click Context Sensitive Help under the Right Mouse Button heading, then exit the dialog box. This assigns the right mouse button to the F1 help hot key.

► *KEYWORD/TOPICS HELP* ►

While in QC, no matter which window is active, the F1 key gives instant help on any keyword and many other topics. Place the cursor anywhere on a keyword (or the space following), and F1 will bring up the specific help screen for that keyword. I am using *keyword* here in a wider sense than the normal C usage. Here, keyword includes not only the ANSI C list of reserved words and the QuickC extensions but also the names of library functions, include files and their manifest constants, and even some of the C operator symbols.

Load the final version of SIGMA.C (Program 11.4 in Chapter 11) and move the cursor to **main( )**. This selected word is called a *topic*. You now have two ways to invoke help on a topic: you can use either the Help menu or the F1 hot key.

You bring up the Help menu with Alt-H. The Help menu shows four submenus:

Index

Contents

Topic: main

Help On Help Shift-F1

Note that the Topic submenu already shows the selection **main**, so you can press T (or use the down arrow to highlight Topic, then press Enter) to display the help window for **main**.

The quicker approach is to press the hot key F1—this will always pick up the topic from the cursor position. If no help is available, you will hear a warning trill. Figure G.1 shows the resulting help display for the keyword **main**.

```
  File  Edit  View  Search  Make  Run  Debug  Utility  Options           Help
 ──────────────────────────── HELP: main ───────────────────────────────┤↑│
│Keyword:│ main                                                           │
│                                                                         │
│Syntax:│  main ()                                                        │
│           (                                                             │
│           <program>                                                     │
│           )                                                             │
│                                                                         │
│Summary:│ The main function is the name of the function that marks the   │
│          beginning of program execution. A program must have one        │
│          function named main.                                           │
 ──────────────────────── E:\BIN\SIGMA4.C ───────────────────────────┤↑├─┤
│/* prog11.4 = SIGMA.C final version 4 */                             │▓│
│/* SIGMA4.C computes sum of first n natural numbers */               │▓│
│/*         with sigma Ø = Ø */                                       │▓│
│                                                                     │▓│
│#include <stdio.h>                                                   │ │
│                                                                     │ │
│        unsigned long sumn(int m);    /* declaration */             │ │
│                                                                     │ │
│        void main()                                                  │↓│
 <F1=Help> <Esc=Close> <F6=Window> <Shift+F5=Restart>        00009:015
```

► *Figure G.1:* Help on the topic **main( )**

You can select a topic from any of the eight standard windows supported by QC, including a help window itself. Just make the window active with F6 and position the cursor prior to pressing F1. If the topic that interests you is not in sight, you can type it (in those windows that allow editing) and then press F1 (since the cursor will be in the space following your entry).

Remember that F6 cycles you through successive visible windows, making each one the current (or active) window. Since the help and Debug windows share the same display area, you may need to use the Ctrl-F6 switch if both are open (more on this in Chapter 11). The other shared windows are Locals/Registers and Notepad/output.

So, you can make the help screen active and select keywords from the help display itself. Any functions related to the target (shown in the See Also box) can therefore be quickly accessed, saving a great deal of page turning and index hunting. You may have already noticed that there is no common index to the three manuals supplied with QuickC!

A mouse makes help selection even easier: point to a word and click the right button.

If the information exceeds the display area, you can use the PgUp and PgDn keys (or click in the scroll bars) to scroll in the usual way or you can temporarily zoom (maximize) the screen using the toggle Ctrl-F10 (or use the View/Maximize menu).

You can also look at the next topic's help screen with Ctrl-F1 or at the previous topic with Alt-F1. Figure G.2 shows that the next topic after **main( )** is help on command-line arguments.

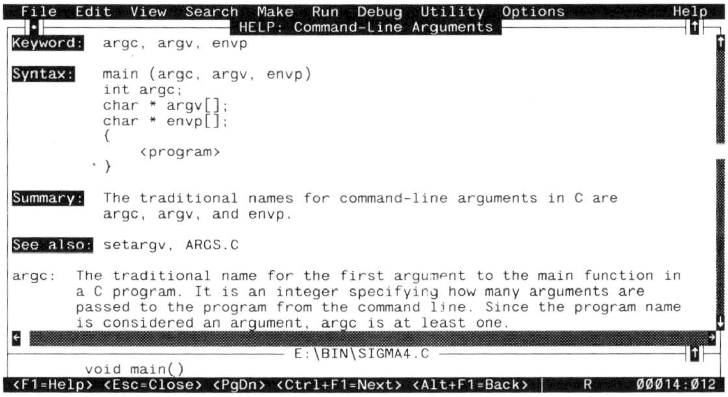

► **Figure G.2:** *Next help screen after* **main( )**: *command-line arguments*

You could now use F6 to activate the help window and select help on
setargv. Use Escape to return to the source window and put the cursor
on **scanf( )**. Pressing F1 will give you the screen shown in Figure G.3.

Note the legends along the top of this help window. These represent
hyperlinks, and they vary according to the target topic. In our case the
<Summary> legend is highlighted, indicating that you are now looking at
the **scanf( )** summary. The other hyperlinks are <Description> and
<Example>. You can access these by positioning the cursor (with tab), then
pressing F1 (or point and click with a mouse). Hyperlinks guarantee that a
help display will be available, whereas a topic may or may not be in the help
database. Typing Kahn, for example, is not going to get you anywhere.

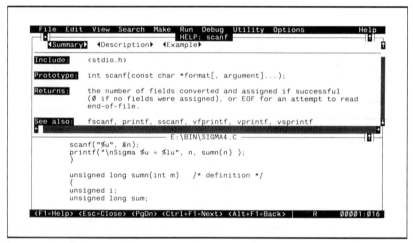

► *Figure G.3:* Help on **scanf( )**

► INDEX/CONTENTS HELP ►

Returning to the Help menu, select the Contents submenu. This menu displays a comprehensive table of topics grouped by subject. You can browse
through this table and select topics from it when you are not exactly sure
which topic names are available. You can position the cursor or mouse-click
on any topic for instant gratification. The Contents window also has four
hyperlinks: Help on Help, Contents (active and highlighted), Index,
and Notes.

You can either browse freely or select Index, which presents the whole
repertory of topics in alphabetical sequence. Here, you can select a letter to
bring up all the topics in that section.

Selecting Notes invokes the Notepad window, just as if you had used the View/Windows.../Notepad menu. You can now use F6 to move back and forth between the Notepad and help windows, make notes, and cut/paste from help to Notepad.

► *Cut and Paste Between Windows* ►

The cut/paste feature also works between the Notepad/source and help/source windows and other fine combinations. Simply select the text from the active window using Shift and the direction keys (this highlights the selection), then copy to the clipboard with Ctrl-Ins. Finally, you can use F6 to return to the target window, then position the cursor and paste with Shift-Ins.

► *ENVIRONMENT HELP* ►

If you highlight any menu or submenu command you can press F1 for a help screen on that command. Figure G.4 shows the result of calling for help on the View/Windows... command. In this case, there are ten screens of help available, so as you scroll up and down page by page, the header reads **Windows Command (3 of 10)**, and so on. Again, you can cut/paste to your Notepad or use PrtSc to capture this information.

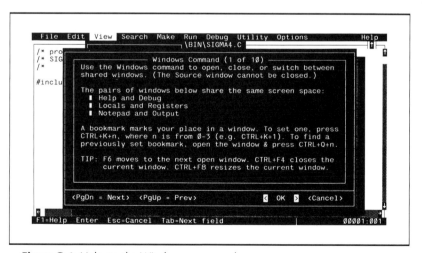

► **Figure G.4:** *Help on the Windows command*

► *ERRORS HELP* ►

Whenever you get an error message in the Error window, you can use F6 to activate that window, select the target error message, and then press F1 for guidance. The resulting help screens will greatly amplify the normally cryptic **Cnnnn:** and **Lnnn:** error messages and will save your leafing through the *QuickC Tool Kit* manual.

► *HELPMAKE* ►

For advanced users, QuickC offers a utility called HELPMAKE that allows you to create and edit your own help database.

► *HELP ON HELP* ►

Finally, in view of the size and scope of the Help system, you may need help recursively! You can use the Help menu's Help On Help command or the hot key Shift-F1.

Table G.1 summarizes the Help and related menus and hot keys.

► *Table G.1:* Help and related commands

Menu Command	Hot Key	Action
View/Output Screen	F4	Toggle between source and user screens
View/Maximize	Ctrl-F10	Toggle-zoom current window
View/Windows...	n/a	Open/close windows
Help/Index	n/a	Help index
Help/Topic:	F1	Context-sensitive help
Help/Help On Help	Shift-F1	Help on the Help system
None	F6	Switch next open window to current window

► **Table G.1:** *Help and related commands (continued)*

Menu Command	Hot Key	Action
None	Ctrl-F6	Switch between a pair of shared opened windows—e.g., Debug/help,Locals/Registers, Notepad/output
None	Ctrl-F8	Resize current window
None	Ctrl-F4	Close current window (source window excepted)
None	Ctrl-F1	Browse forward to next help topic
None	Alt-F1	Browse backward to previous help topic
Edit/Undo	Alt-backspace	Undo previous edit
Edit/Cut	Shift-Del	Delete selected text and copy to clipboard
Edit/Copy	Ctrl-Ins	Copy selected text to clipboard, then deselect
Edit/Paste	Shift-Ins	Copy clipboard text to current window
Edit/Clear	Del	Delete selected text without copying to clipboard
None	Shift+ arrows	Select text

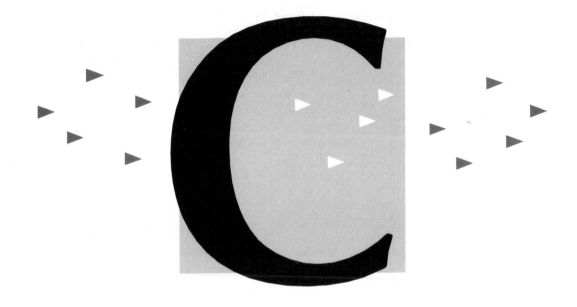

QUICKC RESOURCE LIST

► *APPENDIX H* ►

► *BOOKS* ►

Harbison, Samuel P., and Steele, Guy L., Jr. *C: A Reference Manual*. 2d ed. Englewood Cliffs, N.J.: Prentice-Hall, 1987.

Kernighan, Brian W., and Ritchie, Dennis M. *The C Programming Language*. Englewood Cliffs, N.J.: Prentice-Hall, 1978.

Young, Michael J. *Systems Programming in Microsoft C*. Alameda, Calif.: SYBEX, 1989. (This book has a comprehensive bibliography.)

► *FONTS* ►

Multi-Lingual Scholar and specialized software for exotic alphabets. Gamma Productions Inc., 710 Wilshire Boulevard, Santa Monica, CA 90401; (213) 394-8622.

► *MAGAZINES* ►

The following have regular coverage of C topics with source-code listings:

BYTE. One Phoenix Mill Lane, Peterborough, NH 03458; (603) 924-9281. (See especially "A C Language Primer" by James Joyce in the August 1983 issue.)

Computer Language. 500 Howard Street, San Francisco, CA 94105; (415) 397-1881. (See especially Programming On Purpose, the monthly column by P. J. Plauger and Bit by Bit by Stan Kelly-Bootle.)

Dr. Dobb's Journal. 501 Galveston Drive, Redwood City, CA 94063; (415) 366-3600.

Structured Language World. 175 Fifth Avenue, New York, NY 10010.

UNIX REVIEW. 500 Howard Street, San Francisco, CA 94105; (415) 397-1881. (See especially the monthly column C Advisor by Eric P. Allman and Ken Arnold.)

► MISCELLANEOUS ►

The C Users' Group, *The C User's Journal*, 2120 W. 25th Street, Suite B, Lawrence, KS 66046; (913) 841-1631.

► MISCELLANEOUS SOFTWARE PRODUCTS ►

Complete set of software tools with source code, separate library for each memory model. There are two diskettes and the price is $29.50. The tools are fully described in *Systems Programming in Microsoft C* (see above). Michael J. Young, P.O. Box 5068, Mill Valley, CA 94942.

C Programmer's Tool Box, Volumes I and II. A variety of productivity aids and utilities. MMC AD Systems, P.O. Box 360845, Milpitas, CA 95035; (408) 263-0781.

C-scape/Look & Feel. Interface management system including screens, menus, help support, data capture/verification. Oakland Group, 675 Massachusetts Avenue, Cambridge, MA 02139; (800) 233-3733.

The Heap Expander. Interface for expanded heaps up to 8MB. The Tool Makers, P.O. Box 8976, Moscow, ID 83843; (208) 883-4979.

PEGA Functions. EGA toolkit with 90 enhanced graphics functions. Prototype Systems Ltd., 637 17th Street, Boulder, CO 80302; (800) 628-2828, extension 493.

Screen Maker. Code generator for text files and input/output screens. SoftScience Corp., P.O. Box 42905, Tucson, AZ 85733-2905; (800) 453-5000.

Vitamin C. Screen painter/code generator; window/data, entry/menu manager; help handler. Creative Programming, P.O. Box 112097, Carrollton, TX 75011; (214) 416-6447.

(All the above product names are trademarks of the suppliers.)

► INDEX ►

H

%h for format specifier, 65, 436, 446
H for size field, 436, 446
halloc() function, 497
handles, pointer, 162–163
   See also file handles
haplography errors, 390
Harbison, Samuel P., *C: A Reference Manual*, 227
_harderr() function, 497
_hardresume() function, 497
_hardretn() function, 497
hardware
   errors from, 497
   requirements of, 423
head-of-block declarations, 236
header files, 2, 373–374
heap, 159, 242, 489–490
   checking of, 506–507
   management of, 498
_heapchk() function, 498
_heapset() function, 498
_heapwalk() function, 498
HELLO.C program, 4, 22–40
Help system, 8–9
   commands for, 574–575
   for environment, 573
   for errors, 574
   index/contents, 572–573
   for I/O, 288–289
   keyword topics, 569–572
   for multiple topics, 430
help window, 401–402
HELPMAKE utility, 574
Helv font, 319, 335
Hercules Display Adapter (HDA), 318, 320
   pages with, 360
hexadecimal numbers, 450
   constants for, 62–63, 75
   conversion specification for, 65, 435, 445
   escape sequence for, 29
   test macro for, 100
hfree() function, 498
high resolution, 308
History record, 415–416
Hoare, C. A. R., sort by, 385
hot-key combinations, 6–8
_HRESBW mode, 364
huge memory model and huge pointers,
104, 165–169, 191, 371, 465
hypot() function, 498

I

%i and %I conversion specifications, 435, 439–440, 444
IDE. *See* Integrated Development Environment
identifiers
   duplication of, 71–72, 238–240
   external. *See* extern class specifier
   rules for, 40–41
#if directive, 182–183
if statements, 32–33, 116–124, 129, 151
#ifdef directive, 182, 184
#ifndef directive, 182, 184
images, graphics, 357–362, 535–536, 539–540
_imagesize() function, 317, 357–359, 535
_imagesize_w() function, 535–536
_imagesize_wxy() function, 536
_imagesize_xy() function, 535
implicit declarations, 235
implied bits in FP format, 455
in-line assembly code, 466
#include directive, 2–3, 24, 245–246
include files, 428
   and environment, 19
increment operator (+ +), 52–53, 56, 74–75
indentation for if statements, 117
independent variables, 348
index, help for, 572–573
index registers, 462–464
indices for array elements, 101–102
indirection operator (*), 104–105, 162–163, 206
initialization
   of arrays, 102–103
   and extent, 241
   with for loops, 143–144, 147–148
   of matrices, 175
   of PG functions, 555
   of pointers, 106, 161
   of static variables, 241, 249–251
   of structures, 201–202
   of variables, 61–62, 74
inp() function, 499
input/output, help for, 288–289

Selections from The SYBEX Library

LANGUAGES

Mastering Turbo Pascal 5
Douglas Hergert
595pp. Ref. 529-8
This in-depth treatment of Turbo Pascal Versions 4 and 5 offers separate sections on the Turbo environment, the new debugger, the extensive capabilities of the language itself, and special techniques for graphics, date arithmetic, and recursion. Assumes some programming knowledge.

Advanced Techniques in Turbo Pascal
Charles C. Edwards
309pp. Ref. 350-3
This collection of system-oriented techniques and sample programs shows how to make the most of IBM PC capabilities using Turbo Pascal. Topics include screens, windows, directory management, the mouse interface, and communications.

Turbo BASIC Instant Reference
SYBEX Prompter Series
Douglas Hergert
393pp. Ref. 485-2
This quick reference for programmers offers concise, alphabetical entries on every command--statement, metastatement, function, and operation--in the Turbo BASIC language with descriptions, syntax, and examples cross-referenced to related commands.

Introduction to Turbo BASIC
Douglas Hergert
523pp. Ref. 441-0
A complete tutorial and guide to this now highly professional language: Turbo BASIC, including important Turbo extras

such as parameter passing, structured loops, long integers, recursion, and 8087 compatibility for high-speed numerical operation.

Advanced Techniques in Turbo Prolog
Carl Townsend
398pp. Ref. 428-3
A goldmine of techniques and predicates for control procedures, string operations, list processing, database operations, BIOS-level support, program development, expert systems, natural language processing, and much more.

Introduction to Turbo Prolog
Carl Townsend
315pp. Ref. 359-7
This comprehensive tutorial includes sample applications for expert systems, natural language interfaces, and simulation. Covers every aspect of Prolog: facts, objects and predicates, rules, recursion, databases, and much more.

Turbo Pascal Toolbox (Second Edition)
Frank Dutton
425pp. Ref. 602-2
This collection of tested, efficient Turbo Pascal building blocks gives a boost to intermediate-level programmers, while teaching effective programming by example. Topics include accessing DOS, menus, bit maps, screen handling, and much more.

Introduction to Pascal: Including Turbo Pascal (Second Edition)
Rodnay Zaks
464pp. Ref. 533-6
This best-selling tutorial builds complete

mastery of Pascal--from basic structured programming concepts, to advanced I/O, data structures, file operations, sets, pointers and lists, and more. Both ISO Standard and Turbo Pascal.

Introduction to Pascal
(Including UCSD Pascal)
Rodnay Zaks
420pp. Ref. 066-0

This edition of our best-selling tutorial on Pascal programming gives special attention to the UCSD Pascal implementation for small computers. Covers everything from basic concepts to advanced data structures and more.

Celestial BASIC: Astronomy on Your Computer
Eric Burgess
300pp. Ref. 087-3

A complete home planetarium. This collection of BASIC programs for astronomical calculations enables armchair astronomers to observe and identify on screen the configurations and motions of sun, moon, planets and stars.

Mastering Turbo C
Stan Kelly-Bootle
578pp. Ref. 462-3

No prior knowledge of C or structured programming is required for this introductory course on the Turbo C language and development environment by this well-known author. A logical progression of tutorials and useful sample programs build a thorough understanding of Turbo C.

Systems Programming in Turbo C
Michael J. Young
365pp. Ref. 467-4

An introduction to advanced programming with Borland's Turbo C, and a goldmine of ready-made routines for the system programmer's library: DOS and BIOS interfacing, interrupt handling, windows, graphics, expanded memory, UNIX utilities, and more.

Understanding C
Bruce H. Hunter
320pp. Ref. 123-3

A programmer's introduction to C, with

special attention to implementations for microcomputers--both CP/M and MS-DOS. Topics include data types, storage management, pointers, random I/O, function libraries, compilers and more.

Mastering C
Craig Bolon
437pp. Ref. 326-0

This in-depth guide stresses planning, testing, efficiency and portability in C applications. Topics include data types, storage classes, arrays, pointers, data structures, control statements, I/O and the C function library.

Data Handling Utilities
in Microsoft C
Robert A. Radcliffe/Thomas J. Raab
519pp. Ref. 444-5

A C library for commercial programmers, with techniques and utilities for data entry, validation, display and storage. Focuses on creating and manipulating custom logical data types: dates, dollars, phone numbers, much more.

COMMUNICATIONS

Mastering Crosstalk XVI
Peter W. Gofton
187pp. Ref. 388-0

Recoup the cost of this book in a matter of hours with ready-made routines that speed up and automate your on-line database sessions. Tutorials cover every aspect of installing, running and customizing Crosstalk XVI.

HARDWARE

The RS-232 Solution
Joe Campbell
194pp. Ref. 140-3

A complete how-to guide to trouble-free RS-232-C interfacing from scratch. Indepth coverage of concepts, techniques and testing devices, and case studies deriving cables for a variety of common computers, printers and modems.

Mastering Serial Communications

Peter W. Gofton

289pp. Ref. 180-2

The software side of communications, with details on the IBM PC's serial programming, the XMODEM and Kermit protocols, non-ASCII data transfer, interrupt-level programming and more. Sample programs in C, assembly language and BASIC.

Microprocessor Interfacing Techniques (Third Edition)

Austin Lesea/Rodnay Zaks

456pp. Ref. 029-6

This handbook is for engineers and hobbyists alike, covering every aspect of interfacing microprocessors with peripheral devices. Topics include assembling a CPU, basic I/O, analog circuitry, and bus standards.

From Chips to Systems: An Introduction to Microcomputers (Second Edition)

Rodnay Zaks/Alexander Wolfe

580pp. Ref. 377-5

The best-selling introduction to microcomputer hardware--now fully updated, revised, and illustrated. Such recent advances as 32-bit processors and RISC architecture are introduced and explained for the first time in a beginning text.

Mastering Digital Device Control

William G. Houghton

366pp. Ref. 346-5

Complete principles of system design using single-chip microcontrollers, with numerous examples. Topics include expanding memory and I/O, interfacing with multi-chip CPUs, clocks, display devices, analog measurements, and much more.

HOME COMPUTERS

Amiga Programmer's Handbook, Volume I (Second Edition)

Eugene P. Mortimore

624pp. Ref. 367-8

The complete reference for Amiga graphics programming. System commands and function calls are presented in detail, organized by funcitonal class: Exec, Graphics, Animation, Layers, Intuition and the Workbench. Includes AmigaDOS version 1.2.

Amiga Programmer's Handbook, Volume II

Eugene P. Mortimore

365pp. Ref. 384-8

In-depth discussion of Amiga device I/O programming--including programming with sound and speech--with complete details on the twelve Amiga devices and their associated commands and function calls. Inclues AmigaDOS version 1.2.

Programmer's Guide to the Amiga

Robert A. Peck

352pp. Ref. 310-4

A programmer's hands-on tour through the Amiga system--AmigaDOS, Exec, Graphics, Intuition, Devices, Sound, Animation, and more--packed with in-depth information and sample programs (in Amiga C) showing proper use of system routines.

TO JOIN THE SYBEX MAILING LIST OR ORDER BOOKS
PLEASE COMPLETE THIS FORM

NAME _____ COMPANY _____

STREET _____ CITY _____

STATE _____ ZIP _____

☐ PLEASE MAIL ME MORE INFORMATION ABOUT **SYBEX** TITLES

ORDER FORM (There is no obligation to order)

PLEASE SEND ME THE FOLLOWING:

TITLE	QTY	PRICE
_____	____	____
_____	____	____
_____	____	____
_____	____	____

TOTAL BOOK ORDER _____ $_____

CUSTOMER SIGNATURE _____

SHIPPING AND HANDLING PLEASE ADD $2.00 PER BOOK VIA UPS _____

FOR OVERSEAS SURFACE ADD $5.25 PER BOOK PLUS $4.40 REGISTRATION FEE _____

FOR OVERSEAS AIRMAIL ADD $18.25 PER BOOK PLUS $4.40 REGISTRATION FEE _____

CALIFORNIA RESIDENTS PLEASE ADD APPLICABLE SALES TAX _____

TOTAL AMOUNT PAYABLE _____

☐ CHECK ENCLOSED   ☐ VISA
☐ MASTERCARD   ☐ AMERICAN EXPRESS

ACCOUNT NUMBER _____

EXPIR. DATE _____ DAYTIME PHONE _____

CHECK AREA OF COMPUTER INTEREST:

☐ BUSINESS SOFTWARE

☐ TECHNICAL PROGRAMMING

☐ OTHER: _____

OTHER COMPUTER TITLES YOU WOULD LIKE TO SEE IN PRINT:

_____

_____

THE FACTOR THAT WAS MOST IMPORTANT IN YOUR SELECTION:

☐ THE SYBEX NAME

☐ QUALITY

☐ PRICE

☐ EXTRA FEATURES

☐ COMPREHENSIVENESS

☐ CLEAR WRITING

☐ OTHER _____

OCCUPATION

☐ PROGRAMMER   ☐ TEACHER

☐ SENIOR EXECUTIVE   ☐ HOMEMAKER

☐ COMPUTER CONSULTANT   ☐ RETIRED

☐ SUPERVISOR   ☐ STUDENT

☐ MIDDLE MANAGEMENT   ☐ OTHER:

☐ ENGINEER/TECHNICAL   _____

☐ CLERICAL/SERVICE

☐ BUSINESS OWNER/SELF EMPLOYED

CHECK YOUR LEVEL OF COMPUTER USE

☐ NEW TO COMPUTERS

☐ INFREQUENT COMPUTER USER

☐ FREQUENT USER OF ONE SOFTWARE
    PACKAGE:
    NAME _____

☐ FREQUENT USER OF MANY SOFTWARE
    PACKAGES

☐ PROFESSIONAL PROGRAMMER

OTHER COMMENTS:

_____
_____
_____
_____
_____
_____
_____

PLEASE FOLD, SEAL, AND MAIL TO SYBEX

SYBEX, INC.
2021 CHALLENGER DR. #100
ALAMEDA, CALIFORNIA USA
                    94501

SYBEX Computer Books are different.

Here is why . . .

At SYBEX, each book is designed with you in mind. Every manuscript is carefully selected and supervised by our editors, who are themselves computer experts. We publish the best authors, whose technical expertise is matched by an ability to write clearly and to communicate effectively. Programs are thoroughly tested for accuracy by our technical staff. Our computerized production department goes to great lengths to make sure that each book is well-designed.

In the pursuit of timeliness, SYBEX has achieved many publishing firsts. SYBEX was among the first to integrate personal computers used by authors and staff into the publishing process. SYBEX was the first to publish books on the CP/M operating system, microprocessor interfacing techniques, word processing, and many more topics.

Expertise in computers and dedication to the highest quality product have made SYBEX a world leader in computer book publishing. Translated into fourteen languages, SYBEX books have helped millions of people around the world to get the most from their computers. We hope we have helped you, too.

For a complete catalog of our publications:

SYBEX, Inc. 2021 Challenger Drive, #100, Alameda, CA 94501
Tel: (415) 523-8233/(800) 227-2346   Telex: 336311
Fax: (415) 523-2373

PRECEDENCE AND ASSOCIATIVITY OF QUICKC OPERATORS

GROUP 1 (associates left to right)	
( )	Function arguments: func(arg1, arg2)
[ ]	Array elements: array[20]
.	struct, union member: player.name
->	struct, union pointer member: sptr ->name

GROUP 2 (associates right to left)	
!	Logical NOT: !FULL
~	One's complement: ~i
—	Unary minus: −x
++	Increment: i++; ++j
−−	Decrement: i−−; −−j
&	Address of: ptr = &x
*	Indirection: *ptr
(type)	Type cast: (char) x
sizeof	Size (in bytes): sizeof(int)

GROUP 3 (associates left to right)	
*	Multiply: x * 4
/	Divide: y / z
%	Remainder: tab % 8

GROUP 4 (associates left to right)	
+	Add: a + b
—	Subtract: a − b

GROUP 5 (associates left to right)	
<<	Left Shift: x << 2
>>	Right Shift: z >> i

GROUP 6 (associates left to right)	
<	Less than: if (x < y)
<=	Less than or equal: while (a <= 2)
>	Greater than: if (x > max)
>=	Greater than or equal: while (j >= k)

GROUP 7 (associates left to right)	
==	Equality: if (x == y)
!=	Inequality: while (x != y)

GROUP 8 (associates left to right)	
&	Bitwise AND: x & y